The Money Manias

The Money Manias

The Eras of Great Speculation in America 1770-1970

ROBERT SOBEL

BeardBooks
Washington, D.C.

Library of Congress Cataloging-in-Publication Data

Sobel, Robert, 1931 Feb. 19-.
The money manias : the eras of great speculation in America, 1770-1970 / by Robert Sobel
p. cm.
Originally published: New York : Weybright and Talley, c1973.
Includes bibliographical references and index.
ISBN 1-58798-028-2 (pbk.)
1. Speculation--United States--History. 2. Investments--United States--History I. Title

HG4910 .S58 2000
332.64'5'0973--dc21

00-057976

Reprinted 2000 by Beard Books, Washington, D.C.

Printed in the United States of America

for
Jim Marshall

Foreword

Several years ago, in a book entitled *Panic on Wall Street*, I explored the nature of America's recurrent financial crises, as reflected in activities in the New York securities markets. In it I noted that the tip of Manhattan was only a small part of the nation, and for most of our history had little effect on the daily lives of citizens elsewhere. Only in the last half century have Wall Street and Pennsylvania Avenue come to dominate America's financial and economic destiny.

Yet the kinds of drives for power and wealth that made for panics were and are integral parts of the American character, and tell us much of what made Americans different from other peoples. In a society more egalitarian than most, Americans attempted to "rise above their fellows" through proving their worth in the crucible of competition. Success and failure were not evaluated qualitatively, for even to attempt to do so would be "aristocratic," a term that was anathema to most Americans. Rather, success was measured quantitatively, in terms of dollars and cents. Who but an American would ask, "If you're so smart, why aren't you rich?" As Henry Steele Commager put it almost a quarter of a century ago in *The American Mind,* the American has "a quantitative cast to his thinking," which "inclined him to place a quantitative valuation upon almost everything." When asked what a man was worth, he thought in material terms, and was impatient of any other means of measurement.

Commager believed the drive for wealth and power was more fashionable prior to 1929 than it was in the immediate post-World War II world. But it still exists, one of the more durable strains in the national character. It can be found on Wall Street and in Washington. It was and is present throughout the rest of the country, too, as evinced in various "money manias."

These nonsecurities market manias are the subject of this book. It concerns nine of the more important of them, chosen for their significance and interest, as well as to illustrate aspects of American materialism. The goal of each chapter is to understand how manias developed, trace their courses, indicate the kinds of men involved in them, and show how they ended. In addition, attempts have been made to understand why the manias appeared, where, and how.

Americans both respect and are suspicious of men who make large amounts of money rapidly, as many do in money manias. We admire success and have contempt for failure, and in America it is "all or nothing." Yet most Americans fall in between the poles of wealth and poverty; we are a nation of middle-class people, and we trust middle-class values and accomplishments. To work hard for success is good; to achieve it through a fortunate grab at a "main chance" is suspect. In *A Hazard of New Fortunes,* William Dean Howells has Basil March say:

> And so we go on, pushing and pulling, climbing and crawling, thrusting aside and trampling underfoot; lying, cheating, stealing; and when we get to the end, covered with blood and dirt and sin and shame, and look back over the way we've come

> to a palace of our own, or to the poor-house, which is about the only possession we can claim in common with our brother-men, I don't think the retrospect can be pleasing.

I will leave it to the reader to judge whether or not such is an accurate statement regarding the activities of the men of manias. As far as possible, I have attempted to avoid judging the motives of the central figures in each mania. These are often unfathomable. Actions that appear horrendous in one context may be quite acceptable in others. Risks that result in success may be applauded, while those that end in failure are often condemned. Attempts to pass judgments can be indistinguishable from cheap moralizing after the fact.

Instead, I have tried to view the central figures as protagonists, not heroes or villains, recognizing all the while that no writer can hide his or her sentiments and viewpoints from intelligent readers, even when the author is convinced he is objective.

Many colleagues and librarians have helped me in my researches, and since all know who they are, I will not attempt to list them. Special thanks belong to Truman M. Talley, who encouraged me in my studies of money manias.

Robert Sobel
New College of Hofstra

Contents

Foreword vii
Introduction xiii
1. The Vision of Vandalia 1
2. A Great National Project 33
3. Speculation in Slaves 69
4. The Comstock Lode 99
5. Beef Bonanza 134
6. The Steel Millionaires 173
7. Spindletop 211
8. The Great Florida Boom 250
9. Conglomeritis 297
Conclusion: The Mood for Mania 356
Selected Bibliography 361
Index 381

Introduction

The craving for wealth in its many forms has existed in most civilizations and during all periods of known human history. But it appears to have been more prevalent in America than in almost any other country. It was present when Queen Isabella financed Columbus' voyages to the West, to seek gold in the Orient as well as trade. Failing to discover a route to the Indies, Columbus attempted to uncover gold, precious stones, and pearls in the land and waters of the Orinoco River valley, and when he failed in this and other explorations, he fell from grace.

The *conquistadores* of the sixteenth century plundered Central and South America and explored the southwestern part of North America in their search for gold and silver, in what was the first major money mania in the history of the New World. More often than not they either failed or found very little, and thousands died in the search. But those who succeeded became wealthy beyond their expectations, and because of this, others followed. Later on it would be said the *conquistadores* came for "gold, glory, and gospel." Perhaps. But of the three, gold was by far the most important.

The same was true for the Elizabethan sea dogs and their Dutch counterparts who plundered the Spanish Main. And for the joint-stock companies that established colonies on North America's eastern seaboard, as well as a large majority of those who came to settle. The desire to add to the prestige and power of the mother country was not absent, but wealth was the engine that drove them forward. They came for gold, settled for land, and were part of the beginning of a series of real-estate ventures that are continuing to this day.

America has long been called a land of opportunity by individuals who rarely consider what the opportunity was for. Most who came to America in the seventeenth century and after did so in the hope of bettering their economic conditions. To be sure, the thirst for freedom was also present, but to the Englishman of the seventeenth and eighteenth centuries, the Irish and Germans of the eighteenth, and the eastern and southern Europeans of the early twentieth centuries, freedom meant a chance to break out of the feudal social bonds of the Old World and rise in status and wealth in the New. The Bill of Rights was admired and glorified, but the full dinner pail, the dream of land, and hope for a bank account always seemed more important.*

How could these goals be achieved? In the Declaration of Independence is a statement that all people have inalienable rights, among which are "Life, Liberty and the pursuit of Happiness." Significantly, the Founding Fathers did not consider happiness a right in and of itself, but rather sought to guarantee freedom to pursue it. And Americans have always engaged in the quest, which often had as its goal great wealth.

This is not to deny that Americans were idealists, but rather to

*Of course, the Africans, who had no choice in coming to America, did not share in this motivation. In recent years, however, the capitalist ethic has grown in the Black community, much to the consternation of some Black leaders who consider it degrading, but to the economic advantage of American Blacks.

suggest that they were individualists and, to a great extent materialists.

The country was huge, and for the most part virgin. It contained many natural resourçes, untapped, waiting to be exploited by individuals who came for that purpose. The age of exploration came at the dawn of an age of capitalism, too, which helped break down old social structures in Europe. There was no need of this in America, but rather for the newcomers to rid themselves of preconceived notions as fast as they could. This they did with great alacrity.

Napoleon once called the English a race of shopkeepers. In the same vein, he might have characterized the Americans as a nation of businessmen.

Alexis de Tocqueville, one of the most astute observers of the Americans, noted this in the Jacksonian period. Wherever he went he saw an American penchant for business, profit, gain, to the point of avarice. On his travels he came upon a French farmer who had resettled in the United States a few years earlier. "I was aware that my host had been a great leveller and an ardent demagogue forty years before," he wrote in *Democracy in America*. "It was strange and astonishing therefore to hear him talk like an economist—I almost said a landowner—about the rights of property."

Even more to the point was an editorial in the *New York Sun* in 1838, which lamented that "Americans are not businessmen, but speculators, pure and simple."

> There is scarcely a lad of any spirit who does not, from the time that he can connect the most simple ideas, picture to himself some rapid road to wealth—indefinite and obscure, it is true. . . . He sees the terminus of the race—poverty at the one end, affluence at the other, and jumps the intermediate years. He fancies that the course of amassing will be easy as imagination. He dreams of dashing into a fortune by some lucky speculation. Contentment with competence he learns to regard as slothful vice. To become rich, and, of course, respected—influential, great, powerful—is his darling object.

Americans as individuals have always sought the wealth, status, and power that could be had in the arena of economics and business. From time to time, at least once in a generation, major opportunities would be presented, not to individuals, but to many people, who would rush to take what they could, and hopefully emerge with a prize of great value. These opportunities have been called many names, but may all be included in the general title of money mania.

It may be pointless to consider whether manias of this kind were beneficial or harmful to the nation, since to ask would appear to indicate that we can do something about them, or at least come to a conclusion that may be acted upon. Almost by definition, manias are uncontrollable. We may explore the anatomies of money manias and try to uncover their origins, developments, and culminations. But we cannot stop them, unless and until we drastically change the nature of American society and its economy. These, too, are probably not within the power of men or organizations to alter considerably. As we shall see, attempts to curb manias often result in the creation of even greater ones later on.

The money manias explored in the following pages will tell us much of the American character and value system. Each was unique, although some grew out of the mania which preceded it. And all shared certain characteristics, which will be discussed in the conclusion. Perhaps such knowledge that may be gained through their study will help us to guard against future manias—or at least prepare us to benefit therefrom. This, too, would be typically American.

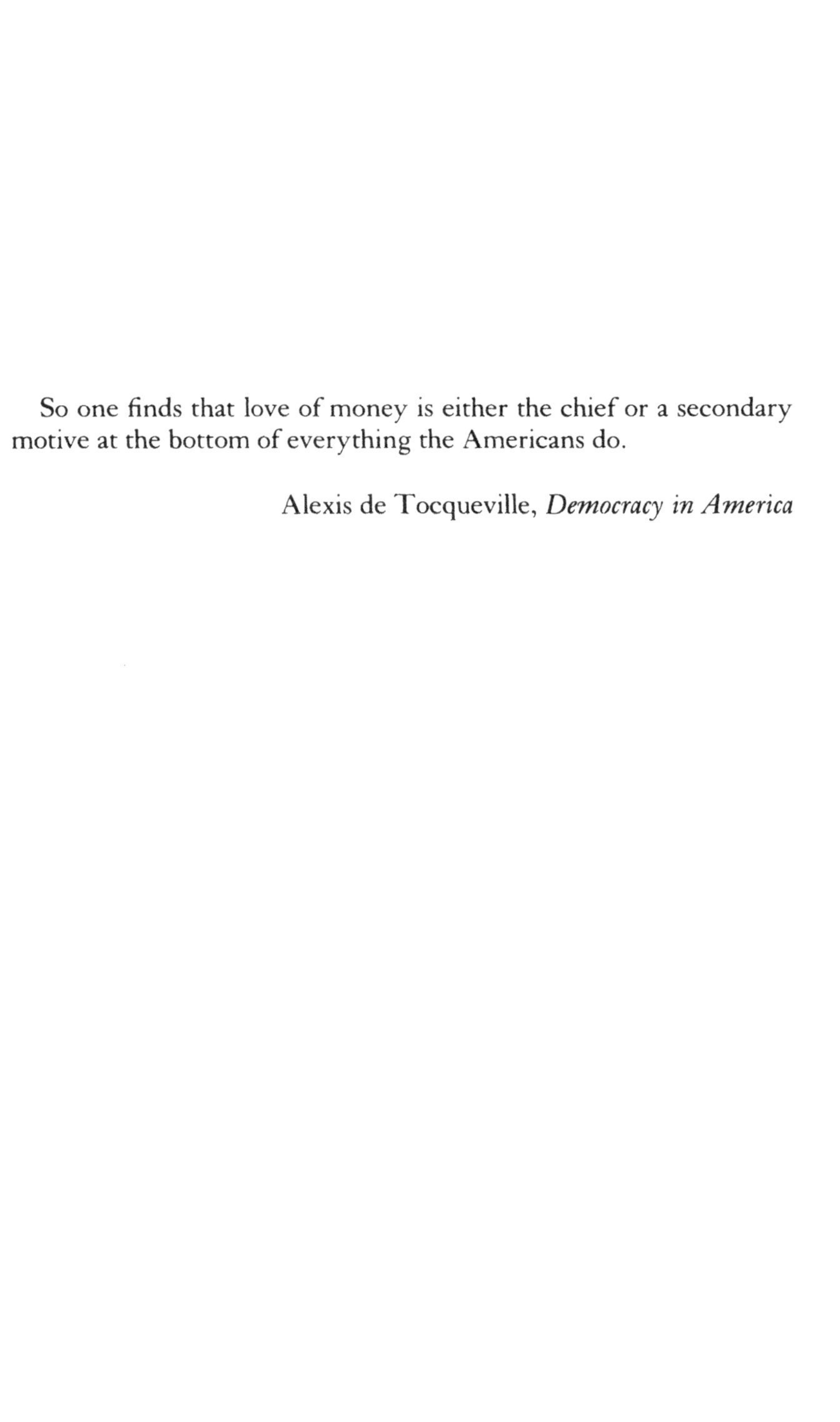

So one finds that love of money is either the chief or a secondary motive at the bottom of everything the Americans do.

Alexis de Tocqueville, *Democracy in America*

CHAPTER 1

The Vision of Vandalia

For centuries people have debated the differences between investment and speculation, and have come to no clear-cut distinction. But all would agree that speculation involves greater risks and hopes of greater rewards than does investment, which is safer if not as promising in terms of financial gain. Individuals with surplus capital in the late twentieth century can pretty well determine the amount of risk they want to take with their money, and act accordingly. And they can select the medium of speculation and/or investment. So it is they can buy blue-chip stocks or lightly funded new issues, high- or low-grade bonds, developed or undeveloped land, in different parts of the country or the world. Art, coins, furniture, commodities, rare books, precious metals, antique autos—the list of items that may be purchased for investment or speculation is large. Given the proper knowledge, the would-be investor/speculator literally has the world at his disposal.

It was not so in the eighteenth century. For a variety of reasons opportunities for investment were limited, while those for speculation—or what we would call speculation today—were far greater than they are now. Today's prudent investor might purchase shares in a well-managed electric utility, and hope for slow but steady growth plus a dividend return of 5 percent or so. His mid-eighteenth-century counterpart might enter into a venture in the field of transport where he might triple or quadruple his investment in a year or two, or go bankrupt. Both men might be cautious, but it is far easier to act on such proclivities today than it was then.

As with most such matters, the reasons for the differences were many and complex. But a beginning of understanding may come with an appreciation of the nature of society and how it was perceived by many investors in the late eighteenth century.

Consider the case of an Englishman of rank and position born in 1727, the year George II ascended the throne, and who died in 1803, the year prior to Napoleon's being named emperor of France. These dates and the type of Englishman were not selected by chance, for such a man did exist—Thomas Walpole—more of whom later. A man of this period would have lived in an agrarian England, most of whose people lived, worked, and died in small farming communities. Trade and transport, usually in agricultural products of one kind or another, were advancing rapidly, but at mid-century affected only a small minority of Englishmen, most of whom lived in the towns. Nor was the total economy growing at a rapid rate. England's economic growth in the first half of the century scarcely averaged more than 0.5 percent per annum, though in the second half it rose to an average of 1.5 percent per annum. Surplus capital was rare, and when it existed, it more often than not was put back into the land in the form of improvements. This was not an industrial country, or even one in which industrialization was proceeding at a rapid pace. Indeed, the technology available to Thomas Walpole when he died in 1803 was not too different from that which had existed at his birth in 1727.* Had Walpole by some miracle been set down in the London of the year 1000, he would have been more at home than he might have been in the city a half century after his death. The "dark satanic mills" would appear after his death, as would interest in investments in such businesses.

Let us suppose, however, that a well-born Englishman of the mid-eighteenth century had cash on hand, more than he cared to spend. What might he do with it? The purchase of shares in textile, mining, road building, brewing, or similar firms was out of the question. There were few such enterprises, and fewer still with shares for sale. England would soon enter its "canal age," but money for the ditches was raised locally, or at the most regionally; the canal builders rarely sought investors in London. Most "industrial" businesses were family owned and operated or the product of subscriptions taken up by their founders, who considered themselves partners, not stockholders. Such individuals rarely sold shares, and so they were not to be found on the market. Nor would corporations often issue new shares to raise capital. Until after the Napoleonic Wars, textile and iron firms considered it prudent to retain well over half their total capital in liquid form, so as to be able to pay for raw materials, labor, shipping charges, and the like. Fixed investment was small, as was the need for expansion of plant. There were no investment bankers as we recognize them today simply because they were not needed.

Our Englishman might take shares in a new company, but there were not many of these. After the South Sea Bubble, Parliament

*This is not to say that change was not taking place. The steam engine was patented in 1769, and even before that important changes were taking place in the textile, construction, road building, and mining industries. But the share of national income taken by mining, manufacturing, and building rose only to 23.4 percent in 1801 from 21 percent in 1688. The share would be 34.4 percent in 1841. Phyllis Dean and W. A. Cole, *British Economic Growth, 1688–1867, Trends and Structure* (Cambridge, 1962), pp. 156, 161, 166. In any case, the technological changes of the eighteenth century did not affect the nonworker *directly*. Such would come in the following century.

passed the "Bubble Act" of 1720, which restricted the formation of new corporations, and it remained law for more than a century. Corporate charters were hard to come by, and so what might be called "the industrial sector" of the securities markets was slim indeed.

Such was not the case in shipping. Our capitalist might take a share of a ship engaged in the North American trade, or the African slave trade. Profits could be large here, but so were risks. Should the ship sink, insurance might cover the investment. But should the cargo spoil, or in the case of slaves, die, the investment could be wiped out. Banks and insurance firms backed voyages, so the individual investor might purchase shares in these and so participate in trade indirectly. But there were only 150 or so banks in England at the time, and all of these without floating shares. The same was true of insurance firms.

There was a market, often lively, in government bonds and some securities. "'Change Alley" in London, where dealers in securities congregated, was considered little more than a den of thieves, however, while "stock-jobbers," the ancestors of today's customers' men, were believed barely respectable if that. In 1721 the House of Commons passed an "Act for the better establishing of Public Credit by preventing for the future the infamous Practice of Stock-Jobbing." Although the bill was defeated in Lords, a second measure, "An Act to prevent the infamous Practice of Stock-Jobbing" was ratified the following year, and was reinforced by other measures later on. The act did not actually forbid trading or jobbing, but did formulate rules for trading, in an early version of Securities and Exchange Commission self-regulation.

It didn't work very well, and jobbing went on, more often than not dishonestly. An investor might purchase government bonds from a jobber, but might not receive delivery of them, would worry about interest payments, and might even be concerned lest the country default. Securities in any case were intangible, and so distrusted. The paper economy was two centuries away for the investor of the mid-eighteenth century. He wanted something more substantial in return for his very substantial gold coins. He could see a ship, visit a bank, explore a mine, walk through a textile establishment, or admire a brewery. But who ever saw a national debt? And even then, the returns on investments in England's gilt-edge "consol" bonds was not very high, rarely rising above 5 percent in the mid-eighteenth century.

There remained, however, one area of investment and/or speculation the men of this period could understand and appreciate: land. Throughout the Middle Ages land had been equated with wealth and status, and the mentality of the eighteenth century was not far from that of the earlier period. Late in the century the French physiocrats would claim that all wealth was derived, ultimately, from land, and this view, too, had emotional if not rational roots in medieval Europe. Many Englishmen believed this, as did such Americans as Washington and Jefferson. Stock certificates were intangibles, government bonds could be defaulted upon, a factory might burn to the ground, and a ship sink or fall victim to pirates. But the land was always there, providing crops for factories and breweries and wealth for the nation. Land could not be destroyed. Nor could it be created.

Or could it? To the Englishman of 1750 the amount of land in Britain was finite, but that in America stretched beyond known frontiers. It excited the imagination, stirred patriotic fervor, and provided a prime area for speculation and investment.

The value of American land depended upon several variables, beside the obvious ones as to its suitability for farming and closeness to transportation. For example, was the land secure? Throughout the eighteenth century, Britain and France clashed, in Europe, Africa, Asia, and the Americas. Not until 1763, with the end of the Seven Years' War, did Britain's American colonies seem safe, and even then there was fear of a renewed French assault sometime in the future. The Indian menace was still present in 1763, and would have to be taken into consideration by any speculator in western lands, and even some in areas which were considered settled in the tidewater area of the South.

Speculators also had to be concerned with movements of emigrants from Europe, the growth of America's population, and the drive westward. The population of British North America, excluding Canada, was some 1.7 million in 1763; in 1700 it had been 250,000. There seemed no reason to doubt that this growth would continue. In this same period the western frontier had moved hundreds of miles, held back only by Indians, Frenchmen, and natural barriers. In 1763 the French were leaving, the Indians seemed controllable, and the natural barriers could be overcome. There seemed every reason to believe that the westward movement would accelerate in the last decades of the eighteenth century.

Land values in almost all parts of British North America appeared to be rising in the eighteenth century, the result of increasing demand. The greatest demand was in the seaport towns and the tidewater South, areas already settled. If one purchased land there and held onto it for a while, profits seemed certain. But still greater profits could be obtained from the western lands. More often than not, land there was not purchased from the government, but "granted" to favored individuals. Such literally could be had for the asking—providing one knew the right person to ask, and greased the path with a few well-placed bribes. After all, without settlers the area was worthless. But with settlement would come demand, and with demand a price for the land. A person or group of people might obtain a grant for no more than bribes totaling a few hundred pounds. These grants could run into the hundreds of thousands of acres.* To be sure, some of the land would be swampy or in other ways unfit for use—the grantees had never seen the place, nor had its new owners, for in their minds it existed only as a slice on a poorly drawn map. But some of it would be good, perhaps even better than tidewater holdings. The richness of Mississippi Valley soils was well-known, and a plantation on the banks of a tributary of that river could in time be as valuable as one on the James River in Virginia. In the 1760s good tidewater land could be had for £10 per 100 acres. Speculators knew this, and made

*To appreciate the low cost of American land even after independence, consider that the 523 million acres acquired by the Louisiana Purchase of 1803 cost an average of 3 cents per acre.

mental calculations as to the worth of a 200,000-acre grant in trans-Appalachia. The figures were impressive.

Would-be land speculators also had to concern themselves with opposition from American fur trappers and their English allies. Fur was big business in the 1760s, and became even bigger after the ending of the wars with France in 1763. In 1760, less than £20,000 worth of furs had been sent to Britain from all of North America, or slightly below the average of the past forty years. Exports reached beyond the £49,000 mark in 1765. Much of the increase was due to the diversion of Canadian furs from France to Britain, but the trappers of western Pennsylvania, New York, and the southern colonies, now freed from fear of war and French-supported Indians, were also prospering. Carolina fur exports in 1760 were valued at only £20 in 1760; in 1765 the figure was £491.

Land speculators considered farmers and, in a few cases, ranchers as their obvious customers, while trappers, who used but did not settle on the land, were their enemies. Fur trappers would do all they could, including uniting with the Indians, to prevent settlement, for they realized farmers would destroy their business. So the trappers had to be crushed and eliminated, or failing in this, taken into alliance.

There was yet another variable the speculators had to consider, and that was title to the land. Colonial charters were poorly drawn and in many cases boundaries overlapped. Pennsylvania and Virginia claimed the same places in trans-Appalachia. Other Pennsylvania claims conflicted with those of New York, while Virginia, Maryland, and South Carolina all had claims to identical parcels. London's claims, too, were considered, for members of Parliament insisted that all of trans-Appalachia belonged to the nation, to be disposed of as the king—or his ministers—thought best. A grant from Virginia would be meaningless if the Pennsylvania claims were upheld in London. Both might suffer if London insisted the land belonged to the Crown. Thomas Walpole and other English speculators had to consider these problems, and they did. Yet they still thought land speculation not only capable of returning large profits, but also safer than many other forms of investment open to them at the time.

The search for speculation and investment in the colonies, though not as intense as that in England, did exist. Almost all American laborers were engaged in work either directly or indirectly connected with agriculture. Tobacco, forest products, grain, furs, indigo—these were prime products. Fish and furs were significant in some parts of the colonies. Whatever small manufacturing did exist was carried on by individual proprietors—blacksmiths, brewers, candlers, nail manufacturers, etc.—or in some cases by partnerships and even a few joint-stock enterprises. There were a handful of local banks and insurance companies, but none with securities available for speculation. The slave trade was most profitable, as was the carrying trade in general and shipbuilding and repair. But there was no way for a person to invest his gold in such enterprises, except as loans at interest. A man with money and his own labor and brainpower could find employment in many areas. But a person with money alone, seeking investments, had few areas to consider—and the best of these was land speculation.

If anything Americans were even more land-hungry than Englishmen. And being closer to the scene as it were, they were more anxious to invest. An English investor might think twice before entering into a trans-Appalachian speculation; a tidewater Virginian, such as George Washington, might have been to the region, known of its potential, and be more willing to take a chance. Distance from speculative ventures often lends glamour to them, but closeness increases interest. The Virginians, Pennsylvanians, Carolinians, and New Yorkers of the mid-eighteenth century were most interested in land. Control of Europe, perhaps even the world, involved Englishmen fighting France at that time. To their American counterparts, control of trans-Appalachia seemed more important.

The colonials also realized the dangers present in trans-Appalachia, and, most particularly, those posed by the Indians. The Iroquois Confederacy was powerful in this area, and the colonists feared it more than they did France. Some Englishmen thought the Indians quaint and interesting specimens of an exotic civilization, but those who fought against the Iroquois said otherwise. Lord Jeffrey

Amherst, the English commander in America, thought them "more nearly allied to the Brute than to the Human Creation. I am fully resolved whenever they give me an occasion to extirpate them root and branch," he swore, and such statements won Amherst favor among Americans in general and land speculators in particular.

The speculators knew the end of the French wars did not mean the conclusion of their struggles against the Indians. Indeed, in 1763 the Ottowa chief, Pontiac, led the tribes in a continuation of their war against the English and their colonial allies, one bloodier in the trans-Appalachia than the French and Indian War that preceded it. Land speculation implied eventual Indian removal. The colonists knew this, as did the Indians. Thomas Walpole, viewing the scene from London, his interest in America increasing, was coming to understand this. George Washington, Benjamin Franklin, and others who dabbled in such speculation, knew it to be so. One who understood Indians better than most Americans and Europeans of this day, George Croghan, was most interested in the possibilities of speculation in land in 1763. In time Croghan and men like him would join with European and American speculators to engage in one of the most ambitious enterprises of its kind in history—an attempt to make fortunes from trans-Appalachia.

Croghan was one of that handful of frontiersmen who trapped, explored, fought, and helped settle trans-Appalachia in the mid-eighteenth century. They served as soldiers, diplomats, translators, speculators, businessmen, and pioneers, often at the same time. Most were illiterate and uncouth. Few left behind records of their actions. They were famous in their lifetimes, but most are forgotten today except by students of the period and place. Only one—Daniel Boone—is clearly remembered. And Boone was an expert at self-advertisement and had friends eager to spread word of his exploits. George Croghan left papers, but no autobiography, and he lacked press agents. He wanted fame, and was pleased when people recognized him. But more than that, Croghan wanted to be rich.

We do not know when Croghan was born, but it was in Ireland, around 1720. He left for Pennsylvania in 1741, the result of one of that country's many famines, and headed for the frontier, where he spent most of the next thirty-five years. Croghan was not interested in becoming a farmer—the work was too hard, and the life dull. He craved excitement, easy living, money, and power. So he became an Indian trader, selling trinkets and tools to the tribes and receiving furs in return. The profits were good, and Croghan spent them on fine clothes, imported wines, and other luxuries. Then, when broke once more, he returned to trading, made more money, and spent it once again, living on what for the frontier was a lavish scale.

Croghan was an obvious confidence man. He came by the talent naturally, and it was sharpened in his dealings with the Indians and other traders. Like most such people, he was charming, a good listener but a better talker, and a man given to exaggeration in all things. Almost all who met him thought he was an excellent companion, but a man not to be trusted. Yet even those Croghan bilked continued to appreciate his company. He had many ex-partners, but few enemies.

Croghan got along very well with the Indians. He not only liked them, but also admired many of their customs. Unlike most Americans of his day, he was willing to learn their languages, accept them as equals, and consort with them. Croghan married an Indian, and for a while lived in her village, at the time serving as secretary to the Pennsylvania Council and as Philadelphia's envoy to the western tribes. He opened one of his letters to the council by writing, "Excuse boath Writing and peper, and gues at my Maining, fer I have this minitt 20 drunken Indians about me. . . ." If Croghan ran true to form, at that moment he was as loaded as any of them.

In common with many frontiersmen, Croghan was interested in land speculation. Such speculation was not new; it had existed since the earliest settlements.* But land speculation was becoming institutionalized in the mid-eighteenth century. In 1744 the English signed

*The purchase of Manhattan Island from the Indians in 1626 was, in part, a speculation in land. As most children know, the price paid by Peter Minuit was $24 in beads and trinkets. This price seems ridiculously low today, but had the Indians been able to invest that sum at 6 percent compounded annually, it would be worth in excess of $17 *billion* today, far more than the assessed value of Manhattan real estate at the present time.

a treaty with the Indians by which it appeared the Iroquois ceded a large parcel of land to them. Soon after four large grants were made to groups of Virginians. These in turn united in 1748 to form the Ohio Company of Virginia, whose members included George Washington and his half-brother Lawrence, Governor Robert Dinwiddie, Colonel Thomas Lee and Richard Lee, Robert Carter, George Fairfax, and other members of leading tidewater Virginia families. In order to obtain the support of London, John Hanbury, a Quaker merchant of that city, was also included, and it was he who used influence at the Board of Trade to secure ratification of the grant.

The company employed Christopher Gist to make a survey of the land, and while on the survey Gist met Croghan, who at the time ran a trading post at Muskingum. Later on, Croghan was employed by the company as one of its agents, placating the Indians and at times working for the company in London. This established a pattern for future land companies. They would be organized by fairly well-to-do Americans along the coast, who established contacts with influential people in London and employed frontiersmen to deal with the Indians. The companies hoped to make profits through trade with the Indians, but the real profit would come through land sales later on.

Other companies were formed in the years that followed—the Susquehannah Company, the Company of Military Adventurers, the Mississippi Company, the Illinois-Wabash Company—and all followed more or less the same pattern of organization and strategy. The Proclamation of 1763 closed trans-Appalachia to settlement temporarily, and although individual families and groups did ignore the proclamation and settled there anyway, they had no title to the land. This also meant the companies with claims in the region could not sell land, but the matter didn't seem important at the time. Land sales could wait until settlement in larger numbers began, and such was not the case in 1763. The shareholders felt that by the time they were ready to sell off their holdings, the proclamation would have been repealed. Meanwhile, they would bide their time. And since the proclamation did not forbid trading with the Indians, they would engage themselves in that pursuit. This would require good relations with the superintendent of Indian affairs, and the man who achieved that post in 1755 was Sir William Johnson.

Like Croghan, Johnson had emigrated to America from Ireland, arriving in 1738 at the age of twenty-three. He went to the Mohawk Valley, and soon became the region's leading Indian trader. The Iroquois called him Warraghiyagey—"he who does much business." Alternating army service with his trading activities, Johnson became wealthy, influential, famous, and honored. He lived in a baronial castle, surrounded by Indian retainers, entertained by jesters, and comforted by his Indian bride. Johnson was responsible for maintaining cordial relations with the Indians, and he was an excellent choice for the post. But he needed help, not only in dealing with the Indians, but also with his colonial enemies and English friends. Croghan was a perfect man for an assistantship, and in 1756 Johnson hired the Pennsylvanian at a salary of £200 a year to act as his deputy, a post he held for fifteen years. Thus Croghan was able to combine government service with his other pursuits as land speculator and Indian trader.

In his work for Johnson, Croghan met Samuel Wharton, of the Philadelphia firm of Baynton, Wharton & Morgan. The firm was one of several trading companies which sent boats down the Ohio to trade with the Indians, selling trinkets and tools for pelts. Some of these firms had gone bankrupt during the French and Indian War, and although Baynton, Wharton & Morgan survived, it was in bad shape. Joining with other similarly afflicted companies, they organized a group known as the "suffering traders," which petitioned Johnson for help. The suffering traders also planned to send agents to London to assist in the work. In the process of their planning, Wharton came across Croghan.

Samuel Wharton was barely thirty-one years old in 1763, when he first met Croghan. Suave, subtle, and knowledgeable, he seemed the epitome of a successful urban merchant, a man who might have little in common with Croghan. But the two men hit it off at once, not only personally, but professionally. Croghan too had lost money because of the war, and was eager to obtain reparations. A connection with the suffering traders might prove advantageous to both. So Croghan began selling land claims to Wharton, purchased trading goods from Baynton, Wharton & Morgan, and with Johnson's permission, acted as the Philadelphia group's agent in seeking reparations. In this way, Croghan furthered his own interests, as deputy, trader, and land speculator.

Wharton and Croghan realized they had little hope of winning a cash settlement from London. But they did think it possible to obtain a large land grant to compensate for their losses. They decided that Croghan should go to London to plead the case before the Board of Trade. Croghan was eager to go, not only for business but personal reasons. For the past few years he had dreamed of making a fortune in America and then returning to Ireland in triumph. He would purchase a large estate and live like a lord. Johnson, who already had his estate in America, was willing to give Croghan leave to go, on condition he attend to Indian business as well. For years the board had been grumbling about administration of Indian affairs. Johnson claimed he needed a clarification of policy, a larger budget, additional deputies, and better communications with London. Croghan could explain this to the board, after settling his own and Wharton's accounts.

Croghan arrived in London in February 1764, barely surviving a blustery and near-disastrous crossing. After settling down he visited the Board of Trade. Its members heard him out, but offered little concrete in the way of assistance. Lord Hillsborough, president of the board, had no use for colonials, whom he considered rude and ungrateful louts. An arrogant and ambitious man who hoped to become prime minister, Hillsborough thought he could further his career by turning the colonies into a large money-maker for the Crown. After all, Britain had expended vast sums of money in winning trans-Appalachia, and the Americans would benefit by the removal of the French. Should not England receive compensation for her efforts? If so, why give the suffering traders land in trans-Appalachia? Why not keep the land, or give it to worthy Englishmen, who could turn a profit for themselves—and prove grateful to Hillsborough when he needed them?

Although the board rejected Croghan's pleas, it did draw up a new plan for regulation of Indian affairs to replace the "present vague and uncertain administration." All authority would be placed in the hands of two colonial officials, one of whom would control the northern colonies, Canada, Nova Scotia, and trans-Appalachia. This official would be in charge of trading posts in the area, and be empowered to grant trading rights to individuals and firms. Implied in the new plan was the possibility of future land companies as well. One might well be in the area known as Illinois. Johnson would be named to that post. Croghan would continue as his deputy. In this, at least, Croghan's mission had been a success.

The board continued to ignore Croghan's pleas for the suffering traders. In addition it rejected his own claim for 200,000 acres of Illinois land, which he claimed had been given him as a gift by the Iroquois in 1746. Writing to Johnson, Croghan said, "The people hear spend thire time in Nothing butt abuseing one a nother & striveing who shall be in power with a view to serve themselves & thire friends and neglect the publick. I am Sick of London & wish to be back in aMerica & settle on a Litle farm where I May forgett the Mockery of pomp & Greatness." Yet Croghan took time off to explore England and Ireland, and select several estates that seemed worthy of the man of wealth he hoped to become.

Toward the end of his London stay, Croghan wrote Johnson he was glad he had visited London, for the trip "will learn me to be contented on a little farm in America." Having failed to help the suffering traders, but after assisting Johnson and himself, Croghan set sail for home in late summer. He now knew the trans-Appalachia interested the Board of Trade. The area would remain in Indian hands for the time being, but in the end it would be given to land companies, some American, some English, perhaps a few mixed. He meant to have a share in several of them. Meanwhile, he would profit from the Indian trade.

Before leaving, Croghan wrote Johnson that Londoners seemed to dislike colonials. "The cheefe study of the people in power hear att present is to lay heavy taxes on the colenys and tis talkt of laying an internal tax on them next cesion of Parliament." The tax was indeed levied. It was the Stamp Act, passed in March 1765. Less than three months later, Patrick Henry denounced King George and Parliament in the Virginia House of Burgesses. The Sons of Liberty organized, acting as a terrorist band at first in some port cities and a debating group in others. The Stamp Act Congress met in Philadelphia in October, and adopted John Dickinson's "Declarations of Rights and Grievances." Soon after, radicals along the coast issued nonimportation orders directed against British goods, and the orders were effective. This was not revolution; probably the vast majority of colonists in 1765 considered themselves loyal British subjects and wanted to remain as such. But it was a greater protest than previously had been heard, and the kind not calculated to please Hillsborough and others at the Board of Trade.

Croghan took little notice, however, since he was busy with Indian affairs soon after his return home. He did clash repeatedly with Colonel Henry Bouquet, a British officer in command of part of trans-Appalachia. Croghan informed Johnson he intended to ignore Bouquet; his visit to London had sharpened his anti-British sentiments, and to Croghan, Bouquet was a typical anti-American stuffed shirt. For his part, Bouquet considered Croghan a "savage," and complained "that powers of so great importance to this country should in this instance have been trusted to a man so illiterate, imprudent, and ill bred, who subverts to particular purposes the wise views of the Government, and begins his functions by a ridiculous display of his own importance." In late 1764, one could see issues that would later cause the American Revolution being developed between Croghan and Bouquet in trans-Appalachia.

Meanwhile, the suffering traders persisted in seeking redresses of grievances. Early in 1765 they formed a more permanent organization, consisting of twenty-three Pennsylvania merchants and firms which held claims totaling around £50,000. They called themselves the "Traders' Company," although some dubbed the organization the "Indiana Company," implying a name for the land grant in trans-Appalachia they hoped to obtain. Each member was to receive shares in the company proportionate to his claim. The largest was to go to the Philadelphia trading partnership of Simons, Trent, Franks & Co. Baynton, Wharton & Morgan was not far behind. And George Croghan held the largest individual claim, and so received a substantial share. So did Benjamin Franklin's illegitimate son, Governor William Franklin of New Jersey. William Johnson had no claim, and so received no shares. But he supported the company with zeal, indicating he was in its employ. Considering his new powers in trans-Appalachia, he seemed a good man to cultivate.

As might have been expected, Croghan was delighted with this turn of events. The Indiana Company would receive Johnson's help in obtaining charters. Individuals in London would also assist, for which they would be paid. The land would be sold in time, reaping large profits, a good share of which would be his.

This would require time, and Croghan was not a person to put things off. His desire for the good life was never stronger. He could not wait longer for his estate in England or Ireland. So he purchased one outside Philadelphia—Monckton Hall—for £900. It would do for a beginning. But he had little time for such affairs in 1765. Almost at once Croghan went to trans-Appalachia to placate the Indians who were still engaged in fighting the colonists and to seek new opportunities for trade. "The Illinois country far exceeds any other part of America, that I have seen—both as to soil and climate," he wrote in 1766, praising the land he saw and expanding on its values for investment. This letter went to the man who replaced him in London as a pleader for the cause of the suffering traders—Benjamin Franklin.

Franklin was certainly one of the most skilled negotiators of his time, and few who followed would equal him in dealing with Europeans. Anticolonial sentiment was growing in London, however, and he had even less success than had Croghan in obtaining a grant from the Board of Trade. In 1767 Parliament passed the Townshend Acts, which resulted in a new set of nonimportation agreements and a further widening of the gap between Britain and America. In writing to William Franklin, Benjamin said, "Great changes being expected keeps men's minds in suspense, and obstructs public affairs of every kind. It is there fore not to be wondered that so little progress is made in our American scheme of the Illinois grant and retribution for Indian losses."

Franklin persisted. Although most in power in London were angered by the Americans, some were sympathetic to their protests. The earl of Shelburne was one of these. Secretary of state for the colonies, he was in a position to help. Shelburne was young and inexperienced. He admired Franklin, and indicated on several occasions his willingness to rely upon the older man for expertise in dealing with the colonies. Shelburne told Franklin of his ambition to push the American boundary westward. Franklin answered that to do this would require land companies, and explained their functions to the secretary. He did not mention his interest in the Traders' Company.

In August, Franklin dined with Shelburne and General Henry Seymour Conway, who had recently been named secretary of state. Like Shelburne, Conway was sympathetic to American needs. Against strong opposition he had moved for the repeal of the Stamp Act, and in other ways had demonstrated a sensitivity to colonist demands. Casually and with great skill, Franklin won the two men to his plans for trans-Appalachia. It would be in Britain's interest, as well as America's, to help Americans and their land companies. Franklin described his conversations in a letter to his son.

> I took the opportunity of urging it as one means of saving expense in supporting the outposts, that a settlement should be made in the Illinois country; expatiated on the various advantages, viz., furnishing provisions cheaper to the garrisons, securing the country, retaining the trade, raising a strength there which, on occasion of a future war, might easily be poured down the Mississippi upon the lower country and into the Bay of Mexico, to be used against Cuba or Mexico itself. I mentioned your plan, its being approved by Sir William Johnson, the readiness and ability of the gentlemen concerned to carry the settlement into execution, with very little expense to the Crown, etc. The secretaries appeared finally to the fully con-

vinced, and there remained no obstacle but the Board of Trade, which was to be brought over privately before the matter should be referred to them officially.

English politics and the rapidly shifting tides of opinion, combined with persisting anticolonial sentiments, smashed this hope. Lord North became chancellor of the exchequer in September, signaling the growing power of forces unfriendly to the colonists. Conway left office. Shelburne gave up management of American affairs, to be succeeded by Hillsborough, the former head of the Board of Trade, still known for his anticolonial sentiments. Hillsborough vowed to end smuggling in the port cities and in other ways punish the colonists for violating the laws. Could such a man be expected to favor the Traders' Company?

Up to this time the Philadelphia group had concentrated its efforts at seeking redress from London in the form of a land grant. Now this hope seemed shattered. Hillsborough seemed interested in settling the western boundary of the colonies once and for all. The Traders' Company, as well as the leaders of the Ohio Company of Virginia and other land companies, felt certain such a line would favor the Indians. If this were so, if the line were permanent, and if the British sent troops to the frontier to enforce it, then the companies and their dreams would be ended. Given the bad relations between the mother country and the colonies in 1767, it appeared Hillsborough would triumph.

The speculators had alternate plans and approaches. Instead of winning London's support and then dealing with the Iroquois, they would first sign a treaty with the Indians, and then seek confirmation from Hillsborough. If Hillsborough's grants to the Indians were rejected by the grantees themselves, what could London do?

Accordingly, Johnson called for a meeting of all interested parties in trans-Appalachia, to convene at Fort Stanwix (near present-day Rome, New York) in the summer of 1768. The meeting began in September, and lasted for more than two months, as not all interested parties were able to arrive in time. Some 3,400 Indian warriors and chiefs arrived, representing the Delaware, Shawnee, Seneca, and other Ohio tribes, as well as the Iroquois and the eastern Indians. Johnson provided them with nightly feasts and barrels of rum—which the Indians believed was a gift from the gods to the white men. The colonies of Virginia, Pennsylvania, and New Jersey sent representatives, and one of them was William Franklin. The Ohio Company of Virginia sent delegates, instructed to make certain its interests were not ignored. The largest colonial delegation was that of the Indiana Company, and included Wharton and William Trent, who represented the largest stockholders in that enterprise. Trent was fifty-five years old at the time, the leader at Simons, Trent, Franks & Co., and a man who knew both trans-Appalachia and Philadelphia society. He was also a sometime friend and business partner of Croghan. Needless to say, George Croghan was at Fort Stanwix, too, participating in most of the conferences and present at all the feasts and parties.

Fort Stanwix was one of the most important meetings in colonial history. It brought together more different groups than any previous meeting, and was intended to settle all outstanding differences among the Indians, settlers, and companies in trans-Appalachia. If it succeeded, London would be presented with a *fait accompli*, one that would strengthen the hands of company representatives in that city. If it failed, war might erupt on the frontier, and the financial dreams of dozens of land speculators would be ended.

In his capacity as representative of the Crown, William Johnson presided over the meetings. He assured all parties that he was empowered to make decisions binding on London, but Croghan, Wharton, and Franklin knew Hillsborough and others could easily overturn any decision made at Fort Stanwix. So did Thomas Walker, who represented the Ohio Company of Virginia. Yet all participated as though the claim were true.

After much ceremony and negotiation, a treaty was concluded on November 3. Under its terms, some 3.5 million acres of land situated on the Little Kanawha and Ohio rivers, along the southern boundary of Pennsylvania, was ceded to the colonial negotiators. Croghan's earlier grant of 200,000 acres was reaffirmed in a separate agreement. Two days later the Indians and Johnson signed another pact, this one for the sale of a large grant between the Alleghenies and the Ohio River, for £10,460.* It was the biggest land transaction conducted in America to that time.

The treaty was signed by Abraham of the Mohawks, Sennghois of the Oneidas, Saquarisera of the Tuscaroras, Chenaugheata of the Onondagas, Tagaaia of the Cayugas, and Gaustarax of the Senecas. Franklin, Walker, and seven others signed for the Americans. Johnson and Croghan were not among the signatories. Neither was Trent, but the Treaty of Fort Stanwix stipulated that he would be the agent for the traders and the tribes in their dealings with London. Thus, the treaty implied that royal confirmation was necessary before it could go into effect.

On December 30, Croghan, Franklin, Wharton, Trent, and other interested parties met in Philadelphia to plan strategy and carve up the grant. They agreed that Trent and Wharton should proceed to London, with the others paying their expenses. Any money forwarded to Trent and Wharton would be repaid at a later date, when the grant was confirmed.

All present felt the urgency of the voyage. Baynton, Wharton & Morgan was in receivership at the time, and Trent's own affairs were going badly. Croghan's funds were tied up in land speculations and his Philadelphia estate. Some Philadelphia merchants, original members of the suffering traders, had been excluded from the Indiana Company, and they threatened action unless the company recognized their claims. Not all members of the Ohio Company of Virginia were pleased with the Treaty of Fort Stanwix, and George Mercer, its London agent, was wary of those who belonged to the Indiana Company. Nor was Hillsborough happy with the treaty, and he gave evidence of wanting to repudiate it. After all, why should a British ministry confirm so huge a grant of what it considered its own

*Interestingly enough, there is grave doubt the Indians present at Fort Stanwix had previous clear title to the land they granted or sold. Thus, the colonists may have been purchasing land, while the Indians were engaging in a confidence game.

land, made by Indians to private companies? Such thoughts and issues were discussed in Philadelphia, and occupied the minds of Trent and Wharton as they journeyed to London in January.

The envoys arrived in London in the spring of 1769, and set about finding English allies to assist in their work. Thomas Pownall, the former governor in turn of New Jersey, Massachusetts, and South Carolina, and at the time a member of Parliament and brother of John Pownall, Hillsborough's secretary, was one of these. So was Lauchlin MacLeane, Shelburne's secretary. Franklin was there to assist through his many contacts in and out of government. Within a short period of time, Wharton was able to influence or convince a large number of government officials and MPs of the worthiness of his cause. The most important of these was Thomas Walpole.

Walpole bore a distinguished name. He was the second son of Horatio Walpole, a member of Parliament before him, and the younger brother of Sir Robert Walpole. His uncle was the famous Robert Walpole, the first earl of Oxford, who dominated English politics for a generation, and one of whose important acts was to salvage the wreckage after the collapse of the South Sea bubble. Horace Walpole, the famed diarist, was Thomas' cousin. Few in England could boast a more illustrious lineage.

In 1749, at the age of twenty-two, Thomas had married the daughter of Sir Joshua Vanneck, one of the wealthiest merchants in Europe. Thereupon he began his business career, engaging in government contracts during the French wars and becoming a director of the East India Company. Walpole entered Parliament as a member from Sudbury in 1754, and would remain there for thirty years, combining politics with business and profiting from both. Rumor had it that he and his associates made fortunes from war contracts, although the charges were never proved.

The end of the French wars left Walpole with much money and few places to invest it. The East India Company also suffered as a result of the peace, and Walpole voiced doubts as to its future solvency. In 1769 he and others like him were actively seeking new areas for investment. As has been indicated, land seemed both safe and lucrative. Such was the case when Wharton and Trent arrived in London. They had land claims and needed friends in power with money and influence. Walpole was searching for individuals and companies with investment schemes. They were natural allies. For the moment, however, Wharton rejected an alliance with Walpole. His price was too high.

As before, Hillsborough was opposed to colonial land schemes, or any plan that might enrich American speculators. For the moment the American "rebels" seemed still, but who could tell when they would begin their work again? Weakness in the eyes of such rabble would be disastrous, he thought. In Hillsborough's view, all Americans were alike—coarse, uncouth, ungrateful, and seditious. Samuel Wharton was little different from Samuel Adams. To assist one would be to reward the other, and Hillsborough had no intention of doing either. As a result, he condemned the Treaty of Fort Stanwix and the land claims resulting from it. Hillsborough wrote to Johnson, criticizing him for exceeding his authority, and questioning Croghan's 200,000-acre grant. He observed that some of the land obtained at Fort Stanwix properly belonged to southern tribes, which might revolt if they learned of the terms of the treaty. This could mean a new British expeditionary force in trans-Appalachia, and he for one would not authorize such a costly expedition. Trent and Wharton were told as much by Hillsborough himself. Trent wrote of his dismay to Croghan, warning that all seemed lost. Wharton, the cooler of the two, arranged a meeting with Walpole.

On June 14 the two men met privately to discuss politics and land. Walpole informed the American that although Hillsborough was powerful, most of the other members of the ministry opposed him. To them the Treaty of Fort Stanwix seemed both fair and equitable. The king himself might be induced to overturn Hillsborough's decision on the land grants. Wharton would need help in contacting the right people in the ministry, however, and those who helped him would expect a share in the rewards. Walpole's meaning was clear; Wharton agreed to an alliance.

Together the two men fashioned a new company, one which

would include prominent Englishmen as well as Americans. Lord Hertford, the lord chamberlain, would be a member, along with Richard Jackson, counselor to the Board of Trade. Walpole would bring in Lord Rochford and Lord Gower of the Privy Council, and George Grenville, the architect of the Stamp Act and a man known for his anti-American sentiments. Directors of the East India Company would be given an interest in the new enterprise. Profit knew no politics; men of all political persuasions would be enlisted, and Hillsborough would be outflanked. By early December they were prepared to confront Hillsborough at the Board of Trade, and knew they had the votes to assure success.

So did Hillsborough, who had not risen to his post without a measure of political sophistication. He surprised Wharton and Trent by his graciousness and willingness to hear them out. Proposals he rejected out of hand a few months earlier he now considered reasonable and wise. The Treaty of Fort Stanwix? He would accept it forthwith. But why stop there? Hillsborough wondered why the petitioners did not seek a much larger grant, one sufficient in size to form a new colony—the first interior colony in North America. Then the company could encourage settlement, deal with Indian affairs on their own, and guard the frontier against any new threats. In effect, Hillsborough was suggesting the creation of a new proprietary colony, one almost as large as Pennsylvania. Handled properly, such a grant could in time reward its owners handsomely.

Why did Hillsborough change his mind so abruptly, and in so generous a fashion? His ability to shift with political winds provides part of the answer, but his knowledge of American affairs offers the rest. This enlarged company grant would include land previously claimed by the Ohio Company, and by the Mississippi Company. Arthur Lee was in London at the time, representing the Mississippi claims, and he, too, had friends in power. So did George Mercer of the Ohio Company, who had been in London since 1763, and whose connections were almost as good as Wharton's. Hillsborough knew Mercer would be furious when he learned of the plan for an enlarged grant that would encroach on Ohio Company claims. He was unable to stop the Wharton-Walpole combine, but Mercer might stymie its plans.

Hillsborough's suspicion was well-founded. As soon as Mercer learned of the plan, he sprang into action, calling upon friends and allies and seeking their help in blocking the grant. Mercer petitioned the board, urging its members to recall that his company had prior claims to the land, and had suffered losses as great as that of the Indiana Company. Indeed, the "military adventurers" of the Ohio Company had been given the grant in recognition of their sacrifices and service during the French and Indian War. Were they now to be cast aside in favor of speculators? Mercer added that he was

> encouraged to hope the Ohio company, who were the very first adventurers, and have expended, so large a sum of money, upwards of 14 years since, on a settlement begun under the sanction of government, will not be prevented, from prosecuting their design, while others of your majesty's subjects, who have lately only formed their scheme, enjoy the benefit of the company's labour, and discoveries. . . .

Other petitions followed, but Mercer, who knew parliamentary politics as well as any American, soon realized his influence could not match that of the Wharton-Walpole combine. He wrote to his associates in Virginia, asking directions and telling them of what was transpiring. Even then he knew he could not expect replies before the board had acted. He would have to proceed on his own, and salvage whatever he could.

On December 27, Wharton, Walpole, and other leaders met at the Crown and Anchor Tavern to ratify what had been a fact for months—the creation of a new company. It would be known as the Grand Ohio Company, but was more commonly referred to as the Walpole Associates. Seventy-two shares would be authorized, with Walpole receiving eight and Wharton five. Trent would get four shares. The other forty-two members would receive one or two apiece. William Johnson, Benjamin Franklin, and William Franklin were among these. George Croghan was not, but it was expected that he would be rewarded with shares in return for his 200,000-acre grant. Walpole, Wharton, Benjamin Franklin, and John Sargent, the last named being a prominent Englishman, were to serve as an executive committee, empowered to negotiate with the Crown. Each member was to contribute £200 for each share held, the money used for expenses. Wharton proposed some of the money be used to obtain the additional land Hillsborough had referred to, and his motion was voted upon and accepted.

The four members of the committee met with treasury officials on January 4, 1770, at which time they offered to purchase some twenty million acres of land within the Fort Stanwix cession. In return for this grant they would pay £10,460—the cost of the purchase, and a quitrent of two shillings for every hundred acres of cultivable land, to begin in twenty years. The officials accepted the price, but postponed final decision due to uncertainty as to the quitrents. The delay may have been a ruse, to allow Lee and Mercer time to work out some kind of deal.

Mercer persisted in his efforts, and although Walpole and Wharton felt they could defeat him, they were too close to their goal to take chances. They approached Mercer and began negotiations for a settlement. One was reached on May 7, by which the Ohio Company of Virginia would be merged into the Grand Ohio Company. In return for relinquishing its claim, the Ohio Company would receive two shares of Grand Ohio stock, while Mercer would receive one for his troubles. Three days later Mercer withdrew his petitions against the Grand Ohio Company, the same day Wharton hinted he might be named as first governor of the new territory.

This seemed to have removed the last barrier to Crown approval. Yet Hillsborough continued to raise new objections, each of which was deflected by Walpole. Now the Virginia government protested the grant, which it claimed would infringe upon its territory. Wharton countered, instructing Croghan to prepare and send "petitions" to Parliament from Americans wanting the scheme to go through. These petitions, supposedly from individuals wanting to settle in

Grand Ohio land, were bogus. Wharton didn't know if they could influence the board, but thought it worth the effort. And at the same time, Wharton entered other land schemes, to have something to fall back on should the Walpole Associates fail.

The contest dragged on into 1772. In June, Wharton, Mercer, and Trent told a committee of the Privy Council that 5,000 families had already settled on the land granted under the Fort Stanwix treaty, and that an additional 25,000 families were in the rest of trans-Appalachia. Wharton introduced his bogus petitions as evidence, along with letters from "disinterested" parties such as Croghan and William Franklin. These people needed protection, he said, and only the company could provide it. To add spice to his argument, he showed the committee samples of a silklike substance he claimed was raised in the area. It was indeed silk, he said. The area was perfect for mulberry trees and silkworms, but cultivation could not begin until the grant was made. England would reap a fortune in trade, said Wharton—but first, the council would have to pass the grant.

On July 1, the committee accepted the petition and sent it on to the Privy Council. Hillsborough made his final stand there. If the council supported the petition and sent it to the Board of Trade, and the board accepted it, the grant was as good as ratified. The political battle raged for more than a month. Then, on August 13, Hillsborough was forced from office for reasons having nothing to do with the Grand Ohio.* He was replaced by the earl of Dartmouth, known to be friendly to the company. The very next day the Privy Council accepted the petition.

*In a letter to William Franklin on August 17, Benjamin Franklin wrote: "You will hear it said among you, I suppose, that the interest of the Ohio planters has ousted him; but the truth is, what I wrote you long since, that all his brother ministers disliked him extremely, and wished for a fair occasion of tripping up his heels; so, seeing that he made a point of defeating our scheme, they made another of supporting it, on purpose to mortify him, which they knew his pride could not bear. I do not mean they would have done this had they thought our proposal bad in itself, or his opposition well-founded; but I do believe if he had been on good terms with them they would not have differed with him on so small a matter. The King, too, was tired of him and of his administration, which had weakened the affection and respect for a royal government. . . . The King's dislike made the others more firmly united in the resolution of disgracing Hillsborough by setting at nought his famous report."

Now the company took its case to the Board of Trade. This caused additional delay, as new opponents appeared, disappeared, and then reappeared once again. As late as April 3, 1773, Franklin wrote:

> The affair of the grant goes on but slowly. I do not yet clearly see land. I begin to be a little of the sailor's mind when they were landing a cable out of a store into a ship, and one of 'em said: 'Tis a long, heavy cable. I wish we could see the end of it.' 'D__n me,' says another, 'if I believe it has any end; somebody has cut it off.'

Finally, on May 6, the board submitted conditional approval of the grant to the king. The new colony, it said, was to be called "Vandalia," in honor of Queen Charlotte, "as her Majesty is descended from the Vandals." Two weeks later the Committee for Plantation Affairs approved the report, and on July 3 the Privy Council ordered the attorney general and solicitor general to prepare the final report.

It would appear that the Walpole Associates had finally achieved its objective. A great land combine disguised as a colony was on the point of being realized. It brought together leaders of Parliament and some of the most powerful individuals in the colonies. The Lees, the Washingtons, the Galloways, and other prominent colonial families had a share in the company. Such an alliance not only promised profits, but also perhaps closer ties between mother country and colony. Much money and more time had been invested in the company by all involved—especially by Wharton and Walpole in London and Croghan and William Franklin in America.

As the last vestiges of opposition were being swept away in London, events in America conspired further to thwart the dreams of Vandalia. The first of these was an Indian uprising in the Ohio Valley. The Shawnee and Delaware were attacking frontier outposts, in what seemed the beginning of a new Indian war. Did this mean English troops would once again be needed in the area? If so, what would the role of the Walpole Associates be? Opponents of the

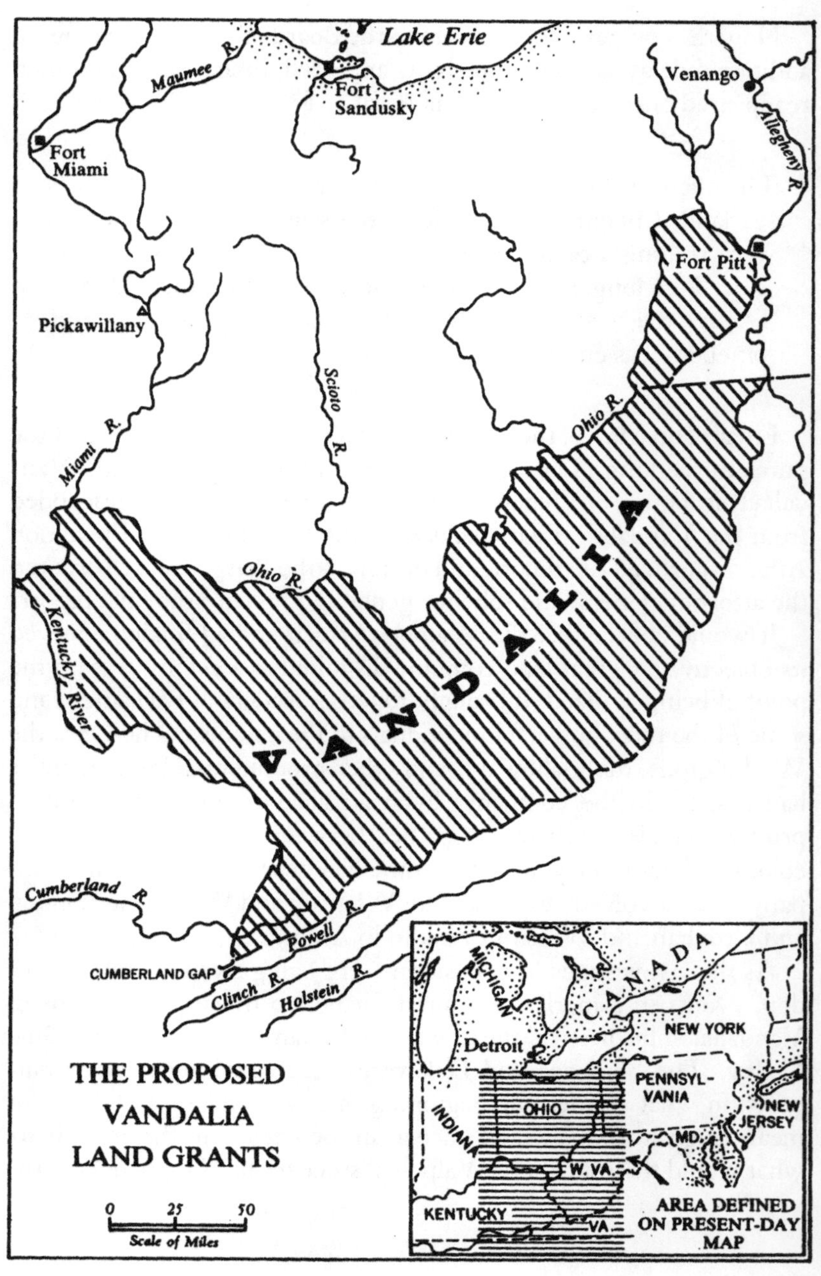

THE PROPOSED VANDALIA LAND GRANTS

company raised these and related questions in the autumn of 1773, causing further delays.

More important was the Boston Tea Party of December 16. Now anticolonial sentiment reached a new high in London. Writing to a friend in Massachusetts, Franklin lamented:

> I suppose we never had since we were a people so few friends in Britain. The violent destruction of the tea seems to have united all parties here against our province, so that the bill now brought into Parliament for shutting up Boston as a port till satisfaction is made, meets with no opposition.

Boston port was indeed shut down, as part of what the colonists called "The Intolerable Acts," which passed Parliament in March-June 1774. This seemed the wrong time for pursuing the Vandalia venture. Wharton's friends in Philadelphia sent urgent letters, asking whether the plan had been accepted. If such were not the case, they said, it might never be revived, for conditions in America were getting worse all the time.

Anticolonial forces now turned on Franklin, who for many years had been the symbol of America in London. They noted that Franklin was a key member of the Walpole Associates. Were they expected to support a scheme to make Franklin wealthy, just as his "friends" were defying the Crown in Boston? Wharton countered by claiming—falsely—that Franklin was no longer associated with the Great Ohio Company, and Franklin even submitted a false letter of resignation from the organization. This did little good. As though this were not enough, Trent learned that his wife, who had remained in Philadelphia, was on her way to London to see what he was doing there. George Morgan, Wharton's partner, sent word that he believed Wharton was double-crossing him. He, too, would go to England, and take matters into his own hands. Morgan all but threatened Wharton's life. Trent would fare little better. "With regard to that contemptible Wretch Trent," he wrote angrily, "my Treatment of him will depend on your Conduct; for of himself he is not worth giving a Kick in the Breech to, or a Pull by the Nose."

To forestall such indignities, Trent returned home in May 1775. Shortly before he left, however, the final passage of the Vandalia measure was achieved. In theory, the Grand Ohio Company was recognized by the Crown. The dream of an interior colony, hatched at Fort Stanwix seven years earlier, was realized.

But not yet. The Crown stipulated that the grant would not take effect until after the cessation of hostilities between Britain and the American rebels. On April 19 British troops had clashed with American rebels in what came to be known as the battles of Lexington and Concord. Although neither side knew it as yet, the American Revolution had begun. The last ties between mother country and colony were being severed. One of the casualties of the Revolution would be the Vandalian vision.

Wharton could not believe this could happen—not after seven years of hard labor and expenses in excess of £10,000. He remained in London, hoping for a quick end to hostilities. In a long pamphlet published soon after news of the battles reached London, he wrote of his dreams for the colony, of its potential wealth, and his plans for settlement once the conflict had ended. But in order to earn money, he joined with Walpole in speculating in English securities. Finally, in the spring of 1779, he was forced to flee to Paris to escape English officials who suspected him of prorebel sympathies and activities. Wharton eventually returned to his homeland, to press his claims to Vandalia before the government of what was now the United States. Then the royal grant was challenged by Virginia. Much litigation followed, but in 1795 the Supreme Court decided against the company. Five years later Wharton was dead, a broken and poor man.

The other leaders of the company fared little better. Croghan fell ill in the early days of the Revolution and never regained his health. Hounded by the Americans for suspected loyalist sentiments and poverty-stricken as a result of his business failures, he finished his life in a small house in the Philadelphia suburbs. Monckton Hall was long since sold to pay debts, and all that remained were his dreams and memories. Croghan died in 1782 and was buried in a local graveyard. His passing was recorded by the sexton, who misspelled his name.

Walpole's fortunes had begun their decline even before the Revolution. Various speculations had failed, so that by 1775 much of his hopes were tied up in the Grand Ohio scheme. He spoke out in Parliament for reconciliation with the Americans, as much to save his investments as anything else. In 1779, one of his business associates fled the country after having stolen some of his funds. Meanwhile East India Company business suffered, causing additional losses. In 1783 Walpole was forced to sell some of his land holdings in England, a certain sign of imminent bankruptcy in those days. Yet he held on, though in 1789 he was forced to ask a friend for a place to stay and a small pension. He received these, and dropped from sight. Thomas Walpole, once a leader in business and politics and the bearer of a famed name, died in near poverty in 1803.

Like Croghan, Trent was accused of pro-British sentiment during the Revolution, during which time his business interests collapsed. Almost destitute, he pinned his hopes on United States recognition of the Vandalia grant. Trent worked with his old associate Wharton in lobbying Congress, and was still at it when he died in 1787.

William Johnson was spared the pain of seeing the scheme fail. In any case, he had so many other interests the losses would not have hurt as much as it did Croghan, Wharton, and the others. Johnson died in 1774, before the Revolution, at the age of fifty-nine, wealthy and respected. Given his close connections with the Crown, he might have been ruined had he lived another ten years. Then again, a man of his talents might have been able to work out some kind of deal with the Americans, and emerged from the Revolution a hero.

William Franklin remained loyal to the Crown during the Revolution, was confined to jail for two years after his capture by the Americans, and, as might have been expected, was estranged from his father. After the Revolution there was a reconciliation of sorts, though the differences between them were never fully resolved. In his will, Franklin left his son some land in Nova Scotia, books, and papers, but the bulk of his estate went to others. "The part he acted against me in the late war, which is of public notoriety, will account for my leaving him no more of an estate he endeavored to deprive me of," wrote Franklin in 1788.

Benjamin Franklin, as always, landed on his feet. He not only survived his many connections with the English, but became a hero of the Revolution and of the difficult years that followed. He died in 1789, at the age of eighty-four. Vandalia had gone wrong for him, but so much else had gone right.

CHAPTER 2

A Great National Project

In 1784 George Washington, one of the greatest land speculators of the day, set out on his sixth and final tour of trans-Appalachia. Washington was fifty-two years old at the time, and in excellent health. He believed his public life had ended; on several occasions he warded off attempts to involve him in Virginia and national politics, and he even left a church office for fear it might be considered in part at least political. Much of his attention since the end of the Revolution had been centered on his home, family—and land.

Washington owned, personally, some 58,000 acres of trans-Appalachian real estate, of which more than 43,000 acres were in the Great Kanawha Valley—the heart of what was to have been Vandalia. The Kanawha originated in the western foothills of the Appalachians, and flowed in a northwestern direction into the Ohio River, which in turn was a major tributary of the Mississippi. The James River began in the eastern foothills, going on to drain central

Virginia until it reached the coast. Washington was aware of this, for river transportation was the prime pathway for individuals wanting to go inland in the late eighteenth century. In 1770, while engaged in the work of the Ohio Company, he noted that his lands were happily situated "upon the Ohio between the mouths of the two Kanawhas, having a front upon the river of fifteen miles and beautifully bordered by it." The location was "river lowgrounds of the first quality. . . . A great deal of it may be converted into the finest mowing ground imaginable, with little or no labor. . . ." It was good, fertile land, perfect for farming. But it was worth far less than worse land along the James, near the seacoast. A farmer there might float his produce downstream to Norfolk, and from there have it sent to coastwise cities farther north or across the Atlantic to Europe. What could a farmer do if his holdings were on the Great Kanawha? He might send his goods downriver, into the Ohio and then to the Mississippi. At the end of the voyage was New Orleans, a Spanish city. The Great Kanawha Valley might be reached through the Great Lakes, still controlled by the British. Thus, the two major transportation lines into the valley were in the hands of unfriendly foreigners.

But the farmer might choose a third route, carrying his goods across or through the Appalachians to the James River, and there load them on boats for the trip to Norfolk, which involved several portages. Land transportation was expensive, as were transfers. Washington and other speculators knew the western lands would not increase in value until the transportation problem was solved.

Prior to leaving for trans-Appalachia, Washington advertised for settlers on his lands. Those who came could live there rent-free for three years, on condition that for every hundred acres taken, five would be cleared and a house erected. After the three years rents would be charged, to reach a maximum of three shillings per acre per year. Leases would be for 999 years, reflecting the optimism of the time.

The trip was leisurely. In his diary Washington noted major stands of lumber, suitable for sale or use. He saw many outcroppings of coal, which appeared to be "of the very best kind, burning freely." But these natural resources were worth little, since there was no way to bring them to market.

One of Washington's objectives on his trip was to visit Gilbert Simpson, who had constructed a mill on his land, on a tributary of the Youghiogheny River. Washington was half-convinced Simpson had been cheating him; he was certain he should have received payments from Simpson, and none were forthcoming. Now he would auction off the mill and other properties in the area. While there he would deal with squatters on his lands, demanding payment for its use.

Washington arrived at Simpson's Mill to find it in bad repair. Simpson complained it had lost money, since there was no way to get flour to market cheaply. Washington knew this, but was determined to sell it anyway. So he organized an auction, and received no bids. Then he tried to sell the mill, and no one came forward. Finally he offered to rent it at a low price, with no rents to be charged for the first fifteen months. Still there were no takers. So Washington was forced to "let her return to dust," and collect what he could from Simpson in the form of flour and wheat. In the end, however, he did not take these products with him to Mount Vernon. Flour was cheaper at Simpson's than in tidewater Virginia, but when transportation costs were added, it came to twice the price.

Washington then dealt with the squatters, Scotch-Irish subsistence farmers all. He offered to sell them the land, at 25 shillings an acre, to be paid in three annual installments. If this were not acceptable, he would rent them the land for 999 years. The farmers wanted to buy, but asked for longer payment periods without additional interest. The general refused to consider this, and since the squatters would not budge, the case went to court. Washington won the suit in 1786, but this victory had little meaning, since there was no way to expel the squatters or make them pay for the land. Nor would it make sense to force the issue, for the land was not that valuable, and the troubles not worth the effort. Again, transportation was the key. Given good transportation from the Great Kanawha to the James, Washington would be rich. As it was, he was "land poor."

There was another, even more important reason to desire such transportation. Without a route to the Atlantic, the Kanawha residents and others who came to the region might see little value in remaining Americans. Under some circumstances, they might seek the protection of the Spaniards at New Orleans, while under others they could turn to Britain. "The western settlers (I speak now from my own observation) stand as it were upon a pivot," he wrote on his return. "The touch of a feather would turn them any way."

For political and personal reasons, then, Washington saw the need for better transportation to trans-Appalachia. This was not a new discovery on his part. Even as a youthful surveyor before the French and Indian War he dreamed of a canal from the Potomac River to the Ohio, which would make Alexandria the greatest port on the Atlantic and the key to trans-Appalachia. While a member of the Ohio Company he had planned a private company, which would construct a canal from the tidewater 150 miles into the interior, and eventually to the Ohio. As late as 1773 Washington spoke of such a canal, the plans for which of course were ended by the Revolution.

After the war several Virginians urged Washington to renew the plan, for the sake of the state. Jefferson thought a Potomac Canal might be "only a dignified amusement to you," but "what a monument of your retirement it would be!" Patrick Henry, who like Washington owned land in the West, said "the finger of heaven" pointed the way. Washington supported the proposal, which was taken to both the Maryland and Virginia assemblies.

The prestige of these three men and others of the revolutionary generation, together with the obvious advantages such a canal would have; made passage of an enabling act possible. Two private companies were authorized. The first, the Potomac Company, was empowered to raise funds to open the river to its highest point of permanent navigation—hopefully, to Fort Cumberland. The company would then construct a road to the Ohio, and in this way give Virginia access to the West. Washington consented to serve as its president, and received fifty shares of its stock. The second company, the James River Canal Company, would construct improvements on that river. Washington received one hundred shares of its capital stock. Fearful of being charged with an attempt to profit from these ventures, he assigned the securities to a fund for the education of poor children, especially those of soldiers who had died in the Revolution. "I would wish that every individual who may hear that it was a favorite plan of mine, may know also that I had no other motive for promoting it, than the advantage I conceive it would be productive of to the Union, and to this state in particular."

Washington threw himself into the projects enthusiastically. The canals of Virginia and Maryland would be only the beginning of a great national project, he thought, one that would bind Americans together and engage them for generations. He urged the Continental Congress to "have the western waters well explored, the navigation of them fully ascertained, accurately laid down, and a complete and perfect map made of the country." In writing to Madison of his hopes, he said, "The mind can scarcely take in at one view all the benefits which will result therefrom. . . . This business wants only a beginning." When completed it would bring "navigation to almost every man's door."

Now that the companies were formed, Washington had to concern himself with the development of the waterways. Two problems presented themselves immediately. The first was that of financing. Could sufficient funds be raised to enable the companies to begin work? Even before the canals were completed they could be used, and so bring in revenues through tolls. That would be a long way off, and until then, additional construction funds would be needed every year. Washington believed the states would not vote money, and the Continental Congress had little cash, even had its members supporting the schemes. Only in Europe could large amounts of capital be raised, and he asked Jefferson, then minister to France, to inquire about interest in canal bonds.

This proved unnecessary. Washington's prestige, added to dreams of success, encouraged Virginians and Marylanders to purchase shares. The state legislatures, eager for profit through tolls and land sales, also supported the Potomac Canal. In 1784, 500 shares at £100 a share were sold, raising enough money to begin work. Approximately half of these shares, and those of later subscriptions, were taken by the states, while private investors, many of whom either lived along the rivers or owned western lands, took the rest. Washington was overjoyed. He held a "turtle feast" at Mount Vernon for the directors to celebrate.

The second problem was not so easily overcome. The technology of the 1780s was crude. Canals had been constructed in England, and most had proved successful. But these had been built on flatland for the most part; those that needed locks were less successful. Too, the Potomac Company hoped to use canals as extensions of rivers, and if canal boats were to be used, they would have to be adapted to the Potomac. This meant they would have to go upstream as well as down. How could this be done?

Washington thought both problems could be solved by David Rumsey, a young man as interested as he in canals. Rumsey showed Washington his model of a new kind of vessel. It resembled two boats in parallel with a waterwheel between them, and poles attached to each boat and the wheel in a complicated fashion. Rumsey placed the model in running water, facing upstream. The water caused the wheel to turn, and the power was transmitted to the poles, which propelled the boat upstream. The faster the water went, the faster the poles would go. It seemed Rumsey had developed a vessel that could go upstream with ease. Washington rejoiced; Rumsey had made "the present epoch favorable above all others."

The model was just that—only a model. When Rumsey tried to construct a prototype he failed. The "Steam Boat Without a Steam Engine" was abandoned.

Rumsey also undertook construction of the canals and improvements on the Potomac. Here, too, he failed. Labor was hard to find and difficult to maintain, supplies were overpriced, and the locks Rumsey constructed fell apart. A section of the canal was completed in 1790, and two others two years later. By then Rumsey had resigned, and the third engineer was on the job. Others would follow.

The company was close to bankruptcy in 1792 and applied to the states for additional funds. Some were granted, though not nearly enough to complete the job. In 1802 additional locks were completed, making the Potomac navigable for nearly 220 miles. Toll revenues were not as great as expected, however, and it seemed evident such waterways could not pay their way. The states refused to subscribe to additional loans. Lotteries were used to obtain funds, but these had limited success. The Potomac Company limped on until 1828, at which time it had debts of over $176,000. The James River Canal Company did little more than preliminary work. Both projects were soon abandoned, or merged into new enterprises.*

These early attempts at canal building in America had mixed results. The Potomac improvements assisted in the economic development of the valley, and were widely used by its residents. In 1800 the company had 296 boats on its canals; eleven years later it had 1,300, after which the number declined because of the War of 1812. Similarly, tonnage hauled on the canals rose from 1,643 tons in 1800 to 16,350 tons in 1811. Almost a million dollars worth of goods were carried in the latter year, returning tolls of $22,542, permitting the company to show a small profit. That was an excellent year, in fact the best in the Potomac Company's history. This would seem to indicate that given the technology, costs, and economic development of the period, canals were at best marginal propositions, and not good investments.

Washington suggested that a canal had to be viewed in the same way as schools, the army and navy, and harbor improvements. Such operations were not meant to show profits, but rather were necessary for the general health of the community and nation. The Potomac Company may not have been successful economically, but its opera-

*The cooperation between Virginia and Maryland continued after the organization of the companies. Hoping to cement the relationship, Washington cooperated in the calling of a conference at Mount Vernon in 1785, to discuss improvements of the Potomac. This led to the Annapolis Conference of 1786, which in turn called the states to convention in Philadelphia to amend the Constitution. The Philadelphia Convention wrote a new Constitution, under which Washington became the first President. There is a tenuous link, then, between the Potomac Company and the establishment of the new government under the Constitution. And the president of the Company became the President of the United States.

tions meant larger incomes for farmers, closer political ties between the people in the area, and higher prices for land in the interior.

Better transportation, then, became the concern of many not directly involved in canals. Politicians eager to unite the nation supported them. Farmers along proposed canal and turnpike routes were happy to see them come, and in time small manufacturers would feel the same. Owners of large land grants situated in isolated areas knew that, until people and goods could move more freely in and out of their lands, their value would be small. All three of these groups wanted canals, and were willing to invest in them and even lose funds thereby if by so doing they benefited in other ways.

Some state and city leaders in the East supported them. The riches of the West were ready to be tapped, and the state and city that controlled the spigot would be the ones with transportation facilities to the area. New Yorkers thought of a canal or a canal-and-turnpike system which would open Ohio to the Atlantic, while Pennsylvania and Philadelphia saw no reason why the Delaware River could not act as the leader for a similar system. Baltimore was uncertain as how to act, and Maryland believed canals could be teamed with primitive railroads to make the city the key to the West. Cities as far north as Boston and as far south as Savannah had similar thoughts. Clearly several important segments of the population wanted better transportation, and canals seemed reasonable to a people used to thinking in terms of water transportation. The questions were how the canals would be financed and constructed, which group or city or state would lead the way, when the work would begin, and where the canals would lead.

All these questions were asked at approximately the same time, and their answers reflected the political and economic realities of the period. Presidents Washington and Adams and their Federalist backers supported internal improvements, while their Republican critics, including Jefferson, questioned their propriety and the costs of such programs. Yet it was during Jefferson's Presidency, as the pressures for expansion grew, that the first large-scale plan was developed. His secretary of the treasury, Albert Gallatin, sold $11.25

million worth of government bonds to help pay for Louisiana, thus going against Jefferson's own warnings regarding a large national debt. In his second inaugural address, in 1805, Jefferson again departed from his previous beliefs in limited government by recommending that surplus revenue "be applied to rivers, canals, roads, arts, manufactures, education, and other great objects within each state." In 1806 Congress authorized construction of a National Turnpike designed to link Ohio to the East, in this case Maryland and Virginia. This caused consternation in the New England and middle states, but two years later Gallatin met objections by setting forth an ambitious internal improvements program to finance transportation throughout the United States.

It inaugurated a period of governmental economic activity unparalleled in American history. For the next generation the federal and state governments spent a larger proportion of the gross national product on these and similar enterprises than ever before or since. Not even during the 1930s and after would the percentage be surpassed.

Gallatin's *Report on Roads and Canals* was a key document and bench mark in opening the canal era. In it the secretary stated, "The general utility of artificial roads and canals is universally admitted." In Britain and other countries, "these improvements may often, in ordinary cases, be left to individual exertion, without any direct aid from Government." But in the United States, government would have to play a major role. This was so because Americans lacked the capital to undertake improvements of this scope, and "the extent of territory compared to the population." Canals in particular would suffer losses. "Some works already executed are unprofitable; many more remain unattempted, because their ultimate productiveness depends on other improvements, too extensive or too distant to be embraced by the same individuals."

Gallatin's *Report* proposed "a tide water inland navigation" from Massachusetts to Georgia, consisting of canals and a turnpike. The greatest work would be the east-west connections. Gallatin believed canals could not traverse the Appalachians "in the present state of science." He called for river improvements from New Jersey to Georgia and roads across the mountains. New York might be served best by a canal to the Great Lakes from the Hudson. To accomplish these projects, Gallatin recommended the authorization of $20 million, to be spent over a ten-year period. Of this amount $4.8 million would go for a Maine-Georgia turnpike. River and harbor improvements would take an additional $1.5 million. Canals in all parts of the country would receive $7.3 million in federal funds.

Gallatin thought the money could be raised through federal surpluses, the sale of western lands belonging to the government, or new taxes. The fund could be a revolving one. Completed and successful projects might be sold "to individuals, or companies, and the proceeds applied to a new improvement." Considering the contemporary belief regarding canals, it seemed few would be profitable and appealing to such private interests that existed. Since Gallatin's improvements would be planned in such a way as to benefit the nation rather than local interests, and the canals in particular were not designed to benefit special interests, they would be all the more uneconomical, or so went the thinking at the time.

Gallatin's ambitious *Report* could not be put into operation at once, as foreign difficulties, especially the War of 1812, made such projects unfeasible. The war did demonstrate, however, the importance of good transportation to the interior. After the war, some parts of the program were acted upon, especially those relating to turnpikes, rivers, and harbors. Few canals received major government support. By 1829 only $1,885,000 in federal funds had been used to purchase stock in canal companies, all south of New Jersey. Of this amount, $1 million went to the Chesapeake and Ohio Canal Company, the successor to Washington's Potomac Company.

Gallatin had planned a national transportation program. Most of the turnpikes and canals aided by the federal government were in the South. Jefferson, Madison, and Monroe, who occupied the White House from 1801 to 1825, were all Virginians, while John Quincy Adams, who served from 1825 to 1829, was a nationalist, and not a partisan of northern interests. Federal assistance was limited in money and location, and this fact was not lost on speculators in land elsewhere in the country. Realizing this, they made their own plans for improvements.

As had been the case prior to the Revolution, land speculation occupied the interests of many wealthy Americans. From Maine to Georgia speculators vied with one another in obtaining large grants at little or no cost from the federal and state governments.* Nathaniel Gorham and Oliver Phelps purchased a large tract in western New York in 1788, and other purchases followed in the state. All states underwent similar experiences, but the Gorham and Phelps purchase set off a race for New York real estate that was livelier and more fraught with possibilities than most. The partners thought New York was the key to the Northwest. One could sail up the Hudson to Albany and then enter the Mohawk River as far as it could be taken. Then a portage would be necessary to Lake Ontario, and another at Niagara to Lake Erie, the gateway to the Northwest. Or the Ontario could be bypassed by a road or canal to what is today Buffalo, on the eastern end of Lake Erie. This route would traverse the Appalachians. A canal through the region might draw water from the Finger Lakes, and would help make New York not only the leading American port, but a world port of some importance. In the process, the Gorham and Phelps lands would increase in value. The partners had pledged to pay $1 million for their grant, later confirmed by an Indian treaty. In all they owned 2.6 million acres. Half the land was considered unsalable because of poor soil of one kind or another. If the other half could be sold at $10 an acre, a not unreasonable price, the net worth would come to $13 million. But such prices could not be realized without adequate transportation.

Robert Morris, "the Financier of the Revolution," was attracted to New York's western lands. Morris had speculated in land during and after the Revolution. His government position brought him in contact

*The history of land speculation and policy in the postrevolutionary period is rich and varied, but beyond the scope of this study. For detailed studies of various speculations, see A. M. Sakolski, *The Great American Land Bubble* (New York, 1932), and Payson J. Treat, *The National Land System, 1785–1820* (New York, 1910).

with Europe's leading financial houses. Some land speculators planned to purchase land at low price, wait until the value rose, and then sell the land to settlers or other speculators. Not Morris. He hoped for a quick turnover. Land would be purchased or obtained in some other way, and then wholesaled in Europe to speculators there. With the profits Morris would purchase new lands, and repeat the operations. A few turns of the wheel and he could become wealthy and retire.

As head of a combine which included several important New Yorkers, he purchased land from Gorham and Phelps and others in western New York. In 1790 he owned some five million acres, after which he approached Theophile Cazenove of J. Henry Cazenove & Co., a Dutch firm which had participated in the financing of the Revolution and had retained interest in American speculation and investment thereafter. Cazenove met Morris in Philadelphia, and the American convinced him of profits to be had in New York land he owned, especially Genesee in the western part of the state. Cazenove sent agents to the area, and they reported it to be rich in soil, lumber, and other natural resources. Convinced Morris was right, Cazenove purchased 1.5 million acres from him in December 1792, for a price of £75,000. Additional land was acquired from Alexander Macomb, William Duer, and Andrew Craigie, New Yorkers who also speculated in western land and who were occasional associates of Morris.* Within a few months Cazenove and other Dutch firms had purchased three million acres. They formed the Holland Land Company, divided its shares between them, and prepared to retail the land to European settlers. Peter Stadnitzki, one of the company's agents, published *Information Concerning a Negotiation of Lands in America,* urging Europeans to come to western New York and acquire homesteads.

Few seemed interested, and sales were slow at first. Better transportation would be needed before the Holland Land Company could show a profit.

*For descriptions of land, securities, and other speculations of Macomb, Craigie, and Duer, see Joseph S. Davis, *Essays in the Earlier History of American Corporations.* 2 vols. (Cambridge, 1917), I, 111–338.

Meanwhile, Macomb and his associates took part of their profits and looked elsewhere for bargains in land. Northern New York, then an uncharted wilderness, seemed attractive. Joseph Totten and Stephen Crossfield, two ship's carpenters from New York City, owned 800,000 acres north of Albany, acquired in 1774. The land reverted to the state after the Revolution, and in 1790 was in the hands of private speculators. The rest still belonged to the state, and Macomb offered to purchase most of it—some 3.6 million acres—for 8 pence per acre. He hoped to interest Cazenove and his associates in purchasing part of it, but the banker was too busily engaged in western New York and the Holland Land Company to take a share. Macomb found others willing to take part of the land, and the state approved the sale.

Most of the land was completely inaccessible. But the southern boundary of the Macomb Grant lay along a line drawn from Albany to Buffalo. Should a road or canal be constructed on this line, at least part of the grant would become very valuable. At the time of the purchase, New York was moving in that direction.

In January 1791, Governor George Clinton delivered a message to the New York legislature, in which he spoke of the state's economic development. Of prime importance, he said, was communication and transportation between New York City, Albany, and other eastern centers and the western part of the state. Unless the Albany-Lake Erie link was approved, he warned, New York City might decline as a port serving the nation's interior. Clinton portrayed a period when the farmers of western New York would send their goods to market in Philadelphia, or even New Orleans. To prevent this, he wanted canals, and so he recommended a study of the situation to begin at once.

A survey was made, followed by recommendations for two modest waterways in the central part of the state. No mention was made of the Lake Erie connection at that time. This proposal met with mild interest. Representatives of areas that would not be affected by canals opposed the measure, while legislators from the New York-Albany-Erie line wanted a more ambitious program, as did landholders in the western part of the state.

Elkanah Watson followed the debates with interest. Like Macomb and Morris, he owned land in western New York, though unlike them he had worked his holdings. Among his other accomplishments, Watson was a sheepman. He had introduced the Merino to America, grazed them on his land, helped found the American woolen industry, and been an early sponsor of state fairs, at which he publicized his products. Watson hoped to sell his wool in Europe, but transportation costs were high. A canal to Lake Erie would change this. He had hoped the legislature would consider construction of such a waterway. When it failed to do so, Watson assumed leadership of the pro-canal forces.

Watson was no newcomer to canals. He had visited Europe during and after the Revolution and studied the canals in England. In 1795 he visited with Washington, and spoke with him of the Potomac project. Afterward Watson traveled extensively through western New York, charting the area's waterways. He concluded then that a few small canals and river improvements, linking the natural waterways, could provide New York with a river-lake-canal system to rival that of England. This would not only open Lake Erie to New York City, but also through the Great Lakes bring Ohio to Manhattan's merchants. "The various rivers, and their branches, lakes, and creeks, are disposed by the *Great Architect of the Universe* just as we would wish them," he wote in 1791. The development of the waterway "will be more precious than if we had encompassed the mines of Potosi." Watson visited the saltworks on Onondaga Lake, "in a rude unfinished state but . . . capable of making about 6,000 bushels of salt per annum which is nearly the quantity required for the present consumption of the country." This salt could not be brought to market economically. "When the mighty canals shall be formed and locks created it will add vastly to the facility of an extended diffusion and the increase of its intrinsic worth."

Conceding that a canal to link the Hudson with the Great Lakes would prove uneconomical at first, Watson went on to say that the issue was irrelevant. While it was true that Britain's canals often were money-makers because they went through developed areas, such need not be the case in America. In New York, canals could cause settlement, rather than reflect it, and bring great economic benefits to the people, the state, and the nation. Should his canal plan be accepted, "a vast wilderness will, as it were by magic, rise into instant civilization."

Some members of the legislature liked Watson's plan. Many were landholders of western grants; most came from upstate, and a few from New York City, which would also benefit from Watson's canal. Led by General Philip Schuyler who owned acreage in Dutchess County and represented Albany in the legislature, they pressed for the "lake canal policy," and won.

In March 1792, New York incorporated two companies, the Western Inland Lock Navigation Company and the Northern Inland Lock Navigation Company. The first was to open navigation from the Hudson to Lake Ontario, and the second to connect the Hudson with Lake Champlain. The western company would benefit Watson, the Holland Company, and the Morris group, while the second would, if successful, raise the price of Macomb's holdings. New York City would become the great port of the world; Albany would emerge as a major water crossroads. The wealth of the Northwest would flow through New York State, giving it political and economic power of unprecedented scope. All would benefit from such success.

None of this could be accomplished, however, without money. Each company was expected to sell 1,000 shares for an initial payment of $25 a share, with additional money to be raised from shareholders as necessary. The state would give each company $12,500 after it had spent its initial capital.

These sums were clearly inadequate, and even then the companies were unable to sell their quota of shares; the Western Company could dispose of only 722 after three months of selling. Then an engineering survey was made of the Albany-Fort Stanwix line, the first step in the Albany-Erie Canal, and the report indicated that almost half a million dollars woud be needed for this waterway alone. The state provided some help, but not enough. The first part of the canal was opened in 1796, and was a failure. The public refused to pay the high tolls charged, the locks broke down regularly, and additional work could not be undertaken for lack of capital. In 1803 canal revenues reached $10,000; almost $400,000 was spent that year in construction and maintenance.

The Northern Canal was not constructed, and that small portion of the Western Canal that went into operation was a dismal financial failure. Without far more capital than could be raised at the time, and better engineering techniques, the Albany-Great Lakes link would remain a dream and no more. Watson's proposals were sound, but the wherewithal was not present at the time he made them. The situation would be different in 1817.

As the Western Company foundered in 1807, Gallatin presented his *Report*, recommending internal improvements throughout the nation. After the War of 1812, other states, especially those in the South, were planning or actually began work on canals and turnpikes to the West. The nation, which had no capital market to speak of in 1800, possessed several by 1817, the most important of which was in New York. Western New York landlords, fearful their lands would actually fall in price should other states capture trans-Appalachian trade, united with Hudson Valley farmers to demand a renewal of canal activity. By 1817 nationalists were firmly in control in Washington, and the last vestiges of laissez-faire Jeffersonianism had been defeated. Canal technology had improved, as American engineers, through studying English methods and developing new ones, were convinced better and more secure locks could be constructed at lower costs. Benjamin Wright, a western New York judge (and landholder) who at one time had been a surveyor, worked on the Western Company's canal, then began a serious study of technology, and by 1817 was perhaps the finest canal engineer in the nation; he was eager to renew the drive toward the new town of Buffalo. Canvass White, who had served as Wright's assistant, had gone to England and walked almost 2,000 miles through the countryside, studying every important canal in that nation, noting their defects as well as their workings. Wright, White, and others were available in 1817, and, together with the landlords, politicians, farmers, and financiers, pressured the state legislature to act.

Still, the question of costs remained a stumbling block. All previous experience had shown canals could not be profitable. Washington had conceded as much in the 1780s, and Watson would only go so far as to claim they would "in time" prove profitable in the next decade. Canals might benefit the state, but could they prove lucrative for their stockholders as well? In the past, canal advocates had argued that farmers and land speculators would purchase canal stock, not in the hope of profit, but rather to better their primary businesses. Yet they had not come forth in the cases of the Northern and Western companies. Would the situation be any different in 1817?

For a time New Yorkers hoped the federal government would finance its canals. Then President Madison vetoed a measure that would have brought the state $1.5 million. This discouraged canal advocates in New York, yet they continued their work. The Presidential veto was sent down on March 3, 1817. Six weeks later the New York legislature adopted a measure providing for a new canal.

This canal would follow the route set down by the Western Company, and complete the work begun a generation earlier. A permanent canal fund was established, which would obtain its income from state taxes (on salt and other goods), lotteries and auction duties, bond issues underwritten by the state, and the collection of tolls. It was estimated the canal would cost $7 million, at a time when the total banking and insurance capital in New York was less than $21 million. Canal supporters thought farmers and speculators would purchase stock and bonds, and the rest would be provided by European investors. Governor DeWitt Clinton, who in 1809 had served on a commission to explore the Albany-Buffalo canal route and six years later had petitioned the legislature for canal funds, was certain money would not be difficult to find.* Like others of his group, he felt that, if all else failed, the land speculators would bear the burden of costs. The Holland Company in particular could be counted upon to use its

*Political considerations also played a role in Clinton's activities. Clinton marshaled the upper New York representatives, the backbone of his power, against the Tammany Democrats in New York, who opposed the bill and the canal as not helpful to the city. If the canal was a success, he could crush the Tammany forces and then go on to win additional power, perhaps the Presidency itself.

European connections to float loans there. Thomas Eddy, a former director of the Western Company and an associate of the governor, indicated as much in a letter to Joseph Ellicott, the agent of the Holland Land Company, in which he urged Ellicott to purchase stock and bonds of the canal company, and make land grants to the state to lower its costs. "If *the whole* should amount to something considerable, there is no doubt that the Legislature would agree to commence the work."

There was good reason to press for such support, as for a while it seemed the canal loan of 1817 might fail. The governor wrote to Ellicott of the situation, saying that "Money is very scarce in this city. If this first small loan should fail, it would have a very pernicious effect on all our future operations." Banker and canal advocate William Bayard reported that the foreign capital markets were not receptive to canal notes at that time. Despite this, the drive for subscriptions began.

The first stock and bond drive went better than expected. Several New York banks, led by the New York State Bank and the Mechanics and Farmers Bank, took large blocks of stock, which they then sold slowly at the New York Stock and Exchange Board as well as to private investors, many of them English. The fact that the state owned 40 percent of the stock of the former bank and 10 percent of the latter doubtless had its effect. The English also took most of the first bond issues. David Bevan of the Rock Life Assurance Company of London invested $34,000 in the first issue, which was set at $200,000, and John Deacon, director of the Royal Exchange Assurance Company of London, invested $40,000 in the bonds. These men had had experience in investment in English canals, and doubtless expected to make large profits on similar investments in New York. Some Dutch bankers took bonds, and the Holland Land Company announced a large land grant to the state to assist in the work.

Work on construction began soon after, and from the first glowing reports were issued from the camps. This encouraged Americans to take shares and part of further bond issues. Now wealthy Albany and New York merchants, becoming convinced the ditch would be completed, rushed to purchase shares and debts. Believing his money difficulties at an end, Clinton boasted that "the state [could] procure money to any amount even possibly under the rate of 6% per annum." Indeed, there seemed so much money available in the New York financial complex that he informed promoters of canals in other states of its potential. Clinton was especially interested in encouraging Ohio interests to consider canals, preferably financed from New York. Already he was looking to the future, when the New York port would drain the Great Lakes, and go on to tap the wealth of Ohio. From Albany he wondered how Ohio's goods could be brought to New York, and concluded that state, too, should encourage waterways. "There is money in abundance to loan in our commercial emporium," he wrote to a W. Steele, who asked the governor for advice in promoting Ohio canals.

The canal—now officially dubbed the Erie Canal—proceeded rapidly. The middle section, which connected the Mohawk and Seneca rivers, was completed in October 1819, and the event was marked by a great celebration at the site. Traffic was admitted the following May, by which time the engineers were pushing ahead to Lake Erie. Now Americans from out of state began to purchase canal securities. Langdon Cheves, president of the Second Bank of the United States and a resident of South Carolina, invested $45,000 in 1821. Prime, Ward & Sands, New York's leading brokerage, took large blocks of stock and issues of bonds, for wholesaling throughout the nation as well as in England. Baring Brothers, the most prestigious English banking firm, entered the lists, as did John Jacob Astor, who took not only new issues, but also began to accumulate older ones as well. The Canal Fund swelled, as toll revenue was better than expected and bonds sold at premiums. The fund deposited receipts in New York banks, which used them to purchase additional bonds for resale or retention, and the cycle began once more. Indeed, the banks had so much money they were able to finance construction, land purchases, and improvements along the canal route. The Canal Fund became the pump for prosperity in the state, a fact noted in European banking circles.

At first most of Erie's paper had been taken by local individuals and firms. In 1822 the English purchases stepped up sharply. The *London Times* thought New York City would become the "London of the New World," and wrote glowingly of Erie's prospects. By the end of 1823 the Barings alone owned almost a quarter of a million dollars worth of Erie stock and bonds. Then came news that toll receipts had been higher than anticipated; the firm purchased an additional $100,000 worth of bonds. By 1829 the English owned a majority of Erie stock.

On November 4, 1825, Governor Clinton celebrated the completion of construction by pouring a keg of Lake Erie water into the Atlantic at New York City. As one contemporary put it, "They have built the longest canal in the world in the least time, with the least experience, for the least money, and to the greatest public benefit." The Erie ran 363 miles, and cost little more than the $7 million originally budgeted. Even before work had been completed, toll revenues exceeded interest charges. Ten years later, when the original bonds issued for construction were selling at comfortable premiums, the Canal Fund prepared to liquidate the last of them through repayment. In the interim, tolls had been reduced twice, and after each reduction traffic increased. The Erie was being deepened and broadened to take care of additional traffic. It made sense to do so. The cost of freight from Buffalo to New York had been $100 a ton in 1818; with the Erie in operation, the figure was $15 a ton, and the time of the voyage had declined from twenty to eight days. Villages sprang up along the route, and old towns became fast-growing cities. The price of farm products declined in New York with the lower transportation costs, and sales shot up, so that in 1827 the total value was twice that of 1818. Of course, land values reached new highs. The speculators were rewarded.

Other eastern urban leaders, watching the Erie's progress closely, were chagrined at its success. New York had been growing at a faster rate than most seacoast cities prior to the completion of the Erie; now its wealth would soar. Convinced not only of the worth of canals, but of their economic feasibility, Philadelphia and Baltimore made plans for links to trans-Appalachia, hoping to arrive there before the Ohio,

Indiana, and Illinois trade was lost irretrievably to the New Yorkers.

Leading Pennsylvanians agreed better transportation to the West was needed, but differed as how to best accomplish the links. The state already had a fine turnpike system, which in the early 1820s carried 30,000 tons of goods annually. The state's mountain barrier to the West was more difficult to conquer than the relatively flat lands of central New York, and so canals through passes would be more costly than the Erie. Some in Philadelphia wanted to ignore canals and concentrate on railroads, which, though small and inefficient in the mid-1820s, seemed "the wave of the future" even then. In the long term, the railroad did indeed offer the most promise. But farmers and land speculators in Pennsylvania's western counties demanded immediate action, as did some leading Philadelphia merchants, led by economist and publisher Mathew Carey. They formed the Pennsylvania Society for the Promotion of Internal Improvement in the Commonwealth, and agitated for a Philadelphia-Pittsburgh waterway at all costs. By 1825 the society had published papers on technical and economic matters, was memorializing the state legislature, and propagandizing among newspapermen. Earlier, on March 27, 1824, the governor signed into law a measure providing for a survey of possible routes. The society's work speeded the effort along, and from it came the Pennsylvania "Mainline," a series of canals to Pittsburgh which, though the survey said they could never handle "the entire commerce of the West," would be profitable and help the Pennsylvania economy.

The difficult work of constructing canals along hilly country began soon after, financed by bond and stock sales the bankers had no difficulty in placing. But if investors had confidence in the Mainline canals, those transportation "experts" who did exist were dubious as to their feasibility. Their doubts increased as news of construction difficulties and delays, broadsides from railroad advocates, and news reports of the Erie's continued success caused hesitation, procrastination, and halfhearted commitments in Pennsylvania's legislature. The *Harrisburg Chronicle,* once a canal supporter, changed its mind early in the game. In late 1825 the newspaper noted that, although

Pennsylvania possessed many advantages, "We will certainly fail to compete with the State of New York for the trade of the West."

The Mainline canals were not successful. Their original cost was $12.1 million, and the final cost an additional $4.5 million. There was a small excess of revenues over current expenses, but the bonds were not redeemed as were the Erie's, and the route was sold to the Pennsylvania Railroad in 1857 for $7.5 million. Nor did the farmers of the interior profit from the canals, whose tolls were too high. By 1839 most farmers of western Pennsylvania were sending their flour down the Mississippi to New Orleans, a far cheaper route. Not even the later attempt to combine canals with railroads could prevent the West from becoming a captive of New York. As Job Tyson, a Pennsylvania writer put it in 1852, "the chain that was to bind Philadelphia with the west was . . . severed, disjointed, fragmentary. It was an amphibious connection of land and water, consisting of two railways separated by a canal, and of two canals separated by a railway—happily elucidating the defects peculiar to both methods of transit, with the advantages of neither."

The history of Baltimore's attempt to emulate New York was not dissimilar to the Pennsylvania experience. Building on Washington's earlier efforts at the Potomac Company, Baltimore's leaders planned a canal to extend from Georgetown to Cumberland, and from there by tunnel to the Youghiogheny River and the West. The company began with capital of $3.6 million, of which the federal government took $1 million, the city of Washington an additional $1 million, and a like amount from other cities hoping to benefit from the canal. Private individuals purchased $600,000 worth of stock. As in Pennsylvania, there was no trouble in obtaining initial funding. Then, as construction delays took place, the debate between railroad and canal advocates began, and as it became evident that New York had captured the Midwest's trade, enthusiasm for the canal dwindled. The Chesapeake & Ohio never went beyond Cumberland. It was completed in 1850, at a cost of more than $11 million, of which Maryland contributed $7 million and the terminal cities an additional $1.5 million. Inability to cross the Appalachians, combined with competition from the Baltimore & Ohio Railroad, doomed the canal to failure. Even as the first spade of earth was turned in 1828, this seemed to be its fate; the canal's promoters appear to have hoped for a miracle to save them, but none was forthcoming.

The completion of the Erie set off a wave of canal construction in America, of which the Mainline and Chesapeake & Ohio were only two of the most ambitious. Every town and village near a body of water seemed to want one; in 1825 over twenty other canals were either beginning or in states of organization. The Erie set off a bull market in the young securities markets of New York and Philadelphia as well as the older ones of London and Amsterdam, as Europeans were eager to take almost any American canal issue that appeared. Western land sales boomed, and owners of New York real estate benefited greatly. The Erie was a great success, but it was more than that. As a symbol of American technology, abilities, promise, and wealth, it acted as a magnet to investors.

The construction of the Erie Canal also sparked a new immigrant wave. In 1819, the year the Erie's middle section was opened, only 8,000 immigrants came to America. The number reached 10,000 in 1825, when the canal was completed. Nine years later, in 1834, 65,000 immigrants arrived.

Most disembarked in New York, Boston, and other eastern ports and ventured only a few miles into the interior. Some went farther, joining Americans lured to the West, now that it was opened by the Erie to New York. Ohio's population, 793,000 in 1820, doubled by 1830 and doubled again by 1840. Indiana's population rose from 581,000 to 1,519,000 in the same twenty-year period, while that of Illinois went from 55,000 to 476,000.

Most westward-bound settlers traveled by wagon, but the transportation boom of the late 1820s made such moves more appealing and seemed to lessen their dangers. The newcomers purchased land, and although there was plenty to go around, prices did rise, especially in settled areas. It was a good time to own upper midwestern real estate, acres in western New York or along the Hudson and Erie, or for that matter, any large slice of land near a canal or proposed canal.

Lake Superior
ST. MARY'S SHIP CANAL
Sault Ste. Marie
WISCONSIN
MICHIGAN
Lake Huron
Lake Michigan
Detroit
Chicago
CHICAGO – LA SALLE
La Salle
Peoria
Illinois River
Toledo
Maumee R.
OHIO & PENNSYLVANIA
Cleveland
Fort Wayne
WABASH & ERIE
Wabash River
LaFayette
MIAMI & OHIO
OHIO
Akron
OHIO & ERIE
Bolivar
Brinkhaven
WALHONDING & MOHICAN
Roscoe
INDIANA
ILLINOIS
Columbus
Cambridge City
Terre Haute
White River
WHITEWATER
Miami R.
Dayton
Carroll
OHIO & ERIE
Scioto R.
Athens
HOCKING
Cincinnati
Lawrenceburg
St. Louis
Portsmouth
CINCINNATI & WHITEWATER
Wabash River
WABASH & ERIE
Ohio R.
Evansville
Louisville
LOUISVILLE & PORTLAND
Mississippi River
KENTUCKY
Cumberland R.
Tennessee R.
TENNESSEE
Kanawha R.

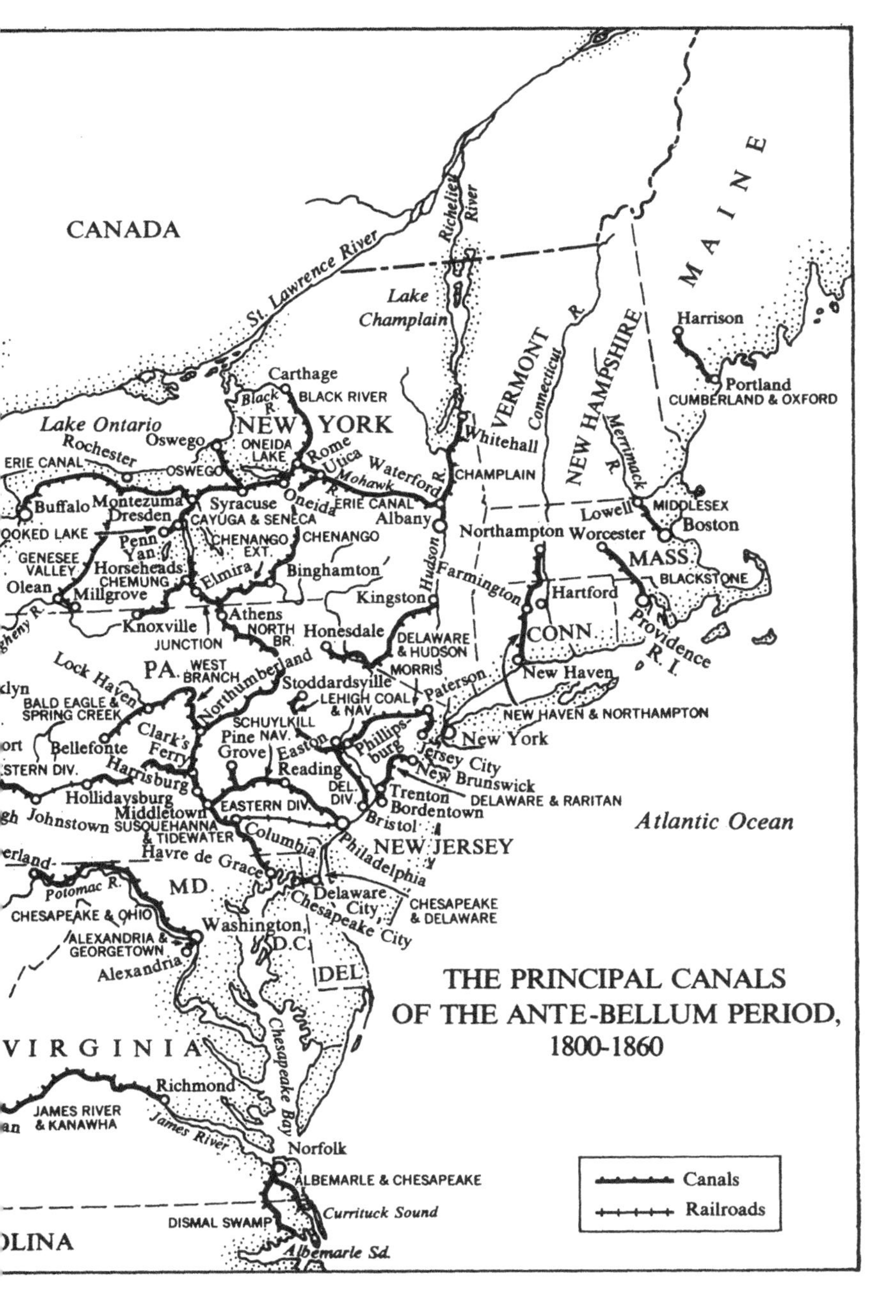

THE PRINCIPAL CANALS OF THE ANTE-BELLUM PERIOD, 1800-1860

The dreams of men like George Croghan and Samuel Wharton for Vandalia were being realized a half century later in Ohio.

As already indicated, Clinton had many reasons for wanting the Erie to be built, and one of these was to tie the Midwest to New York, in an almost colonial relationship. His secretary, Charles Haines, initiated a correspondence with Ohio's Governor Ethan Allen Brown in 1820, in which he spoke of the promise of the Erie, and suggested similar projects for Ohio. "The commencement and completion of the Ohio Canal excite anxious and deep considerations in this State," he wrote. "We see and feel the importance of the work, not only to the great Western section of the Union, but to the country which stretches from the mouth of the Hudson to the Lakes." Haines was only mirroring Clinton's thoughts in so writing. An Ohio canal system would be a continuation of the Erie, "into the heart of a fertile territory, capable of sustaining from ten to fifteen millions of people. When Ohio resolves to make her Canal from the Lakes to the Ohio River, and is willing to pledge her credit for the means of accomplishing the undertaking, it will be done."

Could it be done? The state of Ohio's credit was low, and had been further crippled by the financial panic of 1819. Brown thought "The aspect of affairs rather gloomy" insofar as financing such canals was concerned. Yet the Erie's success was such as to encourage the state's businessmen to support a waterway system, which they believed would soon pay for itself.

In 1825, as the Erie neared completion, the Ohio legislature authorized the building of two canals, both of which were to pass through populated parts of the state. Their names indicated the hoped-for linkage with New York. The Ohio and Erie would extend from Portsmouth on the Ohio River to Cleveland on Lake Erie, and the Miami and Erie would link Cincinnati to Toledo. A board of commissioners was named to secure financing for the waterways. Brown, who entered the Senate in 1822, was named to the board, in the hope that he could obtain federal help. Allen Trimble, a leading Ohio businessman, was another member. Trimble resigned soon after being selected, and was succeeded by a more significant figure,

Simon Perkins, the Ohio agent for the Connecticut Land Company, which owned tracts along the routes of both proposed canals.

Clinton acted as consultant for the board, and strongly urged it to issue bonds secured by the state's credit, so that even should the canals fail, the bonds would be redeemed. This would attract purchasers, he said, as well as lower the interest charges. The board followed his advice, but even then Ohio's businessmen were unable to take the first bond offering of $400,000. Instead, the issue was sold in New York. Rathbone & Lord, a banking firm in Manhattan, took the issue and sold most of it to wealthy New Yorkers and Englishmen. Charles Haines had predicted "that New York capital would sustain the enterprise," and he was right. In all $4.5 million of Ohio canal bonds were sold in New York from 1825 to 1832. Prime, Ward & King took $770,000 for resale in Europe through the Barings, and John Jacob Astor, the nation's leading landlord, purchased $800,000 of the bonds in 1826 and an additional $342,000 two years later, as well as odd amounts of other Ohio canal issues.

Clinton was in Ohio to turn the first spade of earth on the Ohio Canal in 1826, and construction proceeded smoothly. The waterway was completed seven years later. Although not as dramatically successful as the Erie, because Ohio's population was smaller than New York's, the canals were profitable, and so others were initiated. In 1833 Ohio had over 400 miles of canals; by 1850 it had well over 1,000 miles. By far the bulk of the construction bonds had been floated in New York, and a large majority of Ohio bonds were owned by Europeans, especially the English.

Fearful that the New York-Ohio nexus would dominate the Midwest and aware of the enthusiastic reception for canal bonds, Indiana entered the competition. In 1832 construction was begun on the Wabash and Erie, designed to start at Evansville in the southern part of the state and then go north to join the Miami and Erie, so as to drain Indiana's commerce into the Great Lakes at Toledo. This canal, the longest ever constructed in America, was over 450 miles in length and was completed in 1843. This great waterway was never profitable; it was too ambitious, came too late, and in general was the wrong kind of transportation in the wrong place at the wrong time. The Wabash and Erie was not the last great American canal to be constructed; others would follow into the post-Civil War era. But even as it neared completion, it seemed to many that the age of canals was passing.

The canal mania had originated in the desire on the part of political leaders to unite the country through a transportation network. Washington had often spoken and written of this need, and later on Gallatin set forth the master plan for a national transportation system. The federal government did all it could to encourage such improvements until the early 1830s. The Bank of the United States helped the states market their bonds, provided a sense of security for those foreigners who purchased them, and in general promoted an atmosphere of financial responsibility beneficial to such enterprises. The bank acted as an agent for foreign banks and investors; the Bank of England, for example, used its offices to collect debts owed British nationals by American states, localities, and citizens. Federal land policy encouraged sales, and this too helped the canals. Indeed, excessive speculation under the federal land laws contributed to the financial panic of 1819. Even then Congress passed legislation for the relief of settlers. After 1820 one could no longer purchase land on credit, but the price per acre at public auctions was lowered to a minimum of $1.25 and the minimum tract to an eighth of a section. After 1820, a person with as little as $100 could buy eighty acres of land from the government. This too helped fuel the westward movement, and so assisted the canals.

This policy changed with the election of Andrew Jackson to the Presidency in 1828. Jackson's programs differed sharply from those of his predecessors. Opposed to the increased power of the federal government in economic matters and considering federal financing of internal improvements as a possible threat to individual freedoms, Jackson soon made it known he would reverse several key aid programs. In 1830 Congress passed a measure to assist in the construction of a road from Maysville to Lexington, Kentucky. Jackson vetoed the bill, saying the road was purely a private operation and not within federal jurisdiction. Other, similar vetoes were handed down. This did not mean the President would halt all such programs—during his Administration, federal public works cost $25.1 million, of which $6.8 million went to turnpikes and canals—but it did indicate the atmosphere in Washington had changed.

As part of his program, Jackson opposed the Bank of the United States. During the 1836 election he campaigned for reelection on the bank issue, and with his victory the fate of the bank was sealed. Now government funds were deposited in various state banks, called "pet banks" by some since they were usually headed by Jacksonians. By early 1835 thirty such banks had been selected, and others were being considered. State banking grew rapidly in this period, rising from 506 banks in 1834 to 788 three years later. None of these banks had the prestige of the Bank of the United States or its impact overseas, especially in Europe. Although some were well-managed and conservative, most were not. Credit expanded greatly in this period, fueling a major speculative wave.

Shortly before the 1836 election, Jackson solved an embarrassing and, for us today, unusual question. His refusal to fund additional internal improvements, combined with high tariff and other revenues, resulted in a Treasury surplus. In June 1836, Jackson decided to distribute this surplus to the states beginning on January 1, 1837. At the time many states were deeply in debt for having floated many internal improvement bonds. These states used the federal distribution to inflate their debts further, thus feeding the speculation then current.

All of this was reflected in land purchases. Public land sales, which were on the rise due to the transportation boom and government land policies, now soared. In 1836, twenty million acres of government land was sold, bringing in $25 million in revenue; for the first time land sales surpassed customs as the Treasury's chief source of income. This money was deposited in pet banks, and often was lent to speculators to pay for additional land purchases, and the cycle then repeated itself. Most of the land sales were in the West, but all parts of the country shared in the mania. Chicago became a boomtown in this period; New York's assessed real estate rose from $300 million in 1831 to $600 million in 1837.

Believing land speculation harmful and disruptive (although he himself had in the past participated in it), Jackson acted to put a halt to the practice. In July 1836, he issued the "specie circular," which directed that after August 14, 1836, all sales of public lands—except to residents of the state in which the land was sold—would have to be paid for in gold or Virginia land scrip, and that after December 14, all land sales to all individuals had to be paid for in gold or scrip.

The specie circular put an end to excessive land speculation, and dashed cold water to quell the speculative fever. Together with the Maysville veto and the failure to recharter the Bank of the United States, it also served to dampen foreign enthusiasm for American bonds and stocks. And from this came the panic of 1837 and the depression that followed. Thus, political leaders had helped stimulate the canal era, and political leaders helped bring it to a close.

But politics had been only an aspect of the canal mania and related speculation and investment. The desire on the part of land speculators to make their holdings more attractive, of farmers and manufacturers to have better access to markets, and the states to engage in profitable economic enterprises had also played a role. Yet in these areas, too, events conspired to bring the canal era to its end.

Easy money, optimism, the continued success of the Erie and a few other waterways had fueled the canal boom of the early 1830s. This seemed over by 1834. In that year less than $3 million was invested in the waterways; in 1828 the English and other foreign investors seemed to have believed in miracles, and the states were ready to oblige them. Now it was ending.

The boom died hard, however. Even after the 1837 panic some Englishmen continued to purchase American canal bonds. London banker Alexander Trotter, writing in 1839, thought them safer than those of continental Europe, though they had to be watched with great care. The Erie had proved American canals were money-makers, he told his clients; the same could not be said of France's railroads and internal improvements in the German states. Trotter was wrong, of course. A majority of the canals begun after the mid-1830s were ill-conceived. The end of the land boom, the collapse of the banks, the depression, and related factors made a shambles of projections and caused distress in London three years after Trotter's prediction had been made.

Even had the canal builders been correct in their claims, their projects might have failed. This is to say, had technology answered their needs and enabled poorly planned waterways to operate efficiently, they might still have been abandoned. To carry this further, had John Quincy Adams been in the White House instead of Andrew Jackson, and had land development proceeded at a rapid pace with government aid and no panic and depression, the canal era might still have come to an end in the late 1830s, defeated by a superior technology.

Generally speaking, canals were expensive highways, a fact realized even before the Erie was begun. The best stone turnpikes cost from $5,000 to $10,000 a mile; the average cost for a canal-mile was close to $25,000, and the Chesapeake & Ohio cost $60,000 a mile. Furthermore, canals were expensive to maintain. No sooner had the Erie been completed than it was improved through widening, and such costs soon equaled original construction outlays. Canals had to be dredged constantly; since most were not more than a few feet deep, to fail to do so would cause silting and rapid collapse. Finally there was the problem of an adequate water supply. Not all canals had good and constant supplies of water. In times of heavy flooding they became unusable, and needed constant and expensive repairs, while during droughts they became muddy quagmires.

The turnpike did not possess a superior technology, but the railroad offered the promise of one. Given the technological improvements in existence by 1840, railroads were cheaper to construct than canals, less expensive to maintain and improve, did not rely upon water supplies, and were more dependable despite frequent breakdowns. Of course, the early railroads did not operate efficiently by today's standards. Schedules were not followed, engines exploded, tracks needed repairs, and accidents were commonplace. But they were more reliable than canals and swifter than the slow-moving barges. Writing from Walden Pond in 1854, Henry Thoreau, no lover of technology, said, "They come and go, with such regularity and precision, and their whistle can be heard so far, that the farmers set their clocks by them. Thus one well-regulated institution regulates a whole country." This could hardly be said of canals and barges.

Thoreau wrote of the railroad as a symbol of a changing America. A more meaningful symbol was the contest between the Chesapeake & Ohio Canal and the Baltimore & Ohio Railroad. The B. & O. was organized in 1827 with a subscription of $1.5 million from private sources and $500,000 from the city of Baltimore. The following year private investors took an additional $1.5 million in bonds while Maryland purchased $500,000 of the railroad's bonds. Work on both the canal and railroad began the same day—after each was celebrated on July 4, 1828—and each had the same goal: Cumberland and trans-Appalachia. Maryland meant to realize Washington's 1784 dream, and so sponsored the costly "contest."

The C. & O. was completed in 1850; the railroad reached Cumberland three years later. But the railroad had won the more important race, for its rates were lower and transit swifter than the C. & O. The investment community seemed to agree; canal issues languished in the 1850s, while railroad stocks and bonds were sold without much difficulty. Yet before this could happen, both railroad and canal issues had to face the great wring-out process of the early 1840s.

Canal bonds continued to sell in London in 1841 and 1842. This was so more as a result of custom and dreams than knowledge, for London's investors and banks had far more dreams than information.

The first sign of difficulty appeared in Pennsylvania, where the Mainline and other canals were doing poorly. The Pennsylvania state debt, a good part of which had been incurred through the financing of internal improvements, was more than the tax base could support, especially in a depression. At the time, the Pennsylvania debt was $34 million. In mid-1843 Englishmen owned $20 million of this amount, and Dutch investors another $1.8 million, while the total foreign investment was $23.7 million. Pennsylvania interests, in contrast, held only $9.6 million of the state's bonds.

In January 1842, a run began on the United States Bank in Pennsylvania, and on January 31 the institution closed down. The repercussions were soon felt in Europe. Hope & Co., the Amsterdam banker which had sold Pennsylvania bonds throughout western Europe, was threatened by a mob of enraged bondholders, who felt their paper would be worthless. Similar demonstrations took place in London, where the poet William Wordsworth wrote "Men of the Western World" and "To the Pennsylvanians," both of which criticized the Americans for debt repudiation. The Reverend Sydney Smith, a holder of Pennsylvania bonds, led an anti-American movement in England. Writing in the *London Morning Chronicle,* Smith complained that the Americans were scoundrels. How can any American sit down to dinner in England without knowing he owed 2 or 3 pounds to every person in the room? he asked.

> Figure to yourself a Pennsylvanian receiving foreigners in his own country, walking over the public works with them, and showing them Larcenous Lake, Swindling Swamp, Crafty Canal, and Rogues Railway, and other dishonest works. The swamp we gained (says the patriotic borrower) by the repudiated loans of 1828. Our canal robbery was in 1830; we pocketed your good people's money for the railroad only last year. All this may seem very smart to the Americans; but if I had the misfortune to be born among such a people, the land of my fathers should not retain me a single moment after the act of repudiation. I would appeal from my fathers to my forefathers. I would fly to Newgate for greater purity of thought, and seek in the prisons of England for better rules of life.

Holders of Pennsylvania bonds were not lost, however. Aided by the Barings and other London houses, Pennsylvania was able to put its affairs in order and resume payments in 1845. By then, however, its paper was suspect, and foreigners no longer would purchase the state's bonds. The Mainline had failed financially, even though it had aided in the state's economic development.

Maryland underwent a similar experience. In 1840 the state's funded debt was more than $15 million, and interest charges on it, $600,000. The C. & O. accounted for $7.1 million of the debt, the B. & O. another $3.7 million, and other canals and railroads the rest. Maryland defaulted on these bonds in October 1841, and for the next seven years paid no interest on them. As in the case of Pennsylvania, the Barings helped reorganize and refinance the debts, while Maryland passed new tax laws to raise additional funds. Part of the refinancing was a Baring agreement to purchase additional Maryland bonds. By that time the London bankers had fully assessed the potential of both canals and railroads in America. In 1849 the Barings refused to purchase additional C. & O. bonds, deeming the canal a failure. But the house did take $1 million of B. & O. Railroad bonds, indicating more optimism regarding that form of transportation.

Indiana also defaulted, with the same pattern being followed. The Wabash & Erie was a dismal failure, and a drain on state finances. The waterway went through underdeveloped land, and although farmers did settle along its banks, by the time they did, the railroad was also there, to take most of the carrying business. London banks reorganized and refinanced the Indiana debt, but after 1848, would not take canal obligations of that state, concentrating instead on the railroads.

Not only were railroads a superior form of transportation and better investment, but the lines had hired effective lobbyists, while those working for canals could not muster support for their causes in Washington and the state capitals. In 1843 Senator James Buchanan of Pennsylvania protested against the power and influence of the railroad representatives who had managed to lobby effectively both in Pennsylvania and Washington. "If you defeat them at this session, they will be here in greater force than ever at the commencement of the next," he warned. Others said as much, but little could be done to change the situation; the age of the iron horse was dawning, while that of the canal was coming to a close. In 1830 the nation had 1,277 miles of canals and 73 of railroads. Ten years later the figures were 3,326 for canals and 3,328 for railroads. By 1850 canal mileage had stabilized at 3,698, while that of railroads had soared to 8,879.

The canal age brought benefits to the nation. The waterways helped tie America together economically, assisted in the movement west, and in some cases added to production, revenues, and economic well-being. A great deal of money was expended on canals whose costs outweighed benefits; it has been estimated that as much as one-fifth of all such moneys was wasted. A goodly number of canals experienced brief periods of prosperity, only to fail once the railroads came to their regions.

Just how much money was made by speculators may never be known. Few records exist, and estimates are chancy. But the papers of the Holland Land Company are intact, and quotations for its two stock issues on the Amsterdam market, available. The quotations for the latter are a good gauge of hopes and fears regarding land speculation, at least in western New York.

The company had two issues of stock, offered at par (100) in 1796. But as investors learned of the difficulty of selling land in the West, the price fell. Late in 1811, Holland Company stock was quoted as low as 19, with few takers. There is no record of trading during the first year of the War of 1812, when it appeared the United States itself might be no more, in which case the company's claims could have become worthless. Then, with the ending of the war after the defeat of Napoleon, and the coming of peace both in America and Europe, the price rose once again, reaching 57 at the time Clinton obtained passage of the Erie measure in 1817. Although it appeared the canal would benefit the company, the price of its stock moved little during the next eight years. Then, with completion of the canal and the beginning of large land sales, Holland Land Company shares began to move rapidly. Par was reached in January 1829, and a year later Holland stock sold for 126. The 200 level was crossed in November 1834, by which time the company was redeeming shares at a rapid rate, placing further upward pressure on quotations. The high quotes were made in March 1836, when Holland shares changed hands at 1,240, after which the price fell back to 460.

The company paid dividends throughout the post-1829 period, although irregularly as was the custom at the time. The total profits on the original investment were not large. The leading historian of the company estimated that the investment was retrieved "with interest of five to six per cent."* Of course, securities speculators who managed to purchase Holland at its lows in 1811 and then sold in 1836 made tremendous fortunes. There appear to have been few of them. The canal era began at the height of the great age of land speculation and ended just prior to the emergence of the first major period of securities speculation. In time the securities markets would prove a path to profits and power, but land, though often not as glamorous, would never be fully eclipsed as a speculative vehicle.

George Washington, who believed in land speculation, probably would have felt vindicated by the canal experience. Land he thought worthless in 1784, when he visited the Great Kanawha for the last time, was most desirable by the 1830s. Had the squatters with whom he spoke purchased their land, they would have been comfortable, if not well-to-do, by then. Internal improvements made this possible, and the first great national effort in this direction was—as Washington expected it to be—the canals.

*Paul D. Evans, *The Holland Land Company* (Buffalo, 1924), p. 435.

CHAPTER 3

Speculation in Slaves

Like most of the Founding Fathers, George Washington was ambivalent regarding the institution of slavery. On the one hand, he considered it a blot upon the nation and an implied contradiction of revolutionary principles, while on the other he viewed blacks as inferior to whites, and opposed universal, immediate emancipation. Washington hoped the slave trade with Africa could be ended, and viewed both foreign and domestic traders in human flesh with contempt, as did almost all southerners of his class, but he dealt with such individuals, though at arm's length.

In time the institution would die, he believed, but Washington was not certain what could be done with the freed slaves. All he could do would be to take actions leading to its demise, and allow future generations to work out the problems involved in transforming slave areas into free. Toward this end, Washington worked for a more diversified southern economy, one not reliant upon the slavery-encouraging tobacco and indigo crops. Such an economy would make the South more like the North, where slavery either was dying or had never taken root. This was one of the reasons he supported internal improvements, especially canals.

Some others of his generation, men who like Washington despised slavery, had a different view of the institution's future. George Mason of Virginia, who believed slavery destructive of human values, noted that "the western people are already calling out for slaves for their new lands, and will fill that country with slaves." Only poor transportation prevented the West from being settled by southern farmers—and their slaves. "If they can be got through South Carolina and Georgia" slaveowners would dominate in trans-Appalachia.

C. C. Pinckney, also of Virginia, believed better transportation would be a boon to his state. Like Washington, he opposed the further importation of African slaves. Pinckney saw the question not only in human terms, but also in simple economics. "As for Virginia, she will gain by stopping the importations. Her slaves will rise in value, and she has more than she wants."

The cotton gin was invented in 1793, at which time some 10,000 bales were produced in the United States. This invention, which revolutionized the industry, sparked the crop's development in the South. By 1800 production was at 73,000 bales; in 1810, 178,000 bales; in 1820, 335,000 bales, and in 1835 more than a million bales were produced. The 3-million level was reached in 1852, and seven years later more than 4.5 million bales were produced in the United States. The South claimed Cotton was King, and if this were so, slavery was its retainer.

Even before the cotton empire was recognized and established, slavery was spreading beyond the Appalachians. Where the institution spread, the slave trade—small, disorganized, and occasional though it was at first—followed. Slave drivers took their chattel to Kentucky and Tennessee, and later on to western Alabama, Mississippi, and, ultimately, Texas. The drive west—to virgin acres ripe for cotton—became a theme for antebellum America.

At the end of the Revolution a good, healthy field hand could be purchased in Virginia for around $200. By the end of Washington's Presidency in 1797, one could be purchased not far from Mount Vernon for around $250. Southern Virginia and South Carolina were leading cotton-producing areas at the time, and would remain so for decades to come. But the cotton culture was growing rapidly in the Gulf states and Georgia, which contained more virgin territory than the Atlantic states of the upper South and better climate for cotton. The older states had large slave populations but were growing more slowly than the newer states along the Gulf and in trans-Appalachia, where there were shortages of plantation labor. In 1803 a prime field hand could fetch $600 in New Orleans, which had been a slave-trading center in the colonial period and continued in that role until the institution was ended in the Civil War. Six years later several slaves were sold for $1,000 each, at a time when "prime hands" in Virginia were going for less than half that price. By then the slave trade was maturing within the United States, with slaves from the older states being transported to the newer ones—sent to market, as it were. In 1839 Thomas Dew, a leading spokesman for the slavery system, estimated that "upwards of six thousand [slaves] are yearly exported to other states" from Virginia. "Virginia is, in fact, a negro raising state for other states. She produced enough for her own supply, and six thousand for sale."

The cotton empire was expanding, demanding more land. Americans in all parts of the nation were expansionist in much of the antebellum period, but no section was more consistently so than the plantation South. Southern slaveholders supported the annexation of Texas and later on the Mexican War. The elimination of Texas as a potential rival in the world cotton market was one factor in this, while its annexation seemed necessary to open the territory for Virginian and other eastern seaboard slaves.

This was not lost on the Abolitionists, who for the same reason opposed the annexation of Texas and the Mexican War, which they feared would result in the further annexation of cotton land. Deprive the slave states of the means for expansion, they argued, and the price of slaves will fall, until the black plantation worker became a glut on the market. In time slavery will be ended, they predicted, not through war between the states, but rather through the efficient operation of impersonal economic laws. "Texas comprehends a large extent of territory," noted a leading antislavery society in 1840. "It possesses in the judgement of practical men an unrivalled soil for the growth of the very finest kinds of cotton. . . . By some [slaveholders] it has been estimated that the acquisition of Texas as a slave market would raise the price of their slaves fifty per cent. at least."

It was not that simple, though the theory was sound. The price of prime field slaves did indeed rise in the 1850's, reaching almost $2,000 apiece on the eve of the Civil War. By then George Washington's visions of a slave-free South had almost completely faded in that region. Slavery was big business, an area for profits and speculation.

But did this big business pay off in profits? Did it benefit not only the slave dealers, breeders, and plantation owners, but also the economy as a whole? Speaking economically only, was the nation better off with slavery than it might have been without the institution?

These questions have been the subject of prolonged inquiry, discussion, and debate. During the past generation a small army of historians and economists have studied the matter, using sophisticated economic analysis as well as poring over all the records available.* Some have noted, correctly, that much of this work is of little meaning insofar as truly understanding the issue, unless slavery is perceived in its historical context. † The fact of the matter was that many southern slaveholders and writers of the antebellum period truly *believed* slavery was profitable and economically beneficial, as well as a foundation for a truly enlightened civilization. Whether they were guilty of self-delusion and rationalization is beside the

*See the Bibliography for a selection of works on the subject. Of particular interest are Alfred Conrad and John Meyer, *The Economics of Slavery* (Chicago, 1964); Kenneth Stampp, *The Peculiar Institution* (New York, 1956); and Harold Woodman, ed. *Slavery and the Southern Economy* (New York, 1967).

† The key work here is Eugene Genovese, *The Political Economy of Slavery* (New York, 1965).

point; what is significant is that they went to great lengths to prove their contention.

Prior to the 1837 panic many articles and pamphlets were published in the South to demonstrate slavery's profitability. Little was said of the matter for the next seven years, as few businessmen and businesses showed profits in the depression, while the farms too were hard hit. Then the argument reappeared. Some planters and slavers—especially in Mississippi and Louisiana—offered statistics to prove their claims. These were incomplete and biased, as were those of their opponents. But the reports did insist that slavery could not have persisted unless it was profitable, and its very growth was evidence of the case. To this, Abolitionists replied that the Mississippi and Louisiana planters owned some of the best cotton land in the world and that fact, more than slavery, was the source of their prosperity. Nor did the planters spend much time discussing whether or not they would have been better off with free labor than with slaves. Even if the planters' own figures are accepted, however, the record is not impressive.

One of the most complete sets of books for a southern plantation was that compiled for and by the owners and managers of Hopeton, on the Altamaha River in Glynn County, Georgia. Hopeton was established shortly before the War of 1812 by John Couper, a Scots immigrant, who was unaccustomed to working that kind of land and unable to manage slaves. Couper was forced into bankruptcy in 1827. At that time the plantation was taken over by his creditors, but Couper continued on as manager until 1852.

Hopeton grew cotton, experimented with sugar and rice, and was considered one of the finest plantations in the district. Charles Lyell, the British scientist, visited Hopeton in 1845 and commented favorably on what he saw, as did others. From their remarks we may assume that Hopeton's profitability was a cut above the average. Couper's figures show the plantation always managed a profit, even in the last years of the depression, when many other farms were falling under the auctioneer's hammer.

Hopeton Plantation in the 1840s

Year	Capital	Gross Sales	Net Sales	Expenses	Profit	Rate of Profit
1840	$302,617	$26,476	$24,228	$11,276	$12,952	4.2
1841	347,482	30,471	27,975	16,822	11,153	3.2
1842	344,682	18,906	17,232	15,753	1,479	0.4
1843	344,682	23,393	20,770	13,240	7,530	2.2
1844	344,682	30,411	27,700	17,260	10,440	3.0
1845	344,682	26,370	24,436	13,120	11,316	3.3
1846	344,682	41,162	37,603	13,686	23,917	6.9
1847	343,618	29,894	27,335	14,915	12,421	3.6
1848	343,618	30,807	27,811	16,397	11,413	3.3
1849	340,018	36,988	33,281	15,342	17,939	5.3
1850	342,018	35,795	32,572	16,583	15,988	4.7

Source: Thomas P. Govan, "Was Plantation Slavery Profitable?" *Journal of Southern History,* VIII (November 1942), 513-35.

These figures are incomplete, and would not satisfy today's accountants. They do not take into account increases in the value of the land, depreciation of assets, and other costs. Nor do we know the cash flow of the operation.

What of the slave? How much of the productivity and profit of Hopeton could be attributed to the fact that the plantation used slave labor? In fact, how are we to classify slaves? Are they labor? Certainly this was so. But at the same time they were investments in plant, in bookkeeping terms. The slave force had to be depreciated, and children of slaves might be considered incremental assets. Such problems, moral as well as economic, were never considered by Couper and others at Hopeton. They tended to ignore such questions when responding to financial criticisms. Couper must have known, however, that the land was carried on his books at too low a price, since it appreciated greatly in the 1840s, and that this inflated the rate of return on net assets. His entries for expenses were low, not taking into account such matters as depreciation, and this made Hopeton's rate of profit seem larger than it should have been. Nor did expenses include some salaries, including Couper's.

Important though these issues are, they may be ignored for the moment. What does matter, in terms of Couper's presentation, is the belief they held that they were receiving a profit on investment and sales, one on which they based their defense of slavery and the plantation system.

Even in this they were guilty of self-delusion, again considering the economics of the matter and not other factors that went into making the plantation system what it was. Let us assume, for the sake of argument, that Hopeton's owners had liquidated their holding at what they claimed its asset value to have been in 1840, and then put the money obtained from the sale into prime commercial paper in New York or Boston. Such paper fluctuated, but despite this, was far less risky and depended on fewer variables than did the return on a cotton crop. Had they done this, they would have been spared the worry of running a plantation and fears of weather, production, slave management, and the like. In so doing, they would have more than doubled their income.

Comparative Rates of Return on Hopeton and Commercial Paper

Year	Hopeton	60-90 Day Paper, N.Y.	3-6 Month Paper, Boston
1840	4.2	7.8	6.0
1841	3.2	6.9	6.0
1842	0.4	8.1	7.8
1843	2.2	4.5	3.0
1844	3.0	4.9	5.0
1845	3.3	6.0	6.0
1846	6.9	8.3	8.0
1847	3.9	9.6	6.0
1848	3.3	15.1	15.0
1849	5.3	10.0	12.0
1850	4.7	8.0	12.0
Average	3.6	8.1	7.8

Sources: Govan, *"Plantation Slavery,"* and Alfred Conrad and John Meyer, "The Economics of Slavery in the Ante-Bellum South," *Journal of Political Economy,* LXVI (April 1958), 95-122.

In no year of the 1840s did Hopeton do better than the New York and Boston rates. Yet planters persisted in defending their system on economic grounds, and in claiming slavery to be an economical labor system.

What of the productivity of the slave himself? On a well-run plantation, with excellent soil, the cotton production per capita could run as high as eight bales, each weighing 383 pounds. In 1839 a prime field hand cost approximately $1,000, and on such a plantation he could have produced 3,064 pounds of cotton, which at that year's price of 13½ cents would have returned $413.64 to the master. From this must be deducted processing costs of $4 a bale and marketing costs of 70 cents a bale. Slave upkeep was figured at $20 a year, too low and unrealistic, for the food eaten by the slave was usually produced on the plantation and not calculated in the cost, as were other items such as medical care. When all of this is deducted, according to the slaveholder's own calculations, the net return amounted to $356.24, or approximately a 36-percent return on the investment in the slave.

This was the kind of figure slaveholders produced when they wanted to demonstrate the efficiency of their institutions. The return would have been impressive even had the slave been depreciated as though a capital good. In 1850 the life expectancy of a black male slave in Maryland was calculated at 38.47 years at birth, while in Louisiana the figure was 28.89 years. The death rate in the first year of life was very high, so that if a slave could survive to adolescence, he might live to fifty or older. Slaveholders assumed that such a slave, in good health and who would not run away, would have at least forty working years. If straight-line depreciation is employed on such an "investment," the slave might be said to have lost $25 per annum (assuming an initial cost of $1,000). If this is deducted from the net return, the profit per slave would come to $331.24, or 33 percent.

The major fallacy in such reasoning is the failure of the figures to include other factors of production. As was seen, the owners of Hopeton assigned a value of approximately a third of a million dollars to the plantation in the 1840s, did not include charges for their own services, or think of whether or not the plantation could have done better with free labor. A consideration of any of these factors would have lowered the profit margin substantially, and if all were taken into account, the plantation could have showed a loss due to the use of slaves. (Using Hopeton's reasoning, American Beef Packers might have claimed, in 1969, that each employee was bringing in $420,738, the company's statistic for sales per employee that year. In beef packing, large amounts of capital goods are needed with relatively little labor.)

The "rental price" of slaves provides a more realistic method of determining their return on investment. As a rule of thumb, planters would calculate the hire of a slave for a year to be one-eighth the purchase price, so that a $1,000 slave would be rented to a planter for approximately $125. Should the slave die, the contract would be voided, but if he fell ill or ran away, the lessee still had to pay, as well as provide a slave with food, clothing, and shelter during illness. The year in such cases was calculated at fifty-one weeks, for the slave was permitted to go home for the Christmas holiday.

On such a basis, the return on slaves might be figured at 12.5 percent, a respectable figure. Even if depreciation is taken into account, the return would be 10 percent, and this too seems attractive—until compared with the profits to be had by hiring free white workers.

The British actor, Tyrone Power, visited America in 1835 and watched hundreds of newly arrived Irish immigrants digging a canal through a swamp to Lake Pontchartrain. Later he wrote, "Slave labor cannot be substituted to any extent, being much too expensive; a good slave costs at this time two hundred pounds sterling, and to have a thousand such swept off a line of canal in one season would call for prompt consideration." When the Irish laborers fell ill with swamp fever, they were replaced; when they died, they were buried, and that was that. But the death of slaves would have cost the contractor some $900 each, the average price in 1835.

This is not to say such enterprises did not buy and use slaves. One of the reasons their prices rose was the demand for them on the part of large internal improvements operations. The state of Georgia purchased 190 slaves in and before 1830 to use in river and road improvements, but soon abandoned the experiment. The Brandon

Bank, which owned and operated the Mississippi & Alabama Railroad, purchased $159,000 worth of slaves prior to 1839, at which time it went bankrupt because of the depression. The Charleston & Savannah Railroad and the South Carolina Railroad used slaves in construction work in the 1850s. Several manufacturing enterprises purchased slaves, including the Hillman Iron Works in Tennessee and several cotton mills. Most claimed the slaves did their work well and provided good returns on investment. They were sold and their places taken by free labor, however. The reason given was not economic but financial; several enterprises claimed slaves worked better than freemen, but their costs were so high as to stretch to their breaking point the limited financial resources of the firms. In other words, slaves were being priced out of the market.

Here, too, self-deception may have played a role in formulating such conclusions. Most observers agreed with Power's conclusions. Frederick Law Olmsted, writing in the mid-1850s, said that, in his home district in New York, native American farm laborers were paid $10 a month, plus board and lodging, while immigrants were paid even less. In eastern Virginia at the same time, able-bodied slaves were hired at $120 a year, plus board, clothes, and medical services. From the point of view of the renter, it would appear he would have been better off with free laborers, who could be fired if they did not perform well. The slave, on the other hand, could and often did work slowly and still escape being "fired," if indeed it could be so considered. One visitor, writing of plantation slaves, noted:

> Nothing can be conceived more inert than a slave; his unwilling labor is discovered in every step that he takes; he moves not, if he can avoid it; if the eyes of the overseer be off him, he sleeps; the ox and the horse, driven by the slave, appear to sleep also; all is listless inactivity.

Thomas Cooper, a British economist, resided in South Carolina in the mid-1820s, and came to the same conclusion, as did most other writers of the antebellum period.

> The usual work of a field slave is barely two thirds what a white day labourer at usual wages would perform; this is the outside. . . . Nothing will justify slave labour in point of economy but the nature of the soil and climate which incapacitates a white man from labouring in the summer time, as on the rich lands of Carolina and Georgia, extending one hundred miles from the seaboard. In places merely agricultural, as New York, Pennsylvania, Illinois, Indiana, Missouri, slave labour is entirelly unprofitable. It is so even in Maryland and Virginia.

If the hire of a slave hand made little sense for the lessee, the owning of such individuals made less for the leasor. Let us assume he had a surplus of slaves which he hired regularly to neighbors, and that they returned 10 percent on his investment. If he sold them all and put the money into New York commercial paper, his return would have been slightly over 8 percent in the 1840s, and he would have been spared management costs, which were not deducted from the 10-percent rate. He would also be free from what amounted to "pension costs." A free white laborer too old to work was simply fired; the black slave in the same circumstance was retained and supported for life even though he had become nonproductive. The slaveholder who had sold slaves would be spared the fear of losing his investment through death or runaways. These were major considerations. The cholera epidemic of 1833 caused the deaths of slaves worth $4 million at current market value. Two decades later a Savannah broker, who sold slaves in lots, told his client, "the purchaser gave $2,000 more than the asking price for 85 with the privilege of rejecting 10 old people." A Virginian then living in France wrote a relative in 1860:

> Please, let me know the condition of the old negroes at Cherry Grove, and whether there is the remotist likelihood of their cloding this life during the present century. They must be very helpless; and will soon, if not now, require the personal attention of a young negro. Suggest some mode of making them

> comfortable the balance of their lives, and at the present or less expense.

Plantation owners in the seaboard states were aware of this situation. Yet they continued to hold to the idea that ownership of slaves was profitable. To understand this paradox one must consider that the Virginia and border state slaveholders viewed the slaves not only as workers and symbols of a way of life they prized, but also as an investment—in much the same way today's stockholders consider securities, or an art dealer his pictures.

Suppose the owner of a security received a return of 2 percent on his investment in the form of dividends, and was told that, should he liquidate his position and put the money into safe bonds, he could quadruple his return. He might reply that bonds do not ordinarily increase in value, while stocks have appreciation potential. In the aftermath of the 1837 depression, slaves had some of the aspects of growth stocks. It was a period in which a major "bull market in human flesh" developed, the most dramatic in the history of the institution, as the price of a prime field hand went from $600 at "the bottom of the 1844 bear market" to over $1,800 in 1860, the climax of the bull market.

Several factors entered into this price rise, but all may be connected, directly or indirectly, with the ancient forces of supply and demand.

Article I, Section 9 of the Constitution prohibited Congress from interfering with the importation of slaves prior to 1808. This was considered a concession to the southern states, to allow them to "stock up" on slaves before the trade was ended. In 1807 both northern and southern congressmen voted to end the trade the following year, and not until the late 1850s would any significant group of southerners speak in favor of reopening Africa to American slave ships. At the time it was thought the natural increase in slaves through large families would take care of the South's needs indefinitely. Few in 1807 could visualize the explosive expansion of the United States, or the great growth of cotton culture in the next four decades.

The slave population did increase due to natural forces, rising from some 1.5 million in 1820 to almost 4 million in 1860. This was a sizable increment, but still insufficient to meet the new demands for slaves heard from the West.

"Cotton is a frontier crop," said one student of the subject, "restlessly seeking new horizons, and new soil and climate that are favorable to it." So it was that the cotton culture moved westward rapidly after the War of 1812, and the drive continued throughout the antebellum period. Most founders of new plantations attempted to duplicate on the frontier the cultural and social conditions they left behind, and that included slavery. Labor was scarce in the new areas, and this provided an economic reason to seek slaves. Finally, the growing surplus of slaves in the old South, where prices were falling, combined with the demand for them in the newer states, where prices were rising, led to an exodus from the Virginia-Maryland region southward and westward, one that continued for four decades.

There is no accurate count of the number of slaves sold for this reason. The best estimate is that in the 1820–1830 period 124,000 were sent from such slave-surplus states as Virginia, Maryland, Delaware, North Carolina, Kentucky, and the District of Columbia to the importing states of South Carolina, Georgia, Alabama, Mississippi, Tennessee, and Georgia. The prosperous years of the early 1830s caused the movement to grow, and large numbers were sold to Florida, too, while some of the border states, finding themselves with surpluses and unable to resist rising prices, entered the business. Some 265,000 slaves were sold in interstate traffic in the 1830s, the peak for such activity. The hard years of the depression slowed the traffic somewhat, with only 146,000 transferred in the 1840s. Then, as Texas blossomed into a major cotton center and the lower Mississippi became the focal point for the fiber, sales picked up once more. Texas, Alabama, Mississippi, and Louisiana demanded slaves, and they were provided from the older states and border states in great numbers in the 1850s, when some 207,000 "went south" to new homes.

At first most of these transfers were made by families moving west and taking their slaves with them as they went. Individual slaves were sold, too, as parts of estates, surpluses of large plantations, or when a neighbor needed them and offered a good price. On occasion, large-scale sales took place, some of which involved prominent people. In order to raise funds to meet obligations coming due in 1793, for example, Thomas Jefferson sold some of his slaves. In disposing of part of his mother's estate in 1815, Richard Willing Byrd sold more than one hundred of her slaves at auction. Bushrod Washington, nephew of the first President and a Supreme Court justice, sold fifty-four of his ninety slaves in 1821 because he found their use uneconomical on his plantation. None of these men, or their friends and neighbors, would have considered themselves in the slave-trading business. To have called them slave traders would have been a grave insult, one that could lead to a duel.

Paradoxically, the southern plantation owner, who used the services of slave traders, frowned on the practice and the practitioners, in much the same way individuals who purchased liquor from bootleggers in the 1920s considered their sources disreputable men. Later on, the same men who claimed Blacks were not truly human beings castigated slave traders while accepting cattle breeders. They either knew Blacks were human and so disbelieved their biological doctrines, or felt they were truly beasts, but disliked the individual traders. Most likely the former was closer to the truth. Many southern states passed laws against interstate slave trading in the early nineteenth century, only to repeal them later on. Thus, slavery was considered the backbone of society, good both for slaveholder and slave, while commerce in slaves was an evil, though necessary, and one the southerners preferred not to discuss.

Early slave traders took pains to assure buyers and sellers they were moral men. So it was that many advertisements of the pre-War of 1812 period stressed the trader's promise not to break up slave families, and to sell them to plantation owners who would treat them well. Some observed they were acting as middlemen between two farmers, and were not in the business of speculation in slaves; that is, they were not "stockpiling slaves," or purchasing them on consignment. In this way they made a fine distinction between the businessman operating for profits, pure and simple, and the one who provided a needed service in a decent and honorable calling. Yet even those who used the services of these slave dealers would not consort with them outside of business, and to be a slave dealer was considered on a par with today's dealer in heroin as seen by addicts—a needed individual in a hated business. Addressing the Mississippi Supreme Court in 1832, a southern lawyer said:

> I can imagine a man who would hold slaves, who would think it perfectly right to own such property, and cultivate his cotton field by their labor, and yet scorn to make a business of buying and selling human beings for speculation; nay, who would abhor and detest both the speculator and the dealer, and who would shun his society. And I can imagine a community of such men . . . I do not attempt argument before this court to prove the wide differences between a slave holder and a slave trader; such an attempt before this court, who are slave holders, I would consider insulting to their feelings. . . .

After the Civil War, a former plantation owner, writing of the status of the traders, said as much:

> In the South the calling of a slave-trader was always hateful, odious, even among slave-holders themselves. This is curious, but it is so. A trader's children recovered, to some extent, but there was ever a *thin* cloud resting on them, which they could not get rid of. We had two or three slave-traders in this section, and, although their children were taken into society, it was no uncommon thing to hear the sly remark—"his or her father was a slave driver."

Addressing an audience in Peoria, Illinois, on October 15, 1854, Abraham Lincoln, then a former congressman with hopes of a senatorial nomination, spoke of slave traders. Visiting his wife's home in Lexington, Kentucky, he had seen them in action, and had learned to despise them. The Peoria audience was proslavery, but also anti-slave trader. So the audience applauded Lincoln when he said:

> You have among you a sneaking individual of a class of native tyrants, known as the "slave dealer." He watches your necessities and crawls up to buy your slave at a speculative price. If you cannot help it, you sell to him; but if you can help it, you drive him from your door. You utterly despise him. You do not recognize him as your friend, or even as an honest man. Your children must not play with his; they may rollick freely with the little negroes, but not with the slave dealer's children.

Although Lincoln overstated the sentiments, the principle was correct. Still, every plantation area had its share of men engaged in slave trading. In the 1820s most were farmers who found the transactions profitable, and tended to neglect their farms for the more lucrative auctions. Such dealers might be contacted by local plantation owners and informed of their needs or surpluses, and they would make provisions for purchases and sales. They might advertise in local newspapers, asking for slaves to be sold at their auctions, or privately, "at the very best price." Few, however, considered slave trading their major occupation. Or if they did, they told friends and relatives they expected to leave it soon, in order to purchase large plantations and live like gentlemen, something slave traders never could be.

As the great land boom of the 1830s developed, with more and more Americans moving to the Southwest, the demands for interstate transfers grew. Some such sales had been made in the 1820s, and a few traders shipped cargoes of slaves to the Southwest, down the Mississippi, overland in "coffles," or slave gangs, or by sea, around Florida to New Orleans. Such activities required large amounts of capital, since the slaves purchased in Virginia or Maryland could not be sold until they reached Louisiana or Texas months later. They also depended on a network of agents, men to buy slaves in one place, ship them off to a partner or employee in the other, who would sell them at auctions or privately. The possibility of large profits and the existence of a market created such companies.

One of the first of these was formed by John Meek of Nashville, Tennessee, and Samuel Logan of Abingdon, Virginia. Meek had several years experience in slave trading, and had traveled throughout the lower South, holding auctions and taking orders for slaves. Prices were high in Tennessee and the West—a good field hand could be sold for well over $1,200. Profits were lower than Meek thought fair, since there were few slaves to be purchased at lower than the market price.

Logan was a well-to-do lawyer, in partnership with a C. Haynes, who also dabbled in slaves, buying and selling for the local market as a convenience to his clients. Prices were lower in Virginia than in Tennessee, because of an oversupply of slaves on run-down plantations. It was Logan who had the idea of buying slaves in Virginia and selling them in Tennessee. He had learned of Meek from friends, and contacted him in February 1835 with a proposition. Logan and Haynes on the one hand, and Meek on the other, would form a partnership, with the Virginians buying slaves and sending them on to Meek for sale. Realizing this violated the gentleman's code, Logan added that a friend, a man called Magee, would be his "front"; if his law clients learned he was going into slave trading for profits he would lose them. A month later Meek agreed to the partnership, and operations began.

Soon after, the Virginians purchased forty-seven slaves for $19,800, an average of $421 apiece. They pledged the "shipment" would be ready to move on August 10. Then troubles developed. Some of the suppliers demanded payment immediately, and Logan lacked sufficient funds. A few slaves ran away when they learned they would be sent westward. The rest were sent on, and although the correspondence regarding their disposition has been lost, in all probability they were sold at a large profit, for the partnership continued.

Other firms entered the field soon after, bidding the Virginia prices higher. In 1836 Logan purchased sixty-one slaves for $42,420, an average of $695 apiece. All but one were sent on to Meek. The lone exception was a slave who, on learning of the shipment, cut off his hand and had to "be counted as nothing." Logan informed Meek he would make an attempt to exchange him for a whole slave. A few of the slaves ran away once on the road, but a sufficient number arrived to offer a good return on the investment.

The partnership might have continued for many more years, returning profits at both ends, were it not for the 1837 panic, which dried up Logan's source of funds. The Virginian informed Meek he would have to exercise caution that year—cut back on operations. Could Meek forward from $5,000 to $10,000 in gold to him, in order to pay for new purchases? Logan closed by saying, "We are among the damndest population upon the earth for the slander of mens circumstances." By this he seemed to mean his activities had been uncovered, and he was losing clients who disapproved of slave trading.

What followed is unknown, for the partnership ended its correspondence. As long as it had lasted, however, Meek and Logan profited. Other firms, some even larger than theirs, continued, and survived the depression.

Franklin & Armfield was one of these, and in time became known as the largest slave-trading firm in the United States, the best-run, and the most dependable. Fortunately, it was also in the practice of keeping books, most of which survive.

Isaac Franklin, the founder of the firm, was born in Tennessee in 1789, in a frontier community. In 1807, at the age of eighteen, he was employed by his brothers as a trading agent, and spent much of his time in New Orleans, where he also learned the rudiments of slave trading. After a brief service in the War of 1812 he returned to trading and began to dabble in slaves. He would scour the countryside, seeking slaves for sale, and would bring them to Natchez, which at the time was threatening New Orleans as the slave-trading center for Mississippi. Franklin did well, and needed help in his work. In 1824 he met John Armfield, a younger and even more aggressive slave trader, and Rice C. Ballard, who was also in the business. For a while the three men worked together, and in 1825 they formed a trading company known as Ballard, Franklin & Co., which was to concentrate on the Natchez trade.

The business prospered, but not as rapidly as Franklin and Armfield had hoped it would. On their own they began to purchase slaves in Alexandria, in the District of Columbia, and transport them to New Orleans for sale. Armfield was to reside in Alexandria, manage the firm's slave pen there, run auctions, and arrange for the shipment of slaves to New Orleans, where Franklin would sell them, either privately or at auctions.

The two men worked well together. Armfield proved adept at the acquisition of slaves, while Franklin's contacts in New Orleans were of the best. Soon after, Armfield married Franklin's niece, and their relationship grew stronger. Finally, in 1828, they formed the partnership of Franklin & Armfield, which continued until 1841. During this period, the firm was the nation's leading slave trader.

In May 1828, Franklin & Armfield advertised for "150 likely young Negroes of both sexes between the ages of 8 and 25 years." Other, similar advertisements followed, indicating the business was good and expanding. Not content with having only one slave pen, Armfield decided to expand his operations. He contacted several well-known independent traders and offered to advance them funds for their operations, on the understanding they would supply him with "prime" hands, leaving second-rate ones to his competitors. Some accepted his terms, and five agreed to affiliate with Franklin & Armfield, and became satellite firms. George Kephart & Co., of Fredericktown, Maryland, abandoned its coffle-driving business completely to concentrate on supplying Armfield, and did well at the business. In this way, Franklin & Armfield soon had a network in Virginia and Maryland, one which could supply Franklin with all the slaves he needed in New Orleans. Slave pens were established in five cities, and slaves were transferred from one to another when the demand dictated. An indication of the firm's scope may be gathered from the following advertisement, appearing in the *National Intelligencer* on July 2, 1833:

> CASH IN MARKET. We will pay Cash for any number of likely Negroes, of both sexes, from 12 to 25 years of age, Field Hands. Also, Mechanics of every description. Apply to
>
> R.C. Ballard & Co. — Richmond, Va.
> J.M. Saunders & Co. — Warrenton, Va.

George Kephart & Co.	Fredericktown, Md.
James F. Purvis & Co.	Baltimore
Thomas M. Jones	Easton, Eastern Shore of Md.

Or, to the subscribers, at their residence in Alexandria.

Persons having likely servants to dispose of, will do well to give us a call, as we at all times will pay higher prices in cash than any other purchaser who is now or may hereafter come into the market. All communications promptly attended to. —FRANKLIN & ARMFIELD.

Armfield also purchased a small slave fleet. The *Tribune, United States, Isaac Franklin,* and *Uncas* sailed regularly from Alexandria to New Orleans, carrying paying passengers as well as the company's slaves to market. Passengers were encouraged to visit the slave quarters while en route, to see how well the "merchandise" was "packed."* In this, as in other ways, Armfield proved a genius in his field. Passengers often were plantation owners in the market for slaves. When attending auctions in New Orleans, they would seek out Franklin & Armfield slaves, for they knew they were indeed "prime." In every way, then, Armfield was a businessman, considering his merchandise as one might an automobile, house, or suit of clothes.

In 1834, the firm sent from 1,000 to 1,200 slaves from Virginia and Maryland to the Southwest, and the numbers picked up in the next three years. There is no way of knowing exactly how profitable the business was, but at the time, Armfield, a driver ten years earlier, was said to be worth half a million dollars, while Franklin was even wealthier.

By then the senior partner was tired of the business. He yearned for respectability, and such could not be gained in the slave trade. Late in 1835 he informed Armfield of his desire to retire, buy a large plantation in Tennessee, marry and raise a family, and in all other

*Armfield always refused to break up slave families, and was true to his word. This added to his reputation as a gentleman.

ways become a member of the southern aristocracy. Ballard, Franklin & Co. took over much of his Natchez interests, while Armfield was authorized to liquidate his other operations. Franklin & Armfield was dissolved in 1841, with Franklin becoming a planter and Armfield continuing on his own, but gradually withdrawing from trading himself.

Franklin did all he hoped to do—he acquired his plantation, married, and had a family. He died in 1846, leaving an estate worth more than $750,000, and most of it obtained through the slave trade.

George Kephart, who had learned so much from Armfield, now purchased many of the holdings of the dissolved firm. He was a cruder man than Franklin and Armfield and less interested in status than money. During the great surge of buying in slaves that took place in the 1850s, Kephart made a fortune—some say over $2 million. He was still in business in 1861, when United States troops seized his holdings in Alexandria. Kephart fled the town, and was never heard from again.

Franklin & Armfield dominated the Alexandria-Tennessee-New Orleans triangle, but other firms prospered at the same time, and after the depression of the early 1840s was over, more appeared. One of these was Hughes & Downing, established in Lexington, Kentucky, in the fall of 1843. The firm began "small," sending its first shipment of thirteen slaves from Kentucky to Natchez. The total "package" cost them $5,292.50, and was sold in Natchez for $8,695. Transport and related costs came to $257.72, leaving a profit of $3,144.78, quite good by any standard. Among the group was a boy, purchased in Kentucky for $440, and sold in Natchez for $540, and profits from other slaves were equally good. Generally speaking, the firm expected a profit of from $100 to $150 on each of its slaves.

Hughes & Downing was among those companies considered respectable, if such could describe any trading company in the view of white southerners of the period. Lewis C. Robards, on the other hand, was universally despised. By the mid-1850s he was the biggest trader in Kentucky, but also the most unscrupulous. He would sell sick slaves, and when they died soon after, refuse to offer compensation, as did Hughes & Downing, Franklin & Armfield, and other firms. He dealt in young black girls, sold for concubinage, and advertised them as such, contrary to the southern antebellum code. Robards mistreated his slaves, considered bad in itself but also a detriment to good business. Before purchasing a slave at auction, the buyer had the right to examine him. Whip marks on the body detracted from the price, not because it indicated the slave was damaged, but rather because it proved he was a recalcitrant slave, who might run away. At least, this was the case with slaves purchased from most houses; in Robards' case, the opposite might be true, and this complicated the task of would-be buyers.

Robards' dealings continually landed him in trouble, both with the buyers and the law. In the end he went out of business, and few mourned his passing. Were it not for the great demand for slaves in the 1850s, he could not have lasted as long as he did. But the demand was such at the time that even Robards could make a living for a while.

The "bull market" in slaves was caused by the rush to the Southwest following the Mexican War. It came as quite a surprise, even to experienced slave dealers. A Virginia newspaperman, writing in 1844, deplored the falling prices of slaves, and thought "it will be a long time before slaves recover their former prices." A Mississippi planter of 1849, applauding the end of the war, noted the rapid upward move in slave prices, and boasted of having "done very well in the selling of surplus slaves." By then slaves had taken on all the aspects of growth stocks. In 1855 a Georgia commentator remarked that the "upward sweep" could not last indefinitely; a fall was on its way.

> The old rule of pricing a negro by the price of cotton by the pound—that is to say, if cotton is worth twelve cents a negro man is worth $1,200.00, if at fifteen cents then $1,500.00—does not seem to be regarded. Negroes are 25 per cent higher now with cotton at ten and a half cents than they were two or three years ago when it was worth fifteen and sixteen cents. . . . A reversal will come soon.

The decline did not materialize; prices of slaves continued to rise out of relation to the price of cotton. In modern times, it would appear an adjustment in price-earnings ratios was taking place. A New Orleans writer of 1860 tried to justify the high price of slaves, in a way that sounds strongly reminiscent of financial writers in early 1929 or 1966.

> The theory that the price of negroes is ruled by the price of cotton is not good, for it does not account for the present aspect of the slave market. . . . Nor do we agree with our contemporaries who argue that a speculative demand is the unsubstantial basis of the advance in the price of slaves—that the rates are too high and must come down very soon. It is our impression that the great demand for slaves in the Southwest will keep up prices as it caused their advance in the first place, and that the rates are not a cent above the real value of the laborer who is to be engaged in tilling the fertile lands of a section of the country which yields the planter nearly double the crop that the fields of the Atlantic states do. The Southwest is being opened by a great tide of emigration. The planter who puts ten hands to work on the prolific soil of Texas and Western Louisiana soon makes enough money to buy ten more, and they have to be supplied from the older States—hence the prices which rule in Virginia, the Carolinas, and Georgia. A demand founded in such causes cannot fall off for a score or more years, and the prices of negroes must keep up. They will probably advance somewhat.

Slavery may or may not have been an uneconomical institution when compared with free labor, but the fact remains that profits were to be made in the internal slave trade, and some southerners took advantage of the opportunity to become wealthy. Nor is it any wonder that other southerners came to view their chattel as breeding stock, and not workers.

Both before and after the 1837 panic and depression, southern leaders were aware of the fact that slaves were being bred for sale, and that the center of the breeding area was the old South, Virginia in particular. Thomas Jefferson Randolph told the Virginia legislature in 1832 that his state had become "one grand menagerie, where men were reared for the market like oxen for the shambles," and at the same time Thomas Dew claimed "The slaves in Virginia multiply more rapidly than in most of the Southern states; —the Virginians can raise cheaper than they can buy; in fact, it is one of their greatest sources of profit." Edmund Ruffin also noted the situation, but claimed it was a by-product of the Virginia economy; the plantation owners were not breeding slaves on purpose, but merely selling off their surpluses. "No man is so inhuman as to breed and raise slaves, to sell off a certain proportion regularly, as a western drover does with his herds of cattle," wrote Ruffin. "But sooner or later the general result is the same."

This leads to a final consideration of the business of slavery, and the great speculation in slaves on the eve of the Civil War. Did slave breeding produce a satisfactory return on investment? If the labor of the slave was indeed uneconomical when compared with that of free labor, could it not be made up in the sale of slave children? Was this an important consideration in the 1850s?

Attempts have been made to calculate the economics of such sales. One of these assumed that the female slave produced five children, and that females became self-sustaining at age thirteen and males at age nine, and that the slave was purchased at age twenty. Provisions would have to be made for the months a female slave could not work, and for the sake of argument, it was assumed the slave worked land which yielded 3.75 bales per male field hand, with a 7.5-cent per pound of cotton price. Finally, the unlikely assumption was made that all five children survived. If one accepts all these conditions, then the breeding of slaves might appear profitable.

Of course, these figures assume optimum conditions, and do not reflect the actual situation in any part of the South at any time in its history. As such, however, they can lead us to several conclusions and observations regarding the economics of slave breeding. In this hypothetical situation, an $800 investment in a female slave produced $6,012.50 over a thirty-year span, an average of $200 a year, for a net

Return on Investment in a Female Slave

Year From Purchase Date	Personal Field Returns	Child Field Returns	Child Sale Return	Personal Upkeep	Child Upkeep	Net Returns
1	$56	–	–	$20	–	$36
2	40	–	–	20	$50	–30
3	56	–	–	20	10	26
4	40	–	–	20	60	–40
5	56	–	–	20	20	16
6	40	–	–	20	70	–50
7	56	–	–	20	30	6
8	40	$ 3.75	–	20	80	–56.25
9	56	7.50	–	20	45	– 1.50
10	40	15.00	–	20	95	–50.00
11	56	22.50	–	20	60	– 1.50
12	56	37.50	–	20	60	13.50
13	56	52.50	–	20	65	23.50
14	56	75.00	–	20	65	46.00
15	56	97.50	–	20	75	58.50
16	56	127.50	–	20	75	88.50
17	56	157.50	–	20	85	108.50
18	56	191.25	–	20	85	142.25
19	56	225.00	–	20	90	171.00
20	56	180.00	$875	20	75	1,016.00
21	56	210.00	–	20	75	171.00
22	56	157.50	875	20	60	1,008.50
23	56	180.00	–	20	60	156.00
24	56	120.00	875	20	40	991.00
25	56	135.00	–	20	40	131.00
26	56	67.50	875	20	20	958.50
27	56	75.00	–	20	20	91.00
28	56	–	875	20	–	911.00
29	56	–	–	20	–	36.00
30	56	–	–	20	–	36.00

Souce: Conrad and Meyer, *The Economics of Slavery,* p. 63.

return on investment of approximately 25 percent. Naturally, if provision would be made for runaways, deaths, illnesses, and the like, the figure would fall precipitously. In addition, this model assumed a "long-term investment," for the slave would not begin to show a profit until the fifteenth year. Should one or more of her children die prior to the sales or become a successful runaway, or should the female slave herself die in childbirth or any other way—all of which were likely risks in this period—the profitability of slave breeding could fall to nil, or actually show a loss. In today's parlance, the risk-reward ratio in slave breeding was not good.

The slave traders themselves recognized this fact, or at least indicated as much in many public statements. In 1842 the Reverend Jesse H. Turner, a slaveholder himself, told a Richmond audience:

> I keep no breeding woman nor brood mare. If I want a negro I buy him already raised to my hand, and if I want a horse or mule I buy him also. . . . I think it cheaper to buy than to raise. At my house, therefore, there are no noisy groups of mischievous young negroes to feed, nor are there any flocks of young horses to maintain.

Others disagreed. Generally speaking, male slaves fetched higher prices than females, except in the case of those females sold to satisfy the sexual urges of the purchasers. A healthy young female slave was considered as a brood mare, at least in the newspaper advertisements of the time. In 1938 the *Charleston Mercury* ran the following advertisement, typical of many of the antebellum period:

> A GIRL about 20 years of age (raised in Virginia) and her two female children, one 4 and the other 2 years old. She is . . . remarkably strong and healthy, never having had a day's sickness, with the exception of the small pox, in her life. The children are fine and healthy. She is very prolific in her generating qualities, and affords a rare opportunity for any person who wishes to raise a family of strong and healthy servants for their own use. Sold for no fault.

A southern farmer told Olmsted in 1856 that in the cotton kingdom "as much attention is paid to the breeding and growth of negroes as that of horses and mules," while Matthew Hammond, writing of the South a half century later, concluded that in Maryland and Virginia slave breeding was common. "Henceforth slaves were seldom kept in these States for the sake of raising crops," wrote Hammond, speaking of the period when the Atlantic states no longer dominated the cotton culture, "but crops were cultivated for the sake of raising slaves." In other words the rationale for slavery had been turned around. Slaves had been introduced into the South because of a shortage of labor to till the fields. Now the old southern states had a surplus of this kind of labor, and used it to raise cotton, much more of which was being produced than might have been the case had slavery not been present in the 1840s. A half century earlier slavery was an auxiliary of tobacco; now, in some states at least, cotton was a by-product of slavery. Or so Hammond believed.

Some slave traders—the better organized and more sophisticated insofar as business was concerned—looked upon breeding as a "by-product" of their trade. One such firm was that of B. M. & W. L. Campbell of Baltimore, the major slaver of that city in the 1850s. Walter L. Campbell, the firm's leader, scoured the countryside seeking slaves for the New Orleans market, as did others in his business. He advertised his willingness to pay the highest prices, and so he did. Despite this, the Campbells showed higher profits than their competitors. Yet their transportation and other costs were as high or higher than others in the field.

The Campbells' success was due to Walter's activity in New Orleans. Most traders would send their slaves there and sell them as soon as possible, hoping for the best prices at the auctions, and needing the money so obtained for additional purchases in the upper South. Campbell took a different view of the business. He would stockpile slaves, and hold them away from the market until prices were at what he considered a good level. Then he would sell until prices fell once again, and repeat the process. Campbell purchased a large farm about eighty miles from New Orleans, upland where disease was relatively rare. Slaves shipped from Virginia and Maryland would go there first, and, when conditions were ripe, would be taken to market.

Generally speaking, slave prices were highest in early spring, when planters bought them in anticipation of harvests. It was then the Campbell slaves were sent to the auction block. In late spring, when purchasers were scarce, slave prices fell, as traders disposed of their remainders at reduced rates. At such time Campbell would keep his slaves on the farm, away from the market. There they would work in the fields, while slave women were encouraged to have children, who would be sold when market conditions were better. Some slave traders operated only in the early spring; Campbell was different. He advertised in the New Orleans newspapers that he had "negroes for sale all the time." When October came around, and interest in slaves stirred, he would have a hundred or so ready for market, in good shape, while his competitors hastened to drive their slaves to market or ship them to New Orleans.

Campbell was able to advertise that his slaves were acclimated to conditions in New Orleans and were healthy. The same could not be said for a slave fresh from Maryland, encountering the New Orleans climate for the first time. As a result, Campbell was able to get higher prices for his wares than his competitors. And slave breeding added still more to his profits.

But such breeding was only a sideline and not the core of his business. In 1855, at a time when the price of slaves was rising rapidly with no end in sight, females brought only three-quarters the price of males of the same age and health on the New Orleans market, while those described as "good breeders" cost little more than females known to be barren. Most slaveholders in that part of the country were interested in labor, not breeding, and did not want females taking time off to have children, even though they could be sold at a profit.

There can be little doubt that slavery was a big business on the eve of the Civil War.* If we place a value of $1,000 per slave on the 1860

*This is not to say that the question is closed. Ulrich Phillips, the great southern historian of the early twentieth century, believed the slave trade was not as important as pre-Civil War Abolitionists contended it to have been. Three years before Phillips' death in 1934, Frederic Bancroft's *Slave-Trading in the Old South* appeared, in which the trade was slave population of four million—a reasonable sum, since it takes into account women and children, who sold below the going price of approximately $1,800 for an able-bodied male, adult field hand—the net worth of American slaves was $4 billion. Using the same method of calculation, the net worth in 1850 was $1.6 billion. Through natural increases in the slave population—but more through a sharp rise in the price of slaves—the southern financial stake in the institution more than doubled in the prewar decade.

Slaveholders would argue that such a great investment had to be protected, at the risk of war and an end to the Union if need be, even though some of them were coming to believe that if every slave on the face of the nation were to vanish, the South's economy would prosper, and indeed be better off in some respects. In effect, southern planters were paying money for chattel who did them as least as much harm as good, and probably more.

At one time it was assumed that since this appeared to be the case, and demonstrations of the truth existed even in the 1840s and 1850s, southern planters were blind, stupid, or ignorant. Most were none of these. A people that produced a Washington, Jefferson, and Madison, and in the next generation a Calhoun, Toombs, and Andrew Jackson, did not suddenly raise a foolish leadership. In 1846 the South was represented in Congress by John Berrien and Alexander Stephens of Georgia, Pierre Soulé and John Slidell of Louisiana, Robert Walker and Jefferson Davis of Mississippi, Willie Mangum and Asa Biggs of North Carolina, and R. Barnwell Rhett of South Carolina, while Calhoun was the South's leader in the Senate and that body's most formidable intellect. Most of these men were still there in the 1850s. They were individuals of keen intelligence, among the best the South would ever send to Washington.

But they were not businessmen in the nineteenth-century sense of

presented as being of major significance in the southern economy and society, and the Bancroft view is generally held today to be true. Now the Bancroft position is being challenged by scholars contending he overstated his figures, especially for the border states. See William Calderhead, "How Extensive Was the Border State Slave Trade? A New Look," *Civil War History*, vol. 17, no. 1 (March 1972), pp. 42–55.

the term. Unlike the merchants and bankers of New York, Boston, and Philadelphia, they did not judge a civilization or a society in terms of profits and assets. At a time when such matters were becoming increasingly important, the South's leaders opted to remain in a semifeudal state of existence. Isaac Franklin, who made a fortune in the slave trade, wanted nothing more than to be a plantation owner, although there were few profits to be made in such a business or endeavor. Former President James K. Polk, on leaving the White House in 1849, moved his residence—and slaves—from Tennessee to Mississippi, where he, too, became the owner of a plantation. At a time when the nation was becoming increasingly more commercial and industrial, such men rejected these values, while at the same time attempting to prove they were good businessmen on their estates. Their forays into economic proofs of the value of slavery were disasters.

There were, to be sure, some businessmen in the South who profited from the cotton culture by servicing the plantations. The factors in the coastal cities were among this group, as were the representatives of northern business interests. The most vivid example of this genre was the slave trader. He provided goods and services for which there were great demands. A semifeudal society rewarded its retainers, and while recognizing the need for such services, frowned upon those who provided them. When the Civil War began, slave trading declined, so that after a year of fighting all the companies engaged in the traffic were out of business. The plantation South would bemoan the loss of its civilization after Appomattox, but not the institution of slave trading. This it always considered a necessary evil. But many decades would pass before enlightened white southerners would concede that the evil was not in slave trading and the profits from human flesh, but the system that made such men and profits possible.

CHAPTER 4

The Comstock Lode

From time to time there comes a year when several significant movements or events culminate or begin, take place or fail to develop as expected. Often these are described as "pivotal years," in the sense that they provide a point at which the tendencies of the past are diverted into new paths.

One such year was 1848. The Mexican War ended then, opening new territories to the United States and a new chapter in the slavery debate. The Abolitionists turned to increased political activity in the Presidential election of that year, and although the Free Soil Party candidate, Martin Van Buren, ran a poor third, the political structure of the Jacksonian era clearly was eroding. In a sense, 1848 was the last year of the Age of Jackson and the first of the Age of Lincoln.

The most spectacular news of 1848 was that of the discovery of gold at Sutter's Mill in California. Word of the find spread quickly, firing the imagination as it went. Thousands flocked to California seeking wealth in its streams. They came in ships around the Cape of Good Hope, across the dangerous Isthmus of Panama, or by foot and wagon through the Great Plains and across the Rockies and Sierra Nevada. Among them were many young, ambitious men in their twenties and thirties. Most died poor. Few became wealthy in the goldfields. More found their fortunes in supportive enterprises, such as banking, supplies, and construction. Finally, while a handful made a great deal of money in California, more did so elsewhere in the West. For the next half century the young miners of '48 and '49 would roam the mountain and prairie states, seeking "one last stake" before calling it quits.

These men did come for gold, however, and they would seek the metal as the nation became more deeply involved in the tragic questions revolving around slavery. Mineral wealth and slavery would provide the leitmotivs for that generation of Americans. Children who were told of the gold discoveries and the issues of the 1848 election would grow up to fight in the Civil War or go west to seek fortunes. As one writer put it, the streams of the East ran red with blood, while those of the West ran yellow with gold.

He might have added that the western streams also ran white with silver—or, more accurately, bluish-black with argentite and other silver ores. The California gold rush was spectacular and of major importance to the nation and the world, and for these reasons tended to overshadow the silver finds of a decade later. The latter were also of great significance. Almost a half billion dollars in silver would be taken from the Washoe district of Nevada in twenty years, in what was the greatest silver find in history. Like the gold rush that preceded it, the silver bonanza created fortunes and had a major impact on the nation's development. It provided the background for political debates that lasted through the rest of the century, and became a symbol for a reform movement as striking as abolitionism. Even more than gold, silver would make San Francisco the Queen City of the Pacific. The men who came out of the silver rush would dominate Nevada politics well into the twentieth century, and their impact is still being felt today.

The Indians knew of the silver at least a century before the first whites crossed the Rockies. The Mormons also learned of it, soon after settling around the Great Salt Lake in present-day Utah. They were warned away from mining, however, as the elders of the Church of Jesus Christ of Latter Day Saints admonished them to remain tied to the soil as farmers and husbandmen. "The true use of gold is for paving streets," they said. "When the Saints shall have preached the gospel . . . and built up cities enough, the Lord will open up the way for a supply of gold to the perfect satisfaction of his children. . . . Let them not be over-anxious, for the treasures of the earth are in the Lord's storehouse."

Yet the Mormons were affected by the gold rush, since their community stood in the way of those miners headed west to California. Many of them paused to rest in the Carson Valley, south of Lake Tahoe, before crossing the Sierra Nevada into California. They would purchase provisions from Mormons, and speak with them of their California dreams. Some Mormons left their homes to join in the rush, and a party of them was in the Carson Valley in the spring of 1849. While there they made a halfhearted search for gold, more in preparation for work in California than in hope of discovery. One of their number, John Orr, found a nugget under a slab of rock. Another, William Prouse, panned for gold in the Carson River, and extracted a few specks from the wash. The group did not tarry in the Carson Valley, however, but moved on to Sacramento and the richer finds there.

But news of their discoveries spread, so that a year later others came to the Carson Valley, which by then was known as Gold Canyon. Some panned for gold, and although more was found, the miners rarely stayed, and headed instead for California. Others remained and farmed the land, making a good living from selling fresh produce to westward-bound miners who rested and provisioned at Gold Canyon. Some Mexicans arrived in 1850 and panned older streams; they scraped out a living, but little else. Some of the Mexicans had been silver miners, and they recognized the silver ores in the streams. A few of them tried to tell the Americans of their find, but the Americans didn't understand Spanish, and the conversation was limited to gestures, smiles, and nods. So the silver ores were ignored, and the low-grade gold retained.

In 1853 two Pennsylvania-born brothers, Allen and Hosea Grosch, arrived at Gold Canyon, after four years of wandering through Mexico and California searching for a "find." The Grosches knew something of mining, not only through experience, but by reading geology texts. Like the others, they encountered the bluish-black mud in the streams, which they referred to in their journal as "black rock" and "blue stuff." But unlike their fellow miners, they recognized the mud as silver compounds. In 1856 they discovered "two veins of silver at the forks of Gold canyon," and noted that "one of these veins is a perfect monster." The following year Allen Grosch wrote his father that "Our first assay was one-half ounce of rock; the result was $3,500 of silver to the ton. . . . We assayed a small quantity of rock by cuppelation from other vein. The result was $200 a ton. . . . We are very sanguine of ultimate success."

The brothers did not live to enjoy the results of their find. Hosea died of infection from a foot injury, while Allen perished in a storm in the Sierra Nevada late in 1857. The Grosches knew they had found a major outcropping of silver ore, but they couldn't recognize the actual extent of their find.

Henry T. P. Comstock came into possession of the Grosch cabin in 1858, and with it their papers and several boxes filled with the blue stuff. Later on he would claim to have known the silver was there all the time, but Comstock did not seek it. Instead, he panned and dug for gold, as did the other miners in the area. Other miners worked the Grosch claim in Gold Canyon. James Fennimore, a grizzled miner who had come to Nevada after knifing a man in California, was one of them. "Finney," or "Old Virginny," as he was often called, found an outcropping of yellowish quartz along the hillside, and thinking it promising, wrote a location notice on a slip of paper and placed it under a nearby rock—this being the method of posting claims in those days and that place. Finney did no more at the site, and instead moved on.

The following winter, Finney returned, along with several other miners. One of them, John Bishop, washed some gold specks from an outcropping at the northern end of Gold Canyon. Finney and two other prospectors followed, this time posting proper notices. They named the area Gold Hill, and began working their claims in earnest.

The discovery proved minor, but in those days news traveled fast and picked up exaggerations as it went. Now hundreds of miners rushed to Gold Hill, congregating to share rumors in the small town of Johntown, and then traveling to the hill to begin digging.

Some went to the northeast of Gold Hill, to the end of Six Mile Canyon, an area once owned by the Grosches, in the belief the vein might extend that far. Two prospectors, Patrick McLaughlin and Peter O'Riley, dug there for a while with little success. Then they deepened a small spring, hoping to obtain additional water for their washings. By chance they threw some of the mud from the stream's bottom into their rocker, and when the light dirt washed away, they found a few specks of gold.

Certain they had struck a major lode, the two men panned furiously. By the end of the day they had accumulated some $20 worth of specks. It was not a bonanza, but well worth continuing.

Apparently Comstock learned of their find, and he hastened to investigate. Once he realized that gold had indeed been located, he told the prospectors they were on his land, claiming that he, Finney, and another miner, Emmanuel Penrod, owned the spring. McLaughlin and O'Riley protested, but Comstock outshouted, bullied, and threatened them. In the end they accepted his claim and agreed to share the find with Comstock and his two associates.

Comstock bought out Finney's claim for $40 and then he and Penrod went to the camp to help in the panning. Within days it appeared the washings were more valuable than they had first thought. Each day the four washed several hundreds of dollars worth of gold. But the going was rough. The blue stuff, that was first noticed by the Mexicans and later recognized by the Grosches, masked the gold, hindered the operations, and made gold recovery all the more difficult. For more than two months they worked the stream, finding more gold and creating a mound of bluish-black mud. The Ophir, as McLaughlin and O'Riley dubbed the site, would not be abandoned, but unless some way could be found to bypass the blue stuff, its riches would hardly pay for work involved in extracting them.

Rancher B. A. Harrison was also interested in the Ophir. He knew of the Grosches and recognized the mud as the same the brothers had found nearby. Harrison may also have spoken to the brothers, who could have disclosed the fact that silver ores in great abundance were in the area. In any case, Harrison convinced the prospectors it would be worth their while to have an assay done on the mud. By then the four partners were digging into the side of the hill, a costly operation, and would try anything reasonable. The assay was conducted, and the results made known in late June 1859. The blue stuff contained $876 worth of gold—and more than $3,000 in silver. The first stage of the silver rush had begun.

The 1859 rush to the Washoe region of Nevada where the silver had been found attracted thousands of miners from California, British Columbia, and the Missouri frontier, all of whom hoped to find another Sutter's Mill at Six Mile Canyon. Comstock, a natural promoter, created new rumors each day, whipping the rush into a frenzy. He appeared certain the Ophir contained more gold and silver than all of Sacramento, and didn't mind who knew about it. In reality, he was trying to raise the price of his properties so as to make a fortune from their sale. The West was becoming famous for mines that petered out quickly, false gold rushes, and fortunes in mines that dissolved once the veins ran out or the streams failed to yield gold dust. He and his colleagues would get out while the getting was good—at the height of the market.

Comstock promptly dubbed his holding "The Comstock Lode," and hoped the collection of huts that sprang up nearby would also be named after him. Finney beat him to the naming in this case; "Old Virginny" poured some liquor on the ground and shouted for all to hear, "I baptize this spot Virginia Town." At least, this is the legend. Whatever the origins of the name, Virginia City became the hub of the Comstock region of Washoe.

The first owners of the Ophir sold their holdings early in the game, and at the time thought they had bilked the buyers. Penrod received $3,000 for his shares. He took the money and left Washoe for richer diggings, which he never found. Comstock sold out for $11,000, and with the money opened a supply store in nearby Carson City. The store failed, and Comstock returned to mining. Never again would he find a bonanza. Instead, he wandered from camp to camp, all the time speaking of the lost mine in Washoe. In 1870 he blew out his brains with a revolver and was buried in an unmarked grave in Bozeman, Montana. McLaughlin, who sold his share for $3,500, spent his money seeking a new mine and failed in the effort. Then he found employment as a cook, receiving $40 a month for his work. McLaughlin died a pauper in 1879.

O'Riley held his shares longer than the rest, finally selling for $45,000. Like the others, he continued in mining and failed. He wandered to Montana and then returned to Washoe in 1867, with tales of a new mine near the Comstock Lode. There he worked by himself for three years, finding nothing but dirt and rock. O'Riley was trapped in a cave-in and taken to a hospital. He recovered his physical health, but went mad in the process. Like McLaughlin, he died in poverty.

All lived long enough to realize their mistake in selling when they did. Comstock and his partners had believed the Ophir a minor outcropping, several veins that would dwindle to nothing after a hundred feet or so of digging. Actually, the lode was traceable for more than two and a half miles. The silver ores were not distributed evenly throughout the length, however, but were isolated in pockets and branches. Many times a Comstock Mine would close, when only a few more feet of digging would have revealed a new vein or a continuation of the old. This was most unusual in silver mines, as was the nature of the ores, which contained little copper or lead compounds so often found in conjunction with silver.

The true nature of the wealth of the Comstock Lode unfolded gradually, as mine after mine was sunk into the hills around Six Mile and Gold canyons, especially into the face of Mount Davidson, not far from present-day Reno. The final chapter would not be written for a generation, by which time Comstock and his partners had become the subjects of many "might-have-been stories" and all were dead in paupers' or unmarked graves.

By the fall of 1859 Virginia City had been filled with prospectors, who, after hastily setting up tents, rushed to the canyons to stake claims and start panning or digging. Winter came early that year, closing the Sierra passes, while thousands of miners waited on the California side for spring. The passes opened in March 1860, signaling the beginning of the greatest mining boom since the California Gold Rush. More prospectors came, along with others to be found in any mineral rush. There were the more cautious miners with a grubstake, willing to purchase an interest in a going mine and forgo the chance to strike it rich on their own. George Hearst was one of these; he parlayed a $450 investment in the Gould & Curry Mine into more than a million.* Melville Atwood was another investor, and A. E. Head a third. The three went to Washoe from Nevada City on a hunch, as did hundreds more.

Then there were those who hoped to make fortunes servicing the miners. Carpenters and masons charged exorbitant rates for their work, often doing better at it than the men who hired them. Before winter of 1860 there were more than a hundred wooden buildings in Virginia City, most erected by newcomers.† These were occupied by tradesmen and others. The International Hotel was the center of the town's social life, but Berry's Tavern, Nick's Tavern, and other

*George Hearst was the father of William Randolph Hearst, the famous publisher, and the source of the son's fortunes was at Washoe.

†The buildings included: "38 stores, general merchandise, 4 cigar and tobacco stores, 3 druggists' stores, 2 stationers' stores, 2 fruit stores, 25 saloons, 9 restaurants, 7 boarding houses, 1 hotel, 4 butchers' shops, 9 bakers' shops, 7 blacksmiths' shops, 3 tinsmiths' shops, 1 gunsmith's shop, 7 shoemakers' and cobblers' shops, 1 saddler's shop, 2 carpenter shops, 1 paint shop, 1 tailor, 3 watchmakers, 2 barbers, 6 physicians' offices, 1 surveyer's office, 5 brokers' offices, 1 auction and commission house, 1 dressmaker's shop, 4 machine-sewers' rooms, 10 livery stables, 10 laundries, 1 bath-house, 1 theatre, 1 music hall, 1 school-house, 1 post office, 9 quartz mills, 5 lumber yards." Eliot Lord, *Comstock Mining and Miners* (U.S. Geological Survey, "Monographs," IV, Washington, 1883), p. 94.

saloons did good business. The cost of living was high, as was always the case in such places. A bunk for the night was a dollar, or $4.50 a week. One lodging house, the Astor, placed eighteen cots in one room 20 feet by 12 feet, and had no trouble finding occupants. Carpenters making $6 a day didn't mind such charges. Miners, who received from $4 to $6 a day at the Ophir and Gould & Curry, had quarters provided for them at lower rates, while the cooks ($50-$100 a month) often slept in the kitchens.

In November 1860, Virginia City had a population of some 2,200, while nearby towns had 1,200 more. Nevada was not yet a state so no one voted, but in any case there was little interest in politics in that crucial political year. The Civil War would begin and end with surprisingly little disruption of daily life in the mines. Silver, not slavery, was the issue at Washoe, and would remain so for a generation.

The land itself seemed quite desolate. One miner, Almarin Paul, called it "the fag-end of creation." "The Almighty had some great idea when He planned Washoe, but half-way through He forgot. It was never finished. His creative power was exhausted. All that He had left was mineral. Regarding it of the least benefit to mankind He held onto it until He reached Washoe, then He emptied his lap."

Paul was one of the few educated men in Virginia City, one knowledgeable in geology. He saw the Californians try to pan for silver as they would for gold, and knew they would find little that way. Nor could the outcroppings offer much in the way of bonanzas. The Californians would soon learn the need for digging deep into the mountains, taking out carloads of ore, crushing and washing it, and then reducing what remained to silver. So instead of digging, Paul erected a large mill at Gold Canyon, bringing in machinery from San Francisco at $400 a ton and lumber at $300 per thousand feet. In 1861 he erected a second mill, this one at Gold Hill. Both received a good deal of the business of the area, even though Paul had competition. Such men were the first to make fortunes at Comstock, taking the grubstakes of the Californians, most of whom failed to find silver and soon left.* Millowners, tavern keepers, prostitutes, carpenters, and other service personnel considered Virginia City a funnel through which silver earnings would pour into their pockets. And even without such earnings, they would do well so long as the exodus across the Sierras continued.

Others also benefited from the demands of the mineowners. As the managers learned more of the extensive nature of the lode, they dug deeper, following the veins until they ran out, and then going beyond to another one. The Ophir, now owned in part by Hearst, struck an extraordinarily wide vein—at 175 feet it was 45 to 65 feet wide. But the timberings would not hold, and cave-ins plagued the operators and took lives, until few were willing to venture that deep, even when offered bonuses. The owners would not even consider abandoning the lode, and so they sought new solutions. One of them consulted a German engineer, Philip Deidesheimer, who had previously worked in the California goldfields. Deidesheimer devised a new method of timbering for the shafts—square sets—constructed in such a way as to enable the miners to work within wooden boxes, which were added to as the mine went deeper into the ground. The square sets worked, and later were found in most Comstock mines, after which they spread throughout the West, and are still being used today.

Heat presented a second problem. The Comstock mines soon were among the deepest in the nation, and the hottest. The temperature of the air increased around three degrees for each hundred feet, and miners found themselves working in hundred-degree temperature after a while. Ice and snow were brought down from the mountains and sent into the shafts to cool the workers. Few could remain in the mines for more than fifteen minutes at a time, and conditions got worse as the diggings continued. In 1877 the Consolidated Virginia alone purchased 3,439,980 pounds of ice, setting up "ice rooms" below the surface where miners rested between fifteen-minute shifts.

*Mills at the Ophir and nearby mines cost the operators in excess of $10 million by 1870. Supply and manufacturing firms throughout the country benefited from the operations, and during the Civil War pumps needed by the Union armies were diverted to Nevada as a result of higher profits to be made there.

That year some of the operators banded together to build a twenty-five-mile pipeline from the Sierra to the mines, to bring ice water to the miners. The cost was in excess of $2.2 million.

Even this did not alleviate the situation enough to permit continuous digging. By late 1878 some mines were more than 3,000 feet deep, and miners found water at 180 degrees. Several struck the side of an underground spring of superheated water and were scalded to death before they could be dragged away. Soon after, former President U. S. Grant visited the mines and went down one of the shafts. He emerged to say, "That's as close to hell as I ever want to get."

Getting the water out of the mines was even more troublesome than getting ice into them. The problem of flooding was constant. At one point the rich Ophir was closed down for two years before the waters could be removed. Huge Hale & Norcross and Savage pumps, some capable of removing 640 gallons a minute, were brought to Comstock at great expense. These were among the largest of their kind in the world, and yet they could not best the rushing underground springs.

Nor could huge fans and air pumps get sufficient fresh air to the miners. The mules—called Washoe canaries—balked at going underground, and some had to be killed in order to prevent miniature stampedes 2,000 feet below the surface.

One man, Adolph Sutro, thought he had the answer to all these problems. Sutro would construct a four-mile-long tunnel through Mount Davidson, which would drain off millions of gallons of water, ventilate the mines, and in the process uncover new veins. It seemed so simple and intelligent, even though Sutro was proposing one of the greatest engineering feats up to that time. The Nevada legislature gave its approval in 1865, and the Sutro Tunnel Company was formed soon after. According to its terms, each mine would pay $2 per ton for all ore brought from the ground as payment for ventilation and drainage, and an additional 25 cents per ton for ore taken through the tunnel.

But the act was declared invalid, and Sutro had to go to Washington to seek aid. With the help of San Francisco bankers, especially William Chapman Ralston, Sutro lobbied his bill through Congress, and it was signed into law by President Andrew Johnson in 1866. Next Sutro began his attempt to raise $3 to $4 million needed for the construction.

At this point Sutro's San Francisco allies and some of the more powerful mineowners turned against him. Figuring he meant to take control of the Comstock mines, and after calculating his returns on investment, they decided to forgo the tunnel. Also, the waters fell temporarily, and the owners hoped it meant this trouble was ending. Finally, Sutro had expressed the belief the miners were underpaid for their work, and showed sympathy for them during one of their strikes.

Sutro was able to raise $600,000 in subscriptions in Europe, and Eastern businessmen, including August Belmont and Peter Cooper, assured him they could get the rest. Now the Ralston group turned its full attention to the scheme, and informed Sutro they would not pay the assessments as formerly agreed. Angered, Sutro returned to Europe seeking additional funds. This time he failed. Mark Twain, then a western newspaperman who lived in Virginia City and wrote from there during its boom period, reported in the *Alta Californian* that "Mr. A. Sutro of the great Sutro Tunnel scheme arrived yesterday from Europe on the *Russia.* He brought his tunnel back with him. He failed to sell it to the Europeans. They said it was a good tunnel, but they would look around a little before purchasing; if they could not find a tunnel to suit them nearer at home they would call again."

Sutro continued his fight in Washington, San Francisco, and Virginia City. He was able to begin construction in 1869, and continued the work for ten years, with many interruptions. Finally, in 1879, it was completed, and hailed as one of the great engineering feats of all time. Investors in New York and London were excited, and expected profits to flow and the stock's quotation to rise. But Sutro and others on the scene knew the great bonanza days were over at Comstock, and the tunnel could never be expected to show a profit. Armed with this knowledge, Sutro rushed to New York and sold his shares, manipulating the market in them like a master. When he began selling, the price was $6.60; by the time he was finished, it was six cents. Sutro did manage to show a profit of $900,000 on his small investment, but the other tunnel backers were wiped out. One English banking house, McCalmont & Bros., closed its books on the transaction with a loss of $755,000. Later on an American, once a close friend of the promoter, wrote: "Mr. Sutro has accumulated a large fortune, a very large portion of which came out of me. . . ."*

Sutro and others who attempted to provide the Comstock mines with needed services made fortunes from the silver strike. For a while in the 1860s and 1870s such business helped make San Francisco a thriving city, whose leaders owned mines in Washoe, lent money to operators in the area, sold lumber, foodstuffs, mine equipment, and other provisions to the miners, all of which returned good profits. Still larger profits and earnings were made by those who left San Francisco and other parts of California and litigated the claims of rival bands of miners in the 1860s. As one miner put it, "I made a small fortune with pick and shovel. My damn San Francisco lawyer made a bigger one with his quill and ledger."

Whenever a major strike was made in the West, miners would rush to the scene to stake claims. Most claims were filed improperly, and duplicate and triplicate claims were the rule when the lode was rich. In addition, the claims laws varied from place to place and judge to judge. For example, many Comstock miners held to the "one-ledge theory." If a lode had one large vein, they claimed, smaller veins on the same property belonged to the original owner and filer. Other miners held to the "many-ledge theory," which stated that claims could only be honored for veins, and that other veins found on the claimed land were fair game for any who came along and filed for them. Then there was Spanish law, which held that the owner of land had rights to all mineral wealth found below the surface, so that a

*Sutro settled in San Francisco and became a successful real-estate dealer there, but remained interested in Nevada. He ran for the Senate from that state in 1872, 1876, and 1880, without winning. Then in 1881 he moved to Carson City and spent $250,000 to win votes for the post, again failing. Still, Sutro sought elective office. In 1894 he won the mayoralty of San Francisco on the Populist ticket.

single vein might be worked by several different individuals or companies, each with a land claim.

The miners who came in the rush of '59 were accompanied by lawyers prepared to litigate. In 1860 there were more than 50 lawyers in Virginia City; by 1863 the city had a population of less than 10,000, and 215 were lawyers.

No sooner would a miner find a rich lode and stake a claim than others would appear on the scene with their claims. One favorite device was the presentation of an ancient claim, filed by a pre-Mexican War prospector, purchased by another, and dramatically "produced" after the rich vein was made known. There were clashes between the one-ledge and many-ledges theorists that resulted in gunfire and death, but more often than not, disputes were settled in courts.

This presented a problem. In 1859 Washoe was part of Utah Territory, under the control of the Mormons at Salt Lake City. The Mormons sent their judges to Virginia City, and few of them were liked by the miners, mostly because they couldn't easily be bribed. Then President Buchanan sent out a federal judge, who disliked all miners and refused to hold court. Finally, Congress established the Nevada Territory, and Lincoln appointed three territorial judges, who arrived in Washoe in 1861.

Now a large backlog of cases appeared before the judges, who were not above taking bribes. In those days, in the western mining towns, accepting bribes from a lawyer in a case was not considered unethical—failure to deliver or taking bribes from *both* sides were frowned upon, however. Those lawyers who knew how to "handle" judges were prized, while others, who specialized in buying juries, were eagerly sought after. Lawyers had to be adept at bribing clerks to alter records, drilling friendly witnesses and spiriting unfriendly ones from town, and other tactics such as those not usually found in canons of justice. As one Washoe resident put it, "The only sin here is cheating at cards." A California visitor to Virginia City in 1863 wrote that "corruption is at a premium and men's virtue is to be estimated in an inverse proportion to their professions," and the worst was that of attorney.* Charles de Long, a California lawyer who arrived in Virginia City in 1863, wrote to his brother, "I think I have a certain fortune ahead of me in this country. . . . It is the wildest one for law you ever heard of, indeed it is a lawyer's paradise. . . ."

Several lawyers quickly rose to the top in the legal jungles of Virginia City, among them J. H. Hardy, Thomas B. Reardon, Charles H. S. Williams, and D. W. Perley. But the leader of them all—the man who took the most from law and politics—was William M. Stewart.

Stewart was only thirty-three years old when he arrived in Virginia City in 1860, but already was a famous figure in the West. He was a native New Yorker, raised in Ohio, educated at Yale, and intrigued by the possibilities of California. Stewart went to the goldfields soon after learning of the finds at Sutter's Mill, and quickly decided more could be made from law than digging. So he studied law and was admitted to the bar in 1852. That same year, at the age of twenty-five, he was elected district attorney of Nevada City, and two years later, attorney general of California.

Stewart was a tall, rugged-looking individual, smart enough to realize fortunes could be had through litigation and tough enough to stand the gaff of frontier law. Soon he was bribing judges with the best of them. And when a justice wouldn't accept a bribe, he would be destroyed.

In 1864 Stewart represented the Chollar Company in its suit against the Potosi Company, alleging the latter had violated several Chollar claims. It was the usual trumped-up charge, and Stewart might have won were it not for the fact that the case was heard before Judge James A. North, one of the few jurists who couldn't be bought.

*The newspaperman continued: "California in '49 was a kind of vestibule of hell, but Nevada may be considered the very throne-room of Pluto himself. I have seen more rascality, small and great, in my brief forty days sojourn in this wilderness of sage brush, sharpers, and prostitutes, than in a thirteen years experience of our squeamishly moral State of California. . . . The principal occupation of the denizens of this God forsaken angle of creation appears to be the administering to one another of allopathic doses of humbug, which are received with an air of gravity and relish which betokens an abiding and universal faith in their virtue. . . . Mammon is the god of their idolatry, and slavishly submissive to the behests of their demon-lord are all his wretched worshippers."

North found for Potosi, after which Stewart promptly appealed the case to the three-judge supreme court, which consisted of North, Judge George Turner, and Judge P. B. Locke. North's views were already known, while Turner was considered in the hands of the Chollar forces. So the key man was Locke, whom Stewart later characterized as "probably the most ignorant man who ever acted in any judicial capacity in any part of the world."

Stewart and the Potosi lawyers vied for control of Locke. When Stewart learned the judge had arrangements to meet with Potosi leaders at Lake Tahoe, he kidnapped him, entertained Locke at a midnight supper, and would not let him leave until he agreed to vote for the Chollar interests. Soon after, however, the Potosi people threw a party of their own, which changed Locke's mind. Neither side knew how he would vote when the judges withdrew to consider their verdict.

In the end, Locke voted with North to uphold Potosi, but then, after seeing Stewart, he filed an addendum which had the effect of reopening the case. Then the Potosi people got to him again, and Locke revoked the addendum.

Disgusted with a judge who wouldn't stay bought, Stewart retaliated by attacking North. He denounced the judge in several newspapers he owned, and demanded the resignation not only of him, but of all judges in the state. All complied, after Stewart brought sufficient pressure to bear. Then Stewart defeated an attempt to fill the vacancies with people he wasn't sure of. Not until he could name his own men to the bench would he allow the judicial machinery of Nevada to run again.

While engaging in these activities, Stewart found time to participate in the state's constitutional convention, and run for election to the Senate soon after. He won easily in 1864, and was reelected in 1869. Then, in 1875, he stepped down to replenish his fortunes as a railroad lawyer. For the next eleven years he was the Central Pacific and Southern Pacific representative in the Far West. In 1886, when the railroads decided he could serve them better in Washington, he once again stood for the Senate, winning easily. Stewart remained in the Senate until 1905, and he died four years later.

The origins of the Stewart fortune were at Washoe, but he made still more money during his mine-camp days in San Francisco, at the stock markets of that city. Charles de Long made note of the method Stewart and his kind used in speculating at the exchanges. A new ledge would be found, he wrote.

> Then comes some old trumped up title to this newly discovered mine and into the law the whole thing plunges and lawyers are busy hunting up witnesses and this is invariably the case for if there is no outstanding title one will be trumped up and a suit commenced in order to depreciate the value of the claim, and then speculators buy in while it is low, perhaps the very men who started the suit through their agents. . . .

This kind of manipulation was not new, and much of it was done with the full knowledge of all concerned. One went to Virginia City to discover the wealth of silver in America, but if quick profits were desired, the place to be was San Francisco, where the Washoe silver was turned into golden profits. Mark Twain, who for a while worked with Stewart, wrote a "Stock Broker's Prayer," lampooning the situation:

> Our father Mammon who art in the Comstock, bully is thy name; let thy dividends come, and stocks go up, in California as in Washoe. Give us this day our daily commissions; forgive us our swindles as we hope to get even on those who have swindled us. "Lead" us not into temptation of promising wild cat; deliver us from lawsuits; for thine is the main Comstock, the black sulphurets and the wire silver, from wall-rock to wall-rock, you bet!

It was inevitable that San Francisco would become the financial center for the Comstock. The city had grown wealthy during the Gold Rush, and now that the goldfields were ravaged, San Francisco's financial aristocrats sought new areas for investment, especially in minerals, which they knew better than anything else. San Francisco was close to the Comstock, and news from the mines could be sent there far faster than to New York, Boston, or Philadelphia. Many San Francisco bankers and brokers had close ties to eastern investors, and could serve as their representatives when shares in silver mines were required. Finally, San Francisco merchants were among the few in the West able to provision the miners. The city received some competition from Salt Lake, but the miners disliked the Mormons, and preferred dealings with the California commission houses.

There was a small brokerage community in San Francisco in the mid-1850s. Like its counterpart in New York in the 1790s, however, its brokers dealt in municipal bonds, insurance, wharf receipts, grain, and other negotiable securities and commodities as well as stocks. Several New York stockbrokers, among them former members of the New York Stock and Exchange Board, had been drawn to the city during the Gold Rush, and remained to go into brokerage. These men provided the expertise needed in such businesses, and some rose high in the city's aristocracy. One of them, Franklin Lawton, dealt heavily in Washoe shares from the first. Together with another former New York stockbroker, Elisha W. Teacle, he planned to open a securities exchange in San Francisco to deal in mining shares. At first, however, they were stymied, not so much for economic and financial reasons as for those of class prejudice. The San Francisco aristocrats considered brokerage and speculation in shares somehow disreputable. They were willing to accept former miners who had struck it rich, lawyers who represented them, and even mineowners, but frowned on men whose fortunes had been based on buying and selling mining shares.

As the Comstock's riches became better known and more companies were formed, some of the aristocrats began dealing in shares, or "feet."* More joined each week, until by mid-1862 most were

*The reference to "feet" as well as shares requires explanation. At first the mining companies capitalized themselves in terms of the number of feet of frontage at the surface of the claim. Thus, a mine with a thousand feet of frontage would be capitalized at a thousand feet. The owner of ten feet would be entitled to 1 percent of the dividends and votes at the

deep in speculation. *The San Francisco Mining and Scientific Press* noted the phenomenon:

> A few years ago scarcely a merchant in San Francisco could be induced to invest a dollar in any mining enterprise. To do so was to lose *"caste,"* and endanger one's credit "on change." Even our foundrymen could not be induced to invest a dollar in a business to which they were, as now, indebted for almost their entire business. Now things are entirelly changed, and one can scarcely find a man in San Francisco who does not own "feet" in some mining claim.

Shares were traded in the streets, in stores and offices, wherever men could congregate. Again, it resembled New York in the 1790s, when brokers met along Wall Street to pass the time of day and buy and sell securities. But the San Francisco mania was far more intense than that of New York three-quarters of a century earlier. The *Alta Californian*, commenting on this activity, exaggerated its scope, but not by much:

> So far as direct ownership and investment go, San Francisco is interested far more in the silver mines of Washoe than in the gold mines of California. The people of this city own ten times more stock in silver mines than in gold mines. . . . It is a rare thing to meet a man who has not a certificate of stock in his pocket.
>
> Two thousand mining companies have been incorporated in this city within three years—one company for every ten men. Wherever ten men are collected together in San Francisco, there is an incorporated mining company amongst them, on the average with stock to the nominal value of $20,000. Wittington

meetings. If the mine expanded, additional shares would be issued to cover the additional feet of frontage. Later on, stock was issued in terms of shares, but the old terminology remained, and the words came to be interchangeable.

went to London with the expectation of seeing streets paved with gold; if he had lived in California, he might have come to our metropolis expecting to see streets paved with mining certificates.

In the late summer of 1862 Lawton and Teacle convinced forty major San Francisco brokers of the need for a securities market. They joined forces to organize the San Francisco Stock and Exchange Board, which opened soon after. J. B. E. Cavallier was its first president, with Teacle as vice-president and Lawton as secretary.

The market was patterned closely after the New York Stock and Exchange Board. Like the older exchange, it had two auctions a day, with brokers trading on their own in between calls. This was a wild period for securities exchanges. The Civil War was on, and the New York organization was going full blast. Not only that, some twenty new exchanges opened in New York and other eastern cities in this period, including the powerful Gold Room, where the metal was bought and sold on news of Union victories or defeats. One New York market operated around the clock, to overfilled rooms. Yet Howard Cobb, of the San Francisco Stock and Exchange Board and a leading auctioneer of the city, auctioned off more shares in terms of dollar value than any of his East Coast counterparts. During the next ten years there were many days in which volume at the San Francisco market exceeded that at the New York Stock and Exchange Board.* It was a time when New York was in the midst of a gold mania, which would culminate in the Gold Ring of 1869. During the same period, San Francisco was the silver capital of America.

The San Francisco Stock and Exchange Board opened with a fanfare and high trading volume. In October, a Virginia City news-

*Other exchanges were organized in San Francisco after the success of the Stock and Exchange Board. The San Francisco Stock Exchange made its debut in March 1863, and the Pacific Stock Exchange in April 1875. There were at least two stock exchanges in Virginia City, but they did little business, and not much is known of them.

paper correspondent visited the exchange, and reported on his findings:

> Are all the folks on the Bay stock mad? Are you all so rich that you can recklessly create a mania for Washoe stocks? Go it blind, or what is worse, be blindly led into speculation, which will end in ruin, by clever chaps who know a "hawk from a handsaw." . . . But I see you have a board of brokers too. Maybe that accounts for the milk in the cocoanut. . . . Barnum was right. . . . Have the people been insane that they should unreflectingly rush into a financial abyss?

Rush they did, and the miners and lawyers of Washoe were there to capitalize on the situation.

The San Francisco boards were speculative jungles. Wilder and more dramatic rumors were floated there than in New York, this being the nature of mining operations, the people involved, and the West of that day. Talk of a new vein could send several stocks upward in sudden spurts, since a rich find could mean tens of millions of dollars in added value. The mining firms were in the practice of paying out their total surpluses in the form of dividends, so that a rise of fifty points in a stock could be matched by the next dividend. Should a rumor prove false, the stocks would fall to below the original price even more rapidly.

Speculators knew this, and employed a variety of techniques to move stocks one way or another.* The ancient method of salting mines with nuggets was used, as well as false rumors and tales of old Indians who "finally revealed their secret lodes." Speculators sent agents to Washoe to find inside information, which would be relayed

*Contrary to the practice in New York, the San Francisco speculators rarely tried to corner a stock. Most lacked the capital to do so, and in any case, the use of rumors was far more effective at that kind of an exchange. As a result, few "kings of the exchange" or "young Napoleons of finance" came out of San Francisco. Only one, James Keene, made it big in New York after making a fortune in San Francisco. Then Keene lost all, and finished his life manipulating stocks for others.

to San Francisco and translated into buys and sells. The story was told of one agent who, after failing to pry information from a mine superintendent, scraped some mud from his discarded boots and had it analyzed. It proved rich in silver ore, and the information was relayed to San Francisco. By the time news of the discovery reached the city, the speculator had accumulated a position in the stock at a low price. Another story involved a motherly looking woman who had purchased Consolidated Virginia at $600. She visited the mine with her son, looked around, and asked a few simple questions. Satisfied, she turned to the son and said, "George, give me your arm. Let us go home—it will go to $1,000." So it did.

The success or failure of a stock often depended upon the results of a lawsuit. Virginia City lawyers and judges knew this, and speculated at the San Francisco boards armed with inside information.

This was the situation in the famous Ophir-Burning Moscow case. According to the one-ledge theory, the Ophir should have owned much of Mount Davidson, and on this basis brought suit against others working the claim. A group of miners fought Ophir, organized the Burning Moscow Company in 1862, issued 4,800 shares of stock at $100 apiece, hired a lawyer, and contested the claim.

The price of Burning Moscow fluctuated with the progress of the case. The first 140 shares were sold at $50 on August 26. Then, as news out of Virginia City seemed to favor Burning Moscow, the price rose to $75, and then $100. This activity and rise attracted others, so that within days the price was $275.

Then pro-Ophir rumors were circulated. Burning Moscow fell rapidly, hitting $40 in less than a week. At this point another group of speculators moved in and began accumulating the issue. New rumors were floated in mid-September, sending Burning Moscow to $100 once more, which was followed by another slump. This was succeeded by a third rise, to $155. When, on May 14, 1863, the judge issued an injunction against Burning Moscow, the stock fell to $104 in less than an hour. Then the judge resigned and was succeeded by a new one known to be favorable to the many-ledge theory. With this, Burning Moscow rose to $355. When the judge dismissed the

Ophir suit, Burning Moscow went to $1,000, while Ophir fell from $1,700 a foot to $1,430 on a single trade, and then declined further to $1,150. Ophir then initiated a new suit, and the price rose once again, while Burning Moscow fell. This continued for another two years, and ended only when Ophir purchased control of Burning Moscow to finish the matter in July 1865.

Each suit brought new speculative waves to San Francisco's boards. And there were 245 such actions in the five years from 1862 to 1867, making Virginia City's lawyers and judges wealthy, not only through bribes and fees, but their stock dealings as well.

Legal Actions in Virginia City, 1862-1867

Name of Mine	Suits in Which the Company was Plaintiff	Suits in Which the Company was Defendant	Total
Ophir Mining Co,	28	9	37
Yellow Jacket Mining Co,	24	8	32
Savage Mining Co.	22	7	29
Gould & Curry Mining Co.	20	7	27
Overman Co.	18	5	23
Chollar Co.	7	10	17
Potosi Co.	7	8	15
Crown Point Co.	12	3	15
Bullion Co.	11	4	15
Belcher Co.	9	4	13
Sierra Nevada Co.	8	5	13
Hale & Norcross Co.	2	7	9
	168	77	245

Source: Eliot Lord, *Comstock Mining and Miners* (Washington, 1883) p. 177.

The most risky kind of speculation was in shares of abandoned mines. Often these fell to pennies a share and traded irregularly. The speculators knew that the skilled Washoe miners would not leave a mine until they had explored it thoroughly, called in experts, and decided it was just a hole in the ground. But should a new vein be discovered nearby, the price would boom.

One such case involved the Crown Point, which was abandoned in

1870. The mine's superintendent, John P. Jones, felt there might be additional ore, and so he began purchasing shares, at a time when they were being offered at $2 with no buyers. Jones thought it was a bargain; at that price the entire capitalization came to $24,000, and the mill alone was worth around $140,000. He spread rumors of large pending liquidations in Crown Point, new assessments to be made, and in general maintained the aura of gloom, while he bought slowly, on dips, through masked accounts. News of Jones's purchases filtered out, however, and two others, Alvinza Hayward and Charles Low, both prominent speculators, also began to buy, accumulating shares at below $5.

Then, in May 1871, silver was found in one of the abandoned shafts, and Crown Point rose, twenty points at a clip. Late in the month it was quoted at $180. Jones had made a fortune, as did Hayward and Low. Hayward continued to accumulate shares, convinced additional veins would be found.

At this point he entered into a struggle with William Sharon, known as "King of the Comstock," and William Ralston, head of the "Bank Crowd" that controlled much of Washoe, for domination of the mine. In the end Hayward and Jones won. Sharon sold his 4,100 shares to him for $1.4 million. Hayward had the mine and Sharon another fortune. As for Jones, he ran for the Senate from Nevada in 1873, was elected, and remained a senator for thirty years, retiring in 1903.

Sharon was the key Comstock figure in the early 1870s, and would remain one of the most powerful men of the region even after being bested by Jones and Hayward. Yet he, too, had moments of despair. He had arrived in Sacramento in 1849, having come from Illinois to pan for gold. Sharon found little of the yellow metal, and entered the dry-goods business soon after. Then his store was wiped out in the flood of 1849, and Sharon left for San Francisco, where he opened a real-estate office. Business was good and Sharon prospered. By 1858 he was worth $150,000.

Sharon was intrigued with the Comstock, but unwilling to go there. Instead, he plunged into investments in mines. At first he did well. Then, in 1864, he decided to try for a corner in North America Mining, a major operator. At the time the stock was selling for around $280, was a good producer, and had claims on land being worked by Uncle Sam and Overman Mines. Sharon hoped to gain control of North America, sue the other mines, see the stock skyrocket, and then squeeze the shorts.

Needing backing for his venture, Sharon contacted Ralston, cashier of the Bank of California, who backed him. Then he entered the arena and began to buy. He took all that was offered, without checking on ownership of shares, a major mistake in those days. He left the exchange after two sessions, convinced he had control.

Sharon learned the awful truth the next day. Toward the end of his campaign he had purchased his own shares, borrowed by stockholders, at high prices. He had been the victim of a common fraud of those times. Still, there was nothing he could do about it. To renege on purchases would be to end his credit forever. So Sharon settled, obtaining necessary funds by selling his North America shares. Now he had lost his $150,000 as well as his battle for control of the mine. Sharon was broke.

Going to Ralston, Sharon asked for help. At the time, Ralston was engaged in a duel with William Stewart for domination of Washoe, and he saw in Sharon a perfect tool for the job. Ralston offered to make Sharon the Bank of California agent in Virginia City, with the understanding that, once there, Sharon could also deal in business ventures on his own. Sharon accepted and set off for Washoe. He learned all he could about mining and banking, and plunged into his tasks. These he performed well. Sharon would lend money to mineowners at high rates for short periods of time. When the owners couldn't pay their bills, he would foreclose, speculate in their shares, and pocket the profits.

Within a year Sharon was a millionaire, and, as representative of the Bank of California, one of the most powerful men in Washoe. When Stewart went to Washington and his Senate seat in 1865, Sharon took his place as King of the Comstock, a title he held until elected senator in Stewart's place in 1876. While in the East he augmented his income, working for the railroads both in and out of Congress. Sharon returned to San Francisco after a term, and when he died in 1885, he was one of the wealthiest men in the city.

If Sharon was King of the Comstock, Ralston was ruler of San Francisco during the Washoe bonanza. Like most of the others in the Comstock saga, Ralston was born east of the Mississippi, in his case in Ohio in 1825, and came to California in search of gold after news of the '49 strike hit his town. Ralston went by way of Panama, and remained there for a while as an employee of a shipping firm. He arrived in San Francisco in 1853, as the firm's agent. Soon he was mingling with the city's aristocrats, and recognized as one of them. He gravitated toward banking and got involved with several financial organizations. In 1864 Ralston organized the Bank of California which he capitalized at $3 million, and soon after raised to $5 million. Ralston took the position of cashier, and selected as its first president Darius Ogden Mills, a well-known and liked Sacramento banker, who knew little of banking, and was content to allow Ralston a free hand.

Using the bank's assets, Ralston backed a variety of enterprises, and profited from most. Bank of California money helped expand trade with the Orient, allowing Ralston to boast that one day San Francisco would be the New York of the Pacific, and China the Europe. He helped establish several manufacturing companies, taking shares in them for himself. Ralston sponsored a utility which gave San Francisco its first pure drinking water. He erected the Grand Hotel and the California Theater, and even helped found the University of California.

None of this could have been done without silver from Washoe. Ralston and his satellites—the Bank Crowd—came to control much of the district. Ever since he had first heard of the Comstock find, Ralston had been intrigued with Washoe. Indeed, one of the reasons he split with an early partner to found the Bank of California was a difference of opinion regarding loans and investments in miners and mines. The reason Ralston sent Sharon to Virginia City was to help salvage some of the mines which at the time seemed about to fall due to financial stringencies.

After Ralston learned of flooding in the Ophir and other mines he helped find solutions. For a while he was Sutro's most enthusiastic backer. When Sutro left for England seeking funds, Ralston gave him a letter of introduction, in which he wrote, "Too much cannot be said of the great importance of this work, if practicable upon any remunerative basis. We learn that the scheme has been carefully examined by scientific men, and that they unhesitatingly pronounced in its favor on all points—practicability, profit, and great public utility."

At the time Ralston was not only lending Comstock miners funds through the Bank of California, but had an "understanding" with Sharon regarding private investment in mines, and was behind most Sharon enterprises. Ralston later supported his former rival, William Stewart, not only in Washoe but Washington as well, helping finance his political campaigns, backing his litigations, and taking his share when Stewart won.

Through these and related connections, Ralston became treasurer of the Ophir Mining Company, at the time the largest in Washoe, and then took the same post at Gould & Curry and the Savage, two of Ophir's rivals. As Sharon foreclosed on miners unable to pay their debts, Ralston seized their machinery and turned it over to another of his companies, the Union Mill and Mining, which he formed in 1867. The Union immediately became the biggest supplier of goods and services to the miners, and through it Ralston dominated the Comstock. Then, using his connections in the state and federal legislatures, Ralston constructed the Virginia and Truckee Railroad, giving him the main access to Washoe, and tightening his domination of Nevada's economy and politics.

This is not to say Ralston only wanted to milk Washoe of all he could get. Rather, he was a shrewd businessman who, after making his fortune, decided to use his money and talents to create an economic and political empire in which all would benefit. The Union Mill and Mining charged high prices and the Virginia and Truckee exorbitant rates, but these were not unusual at the time, and without them prices at the mines would have been higher than they were and many might have had to be abandoned. Ralston was often accused of having created a "fortified monopoly" with Sharon its executor, and of easing out small operators whenever he had the chance. But the Bank Crowd rarely used underhanded methods, as had so many others in the early 1860s, relying instead upon the calling of mortgages, outright purchases at prevalent prices, and political patronage.

It might be further argued that Ralston saved Washoe in 1869–1872, when the area was in the midst of a severe depression. Floods in the mines, several major fires, miners' strikes for better working conditions and higher wages—all came at the same time. To cap it all, it seemed the Comstock Lode had finally been exhausted. Had Ralston taken the advice of friends and associates, he would have liquidated his assets and taken profits. Instead, he began construction of the railroad, purchased additional mines, hired miners to work at his varied enterprises, and urged others to have faith in the mines. Without his work, the Comstock might have been abandoned around 1870. As it was, Ralston kept the area going, in this way preparing the way for the biggest find of all, which, ironically, helped destroy him.

The first successful attack on the Bank Crowd came from Jones and Hayward, who as we have seen took over the Crown Point and several nearby mines in 1871. Ralston and Sharon didn't fear the Crown Point people, for they had little power compared with that of the Bank Crowd. Indeed, the find attracted people to Washoe, and in this way helped boost the value of Ralston's many enterprises.

James Flood and William O'Brien were also interested in the revival at Washoe. The men were business partners, operating the Auction Lunch Counter in San Francisco, a place where stockbrokers congregated. Both were sons of Irish immigrants, Flood having been born in New York and O'Brien taken there when only a child. O'Brien had come to California during the Gold Rush and stayed to enter several small supply and other business firms. He was a dealer in marine supplies when he met Flood in 1857. Flood worked for a while as a salesman and carpenter, and was just emerging from bankruptcy when he and O'Brien formed their partnership.

The Auction was a success, and the partners prospered. In time they began speculating in securities, acting on tips given them by customers. By 1868 the two men had become so rich they were able to sell the Auction and enter a new business, that of stock brokerage. At this point they met two Virginia City speculators seeking support for a mining venture in Washoe.

John Mackay was born in Dublin and came to America seeking wealth. He went to the goldfields and found nothing. Then Mackay drifted from job to job, never making more than a modest living. He went to Washoe in 1869, working for a while as a miner, then as a timberman, and later on as an independent contractor supplying services for miners. Mackay's work was good, and like other contractors, he was willing to accept as part of his pay certificates and stock in the mines he serviced.

The shares interested Mackay in independent mining once more, and in 1862 he and a partner purchased control of a seemingly worthless mine, the Kentuck, and began expanding operations there. The gamble paid off; the Kentuck became a producer once more, and Mackay took $5 million in silver out of the ground in the next three years.

It was then that Mackay became friendly with James Fair, one of the most knowledgeable miners in Washoe. Like Mackay and O'Brien, Fair was born in Ireland and came to America while still young. He, too, went to California seeking gold, never struck it rich, but remained in the mining camps, working as a laborer, miner, mine manager, mill operator—and all the while learning more about mining than almost anyone else in California. In 1865 he went to Washoe seeking new properties to exploit. For a while he worked for the Bank Crowd as superintendent of the Ophir, but he always sought an independent operation of his own. In 1866 he became assistant superintendent of the Hale & Norcross, and was credited with saving that mine from abandonment by introducing new techniques. Then Fair left Virginia City for new ventures, returning in 1868, at which time the Hale & Norcross was again in trouble. Fair convinced Mackay he could turn the mine around once again, that with his knowledge and Mackay's money they could become rulers of Washoe. The men next traveled to San Francisco, seeking help in winning control of the mine. By then Flood and O'Brien had become powers at the exchange, and the four men united to plan a raid on the company's stock. Mackay would receive three-eighths interest, Flood and O'Brien together an additional three-eighths, and Fair the remaining two-eighths.

Flood and O'Brien did their work well. Within two months they had obtained sufficient shares to control the mine, buying and selling as they went, in such a way as not to arouse suspicion and so raise the quotations. That they could do this in such a manner was all the more surprising when one considers the former controllers of Hale & Norcross—Sharon and Ralston.

As he had predicted, Fair found new ore bodies at the mine, and it became a major producer in 1869–1870. But the vein petered out soon after, and by 1872 Fair was searching for a new mine to develop.

He found one without too much difficulty—in fact, he found two. The Consolidated Virginia and the California were adjacent to one another. Some silver had been found in each, but like the Hale & Norcross, the veins had run out. Mining operations were continuing, but abandonment was also being considered. Because of this, the partners were able to purchase control of the two mines and some additional nearby property for $100,000.

Fair and Mackay began working the mine soon after, and at first found little of value. In March 1873, some ore was found, which seemed at the time a continuation of a vein at the Gould & Curry. A new shaft was sunk, and according to Fair, it was then that he found a "knife thin" vein, which he followed carefully for the next few weeks. Each assay was richer than the one before. By October it was evident that Fair and Mackay had found the richest vein of all at Washoe.

News of the find spread, to Virginia City and then to San Francisco. The exchanges, in the doldrums for more than two years, came back to life. Consolidated Virginia, which had sold for as low as a dollar a share in July 1870, and even in June 1871, could be had for $15, began to rise. In November 1874, it was quoted at $176, and a year later at $780. By then there were predictions that more than half a billion dollars in silver would be extracted from the Consolidated Virginia and the California. Other Comstock mines followed their lead. Just prior to the discovery, Comstock mining shares were selling for a total value of less than $5 million; in January 1875, the value was $262 million. It was the most spectacular stock-market rise in American history.

Production at the Consolidated Virginia was as good as expected. In 1873 the partners took $645,000 in silver from the mine, and in 1874, almost $5 million. Production rose to $16.7 million in 1875, and then leveled off. By the time the veins had been exhausted, $150 million in ore had been removed, and shareholders received $78 million in dividends. It wasn't as rich as the speculators had predicted, but the Consolidated Virginia and California represented the greatest silver find on the continent.

The partners reorganized their holdings to form the California Mining Company, which was more popularly known as the Bonanza Firm. The Bonanza organized the Pacific Mill and Mining Company, Pacific Wood, Lumber & Flume, and even considered constructing its own railroad, to become independent of the Virginia and Truckee. The four partners were now multimillionaires, and would make even more money before leaving Washoe.

As their stocks rose, O'Brien, Flood, and Fair began to speculate wildly at the exchanges, where news of their interest in a security would cause it to leap. So they added to their fortunes in that manner, too. Mackay, who had no interest in speculation, remained close to the mines, although he traveled, became a popular figure in San Francisco society, and one of the most respected figures in the West.* He participated in the laying of the Pacific cable, represented the United States at the coronation of Czar Alexander III, and even

*Speaking of stocks, Mackay once said, "It is no affair of mine. I am not speculating in stocks. My business is mining—legitimate mining. . . . Had I desired to do so, I could have gone down to San Francisco with 10,000 shares of stock in my pocket, and by throwing it on the market at the critical moment, I could have brought about a panic and crash. . . . Suppose I had done so and had made $500,000 by the job—what is that to me? By attending to my legitimate business here at home I take out $500,000 in one week." Dan De Quille (William Wright), *The Big Bonanza* (New York, 1947 ed.), pp. 369–70.

helped one of his former employees, "Gentleman Jim" Corbett, after the fighter became heavyweight champion of the world. At the time of his death in 1902 he was worth between $20 and $50 million.

Flood became a philanthropist with his money, and later on president of the Nevada Bank. He died in 1889, not as wealthy as Mackay, but worth more than $10 million.

Once he became wealthy, O'Brien concentrated on having a good time. Known as "the jolly millionaire," he threw many parties, lent large sums of money to old friends, and provided handsomely for his relatives. He didn't enjoy this life for long. O'Brien fell ill, and died in 1878, leaving his fortune to nieces and several Catholic and Protestant orphan asylums.

Of the four partners, Fair was the most aggressive and ambitious. He led Mackay, O'Brien, and Flood in a contest against the Bank Crowd in 1875. There were troubles at many bank-controlled mines that year—flooding had taken the Ophir once again, and other shafts gave indications of lower yields. Only the Bonanza mines were strong, and showed signs of further promise. Now Fair attacked the Bank of California head on. Together with his partners, he organized the Bank of Nevada, capitalized at $10 million, and took business away from Ralston. The struggle was joined, although later on both groups would deny its existence. At the time, however, the brokers knew of it, and they began dumping Bank Crowd shares in early August. Flood and O'Brien took them up, in this way seizing control of the mines.

Then a run developed at the Bank of California, and despite many efforts, Ralston could not stop it. On August 26, the bank closed its doors. Ralston was ruined, and with him, the group that ran San Francisco for a decade. He resigned the following day, and hours later, went for a swim in the Bay. Either he went out too far or committed suicide—no one really knew. In either case, the former ruler of San Francisco was drowned.

The Bank of California was reorganized and reopened, with Mills and Sharon in command. But its power was broken. The Bonanza Kings ruled in San Francisco, with Fair aspiring to become Ralston's successor.

Soon after the partners broke up, in part due to Fair's aggressive ambitions which the others did not share. Fair went on to gather additional properties, and also developed political ambitions. In 1880 he challenged Sharon for his Senate seat and defeated him. At the time nothing seemed beyond his grasp.

Yet his decline would begin soon after. In 1883, after a long series of squabbles, he was divorced by his wife. Broken and disheartened, he declined to run for reelection in 1886, and was replaced in the Senate by Stewart. Fair returned to business, but was unhappy at it. Nevertheless, his golden touch had not left him. At the time of his death in 1894, he was worth $45 million.

Mackay, Fair, O'Brien, and Flood—they were to be the last rulers of the Comstock, and all died rich. Their stories were quite different from those of the first of the Comstock leaders—the Grosches, Finney, McLaughlin, O'Riley, and Comstock himself all died poor.

There were no great discoveries after the Consolidated Virginia-California. Ralston had died at a time when he himself thought the lode was just beginning to pay off; actually, the panic of 1875 was a foretaste of what was to come. Prices recovered, but never again reached their old highs, primarily because the silver in the mines was running out. Comstock securities, worth in excess of $262 million in January 1875 would be worth less than $7 million in February 1881. The greatest bull market on an American securities exchange had been followed by the worst decline in history. By then, however, Mackay, Flood, and Fair had sold most of their shares, and O'Brien was dead. Those who had purchased their shares and held on to them suffered, some drifting to "Pauper Alley," a narrow street in San Francisco between Pine and California, where old-time speculators down on their luck would congregate and swap stories. A visitor there wrote:

> There, in Pauper Alley, one can walk, any time in business hours, and see creatures that once were millionaires and leading operators. Now they live by free lunches in the beer cellars and on stray dimes tossed to them "for luck." Women, too, form a part of the wretched crowd that haunts the ends of the Alley

> where it joins its more prosperous neighbor streets and beg every speculator to give them a "pointer" or to carry a share of stock for them. These are the "dead mud-hens," as the men are the "dead ducks," of the Comstock share gamblers. Horrible things one sees and hears of here. Old friends you thought were prosperous but had not heard of for years shove themselves out of the huddle and beg for the price of a glass of whisky. There stands a once-prosperous printer, in rags—he took flyers on the street too many times. Yonder beggar lost $400,000 in a single summer, all good gold. The ghost of many a murdered happiness walks unseen among these half-insane paupers as they chatter like apes of lost fortunes and the prospects of their favourite stocks. Really it is a frightful thing to walk there and look at the seamy side of the silken garment of fortune.

The Comstock did not decline rapidly, but over a number of years. Miners drifted away from Virginia City to other western mining towns, in search of new strikes. Colorado, the Dakotas, Idaho, and finally the Yukon, would all witness scenes like those at Virginia City in the 1860s and 1870s, though only the Yukon strike was as dramatic. Even as miners rushed to the Yukon at the end of the nineteenth century, there were rumors of more silver in Comstock, while the Sutro Tunnel Corporation, listed on the New York Stock Exchange, would have speculative flurries well into the new century.

Nevada was established by silver, but the wealth of the state was funneled into San Francisco, and even before statehood was granted in 1864, it was under the domination of the Bay City. This money made possible Ralston's dreams of a New York of the Pacific, and they were helped along by Nevada's senators, all of whom, from the time of statehood to 1903 (with the lone exception of former territorial governor, James Nye) had come out of the East to Washoe, by way of San Francisco. William Stewart, John P. Jones, William Sharon, and James Fair—these men were almost as much senators from California as they were senators from Nevada. Perhaps it would be more accurate to say that they represented the San Francisco-Washoe axis.

Comparative Stock Prices of Mining Shares 1875-1881

Stock	**Price in February, 1875**	**Price in January, 1881**
Union Consolidated	95	8½
Mexican	85	5¼
Ophir	315	5
California	780	1¼
Consolidated Virginia	700	.90
Savage	190	.80
Hale & Norcross	77	2.90
Chollar-Potosi	94	3¼
Kentuck	37	1¼
Segregated Belcher	165	4

Source: Lord, *Comstock Mining and Miners,* pp. 408-409.

It would not be the first time or the last that wealth made during a bonanza benefited people far from the scene. On the other hand, the next great speculative mania, which also took place in the West, saw the opposite situation develop, as western wealth was transformed into eastern and European disaster.

CHAPTER 5

Beef Bonanza

The *Buffalo Live Stock Journal,* a small periodical which had a limited readership in northern New York, was read by dairymen and breeders and few others. It was one of several such newspapers, all of which tended to be optimistic, as was so often the case with trade journals. In mid-1875, however, the editor outdid himself in describing the industry's future. "Cotton was once crowned king," he wrote, "but grass is now. . . . If grass is King, the Rocky Mountain region is its throne, and fortunate indeed are those who possess it." The "boundless, gateless, fenceless pastures" of the Rockies contained the best grazing land on the continent, if not the world. Subscribers were urged to consider relocating there. After a few years in the West they could return to Buffalo, as millionaires. Or should they not want to make the trip, they might send their dollars westward, and see them multiply fivefold in three or four years.

The editor was not telling his readers anything they had not heard before. By 1875 the great cattle boom was on in the mountain states, and meat-packers in Chicago and Kansas City, bankers in London, Edinburgh, Dundee, and New York, railroad tycoons and their agents in Washington, and cowboys and cattlemen on the Texas range, were watching the Great Plains with interest. Charles Dilke, at the beginning of a meteoric political career in England, urged his countrymen to participate in the bonanza and make the American West part of a "Greater Britain." "Nothing short of violence or special legislation can prevent the Plains from continuing on forever that which under Nature's farming they have been—the feeding ground for mighty flocks, the cattle pasture of the world."

This was hyperbole, and the kind investors wanted to hear. Like so many enthusiastic dreams of glory and wealth in that part of the country, the vision was distorted. Dilke, the editor of the *Buffalo Live Stock Journal,* and others who wrote of and invested in the burgeoning cattle empires either did not understand the region or ignored its nature. They would awaken to reality in the late 1880s, after tens of millions of dollars had been lost in the Rockies.

The cattle industry is almost as old as the early settlements. There were cowboys and roundups in colonial Virginia, South Carolina, and Long Island. As Americans moved westward in the early national period, they took their cattle with them, and new ranges were developed—on a minor level, to be sure, but ranges nonetheless. Americans were and are meat eaters, and in the mid-nineteenth century, they would consume meat three times a day.* Although they ate pork, veal, and other meats in great amounts, the staple was beef. So in the days before modern packing and preservation, Americans took cattle with them almost wherever they went.

There were some 11.3 million head of cattle in America in 1850, when the population was 23.3 million. New York, the largest state with a population of 3 million, also had the most cattle—almost a million head. At that time Americans raised cattle locally, slaughtered them, and consumed their products. If the grazing was good, so was

*At present, however, Uruguay and Argentina lead the United States in the amount of beef consumed per capita.

the meat, but if insufficient grass existed, the meat was stringy and second-rate. The same was true for prices of meat. Good grazing land meant low prices, while poor resulted in higher costs at the butcher.

Clearly it paid to raise cattle in good grazing lands and sell them in poor. As the country's other industries came to be concentrated in different parts of America, so did cattle. In 1860, when there were 31.5 million Americans, the nation had 17 million head of cattle. New York was still the largest state, with a population of 3.9 million, but the number of cattle had declined, to 850,000 head. Texas, with a population of only 604,000 in 1860, had over 2.9 million head of cattle that year, leading all the other states. The Texas ranges provided cattle for many parts of the country, and even some for export. Cowboys would round up cattle on the open range, take them to Shreveport, and from there ship them down the Red River to New Orleans. Or they would drive herds to Galveston and send them to New Orleans by ship. A few enterprising ranchers made the long trek to Chicago and California, and some began provisioning Cuba with the tough longhorns.

It was a good and profitable business. The cattle roamed freely on the range, ready to be gathered like wild flowers by the cowboys, who sold them for around $6 a head at the terminals. Some cowboys tried to fatten the cattle before selling them, for "heavy beeves" could fetch upward of $16 each. There were few of them at first; the cowboys of 1860 were out for the fast dollar, and seemed uninterested in establishing ranches.

The Texas cattle business languished during the Civil War, as the cowboys joined the Confederate armies and the cattle roamed unmolested on the range. Some cattle was used to feed the Confederate forces, but for the most part, the young industry seemed dead.

This was the situation in 1866, when the cowboys returned to Texas. The range was swollen with fat, mature beeves, ready for the roundup. The oversupply of Texas cattle and depressed economic conditions in the South meant that they could be purchased for extremely low prices. At the same time, northern prosperity resulted in increased demand for beef and higher prices. This was a time when sirloin sold for the astronomical price of 30 cents a pound in New

York, twice that of prewar days. A mature steer fetched over $85 in Massachusetts in 1866 and almost $70 in New York. The price in Galveston for a similar animal was little over $9. Clearly profits were to be made in the business of shipping steers from Texas to the North.

Other factors combined to mold the revived cattle industry and determine its direction. The discovery of gold in California in 1848 sparked debate on a transcontinental railroad, and five years later Congress authorized surveys of possible routes. Railroads began to probe into the West prior to the Civil War, and even as the fighting reached its peak, the work continued. In 1862 Congress created the Union Pacific and Central Pacific, charging them with the task of constructing a link from Omaha, Nebraska, to the Pacific. This work was completed in 1869, but before then, trains were rolling through Nebraska and Wyoming, tying these states to the East and helping make Cheyenne a major western junction. The Kansas Pacific, taking a more southerly route, went from Independence and Kansas City to Denver, through Kansas and Colorado. This route seemed perfect for the transport of manufactured goods to the West—and cattle to the East.

So thought Joseph McCoy, a cattle dealer from Springfield, Illinois, who went west on the Kansas Pacific in 1867. Earlier McCoy had thought to establish a cattle depot on the Mississippi, where Texas longhorns could be deposited and slaughtered after going upriver on flatboats. His visit to the Kansas plains convinced him that the railroad would be a better means of transport than the river. Cattle could be taken to Kansas, fattened there, and then transported eastward for sale. With this as his goal, McCoy invigorated the town of Abilene, and two years later that town, on the Kansas Pacific, was one of the fastest growing in the nation, and a hub of the cattle industry.

The Indians were a second force that helped mold the postbellum cattle business. The Five Civilized Tribes had fought on the side of the Confederacy, and as punishment all but the Cherokee were forced into new homes farther north and west. In the past the Indians had blocked the Texas drives from eastern regions; now this would be over, or at least so it seemed.

The Indians would not accept removal. The western war, which had gone on even while the Confederacy collapsed, grew in intensity. Red Cloud assumed leadership of the Sioux nation in 1865 and prepared for new conflicts, in which he bested the American armies. The government signed a new treaty with the Indians in 1867, one that was promptly broken by Washington. Now the Cheyenne, Arapaho, and other tribes joined the Sioux in warring against the federal troops.

The Indian wars discouraged the long drives from southern Texas to the North, and favored a policy of raising cattle farther north, near the railroad towns and federal troops. They also meant a strong federal military presence in the West and a continuation of the policy of Indian removal—or extermination. When General George Custer and his troops were defeated and killed at Little Big Horn in 1874, western cattle interests feared for their livestock, but at the same time ranchers knew this would result in a still greater federal effort to destroy the Indians.

This was the case, and the campaign was conducted on two fronts. The federal armies pursued and defeated the Indians, so that the direct menace was all but ended by 1880. Now the ranchers were freed from fear of Indian attacks, from the necessity of paying tolls when taking cattle over Indian lands, and worries regarding Indian thefts of herds.

Equally important was the fight on the second front—the buffalo. Federal and private hunters destroyed entire herds of buffalo, knowing that without the beasts the Indian economy would collapse. They were correct, and a sidelight to the massacres was the emptying of the buffalo ranges, which were quickly filled with cattle.

The third force was the farmer. The farm frontier moved rapidly westward after the war and rarely abated. Kansas had a population of 107,000 in 1860; it reached 365,000 in 1870, and almost a million in 1880. Nebraska's population rose from 28,000 in 1860 to 452,000 twenty years later. Farmers constituted the large majority of these new settlers, and they resented having Texas cattle trampling over their lands. Furthermore, they had clear title to lands cattlemen had previously used for grazing, and given the force of federal marshals, were able to make their claims stick. Barbed wire, first marketed in

1874, was used to fence off farmlands, and deny Texas cattle entry to northern markets. This, too, forced the range westward, and to the north.

Finally, there was "Texas fever," caused by a tick carried by Texas cattle. There had been cases of Texas fever prior to the Civil War, but these caused little comment or fear. This changed after the war, when large numbers of longhorns were taken north. An epidemic erupted in 1867, resulting in the deaths of tens of thousands of longhorns. Word reached the northern cities, and packers refused to purchase Texas cattle or contract for their delivery. Northern states, fearing the infestation of native herds, banned the entry of the Texas cattle and posted guards along state boundaries to make certain none entered. This crippled the Texas industry for a while, and encouraged stock raising elsewhere, especially in the mountain states.

All of these factors helped change the location of the prewar cattle kingdom. In 1865 it appeared high meat prices would result in a flourishing of the east Texas range. By 1875, it seemed clear the range would grow and prosper, but it would be elsewhere—in the Texas Panhandle, Colorado, Wyoming, the Dakotas, and Montana. It was there that the great speculation in beef began in the mid-1870s, flourished in the early 1880s, and died soon after.

The cattle settlement of the Great Plains might have proceeded slowly, taking generations rather than years, were it not for two unrelated events of the early 1870s. The first of these was the enormous success of Abilene, while the second was the financial panic of 1873.

Joseph McCoy had planned his cattle town well. When he arrived there, it was a shambles of huts, some dozen of them, and a saloon, with no discernible future. McCoy recognized that the potential of the place lay in its access to the railroad, but also took careful note of its geography. Years later he wrote, "Abilene was selected because the country was entirely unsettled, well watered, excellent grass, and nearly the entire area of country well adapted to holding cattle." In 1869 only 75,000 head were driven to the town for transshipment; the following year the number was 350,000.

At first the mangy longhorns spent little time in Abilene. Instead, they were held there for a few days, waiting for the trains to take them east for slaughter and sale. The goal was a fast turnover on high volume.

Conditions soon changed, however. As the town became glutted with cattle in 1869, the herds were set to grazing in the open fields, where they were fattened while awaiting shipment. The fatter the steer, the higher the price. Grass and water were free and in great abundance. Clearly, it paid to use Abilene and the surrounding countryside as cattle-raising areas. For that matter, there was no reason why cattle had to be raised in southern and eastern Texas at all, when conditions seemed so much better farther north. So it seemed to McCoy and other cattlemen of the period. The range began to spread northward in the early 1870s at a rapid rate.*

Abilene's immediate success encouraged other Texas drovers to take their herds to the railroad. In 1871 some 700,000 head of cattle went through the town. This caused a glut, which in turn led to falling prices. High beef prices had led to greater production, which in turn resulted in lower prices and hardship for the cattlemen. Almost half the cattle taken to railroads went unsold, and were allowed to winter on the Kansas plains at a loss. Conditions were better the following year, and the Kansas cattle were sold at premium prices; the loss was turned into a profit. The cattlemen got the message, and the northern ranges filled at an even more rapid rate than before.

This created another cattle glut in early 1873. Then, in September, a financial panic hit Wall Street, sending reverberations throughout the nation and marking the start of a depression which would last for six years in some sectors of the economy.

The panic and depression hurt both the Kansas and south Texas ranchers, as cattle companies in both parts of the country went

*With some exaggeration, a leading scholar of the subject has written, "The spread of the range and ranch cattle industry over the Great Plains in the space of fifteen years—the movement was fairly complete in ten or twelve--is perhaps one of the outstanding phenomena in American history. . . . During that period and for ten years after, men, cattle, and horses held almost undisputed possession of the region." Walter Prescott Webb, *The Great Plains* (Boston, 1931), p. 225.

bankrupt. Kansas ranchers had been experimenting with new breeds of shorthorn which produced a better quality of meat than the tough longhorns, and prices for both fell drastically, to the point where they competed with one another at the market. Soon the market for Texas longhorns was so small as to all but kill it.* The 1873 panic hurt the northern range, but at the same time sealed its victory over south Texas, and that of the shorthorn over the longhorn. Furthermore, Kansas beef was able to compete with the eastern product as a result of better and faster transportation. As eastern consumers developed a taste for western meats, the eastern herds suffered. This, too, helped the northern ranchers at the expense of their counterparts elsewhere. Finally, silver and gold mining boomed in the mountain regions, providing an additional market for beef and people willing to pay premium prices for it. All of this meant the beef market in the West was expanding, even while the nation suffered through the depression. Recovery would arrive there in 1876, before it appeared in the rest of the country. This recovery ushered in the golden decade for the cattle industry, and gave it a patina of growth and solidity far beyond its actual potential.

The railroads cooperated with the ranchers in boosting the industry and section. For if the range was an economic success, the railroads would make profits. Jay Gould, who took command of the Union Pacific during the panic, was most eager to exploit the cattle markets. Even earlier, in 1870, the Union Pacific had initiated a publicity campaign designed to attract investors and cattle ranchers to its lands. The company began a search for able publicists. Dr. Harry Latham, a company surgeon, was one of them. He wrote letters that first appeared in the *Omaha Herald* in 1870, and later on were distributed in pamphlet form throughout the country. Latham wrote glowingly of the "succulent grasses" of the plains, which if covered with cattle could feed the nation and even much of the world. The

*Of course, the south Texas range was not destroyed or abandoned, and in time it, too, recovered. But thereafter, domination passed to north Texas and the Great Plains. Some south Texas ranches, through capable leadership and a willingness to innovate, went against this trend. The most important of these, the King Ranch, was the largest in the nation, a rank it holds to this day.

railroad sent him on speaking tours in the West, where he urged his audiences to expand their operations and aggressively market their beeves in the East. "Never cease your efforts till every acre of grass in Colorado is eaten annually; till your beef is consumed in every market," he told the Colorado Stock Growers in 1873.

Latham was only one of several writers in the railroad's employ. Jay Gould hired dozens of them to encourage settlement in the West and larger herds. Robert Strahorn, a Sedalia, Missouri, journalist who settled in Denver in 1870, wrote *The Hand-Book of Wyoming and Guide to the Black Hills and the Big Horn Regions for Citizen, Emigrant and Tourist* in 1877. The work captured Gould's attention, and Strahorn wrote a second one, *To the Rockies and Beyond, or a Summer on the Union Pacific Railroad and Branches, Saunterings in the Popular Health, Pleasure, and Hunting Resorts of Nebraska, Dakota, Wyoming, Colorado, New Mexico, Utah, Montana, and Idaho,* which Gould hoped would encourage tourism in Union Pacific territory. Strahorn wrote of the great profits to be had in ranching. "A steady profit of twenty-five per cent per annum is really a common result," he claimed. "Forty and fifty per cent have been realized, but the writer who lays down such figures as an average is very liable to get his reputation involved."

Far more persuasive, however, were the words of General James S. Brisbin, who augmented his army salary by writing for the Union Pacific. Brisbin's most influential work, *The Beef Bonanza,* appeared in 1881. Its subtitle was, *How to Get Rich on the Plains.*

Brisbin began his book by saying, "The increasing interest felt among all classes of people in the East regarding stock-growing in the West and the profits to be derived from this occupation induces me to offer the public information gathered at various times during a residence of twelve years on the plains among the herds." He then launched into detailed accounts of how others had made fortunes in cattle raising. Mr. R. C. Keith of North Platte, for example, began raising cattle in the fall of 1867 with five northern cows. He purchased additional cows, steers, and yearlings during the next five years, to bring his total livestock costs to $50,000, and in the process acquired a partner, a hired hand, and some part-time helpers. In this period, said Brisbin, Keith showed a profit of $12,000, and owned a ranch plus cattle in value of $109,900. Others had done as well. A Mr. J. L. Brush of Weld County, Colorado, told Brisbin: "I commenced eight years ago with a capital of $400, and I own now, as a result of the increase and my own labor, 900 head of fine cattle, besides having made considerable investments in lands from money taken from the herd. I think the average profit on capital invested in cattle will not fall short of 40 per cent per annum over and above all expenses." Most of the rest of the book deals with similar stories, calculations, and projections, all of which were designed to lure people and money westward, and incidentally help the Union Pacific in its colonization effort.

The western newspapers, never the ones for understatement, cooperated with the railroads by printing stories of fabulous fortunes to be had in western grazing. Many of these were reprinted in eastern journals, and some overseas as well. The *Denver Journal of Commerce* published one such story, which was circulated throughout the nation. Titled, "How Cattlemen Grow Rich," it purported to be an accurate estimate of the way in which one cattle baron started on his way to a fortune.

> A good sized steer when it is fit for the butcher market will bring from $45 to $60. The same animal at its birth was worth $5.00. He has run on the plains and cropped the grass from the public domain for four or five years, and now, with scarcely any expense to his owner, is worth forty dollars more than when he started on his pilgrimage. A thousand of these animals are kept nearly as cheaply as a single one, so with a thousand as a starter and with an investment of but $5,000 in the start, in four years the stock raiser has made from $40,000 to $45,000. Allow $5,000 for his expenses which he has been going on and he still has $35,000 and even $45,000 for a net profit. That is all there is of the problem and that is why our cattlemen grow rich.

This estimate does not take into account cattle lost through disease, theft, bad weather, or other natural disasters common in the plains. Few easterners or Europeans knew much of these problems—they were either ignored or played down by Latham, Strahorn, Brisbin, and the western newspapers—or realized that a combination of them could lead to economic disaster, and often did. To be sure, there were ranchers in the late 1870s and early 1880s who had made fortunes, but there were many more who had lost all they had and gone home broke.

Westerners knew this, and joked about it among themselves. Bill Nye, the western humorist, wrote a tongue-in-cheek article for the *Laramie Boomerang,* in which he spoke of one "success story" involving "a guileless tenderfoot" who three years earlier had come into Wyoming, "leading a single Texas steer and carrying a branding iron; now he is the opulent possessor of six hundred head of fine cattle—the ostensible progeny of that one steer." Eastern farmers laughed at such humor, but eastern investors in New York, Philadelphia, and Boston believed it was a true story. Another such tall tale, which involved a farmer who lost a few cattle in a winter storm and gave them up for dead, but returned in the spring to find a fattened herd, all from his lost cattle, was similarly taken seriously by eastern investors, who had never been farther west than St. Louis or Chicago and couldn't tell one breed of steer from another.

Had they known more of the cattle industry than could be derived from these books and articles, they would have realized that the young and burgeoning ranches of the Great Plains were quite risky investments. The shorthorns prized by raisers produced far more beef than the Texas longhorns, and were free of diseases, but were more costly as well. A loss of several hundred longhorns would be unfortunate; the death of the same number of shorthorns could be disastrous. The tough longhorns could stand harsh winters, while the more delicate shorthorns would die in prolonged periods of blizzard, or come down with pleuropneumonia, which could sweep through a herd as rapidly as tick fever and lead to its destruction. But if the tenderfeet wanted to invest in western ranges, so be it; the cattlemen and railroads weren't going to go out of their way to educate them before receiving their money.

If the East is defined as westerners of that time did—the area on the New York and Chicago side of the Mississippi—then easterners had interests in the Plains from the beginning of the cattle drives. Railroad men, meat-packers, and even an occasional Wall Street or LaSalle Street tycoon dabbled in investments in herds. There had been little of this in the early 1870s, as there wasn't much in the way of ranches or business in the Great Plains at the time, and there was less investment immediately after the 1873 panic, when money went into hiding.

Toward the end of the decade, as business revived throughout the country and especially in the cattle industry, eastern financial and related interests began sending money to the Plains in great amounts. Ranching became the glamour industry of the late 1870s, although no ranch was listed for trading at the New York Stock Exchange or the outdoor curb market. Eastern speculators and investors, most of whom had never been west of Cleveland, spoke knowingly of ranching, studding conversations with "facts" gleaned from Union Pacific publications. They expected to make fortunes in western cattle. Yet profits were only a part of the reason for the investments, and for many people, a small part.

Easterners were intrigued with the Plains. Reports of the Indian wars whetted their appetite for adventure. The generation that hadn't witnessed the horrors of the Civil War rode vicariously alongside Custer and Sheridan in the West. Young men read of western outlaws, cowboys, and Indians with even more excitement than their counterparts today read of moon explorers. Few can hope ever to go to the moon, but to many young men of the late 1870s, a trip to the West was a distinct possibility. The Union Pacific and Northern Pacific tourist trains would take them there, and easterners could hunt buffalo (often while seated comfortably in a slow-moving parlor car) and visit ranches in Kansas and points west.

Some even played at being cowboys. Theodore Roosevelt, settling in the Dakotas in 1883, said he was going there to hunt buffalo before they all disappeared, and he remained to live the life of a rancher for two years. Roosevelt invested in land and cattle and lost about $25,000. Twenty years later he visited the Dakotas, this time as President. Looking about him, Roosevelt remarked, "Here the romance of my life began."

Even without the promise of great profits, easterners might have invested in the West—for this kind of romance, if nothing else. Writers like Brisbin, hoping to attract easterners with lures of all kinds, did not ignore the romantic appeal. In his preface to *Beef Bonanza*, Brisbin wrote:

> The West! The mighty West! That land where the buffalo still roams and the wild savage dwells; where the broad rivers flow and the boundless prairie stretches away for thousands of miles; where new states are every year carved out and myriads of people find homes and wealth; where the poor, professional young man, flying from the overcrowded East and the tyranny of a moneyed aristocracy, finds honor and wealth; where the young politician, unopposed by rings and combinations, relying upon his own abilities, may rise to position and fame; where there are lands for the landless, money for the moneyless, briefs for lawyers, patients for doctors, and above all, labor and its reward to every poor man who is willing to work. . . . It does not matter where the emigrant settles in the West, so he comes; and he will almost anywhere soon find himself better off than if he remained in the East.

Such lines could have been written for Roosevelt, the New York politician and lawyer, and many others like him, who actually made the trip and stayed on. For those who could or would not cross the Mississippi, their money would act as surrogate.

This was also the beginning of the age of Social Darwinism, the application of Darwin's biological theories to society as a whole. If, as Darwin appeared to be saying, there was a struggle for existence in the biological world in which the best emerged victorious, then perhaps the same took place in everyday life. This was the message of Herbert Spencer's *Synthetic Philosophy* and *Progress: Its Law and Causes*. One could prove one's worth by engaging in the struggle, with no holds barred, with the superior individual—or race—defeating the inferior. Spencer seemed to be writing of the Indian wars, or at least that was the implication that many Americans who read his books and articles received from them. In 1866 American admirers sent Spencer several thousand dollars to enable him to continue his work. Later on, when Spencer visited America, he was greeted as the greatest philosopher since Socrates. Those who were interested in the Great Plains before reading Spencer were even more intrigued afterward with the idea of going there and investing. When Spencer wrote of his preference for "anarchy plus the police constable," he might have been thinking of the range and the cattle towns of the West. Romance and the philosophical justification offered by Social Darwinism, added to visions of great profits, impelled eastern Americans to invest in western ranches.

At first most of the ventures were partnerships. Cattlemen in need of funds to establish ranches, buy more cattle, or expand already existing operations, would seek eastern businessmen interested in investment opportunities. Or the easterners would advertise in western newspapers for cattlemen in need of money. They would then contact one another, usually by mail, and form partnerships. The investor would supply the money while the rancher would offer his management skills, and they would split the profits, if any. It was not unusual for the two never to meet—to begin their business, carry on operations, and finally go bankrupt, all by mail.

Such arrangements seldom worked out well. The investors knew little of the cattle business or the Plains, and had to trust the cattlemen in all things, from the purchase of land and steers to their sale and final accounting. Realizing they were dealing with novices, the cattlemen milked them for all they could get. "When we agreed to associate, you said we could establish a company with $40,000," wrote James Gardner of Albany, New York, to his Wyoming cattleman partner, George McClellan, in 1881. "You now have expended almost

$48,000 and still you have the bravery to tell me that the end is not in sight." Gardner offered advice on how to run the ranch and which cattle should be purchased and sold. "Be sure to hire sober men," he wrote. "I shudder at the thought of our cattle running around on the plains cared for by some fuzzy minded cowboy." One can imagine McClellan's reactions to such advice, coming as it did from one who had much money and no knowledge of cowboys and cows. So he sent assurances that all was well and getting better, and asked for more money. In time the partnership failed, as did most of them, to be replaced by firmer organizations, such as syndicates and corporations.

Fresh out of Harvard in 1878, Hubert Teschemacher and Frederic deBillier went to Cheyenne to establish a ranch. Contrary to expectations, the ranch did not return an immediate profit, so in the winter of 1881–1882 Teschemacher returned to Boston to seek additional capital. He must have cut a romantic figure for his friends and former classmates who had remained in the East, and Teschemacher's tales of Cheyenne probably fascinated them. In any case, he was able to raise a quarter of a million dollars for the Teschemacher & deBillier Cattle Company. One friend, banker Joseph Ames, subscribed $10,000 and his father took an additional $10,000 worth of stock. When the son warned the father of the risks, the older man responded, "You couldn't keep me out!"

Some of those approached were not so enthusiastic, at least at first. Boston manufacturer James Converse, who in a long business career had been stung on several occasions in western gambles, told the young man, "Once a fool, twice the wiser the next time. I know your integrity and enthusiasm, but the fact is you cannot guarantee the return I can get in the East." But in the end, Converse took $10,000 worth of stock.

Americans along the eastern seaboard rushed to invest in western cattle. Those who had savings cleaned out their accounts, while others borrowed heavily to obtain shares in ranches. More than a thousand joint-stock companies were established in the Plains during the last two decades of the nineteenth century, and much of the funding came from enthusiastic would-be ranchers from Boston,

New York, and Chicago, who welcomed the opportunity to join in what seemed a great adventure.

The farther one got from the Plains, the fewer and less troublesome seemed the problems connected with ranching, and the greater the profits to be derived from the business. So if the cash-poor gentry of the eastern seaboard borrowed to purchase shares in Wyoming and Kansas ranches, the wealthy and sophisticated English and Scots bankers and investors, even farther from the range, did so with as much enthusiasm and even greater amounts of money.

Private investors, banks, and trusts in the British Isles had long been intrigued with America. From colonial times through the Vandalia scheme and the canal mania, they had poured out their funds for shares in American ventures. More often than not they were wiped out, yet they always seemed to forget the experience and a generation later came back for more of the same.

This happened after the Civil War. Britain had a larger class of wealthy investors than ever before, and they were on the watch for interesting business ventures. India beckoned, as did the Argentine and other parts of the undeveloped world. But none could compare with opportunities in the United States. The postwar boom not only attracted British capital to American railroads and manufacturing companies, but also to the West. In the three years prior to the 1873 panic, sixty-seven British firms registered with the Board of Trade to carry on mining and related enterprises in the Plains and Far West. Railroads and mining seemed certain to succeed, but in the post-panic years, London and Edinburgh turned increasingly to cattle and land.

As had been the case with eastern Americans, the British were attracted to the Plains by a variety of factors, and a combination of business and emotional considerations.

The prosperous British Isles of the 1860s demanded beef for its inhabitants, more than the industrializing British economy could provide. During this period anthrax was striking the European herds, killing off tens of thousands of heads of cattle. The combination of an increased demand and a smaller supply resulted in much higher prices for meat products, and Britain turned to the United States for increased supplies of foodstuffs. In 1870, the United States exported $21 million worth of meat products, much of it to Britain. The development of refrigerated cargo spaces in oceangoing ships was rushed to take advantage of this demand, and to eliminate the need for immediate sale of meat on landing. This enabled the importers to hold back product until prices were right and maximize profits, and exporters to increase their own profit margins.

In the panic year of 1873, the United States sent $71 million in beef overseas, along with thousands of heads of cattle, both for slaughter in Europe and to help restock the European ranges. Meat exports went past the $100 million mark in 1877, $32 million more than the value of American wheat and flour sent overseas. Between 1877 and 1879, shipments of cattle increased almost threefold, with more than 60 percent going to Britain. American meat products were becoming a major item in foreign trade, and the English and Scots were intrigued with the idea of investing in ranches so as to profit better from the increased demand and prices.

Romanticism also played a role in the equation. Like the United States, Britain was caught up in the rush of Social Darwinist thought—after all, both Darwin and Spencer were Englishmen, not Americans. The Empire seemed proof of British supremacy, but new worlds were there to be conquered, and none seemed so attractive as the American West. Cowboy and Indian stories, and tales of western desperado bands, excited the British even more than Americans. Like their American counterparts, British investors became interested in sending their money to the West, even when they themselves could not or would not go.

The very geography of the West attracted the English and Scots. As a nation with an agrarian past and industrial future, the English looked back to the West as a symbol of lost virtues. The Scots had still more reason to feel at home on the Plains. Many Scotsmen who had settled there wrote of how similar it appeared to the Lowlands, and Scots visitors during the 1870s said as much. John Clay, a Scotsman who came to America in 1879 and returned often to oversee western investments, said he was at ease only in Tweed and parts of Wyoming. More than any other European of his day, Clay knew the Plains and loved the region, speaking of its "champagne air." In a letter to an American, Clay wrote, "There was a freedom, a romance, a sort of mystic halo hanging over those green, grassy, swelling divides that was impregnated, grafted into, your system. . . . It was another world." Many years later, Clay reflected on why the Scots were so interested in overseas investments.

> The Scotch, who are supposed to be one of the most thrifty races on the globe, are on the other hand the most speculative. Not the speculation you see at Monte Carlo, French Lick, or Palm Beach—their young men reach out from inclination and necessity. They are progressive and aggressive, and they will venture anywhere in the pursuit of commerce. "Never venture, never win," is printed on their flag. This love of money-making, enterprise you might call it, was not confined to the wanderers on foreign shores. The businessman at home, the staid steady-going yet successful merchant, farmer, lawyer, doctor, down to the candlestick maker, were always willing to invest their bit of money and take a chance.

Or as the *Statist* put it in 1885:

> In Edinburgh, Dundee, and Aberdeen it would be perfectly safe to bet on any man you pass in the street with an income of over three hundred a year being familiar with the fluctuations of Grand Trunks, and having quite as much as he can afford staked on . . . Prairies, or some kindred gamble. A dividend of twenty per cent or more is to a Scotchman of this class a bait which he cannot resist.

The Scots, then, were interested in investment, and didn't mind sending their money out of the country if high interest rates could be obtained there. They were willing to take risks—gambles, if you will—but at the same time retained an element of caution. These factors not only encouraged investment in America, but helped determine the forms.

Scotland had been deeply affected by the Industrial Revolution. Many former farmers had gone to the cities to enter manufacture and commerce and had made fortunes in business. Edinburgh had become a significant capital market. Dundee had large financial reserves, much of which came through involvement with jute manufacture in Scotland and India. Glasgow was equally wealthy and eager for investment opportunities.

Leaders of Scotland's newly arrived commercial and industrial aristocracy also knew their limitations. They wanted to invest in areas and places they knew well, and in businesses they could dominate. They were wary of American investments in the early 1870s. The Americans had a long record of fiscal irresponsibility and took bankruptcy rather lightly. The Americans used greenbacks as well as gold, a certain sign of a shaky financial system at the time. What if American investment turned out well? Would their owners be able to repatriate their earnings in the future if an American Congress decided against it? What of the various states and territories? Might they pass laws against foreign investment the Congress and President could not overturn? Many Scots interested in American investment had a knowledge of banking and foreign trade, but knew little of American railroads, mines, ranches, and the like. Expert knowledge was needed for investment in America, and the Scots were wise enough to realize most of them lacked it. Professional management of foreign investments was not only needed, but the need was recognized.

The Scottish banking system was one of the finest and most secure in the world. The Scots pioneered in the acceptance of small sums for deposit from middle-class pèople, the payment of interest, and the differentiation of accounts and liabilities to accommodate the needs of different classes of depositors. The Scottish banks were safe, and Scotsmen were used to dealing in small bills in ordinary transactions at a time when many people in other countries still preferred gold coins. The banks would take small sums from depositors and use them to lend to incipient capitalists and invest in Scottish and foreign enterprises. As early as 1793, an observer could write, "The general prosperity of the country and the facilities of procuring money on credit has promoted an uncommon spirit of enterprise of late and multiplied and extended manufactures of all kinds." By the early 1870s, the Scots were more sophisticated in banking techniques than almost any other country in the world, and Scotsmen were used to pooling their funds in banks and similar institutions.

The early investment trusts were natural fruits of such conditions. In England joint-stock companies still functioned, and the corporate form was developing. They flourished in Scotland, too, but at the same time a new form was developing: the investment trust, the ancestor of today's mutual funds. Scotland's manufacturers and merchants, eager to invest in overseas enterprises but lacking sufficient expertise to determine which had true merit, would hire professionals in the field to make investments for them. Middle-class Scotsmen would be able to purchase shares in these companies, in much the same way as they deposited money in banks. "In Scotland men who had made fortunes in commerce and industry but who had limited understanding of investment depended upon the counsel of a financial agent residing in London or Edinburgh."*

William Menzies, an Edinburgh lawyer and financier, was interested in the United States as a country with many investment possibilities. He had visited the United States in 1864, 1867, and 1872, and on his return from the last trip wrote:

> The growth of America in population, resources, and wealth, is too well known to require any statement. . . . The wonderful fertility of the virgin soil, the multitude and variety of its productions and manufactures, the rapid development of its railroad system . . . and the enormous immigration taking place in America, all combine to the development of almost illimitable resources and the creation of material wealth.

*W. Turrentine Jackson, *The Enterprising Scot: Investors in the American West After 1873* (Edinburgh, 1968), p. 10.

Early in 1873 Menzies gathered nine of his associates to form the Scottish-American Investment Company, whose purpose it was to invest in American securities. The company's nominal capital was £1 million, divided into 100,000 shares of £10 each. Half the shares were taken up, and £2 called on each.* Scottish-American soon after purchased shares in eleven midwestern and far western railroads, and sought other opportunities elsewhere.

Another company, with different objectives but similar form, was organized by two Chicago lawyers interested in real estate. Recognizing the large pool of untapped wealth in Scotland and high mortgage rates in America, they proposed to bring the two together. Chicago had been swept by the great fire of 1871, and was in desperate need of mortgage money. With this in mind, Henry Sheldon and Daniel Hale, the Americans, approached James Duncan Smith, a Scots lawyer, with their proposal. Together they formed the Scottish-American Mortgage Company in 1874, which was capitalized at £1 million pounds. "It does not require a very intimate knowledge of finances to understand that, if we can borrow in this country at 4½ and 5 per cent and advance in Chicago at 8 per cent there is a substantial profit," said the trust's chairman, James Guthrie Smith. "Any schoolboy could tell that."

Other companies followed, and the Scottish financial invasion of the United States was under way. In 1879 Congress passed legislation resuming specie payments, and this added to confidence in America. By 1880, four Edinburgh trusts had some £2.2 million invested in American securities and notes, while the Dundee-based trusts provided an additional £2 million.

Such was the situation in the late 1870s and early 1880s, when the cattle boom was beginning and exports to Britain increased sharply. After specie resumption, American securities rose sharply, and Scots investors, considering both the high price of securities and the relatively low prices of land and steers, sent agents to America to inves-

*It was the practice at the time for a subscriber to purchase shares and have only a portion of the subscription taken up. The shareholder would then be responsible for raising the rest of the subscription on demand.

tigate the Plains. Soon the prairies were dotted with agents, Scots newspaper reporters, and members of the Royal Commission on Agriculture, which included John Clay as one of its number. The commissioners concluded that the range was abundantly provided with sweet grasses, free for the taking. Water rights were either cheap or free. Government policy seemed geared to Indian removal or extermination, and the buffalo were disappearing from the range, to be replaced by steers. "It is generally acknowledged that the average profit of the stockowner has been for years 33 per cent. No doubt this is the most remunerative branch of American farming, but to secure the greatest return a large amount of money must be employed," concluded the commissioners. "With regard to cattle, for the present the American stockman in the West is possessed of singular advantages; land for nothing and abundance of it." The earl of Airlie, chairman of the Scottish-American Mortgage Company, visited America in 1880, and the following year told his stockbrokers, "It is not uncommon for a cattle breeder to clear 80 or even 100 per cent a year on his capital."

The English were first to act. In London the Anglo-American Cattle Company had already been formed, and the Colorado Mortgage and Investment Company of London had registered the Colorado Ranche Company Ltd. But these had failed because of poor organization and capitalization. The Scots were convinced they could do better.

Several important Scottish firms organized western ranches in the next few years. The Scottish-American Mortgage Company registered the Prairie Cattle Company in 1880, and capitalized it at £200,000. In its prospectus, profits of from 25 to 40 percent were projected. In Dundee the Texas Land and Cattle Company was organized in 1881, and soon after purchased a ranch with 236,000 acres in the southern tip of Texas. The Matador Land and Cattle Company, also a Dundee operation, took over the assets of the Matador Cattle Company, a Texas ranch organized in 1879. Matador was valued by its owners at between $1.2 and $1.3 million, a generous appraisal. Yet the Scots and Texans were able to sell

£400,000 worth of its stock in 1882, and Matador shares quickly rose to a premium. The Hansford Land and Cattle Company followed, as did the Wyoming Cattle Ranche Company, the Western American Cattle Company, the Missouri Land and Livestock Company, the American Cattle Company, and many more, all in the period of less than two years. The boom was on.

Westerners watched the phenomenon with great interest. They had expected the Plains to fill up, and knew profits could be derived from cattle. But the steers had been followed by eastern investors, and selling such individuals land and cattle proved even more lucrative than grazing steers and shipping them to market. Now there was this English and Scots invasion, and the westerners got the message: if the investment communities in New York, Boston, Dundee, and Edinburgh wanted land and cattle, they would sell. Further, they would manage the ranches for sizable fees, market the cattle, and keep books. Regular reports would be sent to the East and Britain. Should the easterners and foreigners want to visit their holdings, or come to the West seeking new lands and beef for purchase, they would show them around and then sell the profit-hungry and romance-crazed dudes all they could take.

The road to ranches led to Cheyenne, which had become the heart of the cattle kingdom of the Plains. The Cheyenne Club, whose membership consisted of the leading ranchers and businessmen of the area, was at the center of town, and it was there the outsiders were taken to be sold ranches and steers. Over caviar, French wines, and thick steaks, hundreds of thousands of acres passed hands, going from west to east, and at the same time millions of dollars were deposited in the accounts of western ranchers, who only a few years earlier had been cowboys working for $15 a month. Cheyenne itself boomed, and was talked of as "The New York of the Mountains." One reporter, viewing the scene in 1882, wrote:

> Sixteenth Street is a young Wall Street. Millions are talked of as lightly as nickels and all kinds of people are dabbling in steers. The chief justice of the Supreme Court has recently succumbed to the contagion and gone out to purchase a $40,000 herd. . . . A

> Cheyenne man who don't pretend to know a maverick from a mandamus has made a neat little margin of $15,000 this summer in small transactions and hasn't seen a cow yet that he has bought and sold.

The new investors were convinced they could become rich quickly in the West. They were correct in believing a great deal of money could be made in the land and cattle business. And westerners would make it, if not from cattle raising, from selling land and cattle to ignorant, uninformed, or naïve outlanders.*

American commission merchants, some of whom were experienced in dealing with the cattlemen, were also eager to work with the easterners and Europeans. Joseph Rosenbaum, a successful Chicago merchant, was one of these, and he handled several eastern accounts. Frank L. Underwood of Kansas City corresponded with English and Scots financiers, invited them to visit the range as his guest, entertained them, and managed to extract millions in investment capital before they went home. The Wood Brothers, also of Kansas City, had several major accounts. Francis Smith & Co., with offices in Indianapolis, San Antonio, and Memphis, was a major factor in the business. Smith visited Edinburgh and Dundee when the boom was first beginning and managed to talk several Scottish firms into giving him their business. The Scottish-American Mortgage Company and the Dundee Mortgage and Trust Investment Company, two of the biggest, were connected with Smith & Co., and at one point Smith was managing between $12 million and $14 million of Scottish and English funds. Smith even managed to talk several prominent Wall Streeters into taking flings in cattle. For a while

*Westerners had obtained experience in selling properties to the British during the mining boom of the previous generation. In 1871 a British traveler wrote: "English capitalists have either become less circumspect and prudent, or else American owners of mining properties have grown more ingenious and plausible, for the eagerness of the former to purchase such properties is only equaled by the readiness of the latter to part with them." Clark C. Spence, *British Investment and the American Mining Frontier, 1860–1901* (Ithaca, 1958), p. 4.

money flowed out of stocks and bonds in New York to the western range. Rufus Hatch, considered one of the the shrewdest market operators of his day, was convinced there was more to be made on the range than among the bulls and bears of Wall Street, and he led others to the same conclusion.

As a result, there were two kinds of speculation taking place simultaneously. Nonwesterners would speculate on cattle in the Great Plains. At the same time, westerners speculated on sales to the eager investors. In the process, the supposedly unsophisticated cattlemen bested the wily Scots, worldly English, and some of the best wheelers and dealers Wall Street ever produced.

Alexander Hamilton Swan, a Wyoming rancher who together with his seven brothers owned a large spread, was one such individual. He was fifty-two years old in 1883 when he arrived in Edinburgh to meet with Scots investors. Himself of Scots and Welsh ancestry, Swan had been born in Pennsylvania, and his family had moved westward soon after. For a while he was in the feed business, and it was there he learned of cattle raising. Swan went west afterward, and by 1872 had become a fixture on the Plains. The Scots considered him a "veteran," and were fascinated by this "Scots-Cowboy."

Swan owned three ranches, capitalized at less than $2 million in 1883. He combined them into the Swan Land and Cattle Company Ltd., and it was this firm he represented in Edinburgh, and shares of which he hoped to sell. The new company was capitalized at $3 million, with 60,000 shares offered at $50 each. In his prospectus Swan claimed to have 108,763 head of cattle and spoke of a range of 4.5 million acres. But not a head of cattle had been counted, and Swan owned only 6,037 acres with an additional 24,813 acres in the process of acquisition. Thomas Lawson, a Scots farmer who worked with Swan, wrote a glowing report of the ranch, which he claimed consisted of a "solid block of land about 130 miles long by 42 miles broad at the east end and widening out to about 100 miles at the west end."

The Scots were convinced Swan was a genius. Colin J. Mackenzie, a landed proprietor and director of the British Linen Company Bank, agreed to serve as chairman of the company. The directors included Hugh Beckett, a director of Nobel's Explosive Company and James Wilson, a merchant with interests in China. Swan was also a director, and would manage the ranch.

The Swan stock sold well. The Scots paid $2.4 million for the property, with the rest being taken up by Americans or retained by the old management. Swan pledged to pay a dividend of 9 percent, small when compared with the 26 percent offered by Prairie and similar rates by other companies. Swan explained that his was a growth situation. Most of the earnings would be plowed back into the company, which he expected to become the largest in America.

The Swan Ranch would never approach in size the XIT of Texas, another American company for sale in Britain. The XIT originated in the late 1870s, when Texas decided to erect the largest and most spectacular capitol in the United States, but lacked the money for the job. The state did own land, 3.5 million acres of which was in the dry and dusty Panhandle. It was decided to offer this land in exchange for construction of the capitol. Advertisements for bids were sent out, and after some spirited give and take, the winner was Taylor, Babcock & Co. of Chicago. As the Texans suspected, none of the firm's partners had seen the land. Indeed, only one partner, Abner Taylor, was a practical engineer. It was he who supervised construction of the capitol at Austin, which was completed at a cost in excess of $3 million.

Amos Babcock, another partner, was an Illinois politician who dreamed of the Presidency. John Farwell, a third partner, was a Chicago merchant prince. The fourth member of the firm, John's brother Charles, was a congressman with ambitions for the Senate, and the company's financial guide.

Charles Farwell organized the Capitol Freehold Land and Investment Company Ltd., and went to Britain to find buyers for its shares. The company was described in glowing terms, with stress on the size of the range, the excellent quality of Panhandle grass, and the number of cattle it could feed once it was stocked. The earl of Aberdeen and Henry Seton-Karr joined the board of directors, while the marquis of Tweeddale, a prominent Scots banker, became its chairman. With their help, Farwell sold his stock, pocketing a small fortune in the process.

The Swan and XIT completed their financings in 1884, which also marked the end of the investment boom for cattle securities in Edinburgh, Dundee, and London. By then some of the problems of ranching were dawning on investors, who in the past had been dazzled by promises. Still, the returns were good in 1884, and would continue to be so in 1885. The owner of a share of Prairie stock, for example, had been called upon to pay only half the share's face value of £10. The company had paid a dividend of 20½ percent in 1883, 10 percent in 1884, and would pay another 10 percent in 1884. These dividends were declared on the face value, not the paid-in subscription, and so the actual return was double the published figures. This meant that the three-year payment on Prairie was really 81 percent of the subscription. Another dividend like that of 1884 or 1885, and the shareholder would have received his total investment in dividends, and still retain a valuable share which was rising in value. The situation at other ranches was good, although none approached the Prairie statistics.

Statistics for Selected English and Scots Cattle Companies Operating in the United States 1883-1885

Company	Total Herd	Shares		Annual Dividends in Percent		
		Amount	Paid	1883	1884	1885
Prairie	124,212	£10	£ 5	20½	10	10
Swan	123,460	10	6	9	10	6
Texas	106,322	10	5	12½	6	5
Matador	94,441	10	6	8	6	7
Hansford	37,734	5	5	6	7	—
Arkansas	24,315	10	5	10	—	—
Pastoral	45,885	10	5	—	8	5
Powder River	48,625	5	5	6	4	—
Western Land	35,469	100	100	15	15	10
Cattle Ranche	13,500	5	5	—	—	5
Western Ranche	18,050	5	5	—	7	4

Source: *London Economist,* March 20, 1886, in Ernest Osgood, *The Day of the Cattleman* (Minneapolis, 1929), p. 82.

There were several reasons for the end of the bull market in American cattle shares. One of these was the glut of shares on the Edinburgh, Dundee, Glasgow, London and other British securities exchanges. Most of those who had wanted such securities were fully invested by 1884, and so demand declined. More important, however, was the steadily increasing price of American beef. The new ranches purchased steers and cows to stock their ranges, thus competing with the meat-packers and driving prices up. The strong demand in Europe earlier in the decade had accomplished the same end, making it possible for European meat to compete with American in terms of price.

The most important factor was the difficulty Scots and English investors had with their American cousins who managed the ranches. Accurate cattle counts were almost impossible to get, and the Americans consistently overstated them. The Europeans were becoming convinced their books were being rigged, and in many cases they were right. Such investors were at the mercy of the ranch managers, and no amount of correspondence would serve to change the situation. In February 1884, the *Economist* noted that although the quotations of some cattle companies were down, sixteen of them—including Swan, Arkansas, Powder River, Matador, and Prairie—were selling above their offering prices. This proved "that a well managed American cattle and land, or ranche, undertaking can be conducted profitably by a British joint stock company." But the English and Scots members of the boards of directors were coming to think otherwise. Guthrie Smith resigned as chairman of the board at Prairie, and others followed. The Wyoming Cattle Ranche was sued by its investors for falsifying books.

Economic and financial difficulties were complicated by political action directed against the Scottish and English companies and ranches. Many westerners, especially the small ranchers, resented the giant firms, which were coming to dominate the range and were controlled by foreigners. They petitioned state legislatures and Congress to enforce alien laws and pass new ones to restrict further investment and control that which already existed. There were rumors that Senator George Edmunds of Vermont would introduce a bill limiting foreign land holdings to thirty square miles. President Chester Arthur was fascinated with the Plains, and was generally pro-cattlemen, but seemed to agree that foreign holdings would have to be held down. Secretary of the Interior Samuel Kirkwood of Iowa said in July 1884 that "It is contrary to national policy, and would be antagonistic to the sentiments of the country, to permit the appropriation of public lands in large quantities, by individuals or corporations, whether native or foreign."

It was an election year in America, and alien rights figured in the campaign. Both parties called for new legislation in this field. Republican James Blaine, after winning his party's nomination, coined the slogan, "America for the Americans," while Democrat Grover Cleveland spoke bluntly of the need to limit foreign land holdings. The Montana state legislature was discussing such restrictions in 1884, and the following year passed one such measure, denying land ownership to corporations whose stock had been sold to foreigners—20 percent such ownership was accepted, but the legislature considered a new measure to deny ownership of land to any land company with foreigners on its board.

The antialien activity would not die with the election of Cleveland.* Instead, it grew in intensity, and Scots and English

* This American fear and dislike of foreign investment in the mid-1880s was similar to Canadian reactions to American investments in their country in the early 1970s. In both cases the foreign money was invited in, but afterward considered an unwarranted intervention in the host country's affairs. *The New York Times,* addressing itself to the Scots and English on April 11, 1887, sounded not unlike Toronto and Montreal newspapers of today.

> Foreign investors should understand the American people do not desire to shut down European capital, but propose that it shall be invested, if invested at all, honestly and in accordance with the spirit of our institutions. They are not willing that it shall be used to support those who steal the public land or for the establishment of vast estates upon which American citizens can live only as tenants of a foreign owner.

And Senator Preston Plumb of Kansas echoed such sentiments. Like *The Times,* he wanted to remain on good terms with the British. But he didn't want them to own too large a share of American land. "If no acre of American soil was owned by a foreigner I should still be in favor of enacting a positive prohibition against such ownership in the future," he said. "I think myself that we offer inducements enough to people to come to this country. . . ."

investors came to realize they were not welcome in the Plains. Anglo-American relations were strained, and shares of international companies fell on the European exchanges. This too acted to dampen the boom in American cattle shares.

Foreign investors were to have difficulties with President Cleveland throughout his first administration, but the ranchers were even more troubled when he came to office in 1885. Arthur had favored the ranchers, at the expense of the Indians and others who inhabited the range, including farmers and sheepmen. Cleveland reversed this policy. The ranchers had taken Indian land, driven them from open ranges, and destroyed their buffalo. Not only that, they had transgressed Indian lands without asking permission, and were violating federal law by grazing cattle on government preserves. When Cleveland learned of this he was irate. General Philip Sheridan, who shared his feelings, was ordered to expel the cattlemen from the lands they had taken illegally, and on July 23, 1885, Cleveland gave them forty days' notice to take some 200,000 head of cattle from Indian and government lands. The order was just but the time limitation severe. The cattle were driven to overgrazed ranges to the south, where many died in the months that followed. This was yet another sign that ranching was as much hard reality as romance.

Cleveland also ordered the army to assist homesteaders against the cattlemen. Farmers had taken land under the Homestead Act, gone west, constructed their sod huts, and then attempted to fence in their holdings. These were cut down by the cattlemen, who argued they were there first, and in any case, their herds could not survive without access to the farmlands. For years range associations had acted in this manner; now they would be stopped.

Land Commissioner William Sparks led the attack. "The demand for free land for the homes of American citizens, which is daily increasing in intensity, can no longer be met, unless unpatented lands now unlawfully held or claimed can be recovered to the public domain, and future illegal and fraudulent appropriations decisively stopped." So said Sparks in his annual report for 1885. Cleveland responded by issuing orders against ranchers who had illegally taken government lands, ordering the protection of farmers, and the cutting down of fences erected on government land by ranchers wanting to keep it for their own. Sparks went about purging his office of procattle employees, ending squatting on federal land, and uncovering previous bribes and wrongdoing. The net result of Sparks's actions was to cripple further the cattle industry and add to the woes of foreign investors.

Adding to the cattlemen's problems was a new outbreak of tick disease. The Texas and Plains cattle carried the tick but were not affected by it. If introduced to the eastern ranges, however, the disease could kill off thousands of head of cattle. In the spring of 1885, the disease appeared in Kansas, and that state banned entry of Texas cattle for the rest of the year. State militia appeared on the border to enforce the rule, which meant that a goodly part of the "crop" had to be kept on the range that winter, causing profits to fall even more.

All of this should have warned not only the cattlemen, but also the foreign and eastern investors as well, that there were problems on the range. Overproduction, disease, political complications, the inability to get good accounting—these were the hallmarks of an industry gone sour. In 1884 the cowboys organized and demanded higher wages, rustling increased as the price of cattle went up, and losses mounted. Yet there remained those who insisted that these problems could be overcome, and they attempted to spark new enthusiasm in the range.

One of them was Baron Walter von Richthofen, uncle of the future German air ace of World War I fame. Richthofen came to Colorado in the 1870s and entered enthusiastically into the bonanza spirit. He organized the Western Land Company and tried his hand at ranching, with mixed success and failure. In 1885, when the business was souring, Richthofen published *Cattle Raising on the Plains of North America,* which enjoyed great popularity in the East and in Europe. The book was similar to Brisbin's and others published earlier, filled with tales of great fortunes made in the past and to be had in the future.

> The immense profits which have been universally realized in the Western cattle business for the past, and which will be

> increased in the future, owing to the more economical methods pursued, so long as ranges can be purchased at present prices, may seem incredible to many of my readers, who, no doubt, have considered the stories of the fortunes realized as myths. Yet it is true that many men who started only a few years ago with comparatively few cattle, are now wealthy, and, in some cases, millionaires. They certainly did not find the gold upon the prairies, nor did they have any source of revenue beyond the increase of their cattle. The agencies producing this immense wealth are very natural and apparent.

Another foreigner, the marquis de Mores, entered ranching in the Dakotas in 1883 and soon learned the hazards of the business. These could be overcome, he thought, if the beeves were slaughtered on the range, processed there, and then shipped east on the railroads. The Northern Pacific was a fine line, ever-growing, and could serve as a perfect vehicle for this beef. Transportation costs would be cut, disease would be a fear of the past, and huge profits could be realized by. owners of processing plants. The marquis envisaged dozens of such plants in the Plains and mountain states, each at the heart of a range, and all benefiting not only themselves, but the ranchers as well. Teddy Roosevelt, still in the Dakotas on his ranch, was intrigued by the plan, and lent it his support. De Mores raised $1.5 million to initiate his program, which was put into operation in 1886.

Richthofen could not have released his book at a worse time, nor could De Mores have picked a poorer year for investments on the range—1886 was to be a disaster, and 1887, even worse.

Cattlemen were troubled during the early fall of 1886. Beef prices on the Chicago market were low, and falling all the time, the result of increased production and lower-than-usual demand. There had been another financial panic in New York in 1884, and although it was not as severe as that of 1873, some effects were felt, lowering meat demand. Cattle evicted from the range by President Cleveland's order were being dumped on the market, and this complicated matters, too. In 1882 steer on the hoof had sold for $9 a hundred pounds. By late spring of 1885 the price had fallen to $5, and then to $3 during the summer. By early fall quotations were at $1.80, the lowest since 1873. Some ranches were failing. Others were on the financial tightrope, hoping to wait out the decline, praying for some kind of respite from economic and financial pressures.

It had been a hot and dry summer, so that the grazing was bad throughout the Plains. Old-time cowhands remarked on the fact, and predicted the winter would make up for it by being particularly harsh. There were signs of this, visible only to such men who were used to seeking them. The ducks and geese, which normally flew south in October, had left a month early. Arctic owls, which usually appeared in Nebraska only during bad years, were seen in great numbers. Deer, antelope, wolves, and horses were growing long coats, a sure sign of bad weather brewing. Halos were seen around the sun in Wyoming, and the superstitious saw these as an evil omen.

The prairie was still that October. The usual wet snowstorms of that month did not come, and instead the air was warm, even balmy. Then came the change, suddenly. At the end of the first week in November, it began to snow in the Dakotas, and the storm quickly spread southward, accompanied by strong winds. It was a fine, powdery snow, that was swept into crevices in farmhouse walls, leaving drifts inside. The drifts appeared in the valleys, some more than a dozen feet deep, trapping steers, cows, and calves in their midst. Many died, suffocated in the snows.

Then the snow stopped, but the winds continued. In the past such storms had been followed by warmer weather, allowing the snow to melt. This did not happen in late November. Instead there was another snowstorm, worse than the first. Houses collapsed under the weight of snow on the roof, and others were blown over. Experienced cowmen ventured into the storm to seek their cattle, and couldn't find their way back to the houses, freezing to death less than a hundred feet from safety. Other storms followed, each worse than the one before. Ranch hands knew the bad weather meant the destruction of hundreds of thousands of head of cattle, but they could only guess as to the numbers, for it was impossible to venture outside for more than a few hours at a time. Some spoke of seeing cattle struggling along on stumps of legs, the hooves having frozen solid and snapped. In the Panhandle the snow gathered by the fences, blocking the way of the herds as they moved about seeking shelter. The cattle stampeded in the storm, and thousands ran off cliffs into ravines, where the carcasses would be found the next spring, heaped one on top of another for many feet. In many western towns the people struggled to churches to pray. The chinook, the warm wind from the north which blew down into the valleys every year to signal the end of winter by melting the snows, was late in coming, and the townsfolk prayed for it. The chinook did not come that February, as had been the experience in the past. An Englishwoman with a ranch in Montana noted the prayers with interest, but was more concerned with the cattle. If ranchers spent more time in tending their herds than in talking, she thought, conditions might be bettered.

> It's a great shame the way people neglect their cattle here. Those which are right back in the hills where the grass is good do well enough; but those which are here among the settlements, where feed is so scarce, ought to be fed. . . . What these cattle live on is a mystery. Certainly they pick over the litter which is thrown out of our stable; that and dry twigs is all they can possibly get. It will be interesting to watch if they get through the winter. If they *do,* I'm sure no one need ever be afraid of cattle not making their own living out here all the year around. I saw in the *Field* the other day, that an English farmer had got three weeks' imprisonment for starving a cow. I shrewdly suspect that a good many Montana cattle-men would spend their whole lives in prison at that rate.

This woman had little idea of how the cattlemen truly felt about the great blizzard. They saw their herds vanish, their houses destroyed, and their fortunes disappear. They took all this well, with the air of a gambler who hadn't drawn good cards, but realized it was the breaks of the game. A typical reaction was that of a Dakota rancher, who wrote to a neighbor who picked the right time to be out of the country.

> Dear Pierre,
>
> No news, except that Dave Brown killed Dick Smith and your wife's hired girl blew her brains out in the kitchen. Everything's O.K. here.
>
> Yours truly,
> Henry Jackson

Or the sentiments of Granville Stuart, a hardy Montana stockman who suffered silently through the storm. Later on, Stuart wrote, "A business that had been fascinating to me before, suddenly became distasteful. I never wanted to own again an animal that I could not feed and shelter." Another rancher put his thoughts to rhyme:

> I may not see a hundred
> Before I see the Styx,
> But coal or ember, I'll remember
> Eighteen-eighty six.
>
> The stiff heaps in the coulee,
> The dead eyes in the camp,
> And the wind about, blowing fortunes out
> As a woman blows out a lamp.

Throughout the late spring of 1887 ranchers gathered their remaining stock and buried the swollen carcasses of the dead, locating them by following vultures that hovered above the bodies, and then swept down to pick at them. Some steers had wandered onto the ice covering a small lake when one of the storms began. Then their hooves froze into the ice and they were stuck there, and died. When the ice melted the bodies filled the lake, creating a horrendous sight and smell. Most water holes and lakes were filled with cattle, and mounds could be seen by ranchers who went there to seek their remaining steers and cows. For years stories were swapped of sights on the Plains in those days. Cowboys claimed they could ride from Kingsley, Kansas, to Colorado, using carcasses as their path and never touch grass, soil, or rock.

After the storm John Hollicot, manager of the great LX Ranch, the queen of the Panhandle, rode out to survey the damage. He claimed to have found an average of 250 dead steers and cows per mile along his thirty-five-foot fence. The dead stock were skinned on the spot—little else could be reclaimed—and the cowhides were cured and sent to town, and from there to the East, in the hope of salvaging something from the investment. Cowhide became a drug on the market, however, and the price dropped quickly. By the summer of 1887 new shipments went unsold, and the steers were total losses.

Some 100,000 head were lost in northern Nebraska alone, while a major Kansas ranch, accustomed to branding 10,000 calves a year, found only 900 that spring. Another which put out 20,000 head to graze in the fall found only 2,500 six months later. The Continental Cattle Company recovered a mere 100 head of its more than 32,000, and the story was the same throughout the plains—utter disaster.

John Clay thought some 30 percent of all northern cattle had been lost, while others offered higher estimates. Later on Clay wrote of the disaster:

> It was simply appalling, and the cowmen could not realize their position. From southern Colorado to the Canadian line, from the one-hundredth meridian almost to the Pacific slope, it was a catastrophe which the cowmen of today who did not go through it can never understand. Three great streams of ill luck, mismanagement, and greed met together—in other words, recklessness, want of foresight, and the weather, which no man can control.

The cattlemen survived, and some even told jokes about the debacle. One that made the rounds was of a cattle king whose entire holding had been destroyed, and whose family and hired help had little food to last until the next train arrived in the spring. The rancher went to church to pray for the chinook, but ended his prayer with one for outside assistance. "Oh, God! Soften the hearts of the people in the East to send us barrels of flour, barrels of coffee, barrels of molasses, barrels of meal, barrels of port, barrels of beans, barrels of sugar, barrels of vinegar, barrels of salt, barrels of pepper . . ."

At this a neighbor interrupted. "That's away to hell too much pepper!"

Another tale was of a group of ranchers who entered a saloon after viewing their range. Cheer up, said a bartender. The cattle may be dead, "but they haven't frozen the books." Show a good report, he implied, and the easterners and foreigners will shower you with new funds.

But the money did not come, and throughout the northern range fears of foreclosure suddenly became real.

Many ranchers went bankrupt in the months that followed, and the great beef bonanza, which had dazzled the Scots and English, was ended. Shareholders rushed to sell, causing major collapses on the Edinburgh and Dundee exchanges. Money seemed to go into hiding, and once highly desirable ranches could be had for mortgage payments.

Quotations for Representative Cattle Company Shares 1886-1887

Company	**Price on February 21, 1886**	**Price on February 21, 1887**
Arkansas	43/9	15/0
Hansford	85/0	30/0
Matador	105/0	72/6
Prairie	80/0	26/0
Swan	105/0	45/0
Texas	87/6	32/6
Western Ranches	70/0	61/0

Source: Jackson, *Enterprising Scot*, p. 121.

Some ranchers were saved from ruin by the agents, especially Clay and Joseph Rosenbaum. Clay reorganized several ranches, including the Swan, and put them back on their feet, while extending aid to others. Rosenbaum's assistance was even more dramatic. On learning of the extent of the disaster, he went to Helena and called a meeting of his clients, all of whom owed him money which had been secured by mortgages. They came, expecting to receive foreclosures. Instead Rosenbaum told them he would carry their notes until better times, and he lent them a total of a million dollars to help restock their range. For the moment, at least, these men were saved.*

One additional blow awaited the ranchers. Gathering what little cattle they could spare, they shipped them to the packinghouses. But the midwestern corn crop had been destroyed by the storms, and the steers had little upon which to feed. As a result, many were rejected, while the rest fetched low prices. Later on, Plains cattle had to compete with the steers from south Texas, which had not been affected by the storms. By October steers were fetching $1.70 per hundred pounds on the hoof while cows went for $1.25.

In time the Plains ranchers would recover, but never again would they experience a boom like that of the early 1880s. Fortunes had been made on the range during that period, and in a very short period of time. Still greater fortunes would be amassed after 1890, but these grew slowly, and they were the fruits of hard work, not stock flotations.

The Scots and English had learned their lesson, and, like their forebears after the canal boom, cursed the Americans and vowed never again to buy an American security. They kept this pledge—but their sons were back in the market in the early twentieth century.

In writing of the range and cattle industry, the *Fortnightly Review* of April 1887 spoke of the future. The journal had faith in the American economy and in the West's potential. Like so many other British publications, it realized a new period was beginning on the range, and a new force had come to replace the cowmen. In his own way, the writer of this article wrote finis to the bonanza.

* The cattlemen never forgot Rosenbaum's help. During the 1907 panic, when Rosenbaum faced ruin, the Montana cattlemen raised a million dollars to help him cover his losses.

* * *

No doubt there is money in cattle yet, but the halcyon days of enormous fortunes rapidly made are past. Well watered and adequately sheltered grazing lands have become difficult to find. Year by year the acreage over which cattle can range decreases. The granger with his spade and plough drives before him the cattle-man, who himself in former years drove out the aboriginal Indian.

CHAPTER 6

The Steel Millionaires

Nineteenth-century Americans are often portrayed as men and women who did not shrink from challenges. They seem to have viewed their country as a wild, untamed place, where opportunities for advancement were more abundant than anywhere else on earth, and where those who could do so clawed their way to the top. Such people would seek challenges. They were born speculators.

To accept a challenge is to speculate on the future. Of course, not all speculations were equal in worth, or all speculators equal in status. The rancher who took the land, raised cattle, marketed them, and in the process created a business empire, was admired. He had produced something worthwhile where formerly there had been a desert, and this was an accomplishment Americans could understand and respect. But what of the banker who backed him, the investment company which purchased shares in the ranch, or the lawyers who helped organize it? These men, too, were risk-takers, yet they were ignored or even despised.

We empathize with the rancher who lost all he had worked for in the great blizzard, yet we think little of the investors whose shares sank to a fraction of their previous worth. But both the rancher and investor were speculators. In fact, the latter may be more deserving of our sympathy. All he was guilty of was greed, while the ranchers were equally greedy, and also fraudulent in many cases. Similarly, we identify more with the miners of Washoe than the bankers of San Francisco, the men who built the Erie Canal than those who financed it, and the Americans who wandered through what they hoped would become Vandalia than the Englishmen who remained in London and helped organize the scheme. Even the southern slaveholders have had their defenders in romantic novels and motion pictures, while few have good words for slave traders.

There are many explanations for these attitudes, none of which is completely convincing. All we are left with is the feeling that Americans admire men and women who create something worthwhile by taking the land or other tangible things and transforming them into assets of great value. We distrust others who amass fortunes or take power by creating something out of what seems to be nothing. When the price of a steer rises rapidly, we praise the rancher for his foresight in raising such animals; when the price of a security doubles, we call its owner "lucky." The steer is useful, worth raising for its own sake, while the security is mere paper, and those who deal in them less worthy of respect than ranchers.

There is another important difference to consider. Those who produce crops, raise herds, and dig mines, often are debtors, mortgaging their land, steers, and mines to bankers, or borrowing from bondholders or selling shares to investors. By their very nature and function, these latter groups are creditors. Both groups are businessmen, but each has a different view toward money. Debtors seek to cut down on repayments, and so are helped by inflation. Creditors have a stake in "sound money," and would like to see the value of their loaned-out capital increase, perhaps through deflation.

The differences between these two groups provided the background for late nineteenth-century politics, when debtor and creditor businessmen faced one another at election times and in between. The silver extracted from Washoe played a key role in this struggle. The miners sold their silver for gold and became wealthy. They could not mint their silver, for after 1873 silver coins were no longer produced. For the next generation the miners and debtors throughout the country fought for the remonetization of silver, winning some battles, but never achieving complete victory. If silver were coined, the nation's currency would be greatly expanded, the value of the dollar decline, and debtors able to pay off their obligations with "cheap money." Retention of the gold standard would make the dollar more valuable, and so benefit creditors. To some this seemed a struggle of the wealthy against the poor. This was a gross oversimplification, one recognized by William Jennings Bryan, the Democratic nominee for the Presidency in 1896. In one part of his famous "Cross of Gold" speech before the Chicago convention of that year, Bryan claimed that the gold delegates had "made the definition of a business man too limited in its application." As he saw it, "the farmer who goes forth in the morning and toils all day . . . is as much a business man as the man who goes upon the Board of Trade and bets upon the price of grain." To him, "the miners . . . are as much business men as the few financial magnates who, in the back room, corner the money of the world."

In stating his case in such a fashion, Bryan indicated his sympathy for "producers" against "the magnates." Later on in his speech, Bryan would contrast "the struggling masses" with "the idle holders of idle capital," and he concluded with his belief that the nation was constructed on the work of producers. "Burn down your cities and leave our farms, and your cities will spring up again as if by magic; but destroy our farms and the grass will grow in the streets of every city in the country."

Yet even as Bryan spoke, the cities were replacing the farms as the focus of American life. The pace of industrial change, erratic at times, nonetheless was quickening. Money and power were to be found in boardrooms in cities, not village town meetings and country stores. Men had made fortunes from the soil in the past, but the truly big ones of the future would come from industry and finance. The issues of 1896 were clear, more so than they had been in any election since 1860 or would be again until 1932. It was the debtors against the creditors—farmers and their silver miner allies against urban businessmen. In the end the miners of Washoe would be defeated by the steelmen of Pittsburgh and the bankers of Wall Street, in a struggle that has come to represent the end of America's agrarian age.

The age of industrialization came slowly, almost with a sense of uncertainty. There had been an industrial quickening in the 1850s, consolidations in the 1860s, a major railroad boom in the next generation, and throughout it all an expansion of the nation's industrial sector. America had 35,000 miles of railroad track when Lee surrendered to Grant at Appomattox; by 1875 the figure was at 74,000, then rose to 128,000 in 1875, and stood at almost 250,000 miles as Bryan received his party's nomination in 1896. The railroad, the nation's first big business, helped create a large internal market for goods produced in America's factories, the number of which doubled in the four decades after the Civil War. In this same period the nation's urban population increased at twice the rate of the rural. In 1870 only 1.6 million Americans lived in cities with populations over 500,000; at the turn of the century over 8 million lived in such places.

Politicians, novelists, academicians, and foreign visitors noted the changes, and most seemed convinced that, for better or worse, America was entering the age of the city and factory. The content of the future seemed certain, but its form was not. What would be the dominant kind of organization? What would be the role of the financier? The banker? The government? Would the nation's power be centralized in Washington, or would it be in New York? Or would there be regional financial capitals, such as San Francisco seemed to be becoming in the 1870s and Denver, Chicago, and Boston were still in the 1880s? Did bigness in business mean efficiency or a hopeless jumble no man could decipher? Were the nation's transportation and communications networks capable of handling the traffic for a national business?

Such questions had been tossed about as early as the administration of John Quincy Adams, and were discussed in half-seriousness by the canal tycoons of the 1820s. In the last quarter of the nineteenth century, the questions were still being asked, but now they were real and pressing, requiring reasoned and realistic answers. Or as an editorial writer for the *New York Herald* put it in 1889, "The future is now."

Steel was the key material of the railroad and industrial age, and so the structure and development of the industry was of major concern to the nation's businessmen. The Kelly and Bessemer methods of producing cheap steel were patented in 1847, yet for more than a decade longer producers concentrated on wrought iron, which though inferior to steel was less expensive. Of the 19,600 tons of steel ingots produced in 1867, only 2,679 came from Bessemer converters, while most of the rest were from the costly crucible method. That year steel rails sold for $166 a ton, almost three times that of wrought-iron rails. Ten years later, as the virtues of the Bessemer process became evident and profits realized, the nation produced 570,000 tons of steel, and 500,000 tons were produced in the Bessemer converters.

The steel industry of that period could hardly be called an industry at all. Plants that turned out plows, horseshoes, wire, nails, and other products requiring iron or steel usually purchased ingots from foundries, which in turn bought much of their raw materials from mining operations. Some firms turned out plate iron and steel, for use in the shipbuilding industry and for urban construction. Such companies might produce all or part of their iron and steel, as would those engaged in the manufacture of railroad products, as rails and rolling stock. Yet even these purchased raw materials from a number of local suppliers. A large order from a construction company or railroad would be received, and then be translated into orders for ingots, which in turn affected operations in the coal and iron mines and fields. In what was still an agrarian age, there seemed little reason to integrate operations, either vertically by the firm producing all of its own steel and operating mines, or horizontally, by producing a wide variety of iron and steel products. Even had they desired to do so, and had the vision to recognize the shape of the future, the plant owners and operators lacked the capital for such integration. Steel manufacturing was an expensive proposition. In 1867, the dawn of the steel age, over a quarter of a billion dollars was invested in iron and steel operations, more than in cotton goods, and almost as much as all leather operations, glass, and petroleum refining combined. Funds for expansion could not be obtained from investment bankers, who in the post-Civil War period continued to concentrate on railroad securities, and considered the steels risky and of little promise.

The judgment seemed sound at the time. In 1870 the British steel firms produced 275,000 tons of steel ingots, compared to the American production of 37,500 tons. The British firms were well-capitalized; the Americans could barely scrape up enough money to continue operations. Britain had cheaper coal prices than America, and that country's labor force worked for lower wages. At the time British steel rails cost less than the American product in Pittsburgh, which even then was emerging as an iron and steel capital.

The Americans realized that the problems of capitalization and foreign competition were intertwined, and that the solution to one meant the end of the other. Unable to resolve the cost situation, they turned to politics, and lobbyed for a higher tariff on imported steel. This they won in 1870, when Congress passed, and the President signed, a tariff raising the duty on steel rails to $28 a ton. Though the British lowered their prices somewhat, the net cost of foreign rails jumped sharply, enabling the American manufacturers to post their own price increases, and at the same time undercut the British in the American market. The profit margins of American iron and steel companies rose. Some were able to purchase the new equipment for turning iron ingots into steel and for the time being ignore the investment bankers.

Several of the larger iron companies ordered Bessemer converters in early 1870. Among these were the Albany Iron Works of Albany, New York; the Bethlehem Iron Company of Bethlehem, Pennsylvania; Jones & Laughlin of Pittsburgh; the Joliet Steel Works of Joliet, Illinois; and the powerful Cambria Iron Works of Johnstown, Pennsylvania.

Andrew Carnegie was interested in the Bessemer converters, even though he hesitated before ordering them, as did many other American iron manufacturers. "Pioneering doesn't pay," he said in the late 1860s. Yet even then he was pioneering in the industry, not only in the technological area, but also, more importantly, in the organization and management of resources.

Carnegie had come to iron and steel through railroads, a well-traveled road in those days. In 1853, at the age of eighteen and only five years after arriving in the United States from Scotland, he became private secretary and personal telegrapher to Thomas Scott, the general superintendent of the Pennsylvania Railroad. Scott rose rapidly in the railroad, and took Carnegie with him. He was named assistant secretary of war in 1861, and helped Carnegie obtain the post of superintendent of eastern military and telegraph lines during the Civil War.

In 1862, while working for the government, Carnegie helped reorganize the Piper and Shiffler Company, which constructed wooden and iron bridges. He realized that iron bridges would be needed in the war effort, and that such a company should have no trouble making a financial success of it. He was correct; Piper and Shiffler flourished and proved a valuable Carnegie investment. With the end of the war, Carnegie turned increasingly to its management, and with Scott's help, reorganized it into the Keystone Bridge Company, with himself in control.

Recognizing the need for a source of iron, Carnegie fixed his attention on Kloman & Phipps, manufacturer of fine railroad-car axles and owners of a modern mill. In 1864 Carnegie had formed the Cyclops Iron Company, and the following year he merged Cyclops with Kloman & Phipps and Keystone to organize the Union Iron Mills, which he expected would take up much of his time from then on.

Throughout this period and for years after, Carnegie considered himself a businessman in the iron field, rather than an iron and steel manufacturer. To put it another way, he was intrigued with the idea of constructing a powerful and profitable company, and chance took him into the iron and steel field. Had the dice been thrown differently, he might have wound up in petroleum or railroads, for he maintained small interests in these fields. In 1869 he joined with George Pullman to gain a monopoly in the field of sleeping cars. Carnegie joined the board of Union Pacific in 1871, and for a while thought he might take control of the line, in which case he would have turned more toward railroading. Carnegie became interested in marketing, serving as Keystone's salesman throughout the country and doing well at it. He even took a turn at finance, especially during his European trips, and by 1873 had sold some $30 million worth of American railroad securities to English investors. Carnegie was in the business of opportunity, and the luck of the draw led him to steel.

At first Carnegie moved slowly, unwilling to assume leadership in the industry, or at least commit Union to that challenge. As he saw it, Keystone was the focus of the iron company, with the other components producing iron for use in bridges. When in 1869 Scott urged him to investigate the Bessemer process, Carnegie showed little interest. "That there is to be a great change in the manufr. of iron & steel some of these years is probable," he wrote, "but exactly what form it is to take no one knows." Why gamble on steel, he asked, when so many others know more of the subject than Union? Why wager at long odds? "There are many enterprises where we can go in even."

But Carnegie was not the man to ignore technological developments that could be transformed into profits. Rather, he would not commit his main efforts to a new process until it was proved. In 1861 he had helped form the Freedom Iron Company, a small factor in iron rail manufacture. Five years later the firm was reorganized as the Freedom Iron & Steel Company, and began experimenting with the Bessemer process. In 1867 Carnegie noted that Freedom was "pushing ahead" with the process, "& is going to be, I think, the only really successful Bessemer Manfr. in the United States. . . ." It would appear that Carnegie was using Freedom as a research and development arm for Union. If and when the process proved out and Carnegie was convinced it was economically feasible, he would bring it to Union.

In 1872 Carnegie visited England and learned more of steel-making. He returned to America convinced steel was the key to an industrial economy, and that the Bessemer process was the key to steel. He was about to abandon the business of opportunity and turn to the business of steel.

Carnegie hoped to convince his partners that it would be in Union's best interests to convert to steel, but he failed in this. Leaving them, he formed a new company, Carnegie, McCandless & Co., obtaining part of the funds from the sale of his Pullman and other interests, and in 1873 began construction of one of the biggest and most modern steel mills of the time, the Edgar Thompson Steel Works.

It was the right move, but many thought the wrong time. The panic of 1873 erupted soon after, forcing hundreds of small firms into bankruptcy. Carnegie was untouched. Whether due to innate financial conservatism or a hunch the panic was coming, his firm was solvent on the eve of the crash. Instead of falling, Carnegie used the panic as an opportunity to buy out others, including some of his own partners. Six of them sold their holdings to Carnegie at bargain prices in 1873, so that when the panic was over, Carnegie had 59 percent of the company's stock, while the company itself was debt-free.

Carnegie's interests prospered during the rest of the decade, and all the while he concentrated on expanding his business and buying out old partners. "So many of my friends needed money that they begged me to repay them," he explained later on. Few were forced from the Carnegie companies; most left of their own volition, leaving Carnegie to reap the harvest.

In 1880 the price of rails soared to $85 a ton, at a time when Carnegie, McCandless was turning out 10,000 tons a month at a cost of around $36. Within eight months Thompson returned enough profits to pay for its entire cost, and the steel works showed a profit of $1.6 million for the year, an unprecedented sum for that time, while the other Carnegie interests reported profits of almost half a million.

In 1881 Carnegie restructured and consolidated his holdings, forming Carnegie Brothers & Co., which was capitalized at $5 million, with Carnegie owning $2.7 million of the stock and taking the post of chairman of the board. His brother Tom received $878,000 of the holding, while the other partners—Henry Phipps, David Stewart, John Scott, Gardiner McCandless, and John Vandervort—shared the rest. The new company owned the Thompson Works, Union Iron, and the Lucy Furnaces, one of the most profitable iron-making facilities in the nation.

The new company flourished, even during the recession that struck in mid-decade, and a slump in the rail business in 1883. The price of rails dropped sharply, and yet Carnegie prospered, as his competitors fell by the wayside or were forced to cut back on operations. Cambria and Jones & Laughlin, initially larger than the Carnegie interests, were forced to the wall. The Homestead Works, one of the finest of its time and Thompson's chief rival, was in financial difficulty, and Carnegie sent out feelers to its managers, hoping to purchase the facility at a bargain price.

Profits of Carnegie Brothers, 1881-1886

Year	Profits	Percent of Return
1881	$2,000,377	40
1882	2,128,423	42
1883	1,019,233	20
1884	1,301,180	26
1885	1,191,933	24
1886	2,925,350	59

Source: Herbert Casson, *The Romance of Steel* (New York, 1907), p. 94.

The company also sought to gain control of its supply of coke, which along with iron ore was a necessary component of steelmaking and iron production. Carnegie Brothers had no coke ovens, having to purchase its coke supply from a variety of companies, the largest of which was Henry Clay Frick Coke Company. Frick seemed intent on becoming the king of coke, just as Carnegie was achieving that position in steel. Each man realized his product was intimately connected with the other's and both Frick and Carnegie seemed interested in expanding into the other's territory, perhaps engulfing the competition.

Carnegie moved first. In 1881 the Frick Coke Company was reorganized, with a capitalization of $2 million, represented by 40,000 shares of stock with a par value of $50 each. Frick received 11,846 shares, while two Pittsburgh financiers, the Ferguson brothers, took another 23,654 between them. The Carnegie forces joined the new firm, subscribing for 4,500 shares. During the next two years Carnegie purchased stock from the Fergusons and was able to obtain additional shares from the company when it recapitalized in 1883, coming out with half the outstanding shares. At that time, too, he was able to buy out the owners of Homestead, who were plagued by strikes and crippled by the depressed prices of steel rails.

Now Carnegie once again reorganized his holdings, forming a second company of his own, Carnegie, Phipps & Co., which included the Homestead mills and the Lucy Furnaces. Together Carnegie Brothers and Carnegie, Phipps dominated the steel industry, but in theory they were separate firms. Carnegie himself owned controlling interest in each. In this way, he once again profited from a recession that harmed his competitors.

When good times returned in 1887, Carnegie was in a fine position to profit from them. Carnegie Brothers showed earnings of $3,441,887 in 1887, or a 69-percent return on capital, an amazing performance even then and under those conditions.

Or was the return that surprising, or indeed that high? There is reason to believe Carnegie consistently understated earnings and net worth throughout much of his business career. He did this not through modesty or financial manipulation—those were the days before income taxes or capital gains levies, and Carnegie showed little interest in the stock market—but rather due to the "partnership" system he introduced at his plants.

Carnegie constantly searched for ambitious young men, who if they showed promise would receive rapid promotions. Some of them would be told stock in the company had been set aside for them, to be paid for out of the company's earnings. In effect, these men were given shares as a bonus, and told more would be coming if earnings and dividends remained high, and their work continued to improve. Carnegie later said that "every year should be marked by the promotion of one or more of our young men. . . . We can not have too many of the right sort interested in the profits." One of these men later said that Carnegie "exceeded any man I ever knew in his ability to pick a man from one place and put him in another with a maximum effect."

It was a simple enough idea, although other industrialists would not adopt it for decades. Carnegie claimed to have come across it from watching commercial fishermen, noting that those who worked for a share of the catch did more than those who were mere wage earners. New partners were not added each year, but some were taken in regularly. In 1898, a banner year for the firm, twenty such individuals received partnerships in the form of stock.

Charles Schwab was the most successful of these Carnegie partners. A former grocery clerk, he asked for a job at Homestead and was put to work as a stake driver at a dollar a day. Within six months Schwab had caught Carnegie's eye, and was named superintendent in charge of constructing a new blast furnace. Schwab was elevated to superintendent at Homestead at the age of twenty-five, and five years later was placed in command of Carnegie's major operations as his right-hand man.

Henry Clay Frick represented a special case, and indeed was an unusual person in many respects. Frick was taken into Carnegie Brothers in 1887, given 2 percent of its stock valued at $184,000, with the understanding that the sum would be paid out of earnings, and not in cash. Two years later Frick was named chairman of Carnegie Brothers, and his interest was increased to 11 percent, more than any such partner before or after. Frick was ambitious, and clearly saw himself as the founder's heir apparent. But Carnegie retained a method of ridding himself of such partners at a time and in a way he controlled.

This was the Iron Clad agreements, first promulgated in 1887. Under its terms, the company could repurchase stock given to partners at book value. If a partner did not turn out well, Carnegie could be rid of him in a matter of months. This encouraged Carnegie to understate the worth of his enterprise, to write off costs as incurred and not over a period of years, as was the practice then and now. As a result, Carnegie's operations were always carried at below their true worth, and so his return on capital was greatly exaggerated.

As Carnegie's power grew, he began to take an active interest in the structure of the steel industry as a whole. As early as 1875 he helped form the Bessemer Steel Association, which also included Pennsylvania Steel, Cambria, Bethlehem, Jones & Laughlin, and Scranton Iron & Steel. The association had many functions, but the most important of these was to bring order to the chaotic and overcrowded steel market, which at the time was suffering from overcapacity. If the companies competed on a price basis, soon they would be selling steel for below cost, and all would suffer. So they combined to set prices and shares of the market—later on such activity would be called a conspiracy in restraint of trade. Carnegie favored such arrangements, and had participated in others on a less formal basis in the early 1870s. But the pool was short lived, as some members refused to abide by its decisions and insisted on competition.

The pool always was a weak reed, capable of rupture at any time. There was no way to enforce its provisions, and members abided by them only so long as they suited their interests. In other words, pools worked when they were not needed, and failed when they might have done some good for the companies as a group. Pools in steel and other products failed in periods of depression, as each company scrambled to sell its product and so maintain liquidity. They fell apart in good times, when markets were expanding and each member felt it could increase its share of the market by nibbling away at the quotas of others. The same was true of prices; aggressive managers could not resist the temptation to undercut weaker units when the opportunity to do so arose. On the other hand, pools might have worked had all the companies been equal in size and power and led by men more interested in order than growth. Of course, few of them were in the unstable industrial climate of the late nineteenth century.

A major pool in steel rails was formed in 1887. Its members

produced more than 90 percent of the country's rails, with the two Carnegie firms receiving 13 ⅝ of the market, the largest share. At the time it seemed the arrangement might work. Indeed, it lasted for five years, something of a record for such agreements. Like the others it fell apart, and for the usual reasons: hard times and the expansion of a member firm.

The key figure here was Frick, who, we have seen, joined Carnegie as a partner that same year. Frick was opposed to pools, correctly seeing them as limiting his firm's growth. Upon becoming chairman in 1889 he set about adding valuable new properties to Carnegie Brothers, and eliminating competitors in a ruthless fashion. Then Frick urged Carnegie to consolidate his holdings into one giant company, and this was accomplished in 1892, with the organization of Carnegie Steel Company Ltd., capitalized at $25 million. Carnegie received 55.33 percent of the stock, Frick 11 percent, Henry Phipps another 11 percent, with nineteen other partners receiving 1 percent each, and the rest set aside for future partnerships.

As expected, Frick was named chairman of the new company, while at the same time remaining president of Frick Coke, still the nation's leading firm in that field, and Carnegie's major supplier. Frick saw Carnegie Steel as a base for an even greater industrial empire, one merged with his own coke interests, which would dominate every aspect of steel, just as Standard Oil had come to dominate petroleum.

Frick was an excellent manager and industrialist, one of the most brilliant of his time. Of course, he was high-handed toward labor unions; witness the famous Homestead strike of 1892, one of the most violent in American history, which climaxed with an almost successful assassination attempt on Frick himself, who was running the company while Carnegie was in Scotland on vacation.

Frick was not alone in opposing organized labor. Carnegie agreed with him on essentials, as did almost all other industrialists of the time. Always a believer in Social Darwinism a la Herbert Spencer, and convinced his partnership arrangements and system of rewards encouraged bright young men to rise in the firm, Carnegie opposed unions as divisive intrusions into his private affairs. Nevertheless, he and Frick did have their differences, and as early as 1892 it seemed the firm, large though it was, could not contain two such strong individuals.

The second factor in destroying the 1887 pool was the depression of 1893, which created hard times in steel. Even before the panic of that year, Carnegie had chafed under the pool restrictions, feeling he could outsell all other members if turned loose from the agreement. "Take orders and run full" was one of his mottoes, and during the recession he was restricted from doing both. So he told another pool member, Abram Hewett, he was withdrawing. When it was pointed out that even under restrictions Carnegie was making good profits, the industrialist replied, "That is not enough. I can make steel cheaper than any of you and undersell you. The market is mine whenever I want to take it. I see no reason why I should present you all my profits."

Carnegie withdrew from the rail pool, thus shattering the arrangement. Carnegie undersold his competition, as he said he would, creating havoc in the industry, joy for Frick, opportunities for further expansion, and concern on Wall Street. Carnegie Steel's profits rose sharply, even more so when good times returned in 1897. The firm earned $6 million in 1896, $7 million in 1897, $11 million in 1898, and $21 million in 1899. In this way, Carnegie was transformed from an admired and accepted member of the business community of steelmen into a marauder, a man seemingly intent on crushing his rivals and creating a huge business edifice such as the world had never seen.

Acting upon this assumption, and at the same time taking advantage of opportunities created in the wake of the 1893 panic, other steelmen and some outsiders acted to consolidate rival steel giants, firms that could withstand Carnegie's assaults.

John Gates was one of the first to see the potential for such mergers. An improbable speculator and inveterate gambler, Gates was also known as "Bet-A-Million." Joining with an old friend, lawyer Elbert H. Gary, Gates brought together five companies in

1892 to form the Consolidated Steel and Wire Company, immediately the largest factor in the barbed-wire business. Gates dreamed of using Consolidated as a base for a steel empire to rival Carnegie's. He would float stock, enlist the aid of investment bankers, manipulate finances, absorb companies through stock deals, and in the process gobble up major non-Carnegie firms. Gates knew Carnegie hated Wall Street, would not recapitalize his own company and sell stock, and so Carnegie would be unable to stop him on his own battleground.

Gates ran Consolidated with skill, forming and breaking pools when the device suited his purposes and forcing rivals to the wall. Then, in 1898, he joined with J. P. Morgan to form American Steel & Wire of Illinois, which absorbed Consolidated and several smaller companies. The new firm was capitalized at $24 million, although it had assets of less than $16 million. Late that year the remaining barbed-wire companies capitulated, and united with Gates in January 1899 to create the American Steel & Wire Company of New Jersey, which produced four-fifths of the nails and wire fencing in the nation. This company was capitalized at $90 million, although it had assets of less than $38 million at the time.

The talks with Gates marked Morgan's entry into the steel picture. He had been involved in small ways earlier, but for the most part had concentrated on railroads prior to 1898. Now that Carnegie seemed on the rampage, Morgan felt obliged to take a hand in setting the industry straight. If there was anything Morgan disliked in business or anything else he touched, it was disorder and chaos. Carnegie seemed to be threatening such chaos, and Morgan wouldn't stand for it.

That Morgan was powerful is undeniable, but he no more controlled Wall Street than Carnegie did Pittsburgh. Rather, the two men were leaders, each in their own sphere, with many rivals, some of them quite strong and independent. Jacob Schiff of Kuhn, Loeb commanded as much power as did Morgan, even though Wall Street of the late 1890s wouldn't accept a German Jew as its hero. As we have seen, Carnegie, too, had rivals, and would never go so far as to claim to be the spokesman for steel. Yet the public made heroes or villains of both men, glorifying or condemning them according to who was speaking or writing.

Morgan was sixty-one years old in 1898, two years younger than Carnegie. Where Carnegie was preparing to leave business for other pursuits, even as he forced his way to the top of the industry, Morgan's great power was still expanding, with the next decade bringing him as much glory and almost as much prestige as the one just past. One reason for this was the difference in the temperaments of the two men. Carnegie always considered business to be one aspect of his life, one way for him to develop and demonstrate his world view. For Morgan, business was all, and power the engine of his life. Even when supposedly relaxing on his art-buying expeditions in Europe, Morgan was the corsair, dealing skillfully, swiftly, and with as much cunning as he did on Wall Street, collecting art the way he did corporations, always with a sense of order, seeking rationality and perfection. Carnegie would pass the time during holidays playing golf at his castle at Skibo in Scotland. Morgan would sit in his Renaissance drawing room, puffing a fine Havana, playing game after game of solitaire, even then bringing order from chaos. There is no record of Morgan ever attempting golf, but it seems likely he wouldn't have liked it—why play a game that can never be fully mastered or perfected?

If Carnegie and Morgan respected one another, it was a grudging respect, and not admiration. Carnegie never had much use for bankers, and considered his activities constructive while those of Wall Streeters were parasitic. For his part, Morgan thought Carnegie a dreamer and perhaps a dangerous radical, who by virtue of his position should know better than to act the way he did, supporting utopian movements and disrupting a major industry like steel.

Neither man knew the other well, and relied upon rumor and hearsay as much as solid information for knowledge of what the other was doing. So as far as Morgan could tell, Carnegie was trying to seize control of the entire steel industry by destroying all rivals, using Frick as his hammer to crush all opposition that developed. If he succeeded, this might lead to government intervention. Already an antitrust act—the Sherman Act of 1890—was on the books. Both men had supported William McKinley in the election of 1896, and McKinley had won. But his opponent that year, Democrat William Jennings Bryan, had stood for control of corporations, and even though soundly beaten, was expected to be the Democratic nominee in 1900. What might Bryan do if elected? The attack on the trusts would be mounted, and if Carnegie then controlled steel, as he seemed capable of doing, it would present a fine target. So for many reasons—the desire for order and stability, dislike of the Carnegie type, political factors, and his own need for power—Morgan entered the steel struggle in 1898.

To counter Carnegie's power, Morgan erected Federal Steel Company by bringing together Illinois Steel, the Lorain Steel Company, the Johnson Company, and the Minnesota Iron Company. Federal also controlled several railroads, the most important of which were the Elgin, Joliet & Eastern and the Chicago, Lake Shore & Eastern, as well as some good ore fields. To head the corporation, Morgan selected Elbert Gary, whom he had come to respect after dealing with him at American Steel & Wire. The book value of Federal's properties came to $56 million. Morgan capitalized the company at $230 million, and sold the securities without much difficulty. This enabled the financier to pay extremely high prices to the former owners of Federal properties and so ease the transition and speed up the mergers. The capital markets were good in 1898, Morgan's name was magic, and there seemed little question that the issue would succeed. As a result, the first group of "merger millionaires" was created.

Financial writer John Moody recounted the story of a party of steelmen, probably tied with the Federal merger, on their way to Chicago after a "buying tour."

> The men had been drinking and were in a convivial mood. Said one, "There's a steel mill at the next station; let's get out and buy it." "Agreed!"

> It was past midnight when they reached the station, but they pulled the plant owner out of bed and demanded that he sell his plant.
>
> "My plant is worth two hundred thousand dollars, but it is not for sale," was the reply.
>
> "Never mind about the price," answered the hilarious purchasers, "we will give you three hundred thousand–five hundred thousand."

The story is exaggerated, perhaps, but such kiting of prices did take place prior to the Federal merger. No one seemed to mind, not Morgan, the former owners, and least of all purchasers of Federal securities, which sold at a premium soon after the public offering. This kind of market encouraged Wall Street in setting the price for American Steel & Wire of New Jersey and subsequent mergers and consolidations, each of which created dozens of paper millionaires.

National Steel Company, a third great consolidation, was the creation of William and James Moore, who like Gates had reputations for wheeling and dealing. The brothers had already organized Diamond Match, involving themselves in manipulations so complicated and shady that their riggings had caused the Chicago Stock Exchange to close down for three months. Then they organized National Biscuit Company in much the same way. The American Tin Plate Company—"the Tin Plate Trust"—followed in 1898. It brought together thirty-nine plants, controlling 279 mills, which produced virtually all the tin plate in the nation, and was capitalized at $50 million, but had assets of only from $10 million to $12 million. Then came American Steel Hoop, uniting nine concerns producing steel bars, hoops and bands, and wire. Capitalized at $33 million, it had assets of less than half that amount. The brothers rewarded themselves in this instance by taking over 15 percent of the stock.

Now they were ready to create National Steel, the work for which was completed in February 1899. National brought under one roof six large plants with fifteen blast furnaces, iron mines in Michigan, and nine lake ships. At the time it was the nation's third-largest steel firm, producing about 12 percent of the nation's steel. Through its close affiliations with American Tin Plate, American Steel Hoop, and another Moore company, American Sheet Steel, National was able to challenge Carnegie and Federal as an equal.

National was capitalized at $61.5 million, and its finances were so convoluted it was impossible at the time to tell how much the plants were worth in terms of replacement costs.

These then were the main challengers to Carnegie's growing domination of steel. American Steel & Wire, Federal, and the Moore companies all contained units which prior to amalgamation had purchased steel shares from Carnegie. Now they were on their own as integrated firms, and announced that henceforth they would produce their own steel, and compete with Carnegie in the open market. Others joined them, in the three great years of amalgamation from 1898–1900, when the structure of the industry changed drastically in the face of the Carnegie challenge and other factors.

In varying degrees, each of these companies were "watered," in the sense that they were capitalized at more than asset value, and often far more than stock quotations at the time the mergers were announced. Speculators at the Boston Stock Exchange, which prior to 1900 was the major market for industrial securities in the United States, made fortunes, as did underwriters in that city. But with the formation of Federal Steel by Morgan in New York, Wall Street entered the industrial field in a big way. Railroads still dominated the underwriting scene in New York, but the industrials, led by the great steel mergers, were becoming more important each year. Recognizing the attraction steel companies had, both in terms of profits and marketability, the major New York firms scoured the country seeking new properties to merge and underwrite. Individual promoters, men like Gates and the Moores, worked in harmony with the Wall Streeters to share the gains, much to the disgust of Carnegie, who looked askance at such activities. Yet the age of the industrialist clearly was passing by 1898, to be replaced by that of the financier. Or to put it another way, the period in which men like Carnegie

Non-Carnegie Amalgamations in Steel, 1898-1900

Year	Organization	Capitalization
1898	American Steel & Wire of Illinois	$ 24,000,000
	Federal Steel Company	230,217,179
	American Tin Plate Co.	50,273,000
	American Car & Foundry Co.	60,000,000
	American Iron & Steel Manufacturing Co.	20,000,000
	Empire Steel & Iron Co.	10,000,000
	National Enameling & Stamping Co.	30,600,000
	Pressed Steel Car Co.	25,000,000
	Republic Iron & Steel Co.	55,000,000
	Sloss-Sheffield Steel & Iron	23,835,000
	U.S. Cast-Iron Pipe & Foundry Co.	30,000,000
	Virginia Iron, Coal & Coke Co.	20,000,000
1899	American Steel & Wire of New Jersey	90,130,656
	American Steel Hoop Co.	33,000,000
	National Steel Co.	61,561,000
	National Tube Co.	80,000,000
1900	American Bridge Co.	70,156,000
	American Sheet Steel Co.	54,000,000
	Shelby Steel Tube Co.	15,000,000
	Crucible Steel Co. of America	50,000,000

Source: Eliot Jones, *The Trust Problem in the United States* (New York, 1921), pp. 189-90.

seemed to be be dominant was giving way to one in which investment bankers like Morgan would rule.

It appeared a natural development. A firm as large as Carnegie Steel needed organizational skills as much as if not more than knowledge of steelmaking and marketing. Large amounts of capital were also needed, and this could only be obtained at the capital markets, dominated by the investment bankers. Carnegie would hold out for the time being, but there weren't many like him.

One member of the old industrial class who also held out, while at the same time seeking his own rationale for the new dispensation, was John D. Rockefeller, the ruler of Standard Oil. Rockefeller combined the best qualities of Carnegie and Morgan as businessmen. His petroleum complex was self-sufficient, well-integrated, and constantly expanding. During the 1880s Rockefeller absorbed several large and many small petroleum producers, combined them with his refining operations, and extended vertical integration to every facet of the business. Rockefeller seemed to hate to buy from suppliers, giving them profits he wanted for himself. He would take them over, and so retain all earnings for the Standard giant.

Carnegie appeared to be taking the same path. In the early 1880s he had taken over Frick's coke and coal operations, a major step in the direction of vertical integration. But Carnegie lacked large iron-ore deposits, and so far had made no move to obtain them.

This was the situation when the great Mesabi range was opened in the early 1890s. The Merritt brothers, Lewis and Leonidas, had obtained a large tract at Mesabi, and in 1892 approached Frick with an offer of partnership. Frick rejected them at first, an understandable stance since he was then completely occupied with the problems of the Homestead strike. Then Henry Oliver, the farm implement manufacturer and a boyhood friend of Carnegie's, took an interest in the Merritt properties, and wrote to Carnegie, offering to make a deal. Carnegie wasn't interested, but by then Frick was. He went ahead and bought the land, giving Carnegie Steel a foothold in what would prove the greatest iron-ore field in North America.

This sparked anew the personality conflict between Frick and Carnegie. Frick held to his dream of making Carnegie Steel the master of the metal, ridding himself of all rivals, and raising the company to the status Standard Oil had in petroleum. Carnegie, increasingly occupied with other matters, didn't seem to care as much about growth as he once did.

While the two men debated the point, Rockefeller entered the picture. The Merritts were struck hard by the 1893 depression, and sought additional financing. Unable to get it from Carnegie, they turned to the petroleum giant, who in 1894 took a major share of their properties in return for funding. Together they formed the Lake Superior Consolidated Iron Mines Co., which controlled the largest single tract in Mesabi; the Bessemer Steamship Company (the largest owner of ore vessels in the Great Lakes); and a key iron-ore railroad, the Duluth, Missabe and Northern.

Rockefeller's entry into the company led to new rumors in Pittsburgh and New York. It was said he would now construct blast furnaces and converters, and then challenge Carnegie for the title of steel king. This was not the case, or at least, so it seemed. Instead, Rockefeller signed a fifty-year agreement with Carnegie to supply him with ore, and made few further advances in the direction of entering the steel business. He remained a potential threat, however, waiting on the sidelines, perhaps preparing to enter the picture when the time was right.

In 1898 Frick felt the time to challenge Carnegie was at hand. He was forty-nine years old, vigorous, ambitious, and aware that he knew more about steel than did Carnegie, and did most of the real work while Carnegie relaxed at Skibo, attended philosophical congresses, and made pronouncements on every subject except steel. Frick was not a Carnegie creation. Alone of the partners he had entered the firm as an equal, after proving his worth at Frick Coke. He chafed at Carnegie's moralizings and resented the insinuations Carnegie spread of his heavy-handedness during the Homestead Strike. Eager to rid himself of the old man and take control of the corporation, Frick prepared to buy Carnegie out. When the two clashed over Frick's desire to expand, Carnegie agreed to set his price.

In December 1898, Carnegie told Frick he was willing to consider a deal. Perhaps a syndicate could be formed, by Morgan or someone else on Wall Street, to take over. Or it could be that Rockefeller was ready to make his move. Carnegie and Frick agreed on a price—$250 million for Carnegie Steel and $70 million for the Frick Coke Company. Carnegie's own share of such a transaction would come to $157 million.

Frick, who by now was joined by Phipps, accepted the offer. "It is surprising the amount of money awaiting investment in the City," he wrote. "On all sides you find people who are looking for investments." Frick had little trouble in forming a syndicate. Carnegie asked for "earnest money" of $2 million, and gave his partners ninety days to raise the rest.

Frick failed in his first attempt. He enlisted the support of the Moore brothers and Gates, but failed to attract Morgan, who refused to enter a syndicate containing men whom he considered gamblers and plungers. On his part, Carnegie was angered on learning that Frick and Phipps would take $5 million as brokerage fees if and when the deal was completed. So he pocketed most of the earnest money, including $170,000 from Frick and Phipps, and announced he had upped the ante for earnest money to $5 million.

Now Carnegie and Frick turned on one another. Carnegie's growing dislike for Frick led to an attempt to force him from the company. Frick resigned—he had often said he would do so if asked—and announced his willingness to be bought out. Carnegie invoked the Iron Clad agreements and said Frick's share should come to $5 million. Frick replied that Carnegie deliberately understated the firm's worth—which was true—and demanded a fair settlement. Lawsuits and acrimonious exchanges followed, and at one point Frick challenged the older man to a fight. But in the end Carnegie settled.

In 1900 the company was reorganized and recapitalized as Carnegie Company of New Jersey. Its total capital was $320 million, the figure the two men had previously agreed upon as its true worth. Stock was distributed to the partners, with no public offering made. Carnegie's share came to $174.5 million, slightly more than he would have received had Frick's deal been consummated. Frick came out of it with $31.3 million, and he left the firm.

Now Carnegie took the helm, with Schwab replacing Frick at Carnegie Steel. Immediately Carnegie launched an aggressive expansion movement, apparently designed to destroy the new combines that had been formed during the merger boom of 1898–1900. He announced his intention to enter the nail, wire, tube, hoop, and other businesses, a clear challenge to Gates's American Steel & Wire and the Morgan-created National Tube. Carnegie would erect a huge tube plant at Conneaut on Lake Erie and a modern rod facility in Pittsburgh. He said he would issue contracts for a fleet of ore carriers to be used on the Great Lakes, an obvious attack on Rockefeller. Then he joined with George Gould to plan a railroad from Pittsburgh to the sea, one which would free Carnegie from the Pennsylvania, which at the time was controlled by the Rockefeller interests.

Carnegie's motives in so acting weren't clear, but two possible explanations were offered on Wall Street. The first was that Carnegie was intent on becoming the czar of steel, forcing other firms out of business. This would create panic on Wall Street and havoc in the industry, two situations Morgan and his friends could not accept. The other possibility was that Carnegie was showing Morgan his muscle, and saying, in effect, "Buy me out at my price or I will destroy you."

Whatever the reason, it worked. By autumn of 1900, Morgan was in the mood to approach Carnegie, or be approached by him, regarding a take-over of Carnegie Co.

The catalyst came on the night of December 12, 1900, when Schwab, at a dinner in his honor, spoke of the future of steel and the nature of the industry. Morgan was there, and listened intently. Carnegie dropped in for a few minutes, perhaps to make certain Morgan was impressed. Schwab talked of the waste of competition, the need for cooperation, and broadly hinted that such a state could be arrived at with Carnegie's cooperation.

After dinner, Morgan took Schwab aside, asked a few questions, and arranged for a meeting at his home in early January. Carnegie had baited the hook with Schwab, and Morgan had taken it.

Morgan met with Schwab soon after, at a meeting attended by Robert Bacon, a Morgan partner, and Bet-A-Million Gates. They talked all night, and in the end Morgan asked whether Carnegie would sell. Schwab replied he didn't know, but promised to find out.

Now the two giants, Morgan and Carnegie, played their game, with Schwab acting as go-between. Perhaps it would be more accurate to say that Morgan thought he was wooing Carnegie, when all the time Carnegie was willing to be taken, but at the right price. The contest did not last long. Carnegie told Morgan—again, through

Schwab—that his price would be $480 million. This was $160 million more than Carnegie had capitalized Carnegie Co. for the year before. The difference between the $320 million and the $480 million consisted of Carnegie's price for getting out of the industry, and for his new projects. If the deal went through, Carnegie's share would come to $225.6 million, payable in 5-percent mortgage bonds.

Schwab took the figures to Morgan, who looked at them briefly, and said, "I accept this price." A few days later the two giants met. Morgan extended his hand. "Mr. Carnegie, I want to congratulate you on being the richest man in the world."

Now Morgan went to work spinning his web, organizing his syndicate, bringing together companies which, when joined to Carnegie Co., would form a new steel giant. The Federal Steel property, still under Morgan control, was taken in, as was National Tube. Morgan accepted American Steel & Wire, but not Gates, whom he disliked. The Moore interests came in, with promises of high prices for securities but no power in the new company. Rockefeller's Lake Superior Consolidated was accepted, also at a premium price, as were other, smaller units. For all of this, Morgan exchanged $550 million of common stock, a like amount of preferred, and $304 million in bonds, for a total of $1.404 billion in securities.*

This was the price Morgan asked for shares and bonds in his new creation, which he called United States Steel. As had been the case with the new issues of 1898–1900, the U.S. Steel securities' prices represented what Morgan thought the public would pay, and not the "underlying assets." A decade later the Bureau of Corporations would estimate the real worth of the properties to have been from $676 million to $793 million, and this would lead to charges that Morgan had "watered the stock" and in effect cheated the public.

Morgan never replied to these charges, as he ignored most challenges to his power. He might have observed, however, that his critics did not understand the ways of finance and the marketplace.

*It was said at the time that Carnegie took bonds instead of stock because he expected the company to fail, after which he would foreclose and take command of the Morgan-created giant.

The concept of "book value," or "underlying assets" was a nineteenth-century formulation, used to figure the "true worth" of a corporation if and when it failed. Such a concept was out of place in the emerging age of industrial securities, when intangibles were at least as important as plants, inventories, and the like. Too, Wall Street was in the midst of a bull market at the time U.S. Steel was formed. Prices were soaring and trading was at a fever pitch. There were days in 1901 when more than three million shares were traded, or 5 percent of all listed shares. A 5-percent day in 1973 would have seen some 200 million shares change hands. Was it any wonder then, in that kind of market, that U.S. Steel could not only be distributed, but also be taken eagerly?

Most speculators and investors of that time agreed that steel was the key to industrial growth, and that U.S. Steel would dominate the market. How much is such a position worth beyond the book value? In 1972, International Business Machines, the leader in computers, had a book value in the area of $65 a share, and sold for over 400, while Xerox, Polaroid, and Eastman Kodak, all with book values of less than $17 a share, sold for well over 100. In contrast, U.S. Steel was offered at two times book value. Looking backward from 1901, one might see the stock as watered and overpriced, a vehicle for Wall Street speculators to make fortunes. But looking ahead to the twentieth century, the price appears reasonable.

The U.S. Steel flotation was the largest in American history to that time, and it created the largest company in the nation. For years after, writers would rhapsodize over the flotation and the company, seeking new ways to describe them. One put it this way:

> Fourteen hundred millions!
> Supposing that this amount represented real capital, it would be equal to the following:
>   One-sixty-seventh of our national wealth in 1900.
>   One-fifth of our national wealth in 1850.
> One-thirtieth of the world's manufactures.
> One-tenth of American manufactures.

One-fifteenth of all the gold and silver mined in the world since the discovery of America.
More than the combined product of all the manufacturing industries, farms, fisheries, and mines of the United States in 1850.
More than the gross receipts of all American railroads in 1899.
One-fifth of the resources of our 3,871 banks in 1900.
All of the savings bank deposits in 1890.
The value of all the animals on American farms in 1880.
Combined value of all our corn, wheat, rye, oats, barley, buckwheat, and potatoes in 1900.
Three times the value of all our cotton and wool in 1900.

And so on. The author went on to claim that U.S. Steel owned as much land as contained in Massachusetts, Vermont, and Rhode Island, employed more men than fought on both sides in the Battle of Gettysburg, and had a wage bill larger than that of the United States Army and Navy combined.*

This kind of analysis went on for years. In 1916 a writer asked his audience to imagine what the total capital of the company would look like if it were turned to gold. It could be a body containing 3880 cubic feet, or a pillar "towering 108 feet in the air; or a Cleopatra's needle of virgin gold six feet square at the base and tapering to a point at a height of over 430 feet!"†

In 1904 the corporation accounted for over 5 percent of all assets of American industrial corporations, and over 20 percent of the total assets of the hundred largest corporations.

It was impressive, but was it good for the nation? This question did not interest most Americans at the time, impressed as they were with bigness, often for its own sake.

Those who organized the trust profited greatly. The Morgan

*Herbert Casson, *The Romance of Steel* (New York, 1907), p. 221.

†Arundel Cotter, *The Authentic History of the United States Steel Corporation* (New York, 1916), p. 17.

syndicate claimed to have raised $200 million in cash to organize "Big Steel." Actually, the members contributed $25 million, for which they received 649,988 shares of common stock and 649,987 shares of preferred. The common came out at 38 on the Curb Market and the preferred at 82. Morgan obtained the services of several "market makers," the most important of whom was James Keene (who had gotten his start in San Francisco during the Comstock bonanza). Within a month Keene managed to raise the common to 55 and the preferred to 101. This gave the syndicate a paper profit of $23 million on top of their large fees and sales of stock at inflated prices to themselves as syndicate managers. In all, Morgan was rumored to have made $45 million for his firm on the flotation.

Naturally, the men who had relinquished their shares in component firms to receive Steel's paper in return did well, and in the same fashion. Estimates vary, but it would appear that from fifty to one hundred millionaires were created by the flotation and the speculation that followed.

This calculation does not include the Carnegie partners, those bright young men who had been sold shares under the Iron Clad agreements. There were some thirty to forty of them in 1901, most of whom were settled in Pittsburgh. Now they were millionaires, and eager to live on a grand scale.

Later on, when the Pittsburgh millionaires were old and settled and their exploits more legend than history, wild tales were told of them. These made them appear as yokels in the big city, barely literate and ready to be taken by any sharp dealer who came their way. It was said that they came to town in a group, and went directly to a public bath, where more than five pounds of Mesabi dust was collected from the drains after they bathed. Lucius Beebe, who collected and believed these stories, wrote that "steel puddlers' wives who only yesterday had been slaving over hot cookstoves to keep their husbands in Cousin Jack pasties at lunchtime blossomed with English butlers and liveried house footmen," and "the toughened offspring of Mesabi iron miners found themselves distressingly poured into Little Lord Fauntleroy suits and their Buster Brown curls ordered by exquisite barbers."* He noted, correctly, that their idol was Diamond Jim Brady, the master steel products salesman who was better known for his penchant for high living than his business activities. Brady liked pretty girls, fine clothes, the company of witty people, and most of all, the best food available, in gargantuan quantities. He became a celebrity in the 1890s, a period of depression and hardship for most Americans. Yet the decade came to be known as the "Gay Nineties," in large part due to Brady's image. Now the steel millionaires would emulate Brady, or so the legend went.

If the Pittsburgh millionaires wanted to live like Brady, they were raised under Carnegie, an entirely different kind of person. And if they were granted partnerships, they were extraordinary men, hard workers, smart, and not at all the sort to squander their wealth. Nor were they hardened, simple workmen, but managers, men in charge of huge steel plants, who in 1900 went to work in suits, not overalls. Alexander Peacock, for example, had been a linen salesman when he came to Carnegie seeking employment. Carnegie liked the young man, who like himself was a Scots immigrant, and gave him a job in sales. Peacock did well, and within a few years was head of the sales department and a partner. As such he participated in the various merger negotiations, usually seconding everything Carnegie proposed, and won a reputation as a shrewd if not intelligent businessman. Peacock owned 2 percent of the Carnegie Steel stock; now he was a millionaire. Then there was William Corey, who began as a laborer at Braddock, rose to head the Homestead plant, and was known for his tough labor practices. Corey was crude, but he also developed new methods for hardening steel which he patented, and which by itself would have made him rich. Corey was a Carnegie partner, and now a millionaire. Peacock and Corey were typical of Pittsburgh's *nouveaux riches*—they sometimes acted like Brady, but under it all, they were believers in Carnegie's philosophy.

Seven of the Carnegie partners set sail for Europe after receiving their shares, and there they were followed by salesmen of every

*Lucius Beebe, *The Big Spenders* (New York, 1966), p. 276.

description, eager to unload "rare art treasures" for exorbitant prices. The partners bought, often with wild abandon, but for the most part showed good judgment in their selections. The story was told of one who asked the secretary of the archbishop of Paris for "the lowest price on that church of Notre Dame, C.O.D., Sewickley Heights, Pennsylvania, good old U.S.A."

The partners all erected their homes in such areas as Sewickley Heights, and these were lavishly built and decorated. Naturally, it sparked a real-estate boom in Pittsburgh, which for a brief instant dreamed of rivaling New York and Chicago for national leadership. Artists, book agents, dealers in antiques, interior decorators, architects, and "home consultants" descended upon the city, and the trains from New York and Chicago to Pittsburgh resembled a gallery show or cocktail party at Rector's. The millionaires wanted a theater district in their city, and for a while planned to bring one intact from New York, actors, designers, playwrights, and all. These men and women congregated in the showy Sewickley Heights mansions, where they and their hosts were attended by squads of maids and butlers, most of whom had been brought over from England. They conferred status on their employers, many of whom had emigrated from Scotland as boys and now enjoyed the idea of being served by the English.

Peacock constructed one of the finest and most ornate of these palaces. He learned of the sale while in California, and hired a special train to bring him home to celebrate, making the trip in the unheard-of time of less than fifty-eight hours. Then he planned his home, Rowanlea, on Highland Avenue. The home was impressive by Victorian standards, with many rare shrubs, fountains, walks, and even a maze. Rowanlea was surrounded by a huge iron fence, which when opened on its casters ushered the visitor to a long walk, at the end of which were the Doric and Ionic columns of the main house. Peacock threw many parties there, inviting his old friends for "bashes" that shocked the older families in that part of town. Clearly Peacock was an *arriviste*. When one of his neighbors told him he had purchased two gold-plated pianos, Peacock promptly ordered four.

He ordered fine art by the yard, and even though he knew little of their worth, liked to show his "finds" to visitors.

Thomas Morrison, another Carnegie partner, lived next door on Highland Avenue. Morrison had begun as a steel puddler and rose quickly to command at the mills. A man of little formal learning but fine intelligence, Morrison soon became known to Carnegie, who used him in a variety of positions. Now that he was wealthy, he constructed an edifice second only to Peacock's in the neighborhood. Nearby was Francis Lovejoy's home, also ornate, with a garage that had room for sixty automobiles. And other partners were in the same area, called at one time "the Carnegie compound." These houses, and others like them, made Pittsburgh real-estate men wealthy, too. It was estimated that over $35 million was spent on land alone, and even more for the homes that were constructed on the scenic acreage.

Carnegie watched his former protégés from afar, and was annoyed by what he saw and heard of their activities. The Pittsburgh and New York newspapers ran many stories about the antics, parties, eccentricities, and purchases of the new millionaires, who for a season were front-page news. Writing to the *New York Evening Post*, Carnegie lamented:

> These young men were models as long as they knew they had to be—besides they had my example & they were poor. Altho making large sums, these went to their credit paying for their interests. Now they see stock gamblers prominent in the Company & behind it. They become demoralized. . . . It is too sad for me to see such ruination morally. You will see I cannot speak of it publicly. My influence is best exerted privately upon the others. I am not in the proper position to play critic to my former associates publicly.

But the new millionaires were not the profligates Carnegie thought they had become. The newspapers exaggerated their antics and wild spending. Almost all survived the financial panics of 1901, 1903, and

1907, and some of their descendants remain prominent and wealthy citizens of the city.

Carnegie was particularly disappointed with Schwab, who had not only taken Frick's place at Carnegie Steel, but also had become the first president of U.S. Steel. In 1902 Schwab took a vacation in Europe, and at one point was in Monte Carlo. While there he took a modest turn at the roulette wheel, one several reporters noted, and which they turned into a gambling coup. According to the newspapers, Schwab had broken the bank, and one had the president of U.S. Steel carrying on at a wild party. Carnegie read the reports and wrote to Morgan of them:

> I feel in regard to the enclosed as if a son had disgraced the family. What the Times says is true. He is unfit to be the head of the United States Steel Co.—brilliant as his talents are. Of course he would never have so fallen with us. His resignation would have been called for instanter had he done so. . . . I have had nothing wound me so deeply for many a long day, if ever.

Schwab wrote to Carnegie, explaining what had really happened, but it is doubtful that the old man ever felt the same about his protégé.

Carnegie also resented the fact that Frick was named to the board of U.S. Steel, and so worked with Schwab. Frick remained interested in Big Steel, acting as a Rockefeller representative on the board. Frick was too independent to wear another man's collar for long, and he drifted from business. His magnificent Pittsburgh mansion—smaller than some of the others but done in far better taste—was abandoned for an equally impressive house in New York. Frick would continue to dabble in business and public affairs, but increasingly he turned to art, and before he died had amassed one of the finest collections in the world, one that rivaled Morgan's.

Frick sold much of his U.S. Steel stock, feeling that the company's management would not be able to weld its many components into a smoothly operating whole. A giant like U.S. Steel required a giant of a man at the helm, and Frick felt Schwab lacked the qualities for the job. Indeed, he was convinced that he was the only person capable of carrying it off. His judgment proved correct, as Big Steel never fulfilled the dreams of its creators. Those thousands of people who had purchased its securities saw their prices slide, while profits tended to follow the business cycle. The other steel companies—Jones & Laughlin, Tennessee Iron and Coal, Bethlehem, Cambria among them—did as well or better than Big Steel, and even after Morgan acquired the valuable Tennessee Iron & Coal properties in 1907 and merged them with Big Steel, the company's returns on investment and general performance were poor. Earnings and securities prices rose after the disastrous interlude of 1904, and the common reached its pre-World War I high of 91 in 1910. In that year Big Steel's return on investment was only 10.7 percent, however, or half of what had been anticipated for it in 1901 and far below the gargantuan returns shown by Carnegie Steel at its prime. This was another sign that Frick's judgment had been sound—U.S. Steel was not then, and for decades would not become, an integrated and smoothly operating company.

This meant little to the Carnegie millionaires, most of whom had diversified their holdings soon after the merger. They continued to

Profits and Securities Prices for U.S. Steel, 1901-1910

Year	Earnings (000 omitted)	Return on Investment	Common Stock High	Common Stock Low	Preferred Stock High	Preferred Stock Low
1901	$ 77,741	14.8	55	24	107-7/8	69
1902	121,502	15.9	46-3/4	29-3/4	97-3/4	79
1903	94,156	11.7	39-7/8	10	89-3/4	49-3/4
1904	62,491	7.6	33-1/2	8-3/8	95-5/8	51-1/4
1905	112,830	12.9	43-1/4	24-7/8	107	90-3/4
1906	143,393	15.1	50-1/4	32-7/8	113-1/4	98-3/4
1907	155,416	14.4	50-3/8	21-7/8	107-3/4	79-1/8
1908	84,793	7.8	58-3/4	25-3/4	114-5/8	78-1/2
1909	120,807	10.5	94-7/8	41-1/4	131	107
1910	127,216	10.7	91	61-1/8	125-3/8	110-1/2

Source: Cotter, *United States Steel*, p. 228, and Jones, *Trust Problem in the United States*, p. 211.

dominate Pittsburgh's society pages for decades, and their children and grandchildren would become the city's aristocracy. Pittsburgh was the steel capital of America, and in 1901 the metal seemed the key to the new century. This was not to be, as other industries outstripped steel. Still, the Carnegie millionaires went into other areas, and for a while Pittsburgh appeared a rival to New York as the petroleum center of America, the place from which non-Rockefeller companies would be controlled, or at least financed. For a generation Pittsburghers held to the dream of greatness, of successfully challenging New York. The dream was not realized, but it wasn't the result of lack of effort.

The great U.S. Steel flotation had significance far beyond that of the company, or Carnegie or Morgan, or even the industry. There had been mergers in American industry prior to the late 1890s, and securities flotations for railroads had made fortunes for promoters as early as the 1850s. But the great merger mania of the 1898–1903 period, one which continued for two more years after the U.S. Steel flotation was completed, was something startling for Americans. It created not one or two, or even a score of millionaires, but hundreds of them, and in a short period of time.

To many Americans this way to great wealth didn't seem right. These wealthy men hadn't made steel, or even managed the re-formed companies. Instead, they had manipulated paper, put together the pieces of a jigsaw puzzle, and then claimed the prize. Many were not certain such activities were moral. Or, as Bryan put it in 1896, on the eve of the merger mania, the men who put together such combinations were "the idle holders of idle capital."

Not Bryan, the American work ethic, or calls for government controls could stop the men of Wall Street who had learned to create fortunes out of paper overnight. The progressive movement, which began on a national scale soon after the steel merger, could not stop it. Land, canals, railroads, mines, cattle—millions had been made in these areas in the nineteenth century. The great fortunes of the twentieth century would be made from paper. This was the lesson of the merger mania which culminated in the steel flotation.

Henry Clay Frick, a man who had created an industrial empire, managed another, and then became a multimillionaire in a matter of days through the transfer of paper, felt ill at ease with all this—as might be expected of a transitional figure such as he. He continued to dislike Carnegie, not only for their clash, but also for his willingness to sacrifice his empire to the pad pushers of Wall Street. Frick had little to do with Morgan, and sniffed imperiously at the whole investment banker gang in lower Manhattan. As for his former colleagues at Carnegie—the Pittsburgh millionaires—he had no use for them either, calling them men with much money and little sense as to how it should be used.

Frick confided these feelings to some of his very few close friends. Andrew Mellon was one of them. He shared Frick's interests in business and art, and the two men had still closer ties in that Mellon's father, Thomas, had backed Frick when he had first started in coke. The friendship of Henry Clay Frick and Andrew Mellon was all the more interesting considering Mellon's position: he was a banker.

The Mellons were an old Pittsburgh family, Thomas settling there long before the Civil War. In 1870 he opened his bank, T. Mellon & Sons, which by the late 1870s was Pittsburgh's leading financial institution. Andrew took command at the bank in 1880, on his return from a European vacation with his friend, Henry Frick.

T. Mellon & Sons flourished under Andrew's command. The new president had a wider vision than his father. He had observed the Wall Street banks in action, learned how they financed railroads by raising funds for them while making huge commissions for themselves. Mellon was also alive to the fact that the nation's industries were growing, seeking capital, and merging, and that with these changes came additional opportunities for profit. In 1889 he learned of the Pittsburgh Reduction Company, which hoped to develop the Hall process for producing aluminum (and which in time became the Aluminum Company of America). Mellon was able to take control of the company in return for an advance of $250,000, and he also became the firm's investment banker. Mellon also organized the Union Transfer & Trust Company, with Frick a power on the board, to signal his own entrance into investment banking and his determination to make Pittsburgh the financial rival of New York. Mellon slowly became the financial czar of Pittsburgh, and at one point went so far as to try to take control of the Pittsburgh Petroleum Stock Exchange, and through it dominate local securities and the prices of non-Rockefeller oil companies. He failed in this attempt, but turned to other fields, even more ambitious.

Mellon backed Frick in his attempted take-over of Carnegie Steel, and when that move failed, helped him form and then supported Frick's Union Steel, a small but efficient and profitable factor in the industry. Then he made peace with U.S. Steel, and by 1902 was assisting in its financing. He worked to form Crucible Steel (not to be confused with the old Carnegie property) and Pittsburgh Steel, quietly but effectively spreading his net over the industry.

Andrew Mellon was also interested in oil. A nephew, William Lorimer Mellon, had entered the field by constructing pipelines and refineries, which he sold out at a large profit to the Rockefellers in 1895. William had learned of a new petroleum discovery in Texas in 1901, at a time when the financial pages were filled with stories of the steel reorganization. Most investors and bankers ignored it; everyone assumed the Rockefellers couldn't be challenged in their own field, since they held a position in oil greater even than Morgan's in investment banking or his new creation would have in steel. If the Texas find were worthwhile, so the argument went, the Rockefellers would soon have it under control. And if they didn't enter the field, it couldn't be that important.

The Mellons were intrigued and decided to explore the situation more closely. So were some of the Carnegie millionaires. Despite Frick's dislike of their antics, Mellon was on good terms with many of them, while they respected his abilities at investments. Now they would join with the Mellons to invest in Texas oil.

These investments paid off, and some of the Carnegie millionaires would make more money from Texas petroleum than they did from Pittsburgh steel. Largely because of the Texas find, Mellon would become one of the three American billionaires (along with Ford and

Rockefeller) of the first half of the twentieth century. His family conglomerate would in time dwarf U.S. Steel and rival that of the Rockefellers. Finally, Mellon would enter politics, and achieve greater power in that field than that enjoyed by any of the Fords or the Rockefellers (including Nelson Rockefeller of New York).

In 1901 Andrew Mellon was known as a friend of the great Henry Clay Frick—a middle-aged man of forty-six at the apex of his career, a big frog in the little pond that was Pittsburgh. Texas oil changed this. A generation later Mellon would be recognized as a power in his own right, while most Americans would associate Frick with his art collection, forgetting, if they ever knew, that its foundations were in coke and steel.

CHAPTER 7

Spindletop

Andrew Carnegie, J. P. Morgan, and John D. Rockefeller all were born within a four-year period in the mid-1830s, and each began his business career on the eve of the Civil War. In 1860 the twenty-three-year old Morgan organized J. P. Morgan & Co., which acted for his father's London-based banking house. That same year twenty-five-year-old Carnegie was elevated by Tom Scott to head the Pittsburgh division of the Pennsylvania Railroad. By the time the war had ended, Morgan was established on Wall Street, largely through his own talents but also because of his family name, while Carnegie had interests in railroading, construction, and iron and steel, all of which grew out of his connections with Scott as well as his business acumen.

Rockefeller's career had a different kind of beginning, and one far from the East. He came from an undistinguished family and lacked powerful friends. In 1857, at the age of eighteen, he helped organize the commission house of Clark & Rockefeller, one of many in Cleveland, Ohio. The firm did half a million dollars worth of business its first year. This was remarkable, all the more so considering that 1857 was a panic year, bad for business generally, but especially so in the Midwest.

Like Carnegie but unlike Morgan, Rockefeller was uncertain as to which field to concentrate upon. Carnegie came to steel slowly, almost reluctantly, and might just as easily have made a career in railroading. Under other circumstances Rockefeller might have become the merchant prince of the Midwest. Bessemer steel changed the course of Carnegie's life. A stroke of fortune, the discovery of oil in Pennsylvania in August 1859, affected Rockefeller in much the same way.

Rockefeller visited the oil field in 1860 and liked what he saw. Although remaining in the commission business during the Civil War, he also invested in the Excelsior Works, headed by Samuel Andrews, and by the end of the war this refinery was the largest in Cleveland. That year—1865—Rockefeller abandoned the commission business, which he realized would decline with the end of the fighting, in order to take personal charge of his petroleum refining interests, which were united under a new firm, Rockefeller & Andrews.

During the next four years Rockefeller established new companies, constructed additional facilities in Cleveland, arranged for eastern sales by setting up a New York office, and even entered the area of international sales. Then, in 1870, he consolidated his various companies into a single firm, Standard Oil of Ohio, which was capitalized at $1 million. The firm owned two refineries, a fleet of oil tank cars, sidings and warehouses in Pennsylvania's oil fields, warehouses in New York, and a barrel-making plant (and timberland to provide staves). Standard of Ohio was primarily a refiner, however, with transportation and distribution playing a secondary role in its operations. Standard owned no oil wells, did not explore for oil, and showed no desire to do so.

There was good reason for this strategy. Rockefeller lacked the wherewithal to establish a transportation network and distribution points, since to do so would mean a frontal assault on the railroads or the construction of pipelines and the development of a costly marketing setup. This would come in time, he thought, but for the moment he would concentrate on refining.

The market for petroleum products—kerosene, lubricants, medicines, paraffin, naphtha, solvents—was growing rapidly, and there was much money to be made by processing crude oil. It cost 30 cents to refine a barrel of crude, which contained forty-two gallons. In 1870, kerosene could fetch a dollar a gallon at the point of sale. This part of the business was constantly expanding and highly profitable.

Such was not the case with production of crude. Exploration and drilling were costly; dry holes seemed a bad investment to Rockefeller. The price of crude fluctuated wildly, dropping when new wells were found, rising sharply when they were not. At the time the first Pennsylvania fields were being explored, crude fetched $20 a barrel. Then a flood of oil came to market, and in two years the price was 10 cents a barrel. It rose again soon after, leveling out at around $7 in 1869, and then fell to below $3 in 1870, at the time Standard of Ohio was formed.

Let others take this risk, thought Rockefeller. In time he hoped to dominate refining, and then distribution and marketing, all of which were the profit centers for the industry. Explorers and drillers would look for and find oil, and sell it to him at his price, since he hoped to be the only big buyer in the field. He could buy when prices were low and store the crude in Standard's tanks. Rockefeller would leave the market when prices rose, in this way forcing the quotations down once again. It seemed simple enough; he would control the industry by owning the spigot, and let others take care of the reservoir.

Rockefeller carried out the first parts of his program with boldness. He forced out competition in the Cleveland area through cutting prices, bankrupting his opponents, and then taking them over. Rockefeller used his increasingly dominant position to extract concessions from those on whom he depended for supplies, transportation, and other forms of cooperation. Should a supplier ask for more than what Rockefeller deemed a fair price, he would be pushed to the wall and forced to surrender. Standard would join with rival companies to sign agreements with railroads, would lead the industry in fighting the lines when the time came, and then, when the arrangement no longer suited the company, would go off on its own again, gobbling up former allies. Rockefeller would give his business to a railroad so long as he received rebates on shipments, a not unusual practice at the time. Should the line refuse, he would use its rivals, take over a pipeline or build his own, and in time either force the enemy to give in or destroy it.

In the 1870s Rockefeller expanded into marketing, acquiring several regional distributing companies and building upon them. As before, he acquired functioning firms at bargain prices and set up rival operations when they would not capitulate. What was already being called "the octopus" overspread the industry, accounting for some 90 percent of refinery runs and setting prices on major products.

By 1880 Standard of Ohio truly was the "standard" for petroleum, even more so than Carnegie was for steel. The company had competitors, but none approached it in size. The rest had been destroyed, acquired, or divided. According to Rockefeller, this was natural and desirable, something that could not be prevented, or if it could, should not be. As he would say later on, the price for having a perfect American beauty rose was the destruction of the lesser buds that surrounded it. No less than Carnegie and Morgan, Rockefeller was a believer in Social Darwinism.

Rockefeller again restructured his holdings in 1882, this time to form the Standard Oil Trust, which consisted of fourteen wholly owned companies, including Standard of Ohio, and twenty-six partly owned firms, ranging in size from the huge National Transit Company, capitalized at $30 million, to the Germania Mining Company, with a capitalization of $30,000. Members of the trust received $70 million in certificates, with Rockefeller and his direct allies receiving a majority.

The trust agreement provided for the formation of a group of subsidiaries, bearing the Standard name, to be established in New

York, New Jersey, Ohio, and Pennsylvania, with each to concentrate its attention in the state named in its title. The structure remained in force for ten years, being dissolved in 1892 as a result of successful antitrust actions initiated by the state of Ohio. Rockefeller, who at that time owned 256,854 of the 972,500 certificates outstanding, reorganized the trust into twenty operating companies, and presided over the distribution. National Transit was to be the largest of the successor companies, with a newly structured and renamed Standard Oil Company (New Jersey) next. The New Jersey firm would become the flagship of the Standard fleet, and the vehicle through which Rockefeller hoped to complete his domination of world petroleum.

Rockefeller and Standard Oil had faced and dealt with a wide variety of problems in the 1870s and 1880s, most of them from rival firms, enraged state legislatures, and technological bottlenecks. All had been overcome, or, with the case of the Ohio antitrust action, sidestepped. In 1892 it seemed Standard would have only minor problems dealing with competing refineries and transit companies. Rival refiners in the Appalachians combined in 1895 to form Pure Oil Company, which announced its intention to remain independent of the octopus and fight it for markets and sales. But Pure lacked the power of Standard, and could not hope to defeat it in head-on combat, at least not without the help of outside forces.

This help was at hand in the 1890s, in the form of a reform movement that singled out Rockefeller as its target in much the same way Morgan would be earmarked during the next decade. The early 1890s was a period of depression and social unrest, much of which was based on the belief that the large corporations were taking control of the country, with the average citizen having no recourse against their power.

In 1890 Congress passed and President Benjamin Harrison signed the Sherman Antitrust Act, which though weak and almost unworkable, marked the entry of the federal government into the battle. There were 1,897 work stoppages and strikes in 1890, a high point in the century, and strike actions would continue at only a slightly lower level for the rest of the decade. In 1892, the year the Standard Trust was dissolved, the silver miners at Coeur d'Alene, Idaho, went on strike, and soon after pitched battles between workers and strikebreakers erupted, resulting in the calling out of federal troops and guerrilla warfare that continued for years after. The Homestead strike at Carnegie followed, the one in which an assassination attempt was made on Frick, and during which battles between strikers and the state militia resulted in deaths.

The Populist party held its first national convention in 1892, demanding social justice and sweeping reforms. "The fruits of the toil of millions are boldly stolen to build up colossal fortunes for a few," said the platform. "From the same prolific womb of governmental injustice we breed the two great classes—tramps and millionaires."

There seemed little doubt Standard Oil was in the minds of the delegates at the St. Louis convention. That year the trust earned a record $19.1 million. The depression would hurt the companies in 1893 and 1894, but in 1895, Standard's earnings topped the $24-million mark. There seemed no way to stop it, except through governmental action.

By that time many Americans were reading Henry Demarest Lloyd's *Wealth Against Commonwealth*. Elaborating upon an *Atlantic Monthly* article first published in 1881, combining it with government reports, court cases, and newspaper articles, Lloyd drew up an indictment against Standard Oil which, though overstated, exaggerated, and inaccurate, was powerful. To him Standard was the symbol of all that was wrong with the country, and he called for its dissolution. "We must either regulate, or own, or destroy, perishing by the sword we take."

> Nature is rich; but everywhere man, the heir of nature, is poor. Never in this happy country or elsewhere—except in the Land of Miracle, where "They did all eat and were filled"—has there been enough of anything for the people. Never since time began have all been shod and roofed. Never yet have all the virgins, wise or foolish, been able to fill their lamps with oil.

* * *

During the previous two decades Rockefeller had engulfed or crushed his rivals. No firm or group of firms could defy him. Now Lloyd and an army of writers, reform politicians, and judges would attempt to do what businessmen could not—contain Standard Oil, or, as Rockefeller might have put it, prune the American beauty rose.

A second threat to Rockefeller's ambitions came from Europe, a prime market for American petroleum products. During the first half of the 1880s an average of $47.8 million in American petroleum products were sent to the rest of the world, more than two-thirds the total for meat exports in that period of the great beef bonanza. Standard dominated the American petroleum export field as it did that of domestic refining, operating through affiliates in every major European nation as well as those in Asia and other parts of the world. But trade relations were not good. Standard charged the Europeans higher prices than it did the Americans, knowing they had no other major supplier. Then, too, the quality of Standard's exports was not as high as the Europeans demanded. For example, American kerosene did not burn well in European lamps.

In 1879 European businessmen convened in Bremen to form a united front against the Americans and to seek a remedy. Wilson King, the American consul in the city, reported, "I regret to say that a bitter feeling towards Americans was somewhat snarlingly expressed by the spokesman of the Hamburg delegation and only very mildly resented by the gentlemen from Bremen and Breslau." Yet Standard did not accept the protests, agreeing to only a few minor changes, and suggesting the Europeans use shorter wicks in the lamps to prevent future difficulties.

It was a foolish rejoinder, for by the late 1870s a new supplier of petroleum products was at hand. Oil was discovered in the Baku area of Russia in 1872, and the following year the first major wells were tapped. These appeared richer than any American wells, with one producing at a daily rate of 43,000 barrels, at a time when few Pennsylvania wells pumped as much as 1,000 barrels, and most were in the 20-barrel range.

The Baku rush drew businessmen from all corners of Europe to Russia. The Nobel brothers, Robert, Ludwig, and Alfred, were the most important, opening their first refinery in 1876 and two years later organizing the Nobel Brothers Naphtha Company, which was capitalized at $2.5 million. The Nobels constructed rail lines and pipelines, built a fleet of tankers, set out to capture the Russian market, and then sell their products abroad. By the mid-1880s they were selling half the illuminating oil consumed in Russia, at a time when that country was self-sufficient in that product, as American imports fell below 10 percent. The total Russian exports of kerosene to Europe were only half a million barrels that year, small compared with American exports of well over 10 million barrels, but the Russian product was growing at a more rapid rate than was the American, and Standard was forced to pay attention to it. So were the Europeans. In 1885 British petroleum expert Boverton Redwood told English importers "not to entirely stop the importation of American oil but to rely more largely upon the Russian product," unless the Americans made adjustments in price and quality, and as he spoke the Russian tankers entered the Thames for the first time.

Nor were the Nobels the only threat. Baron Alphonse de Rothschild organized the Caspian & Black Sea Company, which refined and distributed Russian petroleum. The Shibaieff Company's kerosene competed successfully against Standard brands in central Europe. Oil shale was being exploited in Scotland, wells were being reported in Austria-Hungary, Canada, Japan, and Java. Royal Dutch Petroleum was intent not only on dominating the East Indies oil, but forcing Standard from the Pacific. M. Samuel & Co., which would become Shell Transport & Trading Company in 1897, also explored possibilities in Asia, threatening Rockefeller from yet another quarter.

In 1882 the United States produced 85 percent of the world's oil, with Standard accounting for the largest share. Standard's position in American refining was greater in 1888 than it had been in 1882, but in that year America's share of world production was down to 53 percent. It seemed that although Rockefeller would be able to dominate American refining, he could not hope for an imperial position in Europe and Asia.

As might have been expected, Standard struck back, organizing new foreign affiliates, signing agreements with more powerful distributors, upgrading its products, and lowering prices. In addition, Standard signed marketing agreements with the Nobels, the Rothschilds, and other foreign firms, agreeing to share markets and limit competition. In this way, Rockefeller and his new allies extended the community-of-interests concept to the world itself. Rockefeller was a globalist in the late 1880s and early 1890s, but had no hope of destroying his foreign allies-of-convenience as he had his domestic ones. Foreign competition, together with increased domestic political and legal pressures, complicated Standard's problems in the late 1880s, and were the major storm clouds visible on the horizon.

Meanwhile, Rockefeller and his associates worked to complete their web of domination in the United States. They had what amounted to an effective monopoly in refining and distribution in most parts of the country, but in the past had done little in the area of discovery and production. Now, with petroleum usage increasing rapidly, they reassessed the situation.

Standard's opportunity arrived in the mid-1880s, when a successful well was drilled near Lima, Ohio. It was a moderate producer, yielding around twenty-five barrels a day. Others were drilled, with few producing more than a hundred barrels. This was considered a worthy find, and oilmen from Pennsylvania and other states were drawn to Lima, marking the opening of a new boom. Standard also arrived, and in typical fashion ignored discovery and production to construct the Buckeye pipeline, which Rockefeller expected to be the major conduit bringing Ohio crude to market.

Ohio oil had characteristics that made it less desirable than the Pennsylvania product. It had a high sulfur content and did not refine easily. Kerosene produced from it performed poorly in lamps, crusting the wicks and clouding the chimneys. To solve this problem, Standard selected Herman Frasch, a German-born chemist who had worked in petroleum before (and would later develop the process for extraction of sulfur associated with his name). Frasch succeeded in finding a new method of refining that produced fine kerosene from Ohio crude, and his process was patented in 1887. Soon after, Standard began quietly to buy out producers in the Ohio fields, while other Rockefeller companies, most notably National Transit, did the same.

In 1889 Standard purchased Ohio Oil Company, which held leases on more than 20,000 acres of oil land with 146 wells already in production. Other, smaller acquisitions followed. By 1891 Standard controlled more than half the production of the Ohio-Indiana field, when the field yielded 17.5 million barrels, a quarter of the total United States production. In that year the field had 4,689 wells, producing crude at a daily average of 10.1 barrels a day.

Standard expanded its operations to West Virginia and Kansas in the 1890s, and added to its Pennsylvania holdings. But its main effort was in Ohio-Indiana. Although 1891 was a peak year for Ohio Oil, and output would decline soon after, it still outproduced Standard's other interests in 1899. By then the company was bringing in more than 18 million barrels a year from its wells—almost a third of the nation's production.

Standard seemed reasonably content with what it had—leadership in all three areas of the industry. There was talk of new explorations in California and Texas, but due to local political opposition Standard's executives would not take the company into those states. John D. Archbold, who had battled Rockefeller early in his career and then was "acquired" by Standard, was one of the inner circle that ruled the company. He offered what he said was the last word on the subject when he swore he would drink every gallon of crude discovered west of the Mississippi.

Archbold actually knew better. Some oil had been found in California in the mid-nineteenth century, although serious exploration did not begin until the early 1890s. At that time too there was talk of oil in south Texas. Seepages were found in Hardin, Angelina, and Nacogdoches Counties, and in 1866 the first Texas oil well was drilled at Oil Springs, Nacogdoches County. The well was not very productive, and soon was abandoned, but other drilling followed. From 1886 to 1889, less than 4,000 barrels were produced in the entire state. Texas used little oil in this period—its population was only 1.5 million in 1880, at a time when the nation's population was over 50 million—and most of its kerosene came from other states, a good deal under the Standard labels.

As had several states in this period, Texas passed an antitrust act in 1889. Soon after, Attorney General James Hogg began investigating complaints against Rockefeller practices deemed in violation of the act. Together with Waters-Pierce, which was 60.7 percent Standard-owned, Standard was manipulating the markets for kerosene, granting rebates to companies which discontinued handling rival products. In 1894, Hogg, who was now governor, instructed the attorney general to initiate action against the companies. The result was *The State of Texas* v. *John D. Rockefeller et al.* Indictments were drawn against Rockefeller, Archbold, and other Standard officials, as well as officers of Waters-Pierce. Hogg followed this up by asking New York Governor Roswell Flower to extradite Rockefeller for trial.

Samuel Dodd, Standard's counsel, advised Rockefeller to ignore the order, saying the Texans had "one of those crazy socialistic laws which are unconstitutional." In any case, Flower refused to comply with Hogg's request. The matter did not die there, however, for in 1898 the Texas Supreme Court upheld a lower court's decision to suspend Waters-Pierce's rights to do business in the state.

Throughout the 1890s and into the early twentieth century, Texas was unreceptive to Rockefeller companies. It was one of several states with this policy, at a time when the great Texas oil bonanza was about to begin. The reformers had failed to halt Standard with a direct attack. The Texas approach was designed to limit the firm territorially. It succeeded, far more than the reformers thought it would, and in a totally unexpected fashion and places.

At the time, the men of Standard hadn't heard of Corsicana, Texas, and the citizens of that town cared little for petroleum and knew less.

Ever since its founding in 1849, Corsicana had been oriented toward cotton, serving as a center for the farms of the area. The cotton market was bad in the early 1890s, leading the townspeople to make plans for diversification through attracting new industry.

Corsicana had barely 4,000 people, and was a hot, dusty place, with little to attract new settlers. Water was a major problem. Although sufficient water existed for cotton, more would be needed to serve an enlarged population and new enterprises. So the town's leaders organized the Corsicana Water Development Co. in 1894, and began digging. The driller did not find an underground stream. Instead, at 1,035 feet, he struck oil.

The Corsicanans were disappointed. Work continued until water was found at 2,470 feet. By then, 150 gallons of crude a day were also being collected from the well. Several townspeople organized the Corsicana Oil Development Company but little was done to activate it until the arrival of James McClurg Guffey and John Galey in 1895.

Guffey and Galey were already famous for their abilities at finding oil, operating for the most part in Pennsylvania and based in Pittsburgh. It was the day of the wildcatter, and Guffey and Galey were two of the best. They inspected the site and offered Corsicana Oil a deal. They would drill on the land and bear all costs, in return for which they wanted a half interest in their discoveries, if any. Corsicana Oil accepted, and the team began work soon after. Some oil was found, but not enough to warrant additional investment. Guffey and Galey sold their interest, Corsicana Oil was liquidated, and a new firm, Southern Oil, capitalized at $100,000, was organized to take its place. Other firms, among them Texas Petroleum, were also organized, and they obtained leases and began what for Texas seemed a major drilling operation, but was really small compared to what was going on in Pennsylvania. Still, in 1896 the young Corsicana field produced 1,450 barrels of crude, and the figure rose to 65,975 in 1897.

By then the Corsicana companies discovered they lacked the management skills needed to operate in the industry. Capital had to be raised, perhaps a refinery established in town, and the products had to be brought to market. All of this was foreign to cotton farmers and small-town businessmen and bankers.

The companies began considering bringing in an outsider. They might have sought the intervention of one of the large firms—certainly not Standard, but one of its competitors. But the Corsicanans wanted their interests to be Texas-owned and operated. They wanted a person or people to manage their affairs, not take them over. That is why the approached Joseph Cullinan.

Cullinan arrived in Corsicana in 1897 seeking oil. He seemed friendly, and the Texans liked him, even though his past was unknown at the time. Cullinan preferred it that way, for had the townspeople known he was a former Standard Oil man, he might have been invited to leave. More to the point, Cullinan was there backed by New York capital—Standard Oil money, it would appear. Henry Folger, secretary of Standard's manufacturing committee and at the age of thirty-three already earmarked for future leadership, and Calvin Payne, director of five Standard companies and Rockefeller's pipeline expert, had "invested" in Cullinan, using their own money, not Standard's. But the connection, and its implications, seemed evident. So for the moment, at least, Cullinan said nothing of Folger and Payne.

Cullinan, supposedly an independent, surveyed the field, spoke to suppliers and refinery outfits, and returned in 1898 with a proposition. He would contract with the three largest producers—Texas Petroleum, Southern Oil, and Oil City—to purchase 100,000 barrels at 50 cents a barrel over a period of two years. At the time Pennsylvania crude was fetching a dollar a barrel and more, but the Corsicanans accepted, since they felt they had no alternative but to enter the business themselves, and that was beyond their scope. But many didn't like the deal. Already rumors of Cullinan's Standard affiliations were being spread, at a time when the Waters-Pierce case had just been decided by the state Supreme Court. Still, Corsicana remained true to Cullinan, and honored the contract.

At the same time Cullinan signed an agreement with Folger and Payne, setting up a company to be known as J. S. Cullinan & Co., and incorporated at Corsicana. The firm was capitalized at $100,000, with the Standard partners providing the money, and Cullinan the leadership, at a salary of $5,000 a year. Now Cullinan proceeded with his plan, constructing a pipeline and starting work on a refinery. Then, as though in imitation of Rockefeller, he announced he would only process and send the 100,000 barrels agreed upon; the smaller Corsicana outfits would be denied access to markets, and so be destroyed.

The town rebelled at this, forcing Cullinan to back down. Turning to a flanking operation, Cullinan organized Corsicana Petroleum Company, capitalized at $300,000 and the largest in the region. Payne, with the backing of Standard Oil executives, took 2,500 of the 3,000 shares, while Cullinan and a friend obtained 125 each, with the remaining 250 distributed to local businessmen whose help had been given in the past and who could be counted on for future favors.

Corsicana Petroleum took over other producing firms in the area, and by the turn of the century was the dominant force in Texas oil. In time, perhaps, when antitrust tempers cooled, Payne, Folger, and Cullinan would merge into Standard of Jersey. At least this seemed a possibility. If this happened, Texas oil would join Ohio-Indiana and Pennsylvania as Standard fiefs.

A handful of men shattered the pattern, and they did this in Beaumont, Texas.

Like Corsicana, Beaumont was a small, unimpressive town, one of those seeking revitalization in the face of the depression of the 1890s. It was twenty-one miles inland from the Gulf of Mexico, on the Neches River—Beaumont was called "Queen of the Neches"—and northeast of Galveston, not far from the Louisiana border. Its major industry was lumber, with rice a close second. Over 60 percent of the state's rice was grown in the swampy land near the Neches, and Beaumont's citizens planned for the day when they could dredge the river and so send their rice and lumber into the Gulf, and from there to other parts of the Southeast, making their town the rice capital of Texas and the region.

Beaumont's citizens knew of Corsicana oil, but few thought their land contained deposits. The geology was all wrong. Petroleum had always been associated with rock formations, and there were none in or near Beaumont—only large salt mounds, forests, prairie—and swamps.

The swamps were well known, as were some springs. There was one near Big Hill where "sour water" came from the ground, blue, green, and at times yellow in color, smelling somewhat like kerosene, and, at times, rotten eggs. The sick would bathe in the waters, and some would drink them, in the hope that they would prove curative. Such springs—and there were several in the area—became a poor man's spa, but only during the day. There were supposed to be ghosts in Big Hill. Some swore they saw them, although the more scientific believed it was St. Elmo's fire, a natural phenomenon associated with gas. Natural gas in turn was associated with oil, and the waters seemed to contain the substance.

A few knew of this, and tried to profit therefrom. In 1866 a Dr. B. T. Kavanaugh came upon the "medicinal spring" at Big Hill and another at Sour Lake. He recognized the waters as containing crude. Later on he wrote, "Here I found some fine veins, one passing under the sour wells some mile or two southwest of Beaumont. Also I visited Sour Lake, where I found oil upon the surface in greater quantity than at any other point." Kavanaugh explored farther, going to the coast, where he found a substance "in lumps like wax, which the people call 'sea wax.' When examined, this wax is found to consist of bitumen and paraffin. The petroleum being a thin liquid, is washed out of the mixture, leaving the bitumen and paraffin as a wax or gum which is found on the beach."

Kavanaugh drilled the first oil well in town, but he could not go beyond 142 feet, quitting because quicksand clogged his rig and his money ran out. He stayed in the area for a while, and came across more evidence of petroleum. Kavanaugh learned that Spanish survivors of the De Soto expedition washed up on the coast near Beaumont in 1543, and there discovered tar with which to caulk their boats. In the nineteenth century, shipmasters reported "an immense oil pool, about a mile and a half in width and four miles in length" off the coast. Many in Beaumont knew of this, but none did anything about it.

Pattillo (sometimes spelled Patillo) Higgins was one of those who heard the stories and meant to act upon them. A self-made man who had gotten his start in lumbering and from there had gone on to do fairly well in real estate, Higgins owned several hundred acres near Beaumont on which he found good brick clay. He explored the possibility of starting a brickworks in town, and in the process visited several elsewhere. He was intrigued to learn that a few had converted from wood and coal to oil. Higgins was told that oil was a superior fuel; it burned at a constant temperature, was a more efficient source of heat than coal, and could be stored more easily than other fuels. Nothing came of the brick venture, but it served to interest Higgins in petroleum. He read all he could find on the subject, and in the process became convinced that there was oil under Big Hill, near Spindletop Springs, on the outskirts of town.

In 1892, Higgins obtained an option on a thousand acres of land near Spindletop Springs, and soon after organized a company, Gladys City Oil, Gas and Manufacturing, which was capitalized at $200,000. There was no Gladys City—the company was named after Gladys Bingham, a childhood friend, and at the time of its founding, the firm had no manufacturing facilities or the indication that gas or oil was under the land. Yet Higgins was able to interest some of the townspeople in taking shares, and began exploratory drillings.

Higgins did not find oil, or gas, or initiate manufacturing facilities. And Beaumont was struck by the ripples from the panic of 1893, causing the lumber industry to decline. The investors sold their shares and took losses; even Higgins was obliged to sell off most of his holding.

But news of the drilling spread, and in 1895 Savage & Co. of West Virginia entered the scene, offering to bore new wells in return for a 10-percent royalty. Higgins agreed, reluctantly, for he had hoped to bring the well in himself. Savage was granted an option, but did not find oil in the time specified. Then a second option was granted, this time to the Texas Mineral Company—really Savage in a different corporate disguise—and once again the drilling failed. With this, the outsiders left the scene.

Higgins' confidence was shaken, even if his faith remained strong. He asked the Texas state geologist, Robert Dumble, to look the situation over. Dumble sent an assistant, William Kennedy, to Beaumont. Kennedy went to Spindletop Springs, walked around Big Hill, stood atop Sour Spring Mound, a rise in the land, and pored over the records. Then he told Higgins there definitely was no oil in Beaumont. Oil was found under rock, and there were no rock formations in the area. A few years earlier a 1,400-foot water well was dug at Beaumont, and even this hadn't struck rock. With this, Kennedy left town.

News of the report reached the Gladys City investors, and they abandoned the company, determined to write off their losses. As for Higgins, he continued to hope. He advertised for wildcatters, offering a lease on Gladys City land in return for an interest in what was discovered beneath it. In early 1899 Higgins received a reply, from a Captain Anthony F. Lucas.

Lucas was an unusual man, and, to the Texans, a true exotic. He had been born in Dalmatia, then part of the Austro-Hungarian Empire, as Anthony Luchich. After graduating from the school of mining engineering at Gratz, he entered the Austrian Naval Academy, and upon completion of his studies was commissioned a lieutenant in the Austrian navy. Before reporting for duty he visited an uncle in Michigan. Luchich liked the United States, so much so that he decided to stay. He applied for American citizenship, changed his name to Lucas, gave himself a promotion to captain, found employment as a mining engineer, and married the daughter of a Georgia doctor.

Lucas specialized in petroleum discovery and made a reputation in the field for bold and daring ideas. Once, while in Louisiana, he visited the salt domes near the coast. These were formations not very different from those Higgins had seen in and near Spindletop Springs. Lucas found traces of oil in them, just as Higgins had found some in the bubbling waters of the springs. He concluded that the domes capped large oil deposits, larger perhaps than those found in the rocky formations in Pennsylvania and Ohio. In other words, the captain and Higgins had come to the same conclusion by different means, and this was why Lucas answered Higgins' advertisement.

Lucas visited Beaumont, spoke with Higgins, and the two men went to look over the situation at Spindletop. The captain was satisfied the region had oil. Together they approached the Gladys City investors, and with Higgins' help, Lucas was awarded an option to drill for oil. The investors would receive a total of $31,150, and Lucas would assume all costs of operations.

The captain began work the last day of June 1899, and from the first had trouble. The methods he had used to drill for oil in Pennsylvania didn't work in the marshy land at Spindletop. He was plagued by quicksand, clogged pipes, and sludge deposits, which caused operations to go slowly. It had not at all proceeded according to plan.

Late in 1899 Lucas was out of money. He asked Higgins to approach his Beaumont contacts to ask for new financing, but the Gladys City group was unwilling to put more into what they already considered a useless venture. Then Lucas traveled to Washington and New York, seeking outside support. Congressman Joseph Sibley of Pennsylvania, a large oil investor, listened to Lucas, but nothing came of their meeting. Then Lucas traveled to Standard headquarters in New York, and met with Payne and Folger. At that time the Corsicana refinery was nearing completion, and the partners knew that Cullinan needed additional crude to run it at full capacity. They were sufficiently interested for Payne to go to Beaumont in late February, 1900, where he and Cullinan inspected the Lucas well. Neither man was impressed. Cullinan said little, while Payne told the captain that he had seen wells in all parts of the world, and knew that no crude would be found under the Spindletop salt domes.

Two months later C. Willard Hayes of the United States Geological Survey came to Beaumont, and he verified Payne's judgment. Hayes added that a 3,070-foot well had been drilled at Galveston, at a cost of a million dollars, and that no oil had been found. That well was around forty miles from Spindletop. Hayes advised Lucas and Higgins to cut losses and use the land for other purposes.

Lucas did receive some encouragement from William Phillips, a professor of geology at the University of Texas. Phillips thought Lucas might be right, and he offered to put the captain in touch with some men who might help him. These were Guffey and Galey, who had returned to Pittsburgh and the Pennsylvania fields after selling their Corsicana interests. The partners knew of the Corsicana operations, and realized they had given up too soon. Perhaps they were ready to return to Texas for another try.

Guffey and Galey indeed were interested. They would back Lucas if the captain could offer more substantial proof that there was crude under Spindletop Springs, and would give him until July 1900 to do so. If and when this happened, they would invest $300,000 in the operation. Guffey and Galey would obtain the services of Al and Curt Hamill, then in Corsicana, and known as the best drilling team in that part of the country.

There was one additional condition. Guffey disliked the Texans, and would have nothing to do with them. As far as he was concerned, his deal was with Lucas. If the captain wanted to share with Higgins and others of the Gladys City group, that was his concern. But Lucas was not to tell Higgins of the deal, at least not until the well was brought in.

Lucas accepted. After his experience with Payne and Folger, he had been discouraged. Now he had new hope. In this way, Standard missed its chance to obtain control at Spindletop, and Pittsburgh began its career as not only the steel capital of the nation, but a rival to Cleveland and New York in petroleum.

The captain rushed back to Beaumont, obtained additional leases, sold his furniture and anything else that might command a price, and with the money traveled to Corsicana to meet the Hamills. Meanwhile Galey went to Beaumont, secretly so that none in town would know he was there, and looked at the well. He left instructions with Mrs. Lucas to begin a new well on the south side of

Spindletop, a distance from the original site. "Tell that captain of yours to start that first well right here," he said. "And tell him that I know he is going to hit the biggest oil well this side of Baku."

When Lucas and the Hamills returned they lined up pipe and lumber suppliers and started in at the new site. Early in October the work began, with Lucas applying lessons he had learned from his first well. "At first I employed the system of boring which I had previously used in the Louisiana salt deposits. But I soon found this method was inadequate, without modification, to deal with the quicksand. Accordingly, I adopted the use of large and heavy castings and pipes of 12, 10, 8, 6, and 4 inches in diameter, successively telescoped one into the other."

Yet like the first hole, this second one caused trouble from the start. Breakdowns, small blowouts, and clogged pipes plagued the Hamills. Small quantities of oil came up on the sludge, and some seeped to the surface. Lucas and the Hamills were encouraged, and they pressed on.

Work was going well in early December, when at 880 feet the bit struck a hard formation. Weary and somewhat discouraged, the workers halted operations for a Christmas break. They were back on the job on New Year's Day, 1901, and quickly struck gas. The captain ignited the gas, causing the sky to be illuminated. This was considered a good omen, and the tempo of work picked up.

At 1,020 feet the bit struck a crevice and was forced off center. Al Hamill wired a third brother, Jim, in Corsicana, for a new fishtail bit, hoping that with it he could drive through the blockage. The bit arrived the morning of January 10, was installed, and lowered into the well. At a depth of 1,700 feet, the rotary mud began to rise, increasing at a more rapid rate than expected—more rapid, in fact, than any Curt Hamill had ever witnessed. The flow subsided, and the workmen began to move back to the rig. Then the ground began to shake, and in amazement the drillers watched mud, water, pipe, rigging—and crude—push toward the sky, in a geyser of oil.

None of the men had ever seen its like. There had been talk of such strikes in Russia, but they were believed exaggerated. Now they saw it with their own eyes. More crude rushed from the Spindletop well than came from many Pennsylvania fields; indeed, the crude released that first day was more than most Pennsylvania wells were capable of producing in a year.

It has been called the gusher heard round the world. At the time it seemed a great petroleum bonanza, one that might shift the center of production from Ohio-Indiana to Texas. It was far more than that, however. The Spindletop discovery marked the beginning of the greatest mineral rush since the Klondike in 1898, and the most important oil discovery the nation had known since Colonel Drake's first find in Pennsylvania. The mania for oil was sparked, and before it ended Texas crude would help create huge business empires and hundreds of millionaires, and in the process destroy the Standard Oil quasi-monopoly.

For the moment, however, Beaumont became the oil capital of the world, as wildcatters from all parts of America and Europe too, scrambled for places on ships and trains going there. Beaumont's population rose from barely 9,000 in January 1901 to 50,000 two years later. Old-time gold and silver miners in San Francisco read that Texas was "oil wild and land crazy," and chartered trains to take them there for one last fling. Texas railroads did a bonanza business, welcome after a period of near-bankruptcy. "In Beaumont, You'll see a Gusher Gushing," they advertised, and hundreds of tourists came in the first months to see the new marvel.

As the field developed and other derricks were constructed, wildcatters would stage contests, releasing their wells and betting on which gusher would rise the highest. In so doing they wasted more crude than the state had produced in any single year prior to Spindletop. Swindlers, promoters, and brokers flocked to buy and sell lease rights, and with them in hand would form companies, sell shares, and make fortunes in a matter of days or weeks. In 1901 over $200 million of the stock of more than four hundred companies was issued. Stock exchanges were formed in Beaumont, Houston, and Galveston, and for a while did a bigger volume of business than any of the regional markets. The Houston market alone recorded sales of 7.2

million shares in its first eight months, and although there are no records of the Beaumont Stock Exchange, it probably did better than that. Indeed, Beaumont was the place to buy and sell oil shares; New York's Curb Market was far behind, as were other secondary securities exchanges.

Texans were known even then for tall tales and tongue-in-cheek exaggerations, but none of this was necessary in east Texas in 1901. A *St. Louis Post-Dispatch* reporter told of getting off the train and, before leaving the station, being offered a lease for $1,000. He refused, but another passenger took it, and within the hour resold it for $5,000. Soon after, the lease was transferred at $20,000. At the peak of the oil rush, Beaumont land was selling for $1 million an acre, and even rights to drill in the streets were sold.

Provisioners set up shops in town, and charged three and four times the going prices for their wares. Beaumont's drinking water supply was limited, and soon water was more expensive than imported wine, at a time when crude oil was selling for 3 cents a barrel. Restaurants charged $10 for a meal, and waiters expected even more than that in tips. Prostitutes did a round-the-clock business, and news of their success reached the big cities farther north, draining them of their ladies of the evening, who went to Beaumont to put in double and triple time at ten times their customary rates. Fortune-tellers came to town, promising to foresee where the next big strike would take place. They didn't do well, for it seemed that every driller was hitting oil. Later on, however, a boy who claimed to have X-ray eyes and could see beneath the surface did better.

In short, Beaumont was a boomtown, much as Virginia City had been during the days of the Comstock Lode. The money mania had come to east Texas, and those who participated predicted it would last for years. For once, wild predictions such as these fell short of the mark.

Fortunes were made in securities, provisions, oil field services, transportation, housing—in fact, in every area needed by those seeking oil. But the really big money was not made in the fields. Rather, it gravitated to boardrooms in New York, Pittsburgh, London—and Corsicana.

During the next few months the Hamills and other drillers brought in additional wells. Meanwhile, company formation, maneuvering, combination, and transformation proceeded, with each of several groups of men jockeying for position, trying to ease the Lucas-Guffey-Galey combine out of Spindletop and the Beaumont region, or failing in this, getting their shares or working out a deal with the partners.

In other times, with a different product and different men, Guffey and Galey might have attempted to make their fortunes and then retire to new fields. But these men, the most experienced in petroleum in America outside the Standard Oil complex, knew better than Lucas, Higgins, the wildcatters, and even Cullinan that though Spindletop would pose many problems and require heavy financing—more than they could afford—it was no single-shot bonanza. In 1901 many industries were considering converting to oil for power—Higgins had seen it occurring with bricks. Already steamships and some railroads were using the fuel, since it was more dependable than coal or wood, more compact, and less troublesome. The market for kerosene was constantly expanding in Asia and Africa, though electricity had cut back on its use in Europe and America. Even then, oil, and not coal, seemed the desirable fuel for electric power plants far from waterpower sources. Lubricants were needed in ever-increasing quantities by factories. In 1900 only 8,000 automobiles were registered in the United States, but the number rose to 14,800 in 1901 and 23,000 the following year. This gasoline-burning vehicle would almost certainly consume larger and larger amounts of fuel each year, and would be a bonus to the industry—in 1901 few thought it would be more than that, though.* Guffey and Galey had spoken of this situation in the past, and would refer to it in the future, when attempting to raise money to finance their operations.

*By 1907 there were 143,200 motor vehicles registered in the United States, and in that year 43,000 passenger cars were produced. Yet even then gasoline was considered a by-product of kerosene. Although it was costly, the price was set artificially, in the face of excess supply. In that year tankers would dump gasoline in the ocean as a waste product, a practice of many years standing. But that was the last year it was done.

In 1900 several oceangoing ships had experimented with oil power and naval authorities were interested in its use in war. Some railroads were considering it, since oil was a cleaner fuel than coal, more efficient, and, under some circumstances, cheaper. Guffey and Galey hoped that Spindletop—which, if up to expectations, would provide a regular supply of crude, lead to lower prices, and spur an aggressive marketing effort—would hasten the conversion.* On his first visit to the Lucas gusher, Galey told a reporter:

> We must demonstrate the permanency of supply and accumulate stocks, however, to be able to contract with fuel users for fifteen or twenty years before we can expect them to change their boilers from coal to oil. This will mean the investment of millions of dollars. It will mean that this well, the most wonderful thing I have ever seen in my life, must prove itself. Right now our problem is to get the flow under control. This waste can't go on.

Galey noted the pandemonium in Beaumont, with hundreds of small companies being formed to produce crude from quarter-acre lots. There was the Lucky Dime Company, organized by Galveston promoters, selling shares for 10 cents. Some Beaumont and New York women organized the Young Ladies Oil Company, appealing to the feminists of that day to back those of their own sex. Wherever Galey went he heard Texans talking of the importance of keeping the companies then being formed in the hands of natives—to them, the Standard Oil monster had to be expelled.

John Galey knew of Cullinan's efforts in Corsicana, the most successful effort in Texas prior to Spindletop, as well as remembering the Lucas visit. The wildcatters and others forming companies seemed under the illusion that all they had to do was strike oil to

* Of course, the picture was not completely bright. Certainly it was true that oil had advantages over coal. But it was more expensive than coal, the supply less dependable, refinery runs insufficiently precise as to quality, and petroleum products often not available when and where needed. Not even Rockefeller had been able to solve all of these problems to the satisfaction of users.

become millionaires. Didn't they realize the need for refineries, storage facilities, a railroad or pipeline to a port, tankers, distribution centers, and the like? All this would cost money, and there wasn't enough of it in Texas. Financial leaders in only two cities had the funds, interest, and aggressiveness needed to exploit Spindletop, thought Galey. First and foremost, there was New York, the home of the Rockefellers who went there after their trust had been reformed. The second city was Pittsburgh, Galey's own home, and that of the Mellons. Pittsburgh was a wealthy city, and would be richer still once the U.S. Steel flotation was completed and the Carnegie partners sold their holdings. Guffey and Galey meant to tap the U.S. Steel well by interesting some of the partners in Spindletop. Already some of the partners had contacts with the oilmen. James Galey, one of Carnegie's bright young men, was a relative of John's.

Pittsburgh's old money—the Mellons—also had contacts with Guffey and Galey. At the time Guffey told Lucas he would back him to the extent of $300,000, the Pittsburgh partners had nowhere near that amount. They knew, however, that the Mellons, already having had a successful experience in oil, might be interested in taking a share in the venture. During the past two decades they had backed other Guffey and Galey wells, and more often than not had emerged with good profits. Now Guffey told Andrew and William Mellon of his belief in Beaumont. They agreed to back him in the formation of the Guffey Petroleum Company, and also accepted Guffey's suggestion that the deal be secret, so that the Texans wouldn't learn of outside influence in their affairs.

The investment proved out in less than a year. Guffey returned to the Mellons to consider the next step, now that several wells were in and additional capital needed for refineries and transportation. Andrew, William, and Richard (Andrew's brother) met with Guffey, and formed the J. M. Guffey Petroleum Company, capitalized at $15 million, with 150,000 shares at $100 par value. The new company would purchase the entire stock of the old; in effect, engulfing it. In order to raise the money for the purchase price of $1.5 million, the new company would sell 50,000 shares at $30 a share.

The Mellon brothers took 20,000 of these, while a group of Pittsburgh businessmen and politicians purchased the rest. The $1.5 million was given to the Guffey-Galey-Lucas group in return for their stock in the old Guffey Petroleum, which then went out of existence. Of the remaining 100,000 shares, Guffey was to get 70,000, while 30,000 went into the treasury for future use. According to the plan, Guffey was supposed to use his shares to take care of his partners and satisfy their interests. Galey proved willing to sell out for $366,000 and some stock in other ventures. Lucas received $400,000 and 1,000 shares of Guffey's stock in the new company, as well as a contract and agreement for additional exploration work elsewhere in the country.

Then the Mellons arranged for the disposal of the 30,000 shares of treasury stock, which they sold at $66 a share to the Carnegie partners, friends, and politicians. The former steelmen, flushed with their new wealth, invested blindly, in much the same way they had purchased art and homes. Luckily for them, the investment was sound. Those who held on made many times more money in oil than they had in steel.

In June 1901, Guffey and the Mellons planned for expansion in Texas. Refining facilities would have to be built, and an outlet to markets considered. Cullinan controlled the largest refinery in the area, and already was making plans for the development of Port Arthur, the logical outlet for Beaumont crude, since it was only sixteen miles from Spindletop. Guffey Petroleum purchased 375 acres in Port Arthur, to be used for the construction of storage facilities, and money was to be raised for a pipeline from Spindletop to the port.

As a beginning, Mellon interests and Guffey formed the Gulf Refining Company of Texas, so named to satisfy local pride and mask the fact that it would be Pittsburgh-controlled. Guffey received the largest share of stock in the new company, which was capitalized at $750,000, with the Mellons once again in second place. The rest was taken by the Carnegie partners, including Charles Schwab, A. R. Peacock, and James Galey. Guffey was to be president of Gulf, with

William Mellon, the family's oil expert, as vice-president of both firms.

Guffey was a plunger and an excellent oilman, but he was a poor manager and worse at finances. He acquired additional leases, began work on the refinery and pipeline, and in the process quickly spent all his capital. In June 1902, the Mellons took a $5 million bond issue from Guffey Petroleum, and with this began to take a more serious interest in their investment.

In the summer of 1902, without warning, the Spindletop wells stopped flowing as rapidly as they had in the past. This was due in large part to wastage, poor drilling, and the bane of wildcatting, placing wells too close to one another and extracting crude too rapidly. At the time, however, it was feared the oil field was worked out, which would mean the great investment in refineries and pipelines would be wasted.

William Mellon visited Beaumont to look things over. He was convinced "there was still a lot of oil underground," but equally certain Guffey was doing a bad job at management. Mellon thought the company would need an additional $12 to $15 million. By raising this amount, the Mellons could take control of Guffey Petroleum from its founder. Then they could put it into good shape, and sell out to another firm before the Beaumont wells went dry. William had once before sold his oil interests to the Rockefellers. Perhaps they would once again be interested in a deal.

The Mellons approached the Rockefellers to sound them out in the matter. They met with almost total uninterest. "After the way Mr. Rockefeller has been treated by the state of Texas," said one Rockefeller leader, "he'll never put another dime in Texas. You'll just have to do the best you can with it yourselves." This was not the major consideration, however; Standard never was a company to let personal feeling dictate business. Rather, Standard was not certain Texas was worth the bother in terms of production. The Texas crude produced a poor quality of kerosene, and there was doubt even the most modern refineries could produce good fuel oil from it. Besides, Standard had what was believed to be good long-term reserves in

Ohio and Indiana, while Archbold was reporting good results from preliminary explorations in Kansas. California seemed at least as promising as Texas, and indeed would soon outrank the Beaumont field and go on to national leadership. With crude gushing in these areas, why should Standard go to Texas?

So the Mellons were on their own. They meant to protect their investment in Spindletop, and this meant the replacement of Guffey. William Mellon settled in Beaumont and began taking control from Guffey in 1902. Mellon acquired new land, arranged for additional financing through his uncle, expanded refinery and port facilities, and in the process made Guffey Petroleum a major factor in the region.

By 1906 the Mellons were ready to take the final steps, beginning with the ouster of Guffey himself. In the fall of that year they organized Gulf Oil Corporation, capitalized at $15 million, which was to take over the assets of Guffey Petroleum and Gulf Refining. Guffey fought the plan, but the Mellons had the votes. On January 30, 1907, Gulf Oil was a fact. Andrew Mellon was its first president, with William Mellon the true operating head. Two years later William became president in fact as well. The first of the Texas giants had been born, and it was controlled from Pittsburgh.*

A second giant was intimately connected with the rise of Gulf. At the time of Spindletop, London was concerned with the health of Queen Victoria, who would die on January 22, 1901. As England mourned her death as the end of an era, Marcus Samuel, head of Shell Transport & Trading, sent agents and cables to America, to prepare Shell for the beginning of a new age.

Samuel had dreams of the Royal Navy converting from coal to oil, of the merchant marine doing the same, of Britain continuing her domination of the Atlantic, a key to which would be the fueling of her ships at Shell facilities at Port Arthur. In addition, Shell had four new tankers of the most modern design, and these were not being used

*Guffey sold out, took his money, and began speculating in coal. He lost, and never again rose to prominence. John Galey wildcatted for a while, found little, and died poor. Higgins formed his own company, tried to fight the leaders and failed, and, although recognized as the true founder of Spindletop, received more recognition than money. He did sue Lucas for $4 million, however, but settled for a far smaller sum.

because the company was short of crude. They would be sent to Texas, loaded, and returned to England, where the crude could be refined and then converted to Shell products, sold on the continent in competition with Standard and the Russian companies. The key to all this, of course, was an arrangement with Guffey or some other Texas promoter.

On April 4, a Samuel representative contacted Guffey, asking him to: "Telegraph immediately lowest price f.o.b. Port Arthur one hundred thousand tons year for five years fuel-oil." Soon after, Guffey received a second communication: "We are desirous of obtaining a source of fuel-oil supply in Europe, because it is impossible to bring the eastern supply through the Suez Canal, and we must have a supplementary supply for the steamers at this end."

Guffey was agreeable to the bid, and instructed Shell to contact his representative in London, John Hay. Samuel had Hay investigated, and found him to be an obscure individual who dealt only occasionally in oil. Hay seemed unwilling to meet for a discussion, and Samuel dug deeper into his past, finding that Hay, who was supposed to represent Guffey, also acted for Anglo-American, the London subsidiary of Standard of Jersey, and was, it would appear, a man determined to block any deal that might benefit Shell.

Now Shell contacted Guffey again, and, without mentioning the Anglo-American connection, asked for a more direct contact. The company, the second-largest oil concern in the world, "cannot afford to associate with a small broker who has apparently simply obtained some option from you with a view of establishing a company." In the back of Samuel's mind, however, was the suspicion that Guffey had already worked out some kind of deal with Rockefeller. Of course, he had no knowledge of prior dealings between Guffey and Standard, the role of the Mellons—or indeed, much about Standard's difficulties in Texas and the nature of American federal government.

These suspicions were eased when Samuel received a cable from one of his representatives indicating that Guffey was ready to discuss a contract with Shell. Negotiations began soon after, and in June 1901, Shell contracted to purchase 4.5 million barrels of oil over a twenty-five-year period at a price of 25 cents a barrel, plus 50 percent of the profits from the sale of the oil.

The Guffey contract seemed Shell's salvation, for the company's affairs were going poorly in the East Indies and elsewhere. Samuel ordered construction of four additional tankers, and the focus of the company turned from the Pacific and Indian oceans to the Atlantic.

At the time of the signing, the contract seemed a good deal for all concerned, but it had been based on Guffey's overly optimistic assessment of the situation at Spindletop. Oil wells were sprouting like weeds in 1901, and by the end of the year Texas crude was selling for 3 cents a barrel, practically giveaway prices. Guffey thought the average price for the next twenty-five years would be around 10 cents, what it was when he signed the contract. In effect, he had been a victim of his own wildcatter's propaganda. When the Spindletop wells began to dry up in 1902, the price rose, and early in 1903 it reached 25 cents a barrel, the contract price. If this continued, Guffey Petroleum would either have to renege on its contract, in this way inviting lawsuits, or sell at a loss, in which case the company would soon go bankrupt. Whatever happened, there seemed a chance Guffey Petroleum would pass into the control of Shell. It was this blunder, among others, that led the Mellons to take a direct hand in the company's business, and resulted in Guffey's ouster.

Samuel was in a difficult position. He needed the Texas crude as a lever in his international dealings, and at the same time wanted to hold Guffey to the terms of the contract. But if he did so, it would mean a lawsuit in Texas, and who knew how that would turn out? If there was anyone the Texans hated more than a "northerner" from New York or Pittsburgh, it was an Englishman, especially one who was Jewish. So he decided to renegotiate the contract. In 1903 Andrew Mellon traveled to London to meet with Samuel. He told Samuel that Guffey Petroleum was showing no profits, and indicated this could not continue. A new deal would be needed.

Samuel agreed to renegotiate. The old contract was canceled and a new one, providing for smaller sales at higher prices, concluded. In fact, little Guffey (and later Gulf) crude or refined was sent to Shell during the rest of the contact's life.

Despite this, the Shell-Guffey deal did have major long-term implications. It helped Shell at a time when it needed a boost, and served to introduce the company to America. Samuel would again turn eastward after 1903, but now he understood the Americans somewhat better, and was interested in exploiting the market. From the Mellon visit onward, Shell and Gulf have had excellent relations, even as Shell served notice it was in America to stay.*

A third Texas giant, more a product of Texans than Gulf and certainly more than Shell, was unknowingly started by former Governor Hogg, the man who helped send Rockefeller from the state and then tried to bring him back for trial. Hogg visited Spindletop soon after the Lucas well struck, and returned again to take in the scene and explore the business opportunities. Other Texans were there, and they would meet at night to swap stories and talk of the future. James Swayne was one of them. He had served in the state legislature and had been Hogg's floor leader in the House of Representatives a decade earlier. One spring night Hogg, Swayne, and others met to talk of Beaumont, Spindletop, oil and investments. The exact sequence of events is unknown, but it appears Swayne wanted to form a syndicate to buy land in the area, exploit it, sell to speculators—he was not exactly certain of what he wanted—and make money. Hogg and the others were interested. They pooled their resources, and the Hogg-Swayne syndicate was formed.

Together, Hogg, Swayne, and three others put up $40,000 and began looking for bargains. These were men of prominence, individuals who could borrow additional money if the right deal came along. James Guffey offered them such a deal.

Guffey Petroleum, which owned the prime acreage and drilling rights in the area, offered to sell Hogg-Swayne mineral rights on fifteen acres for $180,000. It was a bargain; the partners realized this, and Guffey must have also. Why did he do it? Guffey later said,

*In 1902, Shell, Royal Dutch Petroleum, and the Rothschilds signed a marketing agreement, which was the beginning of the Royal Dutch Shell combine. The new organization invaded the American market directly in 1911, and soon after its American Gasoline Company was in operation. Today many Americans are unaware that Shell is a product of Anglo-Dutch cooperation, just as many Texans assumed Gulf was really a Texas-based company, and not one controlled from Pittsburgh.

"Northern men were not very well respected in Texas in those days. Governor Hogg was a power down there and I wanted him on my side because I was going to spend a lot of money." Perhaps so. Guffey claimed the Mellons had backed him in the transaction, but later on it seemed so bad that they must have begun to have their second thoughts about Guffey as a manager.

Hogg-Swayne took the land and began to deal for it. Their first sale—two and a half acres—brought $200,000. Then the Texas Oil and Development Company purchased a twentieth of an acre for $50,000. The syndicate now realized that small lots were salable for what at Spindletop were low prices. They subdivided madly, selling "doormats," or extremely small plots, just enough for a well and no more. A twenty-fourth of an acre fetched $15,000 a week later, and the doormats proliferated. It set a trend. Blocks of land 25 × 34 feet brought from $6,000 to $40,000 during the boom, and on paper at least the syndicate members were millionaires.

That was the trouble. Hogg-Swayne sold leases for nominal cash payment, agreeing to accept most of the contract price in oil. Unless crude were found, they would have nothing. And by itself crude was worth only a few cents a barrel. A refinery would also be needed, along with marketing facilities and the rest. None of the Hogg-Swayne members knew much about oil, refining, or drilling. Unless an expert in these areas were brought in to manage their interests, they could lose all—even the initial $40,000. So they approached an expert, Joseph Cullinan.

Cullinan was tending to his Corsicana interests when he learned of the Spindletop bonanza. Together with other Corsicana oil men and Mayor Samuel M. Jones of Toledo (one of the nation's leading oil field equipment manufacturers), Cullinan surveyed the possibilities. He was impressed, and hoped his Standard Oil backers would become interested in Spindletop. But they were not, perhaps because of their current problems in Texas.

Cullinan decided to go it alone, but in a small way. Realizing he could not compete for leases and drilling rights, and that the area needed refining and transportation facilities more than anything else, he incorporated the Texas Fuel Company, capitalized at $50,000, which would purchase crude from producers and refine and market it. As he had done with J. S. Cullinan & Co. in Corsicana, so he would with Texas Fuel in Beaumont: Cullinan would imitate the Standard Oil pattern, letting others drill, and reaping the rewards from processing and transportation.

Through their leases, Hogg-Swayne controlled a great deal of crude and didn't know what to do with it. Cullinan, who already had the knowledge of oil, owned a storage facility, was entering into arrangements with railroads, and was an expert in refining, was the answer to the syndicate's problems. It was a natural combination. The two forces agreed to merge interests. Hogg-Swayne would transfer part of their holdings to Texas Fuel, and in return receive $25,000 worth of its stock. This pooling of interests made Texas Fuel second only to Guffey in Beaumont, and made it possible for Cullinan to consider an integrated petroleum company.

Plans for one began immediately. Cullinan planned for a pipeline to Port Arthur, seven new storage tanks, and contracted for a refinery. Then he purchased 350,000 barrels of crude for future delivery at from 3 to 10 cents a barrel. Other contracts followed, so that by April, 1902, Cullinan had contracts for 1.2 million barrels, which he would refine, ship, and sell at large profits.

All of this required money, far more than he or the syndicate controlled. Standard would have been the most logical source, but the company shied from Texas. So Cullinan sought backing elsewhere.

In the fall of 1901 the Lapham brothers of New York, who controlled United States Leather Company (also known as the leather trust) met a Cullinan partner, and became interested in Spindletop. The Laphams had many businesses other than leather. They owned the small Elcho Oil Company of Pennsylvania and the American-Hawaiian Steamship Company, both of which were managed by Arnold Schlaet, a German-born executive who was considered a near-genius and bold innovator. Already Schlaet was experimenting with fuel oil on the steamships, and he, more than the Laphams, wanted to know more of Spindletop.

Schlaet visited Beaumont and met Cullinan, who showed him around. He was impressed by the way Cullinan had contracted for crude deliveries, calculated the profits to be made, and initiated operations at Texas Fuel. Schlaet returned to U.S. Leather's New York offices with a recommendation that the Laphams invest in the operation.

Meanwhile, Cullinan met with other interested investors. He had an option for land in Port Arthur, on which Texas Fuel was supposed to construct a refinery. The land was owned by the Port Arthur Land and Townsite Company, one of the many firms controlled by John Bet-A-Million Gates, fresh from his successes and failures in the U.S. Steel merger, and eager to find new fields to conquer.

Gates knew Texas from the days he sold barbed wire there. The Texans accepted him as one of their own, admiring his daring, ability to tell a tall story, and general good nature. Gates controlled the Kansas City and Southern Railroad, which he hoped would connect the Texas Gulf coast to the nation's interior. Port Arthur Land was part of the complex which Gates felt would make him master of the territory. Now that oil was discovered, Gates altered his plans. Always an opportunist, he would seize the opportunity. He sold the site to Cullinan, and soon after met with him. Under the right circumstances, he would join in the oil business.

Thus, Cullinan was dealing with three groups at once—Hogg-Swayne, Gates, and the Laphams, represented by Schlaet. The Texans didn't like Schlaet, and Schlaet knew of Gates's reputation and didn't want to be a part of a company with him in it. Gates, on his part, would work with anyone so long as it was profitable and interesting. Hogg-Swayne didn't know much of what was going on, but would accept Cullinan's advice so long as their members made money. Gates, always thinking on a large scale, wanted to form a large petroleum company that would challenge Rockefeller. Schlaet preferred Cullinan's original plan for a refining-distribution company, and had no desire to back drillers.

Cullinan tried to satisfy each group and allay suspicions all around. In January 1902, he formed the Producers Oil Company as an affiliate of Texas Fuel. The new firm, capitalized at $1.5 million, was chartered as a discovery and producing company. Gates organized a syndicate including New York and Chicago bankers and took a majority of the stock, while Hogg-Swayne received its share in return for transferring land to Producers. One of the bankers, James Hopkins—who was also president of Diamond Match Company—became Producers' first president, while Cullinan served on the executive committee. As for Schlaet, he took an interest, and the Laphams a share, in Texas Fuel.

From the start it was clear that the small Texas Fuel could not direct the actions of the ambitious Producers Oil. In March 1902, the directors of both firms met and agreed to a merger plan. Under the proposal a new entity, the Texas Company, took over the assets and liabilities of both Producers and Texas Fuel. The Texas Company, capitalized at $3 million, was officially incorporated on April 7. Under Cullinan's direction, it found new fields in the Beaumont area, reinvigorated the region, expanded rapidly (and soon outdistanced even Gulf), and in time, under the name Texaco, fulfilled Gates's dream of challenging Standard of Jersey.

Other companies would emerge from the Beaumont fields. Sun Oil, a small operator prior to Spindletop, would enter and become a major producer. In time Humble Oil would be formed, Rockefeller would take it over, and so gain entry to Texas. Magnolia Oil, Amerada, and a host of others would explore and exploit the area around Spindletop, and from there go on to find petroleum in other parts of Texas.

Few mineral fields have been as dramatic as the uncorking of the Lucas well at Spindletop. The discoveries on the Gulf coast indeed drove down prices, encouraged users to convert to fuel oil, and so created new markets for the product. It was vital for the automobile age, and for the age of energy in general. Yet Spindletop's moment of glory was brief. In 1901 the United States produced 69.3 million barrels of oil, and Beaumont contributed 6.1 million. For 1902 the figures are 88.7 million and 17.4 million. Then, in 1903, when the east Texas fields ran dry temporarily, Beaumont contributed 8.6

million barrels while American petroleum rose to over 100 million for the first time.

Gulf crude would remain important for years, and is still a significant source of oil for the nation. But rival fields would eclipse it. Even when the entire Beaumont area is taken, including Sour Lake, Saratoga, Humble, and Batson, it was not as important as California, the midcontinent fields (Oklahoma and Kansas), and, for a while, Illinois. In only one year of the first two decades of the twentieth century—1905—did Gulf coast crude lead the nation's producing areas.

Domestic Crude Oil Production, 1900-1919 (millions of barrels)

Year	Appalachian	Ohio-Indiana	Illinois	Mid-Continent	Gulf	California
1900	36.3	21.8	—	.9	—	4.3
1901	33.6	21.9	—	.8	3.7	8.8
1902	32.0	23.4	—	.7	18.0	14.0
1903	31.6	24.1	—	1.6	18.4	24.4
1904	31.4	24.7	—	6.2	24.6	29.6
1905	29.4	22.3	.2	12.5	36.5	33.4
1906	27.7	17.5	4.4	22.8	20.5	33.1
1907	25.3	13.1	24.3	46.8	16.4	29.7
1908	24.9	10.0	33.7	48.8	15.8	44.9
1909	26.5	8.2	30.9	50.8	10.9	55.5
1910	26.9	7.3	33.1	59.2	9.7	73.0
1911	23.7	6.2	31.3	66.6	11.0	81.1
1912	26.3	4.9	28.6	65.5	8.5	87.3
1913	25.9	4.8	23.9	84.9	8.5	97.8
1914	24.1	5.0	21.9	98.0	13.1	99.8
1915	22.9	4.3	19.0	123.3	20.6	86.6
1916	23.0	3.9	17.7	136.9	21.7	90.9
1917	24.9	3.6	15.8	163.5	24.3	93.5
1918	25.4	3.2	13.4	179.4	24.2	97.5
1919	31.8	2.8	12.6	193.1	23.4	101.2

Source: Williamson, Andreano, Daum, and Klose, *The American Petroleum Industry: The Age of Energy* (Evanston, Ill., 1963), p. 16.

Standard maintained its grip not only on refining and distribution, but on production as well. Though not a big factor in Gulf coast production at the time, it dominated the rest of the country. Standard would never again hold the commanding position it had prior to the east Texas discoveries. Its share of the market declined, not only in refining, but in kerosene, fuel oil, and gasoline. Yet the industry itself was expanding so rapidly that the company did not suffer. Instead, it came to occupy a position in oil much as that of U.S. Steel in steel—the first and foremost, but with several strong competitors.

Spindletop was proclaimed in the same year J. P. Morgan created U.S. Steel. At the time the steel merger seemed the more important event. Big Steel represented the culmination of an industrial epoch more than a new beginning—the apex of corporation creation rather than its start in steel. Spindletop was a major watershed for the age of energy in America and the world. Seven decades later, U.S. Steel would be the thirteenth-largest American industrial corporation. General Motors and Ford, creatures of the petroleum age, occupied first and third positions. Texaco and Gulf were larger than U.S. Steel, in eighth and eleventh place respectively. Shell, in sixteenth place, probably will be larger than Big Steel by the end of the 1970s.

Antitrust suits against Standard Oil were filed regularly in the early twentieth century, even though it was clear the Rockefeller grip on the industry was not as strong as once it was. Anti-Standard books and articles proliferated, the most important of which, Ida Tarbell's *The History of the Standard Oil Company,* appeared in serial form in *McClure's Magazine* in 1902. These were attacks more on what the company had been, rather than what it was and would be after Spindletop. In 1911, the Supreme Court found Standard guilty of violations of the antitrust act, and in July of that year the Rockefeller executives announced dissolution plans. This did not mean the company would vanish, or that the Court had brought competition to the industry. Spindletop and other fields did far more in this direction than any court decree could. In 1971, Standard Oil of New Jersey, one of the successor companies, was the second-largest industrial firm in the nation, while another successor firm, Mobil Oil, was in sixth

Standard Oil in the Petroleum Industry, 1880-1911

	Percentage Control Over Crude Oil Supplies			
Fields	**1880**	**1899**	**1906**	**1911**
Appalachian	92	88	72	78
Lima-Indiana		85	95	90
Gulf Coast			10	10
Mid-Continent			45	44
Illinois			100	83
California			29	29
	Percentage Control Over Refinery Capacity			
Share of Rated Daily Crude Capacity	90-95	82	70	64
	Percentage of Major Products Sold			
			1906-1911	
Kerosene	90-95	85	75	
Lubes		40	55	
Waxes		50	67	
Fuel Oil		85	31	
Gasoline		85	66	

Source: Harold F. Williamson and Ralph L. Andreano, "Competitive Structure of the American Petroleum Industry, 1880-1911," in Harvard Graduate School of Business Administration, *Oil's First Century* (Cambridge, 1960), p. 74.

place. Two more—Standard Oil of California and Standard Oil of Indiana—were in twelfth and fifteenth places. These are independent companies today, and hardly weaklings by any measure.*

The petroleum industry created many more millionaires than had steel, and a goodly number of them owed their beginnings to Spindletop. More emerged from the Standard Oil complex, however, where hard work, the Puritan ethic, shrewdness, and an ability at teamwork could return astronomical dividends. One such individual was Henry M. Flagler, a man who discovered the business when it first began, and one of the few whom Rockefeller considered a close personal friend.

*"The 500 Largest Industrial Corporations," *Fortune*, 85, no. 5 (May 1972) p. 190.

In 1850, at the age of twenty, Flagler entered the grain commission business and had a small interest in a distillery in Bellevue, Ohio. Three years later he married Mary Harkness, the daughter of a wealthy distiller, and it appeared Flagler was on his way to a distinguished career in liquor.

In the course of his business Flagler met Rockefeller, and the two men entered into several transactions. Both men moved to Cleveland prior to the Civil War, and their relationship grew in this period. When Rockefeller went into oil, Flagler followed, investing $70,000 in Rockefeller & Andrews and so becoming one of the founders of Standard Oil.

Flagler specialized in transportation as well as taking a hand in legal affairs. He helped form Standard of Ohio, brought other companies into the Rockefeller maw, and in 1882 was named the first president of Standard of Jersey. Flagler would remain a key member of the firm for most of the rest of his life. But he had other interests as well. Mary Flagler was ill in the early winter of 1878, and at her doctor's suggestion, the couple went to Florida for her health. This trip would be the origin of a land mania as dramatic in its own way as Spindletop and the Comstock Lode, and one that has not yet ended.

CHAPTER 8

The Great Florida Boom

There was not much for the Flaglers to see or do in Florida at the time of their first visit to the state in 1878. Florida boasted of the health of its residents, and a popular guidebook of the day spoke of it "as a resort for those suffering from pulmonary disease." The sulfur baths at Green Cove Springs, on the St. Johns River, were visited by those afflicted with rheumatism, while St. Augustine had a regular clientele of asthmatics. Parts of the state had good fishing and hunting, and these drew a handful of sportsmen and vacationers in search of a place more exotic than the resorts farther north. Even then, Florida boosters spoke of the climate, which the guidebook predicted "is destined to make it to America what the South of France and Italy are to Europe—the refuge of those who seek to escape the rigor of a Northern winter. The sudden changes experienced at Nice or Florence are unknown in Florida."

The Florida of which they spoke was the northern coast and the interior, along the St. Johns and Ocklawaha rivers. St. Augustine alone drew tourists to the Atlantic coast, while Tampa was not much of a draw on the Gulf. The fastest-growing vacation spot of the day was Palatka, on the St. Johns, where the Putnam Hotel, with its forty rooms, was considered a "queen of hotels." The waters near Palatka, which were really sulfur springs, were claimed to be "efficacious in all forms of consumption, scrofula, jaundice, and other bilious affectations; chronic dysentery and diarrhea, diseases of the uterus, chronic rheumatism and gout, dropsy, gravel, neuralgia, tremor, syphilis, erysipelas, tetter, ringworm, and itch. . . ." This was the Florida that drew the Flaglers and others like them in the 1870s.

Even then some went there for pleasure and a handful for land speculation. The post-Civil War rich, eager for travel but unwilling to take the long and chancy ocean voyage to Europe, and at the same time curious about the defeated South and wanting to see it at first hand, would travel by train to Atlanta, stay there for a few days to see what Sherman had done to the town, and from there trace part of his route to the sea, winding up in Charleston or Savannah, which in the winter entertained many tourists from both North and South. The Florida Steamship Line vessels, including the "New-York built steamers" *Dictator, Capt. Vogel, City Point,* and *Capt. Fitzgerald,* left from their docks regularly, taking tourists and vacationers to Fernandina or Jacksonville, the latter being the key transfer point and the best-known city in the state. Passengers would transfer to paddle-wheelers which would take them into the St. Johns River, the heart of the tourist belt in the 1870s.

There was a railroad from Fernandina to Cedar Key on the Gulf coast, but it was uncomfortable and undependable, and in any case did not go very far south. St. Augustine on the Atlantic and Tampa on the Gulf were reachable by roads—not very good ones—or the steamers. For the most part, however, three-quarters of the state was isolated at this time, and visitors from even other parts of Florida would be talked about for days.

The lack of transportation hindered Florida's development. Even the lines in Georgia and Alabama were poor, so that visitors from

New York and Boston were better off with steamers than railroads. Every Tuesday, Thursday, and Saturday at 3:00 P.M., a Charleston-bound steamer would leave Pier 29 in New York, and in the winter these would carry many Florida-bound vacationers, who came to New York by passenger train and then took the horsecars to the dock. There was no direct rail connection from the city to Savannah or Charleston, and there wouldn't be one for many years. So northerners wanting to go to Florida had no alternative but to take the steamers, which were well-made ships, but unable to smooth out the storms. Often passengers going to Florida for their health would arrive in far worse condition than they might have been in had they remained at home.

Given this poor transportation, it is surprising tourists considered Florida vacations. There was not much to see in the state in the 1870s and 1880s, besides the sulfur springs and swamps. Then, too, Florida insects and other pests were famous for their size and ferocity, a situation the tourist agents tried to ignore. Even then, Florida wanted visitors, and guidebooks of the period spoke of the state in terms that would be repeated for decades to come. It was "the spot for the jilted lover to forget his idol, and the disconsolate lady her imaginary devotee; for those fretted by the rough edges of corroding care to retire and find a respite from their struggles." Florida was "the store-house of the fathomless deep, where we can contemplate that great image of eternity; 'the invisible, boundless, endless, and sublime.' "

We don't know whether Henry Flagler considered these problems and visions when he first came to Florida, or thought of them on his second and third visits in 1879 and 1880. But he did like the state. Even after Mary Flagler died in 1881, Henry would travel the uncomfortable route, a measure of his enthusiasm, since he was used to first-class treatment in other parts of the nation. Perhaps he decided then that transportation was the state's great need. In any case, it would be one of his greatest gifts to Florida, and one that marked the first of the three great stages in the state's modern growth.

Flagler remarried in the spring of 1883, and took his second wife, the former Ida Alace Shourds (who had been Mary Flagler's nurse in her last days), to St. Augustine for their honeymoon. Combining business with pleasure, the fifty-three-year-old tycoon looked the area over for investment possibilities. Already he was somewhat bored with the petroleum business; at the time Flagler had a case of what today would be called "male menopause." To go with his new wife, he wanted a new career. Flagler would remain high in the Standard Oil hierarchy, but from that time on, the development of Florida land and transportation would consume most of his spare time.

At the time St. Augustine was one of Florida's leading tourist centers, and its most important one on the Atlantic coast. Its climate was good, the city itself was quaint and interesting, and the atmosphere relaxed. But it was no Newport, then the leading watering place of the rich, and showed little promise of becoming one. St. Augustine lacked the kind of facilities geared to capture such individuals. The Magnolia Hotel, a prewar relic, had been renovated in the mid-1870s, but was populated almost entirely by invalids, hardly the kind of place Henry Flagler's friends would enjoy. The St. Augustine Hotel was tacky, the Oriental House stodgy, and the Florida House decidedly bourgeois. There were several fine private residences in St. Augustine, but few of the millionaire variety. The city couldn't even match Jacksonville in this regard. The Grand National, the St. James, and the Metropolitan of that city were fairly good, if not ornate. Yet Jacksonville was not as pleasant a place as St. Augustine. It was a lumber town, had a decidedly commercial atmosphere in its downtown, and by rights should have lost its tourist trade to St. Augustine.

It didn't, and the reason for this was transportation and communication. The train service in Jacksonville was good for that part of the country. The mail came regularly, and northern newspapers, only a week old, were available in several parts of downtown. Jacksonville boasted a direct telegraph line to New York.

St. Augustine had none of these. Northern visitors would go to Jacksonville, and if they wanted to proceed to St. Augustine, would do so by an antique, narrow-gauge railroad or paddle-wheeler.

Flagler thought the situation could be remedied by a fine hotel and a better railroad. In 1884 he embarked on a program to provide St. Augustine with both.

Early in the year Flagler announced his purchase of land in the city, on which he would construct the Ponce de Leon Hotel. It would be the finest anywhere, he said. Money was no object. When finished, boasted Flagler, St. Augustine would rival Newport. The Ponce, as it was called, lived up to expectations. Construction costs alone were said to have been in the neighborhood of $1,250,000, while landscaping and extras doubled that price. The Spanish-inspired hotel had 540 rooms, each with electric lights, and furnished at a cost of $1,000 each. The casino was large and ornate, designed to appeal to Flagler's wealthy friends. There was a large sulfur pool on the grounds for those who came to Florida for health reasons, and many recreational facilities, including golf and tennis.

While supervising construction of the Ponce, Flagler also arranged for the purchase of the thirty-two-mile Jacksonville, St. Augustine, and Halifax Railroad, which would connect the Ponce to the Jacksonville railhead. Flagler ordered a new roadbed, rails, and rolling stock—indeed, he constructed a new line rather than improve upon the old. He enjoyed this work almost as much as that on the hotel. Flagler took great joy in riding the cab, donning an engineer's cap, and blowing the whistle. He liked the small line so much he purchased another in 1888, the St. Augustine and Palatka, which tied his town to the interior, and then a third, the St. John's and Halifax, which extended the Flagler transportation complex as far south as Daytona, which he already had marked for future development.

Flagler arranged for special through trains to leave New York for St. Augustine during the season. The "Florida Specials" were first class in every respect. They were lavishly decorated, with plush club cars and luxurious Pullmans. They made the trip in thirty hours, a respectable time even now, but amazing in the 1880s. The first Florida Special arrived in January 1888, in time for the Ponce's opening. Florida's age of wealthy tourists was now properly begun.

Flagler scarcely stopped to enjoy his first success in tourism before he entered a new phase of the business. He purchased a hotel in Ormond, just north of Daytona, added a golf course and in other ways modernized the place, and then reopened it to tourists. Flagler's friends had gone eagerly to St. Augustine, but Ormond was a different kind of resort. It attracted those who sought privacy, or at least quiet and rest. It did succeed, however, and provided the impetus for the next stop: Palm Beach.

It was quite a jump. Ormond was only fifty miles from St. Augustine, while Palm Beach was over two hundred miles south of Ormond. Although the Palm Beach area was settled, and several large estates and citrus fruit interests well-established, it was isolated, with the Atlantic to the east, and tropical forests on the three other sides.* Constructing a railroad through the forests would be a difficult task, though not too forbidding, since worse obstacles had been overcome in the past, both in North and Central America. But it would scarcely pay to construct a line merely for tourists, even the wealthy ones Flagler hoped to attract, men and women who would think nothing of high fares so long as the service was good. The "season" lasted but two months; what would the line do the rest of the year? The answer was, transport Florida citrus fruits to Jacksonville and farther north, expanding the market for these products, which in the 1890s was still small.

Flagler knew what he was doing; he was to create an economic empire, on foundations of tourism, railroads, and citrus. At the same time, he would attend to Standard Oil business. Florida would be his hobby, on a part-time basis. In the 1890s, America's superpowerful capitalists could afford such pastimes.

Flagler's Palm Beach project began in 1893, when he influenced the Florida legislature and the state's aristocratic Governor Francis Fleming to grant him a charter to construct a railroad paralleling the Indian River as far south as Miami. Flagler had no intention of going that distance; his ultimate objective was still Palm Beach, and at the

*The place was called Palm City when Flagler arrived. He renamed it Palm Beach at his wife's suggestion.

time he knew next to nothing of Miami. In addition to the franchise, Flagler was granted 8,000 acres of land per mile for all construction south of Daytona. This was a not unusual practice, and even those who opposed Flagler did not consider it so, while his supporters and individuals who contributed land were enthusiastic about the line, which they felt would bring prosperity to the region.

While shepherding the measure through the legislature, Flagler set about buying land in Palm Beach. His coming sent real-estate prices soaring; land that went for $150 an acre in 1892 sold for over $1,000 four years later. The rest of the country was in a depression, but it did not hit the Florida Gulf coast.

Flagler was not interested in land speculation, though he might easily have made a fortune at it. Instead, he concentrated on construction and promotion, and these more for indulgence than profits. He purchased the estate of Robert McCormick, the farm equipment heir, for $75,000, and put together almost 1,700 acres of land fronting on one of the finest beaches in the nation. Then, when he owned sufficient land for his purposes, Flagler announced his plan to construct a new hotel, the Royal Poinciana, which would rival those of the Riviera. "I shall build upon this spot a magnificent playground for the people of the nation," was the way he put it. It was a time, however, when most workers had a six-day week and no vacation, if they were fortunate enough to have jobs. Even had they been able to go to Palm Beach, they could not have afforded the prices Flagler planned to charge. It would be a playground for the rich, and for no one else. In that era, only the rich had playgrounds, and Flagler could not imagine others wanting ones.

He did propose to construct facilities for the less fortunate, however. Flagler acquired land in what is now West Palm Beach, which he said would be used for light industry, the loading of citrus fruit, and the storage of supplies, as well as rows of small houses. "That is the city I am building for my help," was Flagler's explanation.

Construction work on the railroad and the hotel began in May 1893. The Royal Poinciana was ready for occupancy in February of the following year, at which time the railroad had reached West Palm Beach. The hotel was made of wood, to blend in with the scenery. It was six stories high and covered a huge expanse of ground. In part this was necessary to provide for the 1,750 guests Flagler planned for, but it also served to keep the employees' quarters far from those of the guests. The Royal Poinciana had a dining room capable of serving 1,600 guests at a time, with one waiter for every four tables. There were tennis courts, an auto racing track, and a fine golf course, as well as pools, archery ranges, and a gambling casino that soon became the most famous in the nation. Rooms went for $100 a day, but those who took them were of the type not to worry about price; they were occupied throughout the season, which ran from December to April. The Royal Poinciana was closed for the rest of the year, and deserted except for a small maintenance staff. Even running less than half a year, the hotel was profitable, so much so that in late 1894 Flagler planned for a second hotel, The Breakers, which opened in 1895 and soon became almost as famous if not as exclusive as the Royal Poinciana.

The Flagler compounds at St. Augustine, Ormond, and Palm Beach, were just that—compounds for the wealthy and their servants. As far as they were concerned, the back country, the rest of Florida, did not exist. But the Florida economy was important for the railroad, which Flagler now named the Florida East Coast, and which had over 700 miles of track and served the citrus industry as well as the hotels. The line was not profitable, and was expected to run at a small loss, which would be made up by hotel profits. Flagler believed 1894–1895 would be a turnaround year for the East Coast, but instead it showed a large deficit. The hotel business was good, but citrus fruit shipments fell drastically. The reason was a frost, which killed the orange crop, caused the bankruptcy of hundreds of growers, and brought the depression to the non-Flagler Florida. Conditions were fine at the hotels, where some of the guests grumbled about the early-morning cold but reflected that the weather was far better than in New York, Pittsburgh, or Boston. Beyond their compounds, however, people were starving.

The frost was disastrous for north and central Florida, but it did not strike in the area south of Palm Beach. This was a region that Flagler had ignored in the past, but which now intrigued him. "If my life and health are spared," he said in 1892, "it seems more probable that I will extend the road to Miami within a few years." Flagler was sixty-five in 1895, and somewhat reluctant to continue his southward advance, but the frost and reports of fine weather and crops in Miami spurred him on. Already he was becoming bored with Palm Beach and seeking a new interest. Now Flagler determined to extend his railroad to the end of the Florida Keys, along a series of bridges that would become one of the wonders of the world and provide a fitting monument to his reputation. He made plans to extend the Florida East Coast south of Palm Beach in the summer of 1895, and work was begun in September.

Mrs. Julia Tuttle greeted the news with satisfaction, as she had tried to interest Flagler in Miami since 1893. The elderly widow owned 640 acres of prime land in Miami, and in her small way was attempting to do for her city what Flagler had done for Palm Beach. There was much to recommend Miami. Its climate was as good as Palm Beach's in the winter, although summers were stifling. It was located on the beautiful Miami River, which emptied into Biscayne Bay, a lovely tropical lagoon. But the city was isolated, with the only link to the rest of the world being boats and ships which made occasional calls.

Mrs. Tuttle and another landowner, W. B. Brickell, offered Flagler land if he would take the Florida East Coast to Miami. News of his acceptance, coupled with word that actual construction had begun, delighted Mrs. Tuttle, who, along with others in Miami, prepared for a boom. Land speculators, who had seen values rise at St. Augustine, Ormond, and Palm Beach, now rushed to Miami, hoping to pick up prime lots at low prices and then turn around and sell them for large profits. Mrs. Tuttle obliged them, constructing the Miami Hotel, a rickety structure but good enough for the speculators, charging exorbitant prices for food and lodging, and, joining the throng of salesmen, becoming one of the town's leading dealers. She helped the city incorporate itself in July 1896 and moved to make it the county seat. Mrs. Tuttle and other Miami realtors worked with Flagler's men to plan a new Miami, which would rise from the old, with newly designed streets, parks, and stores, as well as a modern new railroad station. The focal point of the new Miami would be the Royal Palm Hotel, not as imposing as those Flagler had built elsewhere, but magnificent by Miami standards. Flagler also arranged for dredging in Biscayne Bay and the Miami River, so as to be ready for the Royal Palm's opening in January 1897, by which time the railroad linkage was set too. He offered special rates on the line and made up for them by charging more at the hotel. It was a pattern that worked well elsewhere, and Flagler had no reason to doubt it would apply in Miami.

It didn't. Although successful, Miami did not become the "in" resort of Florida, a title that remained with Palm Beach. Later on it was said that Palm Beach had all the naughty millionaires, while the nice ones went to Miami. At the time, this could be translated as meaning that Palm Beach was exciting and "social," while Miami was somewhat stodgy. It also meant the land boom quickly died, causing severe losses for those who had purchased options and now had to make them good. Mrs. Tuttle herself lost a fortune, one she never really had, since it all was on paper anyway. Although Flagler never regretted his move to Miami, it marked the turning point in his Florida career, after which most of what he did went sour.

In 1896 the state established a railroad commission that had the power to regulate rates, schedules, and services. Freight rates were cut sharply, and this hurt the East Coast. In 1901 the growers formed the Fruit and Vegetable Growers Association, which battled Flagler over costs and subjected the line to heavy criticism. Then there were Flagler's personal problems. His second wife suffered a nervous breakdown in 1894 and five years later was declared legally insane. In the meanwhile Flagler was romancing Mary Lily Kenan, and around 1900 the seventy-year-old millionaire asked her to marry him. Miss Kenan agreed, and Flagler set about getting a divorce in New York. After failing in this, he changed his legal residence to Florida, and by using influence in the legislature, was able to have a new divorce law introduced and passed within the unusual time of a week. He then applied for a divorce, was granted one in a matter of hours, and promptly remarried. The law was roundly criticized and offered as proof Flagler had the state in his hip pocket. The divorce law would be repealed in 1905, by which time he couldn't care less.

Flagler was busily at work planning the extensions of his railroad to Key West, only ninety miles from Cuba. He hoped to construct a modern port there, one that would attract Cuban tobacco and sugar imports, and provide facilities for the export of American manufactured goods to the island. He saw a booming business in store, one that would make the railroad his most profitable Florida venture, and his monument.

The task took seven years to complete. The Miami-Key West link was 156 miles long, with half of these over water. It cost $20 million, money which Flagler believed well spent and invested. The first cars went over the spans in January 1912, with Flagler and state leaders on hand to cheer them along. By then most of his difficulties with opposition legislators had been forgotten, and Flagler was hailed as the first citizen of the state.

It was difficult to say exactly how much money Flagler invested in Florida. Most estimates were in the $50-million range, but this figure obviously includes reinvested profits and part of the cash flow. Probably it was less than that, but still an impressive amount of money. Flagler left an estate of more than $100 million on his death in 1913, at the age of eighty-three. So Mary Flagler, already famous for her lavish spending, had no need to worry about his Florida investments.

Flagler, who dominated the first of modern Florida's three growth stages, left the state three major legacies. He had opened it up to the rest of the country by constructing the Florida East Coast Railroad. More than that, he had encouraged utility companies to expand in the coastal area, helped banks, and in general provided the state with an economic infrastructure it previously had lacked. Then he had made Florida the playground of the wealthy, as only a man of his means, reputation, and influence could. Palm Beach had begun to eclipse Newport, and even some Riviera vacation spots. Foreign yachts were seen there in the pre-World War I period; they would never have come had not Flagler made it an "in" place.

Finally, Flagler gave Florida the reputation of being "the state of the future," with many untapped sources of wealth. Tourism was rapidly becoming Florida's key industry, but along with construction and land speculation came advances in cattle raising, agriculture, and other enterprises, without which Florida might have become a *de facto* colony of the northern millionaires instead of an independent entity.

This growth during the Flagler era was impressive, though few noted it or spoke of the development outside of Florida itself. It could be seen in the railroad statistics, where growth of revenues was more

Operating Statistics of the Florida East Coast Railroad, 1896-1913

Year Ending June 30	Total Operating Revenues Per Mile of Road (Unit: $1,000)	Tons of Freight Traffic (Unit: 1 million tons)	Number of Passengers Carried One Mile (Unit: 1 million passengers)
1896	1.697	20.223	10.238
1897	1.951	16.819	11.025
1898	2.289	19.374	14.320
1899	2.727	23.642	17.368
1900	2.586	31.362	15.724
1901	3.266	38.540	19.462
1902	3.994	43.330	22.852
1903	4.161	43.106	25.946
1904	4.790	54.819	27.869
1905	4.649	46.527	32.263
1906	4.942	52.146	32.720
1907	5.912	80.744	41.842
1908	5.160	69.979	39.114
1909	5.784	87.555	41.949
1910	6.324	95.210	46.479
1911	7.172	121.013	60.371
1912	6.896	118.456	63.426
1913	7.823	143.200	69.202

Source: Homer B. Vanderblue, "The Florida Land Boom," *The Journal of Land and Public Utility Economics*, Vol. 3 (May 1927), p. 116.

closely tied to freight traffic than to passengers. The 1907 financial panic hit Florida the following year, for example. The passenger traffic fell only a bit, as few of America's wealthy did without their winter vacations due to financial stresses. But the freight traffic collapsed, as did railroad revenues. The same could be seen in clearinghouse exchanges at Jacksonville, the state's financial center and banker for most of its small agricultural and beef firms. Business boomed in the Flagler era, in part from tourism, construction, and the railroad, but largely due to the rise of the Florida economy as a whole. Not all of those who went to Florida did so because of the Flagler phenomenon. Some made the move for reasons having nothing to do with tourism.

John S. Collins was one such individual. He arrived in Miami in 1896, at the height of that city's land boom. Collins was a fifty-nine-year-old New Jersey farmer, who had experimented successfully

Clearinghouse Exchanges in Jacksonville, 1897-1913

Year	Exchange (Unit: $1 million)
1897	8.2
1898	10.8
1899	11.6
1900	12.7
1901	15.2
1902	19.2
1903	21.2
1904	41.0
1905	55.6
1906	65.6
1907	75.4
1908	70.7
1909	85.6
1910	117.1
1911	141.4
1912	165.4
1913	174.0

Source: Vanderblue, "*The Florida Land Boom,*" p. 118.

with fruits, and later on entered the lumber, coal, and building materials fields as well. He had never been to Florida, but had read of its climate and farming possibilities. Collins learned of an attempt to grow coconuts on Miami Beach, and since it seemed like a good idea, he invested $5,000 in the project. Had he seen the place first, he might not have been so eager to enter the business.

Miami Beach was a long, narrow neck of land, connected to the mainland and running south, with Biscayne Bay being formed in between. Calling it land would be to stretch the point, since it was mostly sand and mangrove swamp. The swamps were alive with vegetation and mosquitoes, crocodiles, and other tropical life. Yet Collins and some sixty others had joined together in 1882 in an attempt to grow coconuts on the desolate strip.

The venture failed, due to storms and poor management. Now Collins came down to see if anything could be salvaged from the operation. He wasn't impressed with the coconut business, now that he saw it at first hand, but he liked the Beach. There was some fertile mangrove land there, although the narrow strip of land didn't seem useful for anything but the growing of exotic, high-priced fruits. But with the railroad nearby, such a business might prove profitable. It may have been an excuse to stay; Miami Beach was quite a change from Moorestown, New Jersey, and like Flagler, Collins wanted a change of pace and a new challenge in his later years.

Collins returned to Florida on several occasions in the next few years, and finally entered into a partnership with Elnathan Field, one of the founders of the coconut business. They would purchase land on the Beach and grow fruits. Field opted for grapefruit, while Collins wanted avocados. The argument couldn't be resolved, so Collins purchased Field's interest, and in 1907 began work on his avocado farm. It was a strange operation—a mile long and seven hundred feet wide—and from the first Collins had many problems. The insects were fierce, and mangrove jungle threatening, and Collins himself not certain exactly what he wanted. He experimented with bananas as well as avocados, hired crews of men to clear additional land, brought in construction equipment, and all the while supervised operations from his home in Miami, crossing Biscayne Bay daily by ferry to see what was happening.

The money ran out in 1911, at which time Collins wrote his family for additional funds. His four children were concerned, not only for their money, but also the sanity of their now-seventy-year-old father. Collins talked of the need for a canal through the mangroves and additional large-scale operations, at a time when he hadn't sufficient funds to continue his original projects. So the family decided to leave New Jersey and join Collins in Miami. They came in the summer of 1911, along with the children, furniture, and other remembrances of what must have appeared a happier and more substantial New Jersey past.

Collins' two sons and one of his two daughters did not share his enthusiasm for avocados or the Beach. They went through the swamps, saw the crocodiles, snakes, and rats that inhabited them, and decided to return to the quiet and safety of New Jersey. The other daughter, Katherine, and her husband, Thomas Pancoast, decided to remain, but not for the purpose of farming. The Pancoasts knew of middle-class resorts in New Jersey, such as Seaside Park and Ocean City, that had been quite successful. Maybe the same kinds of places could be constructed in Florida, at Miami Beach. With Collins' blessings, Pancoast organized the Miami Beach Improvement Company and set to work. Collins' canal would be constructed, not only for farming purposes, but also to make the Beach more attractive to settlers. While construction was taking place, Pancoast would try to clear the place of at least some of the animal and reptile life, and at the same time clear the Atlantic coast side of the Beach for settlement. Finally, he would construct a wooden bridge to connect the peninsula to Miami, and so make the sites more accessible.

Work began early in 1912, at a time all Florida was talking of Key West. Troubles developed at the canal and in the clearance operations, but the major difficulty was with the bridge. After six months of hard work and the expenditure of $100,000 it still wasn't finished, and Collins and Pancoast were broke. The development plan might have been abandoned, with the Pancoasts returning to New Jersey farming, had it not been for the fact that Carl Fisher, on vacation in Miami, went out for a spin in his motorboat, lost his way seeking Biscayne Bay, and happened upon the Collins-Pancoast development.

Fisher, who arrived in Florida shortly before Flagler's death, was not as wealthy as the Standard Oil tycoon, but was more imaginative. He possessed a flare for showmanship Flagler lacked, and although both came from modest families, Flagler seemed always a gentleman, while Fisher would always impress people as being brassy and loud. Flagler was a Victorian; Fisher was a man for the 1920s, a period when men like Flagler would seem antique. Yet there was a striking similarity in their approach to Florida. Both believed transportation was needed to bring a certain class of people to the state's east coast. Flagler thought in terms of a railroad, and the people he wanted in his hotels were those with established wealth, or at least what passed for such in a newly rich country. Fisher was a man of the automobile age. In no way was he genteel, and Fisher made no attempt to appear anything other than what he was. Flagler was a man of brandy and cigars after dinner; Fisher was more at home with a double martini and cigarettes, a character out of F. Scott Fitzgerald or Ernest Hemingway. It was the difference between Victor Herbert and George Gershwin—or more to the point, between Palm Beach and Miami Beach. Fisher's wife, Jane, hit upon it years later when she was asked why Carl liked Miami and had little to do with Palm Beach. "Oh, Palm Beach," she said. "They thought we were just scum. We were *nouveaux riches,* you see. New money from the Midwest, automobile money from Indiana and Michigan. They were old money from the East, bankers and railroads. You know—*Easterners.*"

Fisher was born in Greensburg, Indiana, in 1874. He left school in his early teens to become a candy butcher on a train, and from that drifted into other jobs until winding up as proprietor of a bicycle store. Fisher purchased automobiles with the store's profits, raced them, took them apart and put them together again, and then sold cars to the unwary—in fact, spent most of his time learning about automobiles and dealing in new and used cars. He formed the Fisher

Automobile Company (not to be confused, although it often was at the time, with Fisher Body Company, run by the famous Fisher brothers who were then in Norwalk, Indiana), and became one of the biggest dealers in the state, as well as a race driver of national reputation.

In 1904 Fisher joined with some friends to form the Prest-O-Lite Corporation of America, which was devising an automobile headlight that used compressed acetylene rather than kerosene, and gave off a more brilliant glow. The light was erratic but the company profitable, and in 1911 Fisher and his group sold out to Union Carbide for $9 million, of which Fisher received $5.6 million.

While working at Prest-O-Lite, Fisher also found time to help organize the Indianapolis Motor Speedway, dabble in balloons and airplanes, motorcycles and speedboats, and in the process become a minor American hero. He and Jane would flit around the country, attending races, promoting deals, and in general doing whatever pleased them.

In February 1910, the Fishers went to Miami for a short vacation and liked the place. Fisher purchased a winter home and planned to work on speedboating while there. His Florida trips were filled with meetings with friends and business associates, and Fisher would stay up through the nights with them, planning new activities, both for profit and amusement. Since most were in the automotive field, the plans usually dealt with cars and transportation.

In early 1912, his fortune assured, Fisher began talking of a coast-to-coast highway, and in October he presented the idea to a group of friends in Indianapolis. The "Coast-to-Coast Rock Highway" would cost $10 million, he thought, and would take three years to complete. That event would be marked by a parade of thousands of automobiles to the San Francisco Exposition, scheduled to open in 1915. The idea was attractive, and won support from Frank Seiberling of Goodyear Tire & Rubber, officials at Packard Motor Car, Willys-Overland, and Hudson. Thomas Alva Edison offered encouragement, as did former Senator Albert Beveridge, former Vice-President Charles Fairbanks, and former President William Howard Taft.

While working out details for his highway, Fisher found time to speculate in real estate. The Lummus brothers, who owned large holdings in the area, needed a great deal of cash, and quickly. Collins lent them $150,000, and as a bonus received 150 acres of land on the southern end of Miami Beach, land which the Lummuses, like all Beach landlords, except Collins, had ignored. Fisher obtained a mortgage on other Lummus properties and purchased some sixty acres outright. Without giving the matter much thought, he had become a major holder of Miami Beach real estate.

One day, while wandering about in their speedboat, the Fishers spied Collins, walking near what is now Indian Creek. They asked for directions to Biscayne Bay, received them, and went off. Fisher returned a few days later and talked with Collins, learning of his plans for Miami Beach, and, particularly, of the unfinished bridge, which he later motored over to see. After some further discussions, Fisher offered to back Collins to the extent of $50,000, with the bridge as collateral, and a bonus of 200 acres owned by the Miami Beach Improvement Company. The deal was similar to that entered into earlier with the Lummuses. Collins accepted, and with the two deals completed, Fisher's interest in the Beach began to grow rapidly.

Still, Miami Beach played second fiddle to the highway. Fisher planned to improve his property and then, with the bridge completed, sell it off at a large profit. This money would be used to back the Coast-to-Coast.

Fisher was not a man to enter any deal in a halfhearted fashion. In order to make the land more attractive, he hired a small army of earthmovers which began work in the early summer of 1913, soon after completion of the bridge on June 12. Dredges were brought in to bring up much of the bottom of Biscayne Bay, and this was used to fill in the mangrove swamps. Sand from the Atlantic was sucked up and deposited on the beaches to make them more attractive. Several man-made islands were created at the mouth of Biscayne Bay, as the forerunner for lagoons Fisher thought would please prospective buyers. Fisher's pile drivers bulkheaded the Biscayne side of Miami Beach, in preparation for the first sales, which he hoped would take place the coming winter, when Florida filled with vacationers and tourists.

His first subdivision, Alton Beach, wasn't ready by then, but Fisher went ahead anyway, advertising it in northern newspapers as a "place to escape from winter," and planting stories in the Florida press. He promised buyers they would have electric lights and telephones in 1914, and city water and sewers two years later, as well as golf courses and fishing facilities. Then, to amuse them while they considered purchases, Fisher staged regattas, talked some of his famous friends into showing up on their yachts, and even had an auto race.

The promotion was only a limited success. Fisher's Alton Beach and Ocean Beach realty companies were after all selling what amounted to undeveloped land, and many would-be buyers wanted to see if the necessary utilities would indeed be provided before they signed contracts. Undaunted, Fisher joined with Collins and Pancoast to form the town of Miami Beach in 1915, and petition the state for recognition, which was promptly granted.

While supervising construction at the Beach, Fisher proceeded with his plan for the transcontinental highway. For political reasons he renamed it the Lincoln Highway, and then assembled a roster of notables who helped him lobby for the project. The work proceeded according to plan, although it was evident it would not be finished as soon as Fisher had originally hoped. But long before it was done, Fisher turned to a new idea, one that would harmonize with his Florida interests. He called it the Dixie Highway, which he planned to run from Indianapolis to Miami, Fisher's two favorite places. In October 1915, Fisher took off on what he billed as the "Dixie Highway Pathfinders' Tour," traveling through cities and towns along the route of what he said would be the finest two-lane road in the nation, one that would finally signal the end of the era of bad feelings caused by the Civil War.

Then, returning to Florida, Fisher embarked on a campaign to convince the state and federal governments to support a new plan for causeways from Miami to Miami Beach. While doing this he planned several new islands for the entrance to Biscayne Bay, and he talked of deepening the shallow channel at the Beach's south end—the Government Cut—and digging a canal at the north end to provide easier access to Biscayne Bay, in the process making Miami Beach a true island.

All of these projects were either put off because of World War I, or begun in a halfhearted fashion, to be completed after the Armistice in 1918. But they remained Fisher's blueprint for the future, which would come in the 1920s.

The war proved a boon to Miami Beach and Miami. Wealthy Americans who could no longer travel to Europe on vacations now considered Florida, especially after the sinking of the *Lusitania* in 1915. Most of them went to Palm Beach or St. Augustine, with some of the others going to other coastal resorts north of Palm Beach or on the Gulf coast. Only a few went as far south as Miami. But the *nouveaux riches,* those who made their big money on war contracts and related business, and who before then hardly went on vacations at all, were a different breed. They would have felt out of place at Palm Beach, even had they been admitted. They went to Miami, and while there, they visited the Beach. A handful purchased land from Fisher or one of the other real-estate interests. Almost all returned home impressed with the area and wanting to return on future vacations, at which time they might be in the market for a plot.

Meanwhile, Fisher would continue his filling and construction at the Beach, and work at publicizing it in Florida and the North. The land boom was gathering steam—he was convinced of this. The state's economy was humming, especially on the Atlantic coast. The railroad was not only operating at close to capacity, but was building new spurs, while the Seaboard Air Line Railroad expanded at an even more rapid pace. All the preconditions for a bonanza were present. All that was needed to bring it about were peace and prosperity, completion of Fisher's construction programs, especially the Dixie Highway, and a little luck.

In preparation for the boom, Fisher began two projects indicative of his view of what the future would bring to the Beach. In 1918 he

Operating Statistics of the Florida East Coast Railroad, 1913-1919

Year Ending June 30	Total Operating Revenues Per Mile of Road (Unit: $1,000)	Tons of Freight Traffic (Unit: 1 million tons)	Number of Passengers Carried One Mile (Unit: 1 million passengers)
1913	7.823	143.200	69.202
1914	7.665	149.521	76.076
1915	7.400	163.705	69.390
1916	9.670	281.387	73.687
1917*	9.032	335.695	85.477
1918	9.809	380.678	81.631
1919	11.231	411.894	101.222

*For 1917–1919, data are for years ending December 31.

Source: Vanderblue, *"The Florida Land Boom,"* p. 116.

began work on a polo field, in the hope it would attract his wealthy sportsmen pals to the area. His friend, Harold Talbott, Jr., was a polo enthusiast, and he cooperated with Fisher in planning and constructing the field and necessary satellite operations. "If we are able to get any of these men here, I am satisfied that they will be so enthused that later there will be more to follow them," he wrote. "I hate to see you going to the expense of putting up stables, houses for the grooms, etc. in view of the uncertainty of the situation, but I feel that even if things do not turn out successfully this year, that we will be able to do better the next." Tom Pancoast frowned at the idea, and Fisher tried to calm him down by observing that "We are having an enormous interest in Polo from the very best people in the country, and as long as these people are willing to ship their ponies down to Miami at an annual expense of several thousand dollars, it is the proper thing for us to provide barns for them, since they afford us a big part of our attractions there during the Winter, and draw the kind of people we want to sell houses to."

The second project involved annual regattas, and for this purpose Fisher attempted to deepen Biscayne Bay and its entrances, as well as speed work on what would become Baker's Haulover Cut, which separated the Beach from the mainland in the north, but would not be completed until 1923. Then, to enhance the value of Miami Beach property further, he speeded work on utilities installations, especially near the polo field and marinas, which Fisher felt would become the focus of Beach activities.

These moves indicate the direction of Fisher's thinking on the eve of what would become the greatest land boom the nation had witnessed to that time. He seemed to believe Miami Beach would serve his fast-living friends—one might go so far as to describe them as the "jet set of the 1920s"—in much the same way St. Augustine and Palm Beach were designed for Flagler's circle years before. Given Fisher's own background, the nation's past history and that of Florida, and his knowledge of both, along with forecasts made by respectable pundits as to what the 1920s would bring, his plans made sense. Like everyone else, Fisher was a product of his time and place. But his vision, like that of more thoughtful men, was astigmatic. The boom would come, and Fisher and others would profit from it, but its shape and magnitude would be quite different from anything they expected on Armistice Day, 1918. Other forces, ignored by some at the time, were also at work, and they would combine to create a mania quite new in American history, one that had implications for the American people quite beyond the narrow confines of Miami Beach.

Foremost among the forces Fisher understood and did reckon with was the automobile. At the turn of the century only 8,000 motor vehicles were registered in the United States. In 1912, the year Fisher met Collins, the number was 944,000, and 356,000 passenger cars were produced that year. Registrations were at 5.1 million by 1917, the year America entered World War I, and production of passenger cars stood at 1.7 million, after increasing every year in the century. Production fell for the first time in 1918, but then recovered, reaching 1.6 million in 1919, when registrations were at 7.6 million. In 1925, as the nation went Florida-crazy, production stood at 3.7 million passenger cars, and total registrations at 20 million.

There was little in the way of highway construction in the late nineteenth century, but by 1914 the individual states were spending

$53 million a year for roads and bridges, a figure that would rise to over $400 million by 1925, a year in which state road construction alone was more than 23,000 miles, and federally aided highways included 179,000 miles of road. Additional automobiles created the demand for more highways, which in turn encouraged people to buy more cars, and then the process repeated itself. It seemed an endless cycle during much of the 1920s, one that would benefit Florida. The Dixie Highway was completed in time for the boom, and it would be clogged with vacationers and tourists from all parts of the country, who had heard of Florida and wanted to see it with their own eyes.

Florida's political leaders were keenly aware of the benefits tourism would bring to the state, and recognized that without good transportation outsiders would not come. They were particularly concerned about the inadequate roads. Florida had a reputation of being one of the most miserable states in the nation in highway and road construction, understandable in light of its essentially rural nature. Flagler could build his railroad along the East Coast, and other tycoons could take care of the West Coast and even attempt to build feeders to the interior. But the state itself would have nothing to do with them, or with Fisher when he asked for help on the Dixie Highway.

Governor Sidney Catts, who had campaigned for the office in 1917 on the promise of building roads but not raising taxes, tried to keep both pledges. In 1917 the state appropriated only $55,976 for road construction. The figure was low, to be sure, but defenders of the small budget noted that the roads were constructed for the most part by convict labor, and cost next to nothing. Catts managed to more than double the appropriation for 1918, helped in part by the need for better transportation because of the war. His road budget for 1919 topped $744,000, and went beyond the million mark for the first time in 1921.

Catts stepped down in 1921, the same year Congress passed and the President signed the Federal Highways Act. Governor Cary Hardee, who like Catts was an advocate of better roads, won approval of a $1.1 million construction grant in 1922, and the following year was able to extract almost $5 million in federal aid, an extraordinary feat considering the total federal grant budget for roads that year was only $74 million nationwide. But the state legislature rebelled against increasing construction budgets, and Hardee proved less successful than Catts in wheedling votes for the measures.

Governor John Martin, who took office in 1925, was more adept at twisting political arms. Warning that the real-estate boom would falter unless roads were built, he won approval of several major appropriations measures. In 1925, contracts for 335 miles of road and 5,400 feet of bridges were entered into by the state. The following year the figures were 605 miles and 9,300 feet, while appropriations rose from $5 million to $11 million.

Fisher applauded these moves, and like other developers did what he could to influence legislators to vote for better roads.* Florida real-estate advertisements in northern and midwestern newspapers often spoke of the fine road system which led to balmy resort areas. They did not mention that most of the roads, like the resorts they ended in, existed only on paper in the mid-1920s. Still, the motorists came, as much for the tour as its destination.

T. H. Weigall, fresh from London in 1925, was one of them. A popular journalist seeking stories of America, he hit upon the idea of going to Florida while seeing the *Ziegfeld Follies* in New York, which had several sketches dealing with the land boom. Weigall boarded a Florida-bound train, which stopped at several resort cities, and he wrote of what he saw. At West Palm Beach, for example, "there were a few buildings in the background, and a huge assortment of cars; a few young men were running about with papers, but most of them seemed to have nothing particular to do. There were quite a number of large racing automobiles, most of them occupied by

*Florida real-estate interests did not press too hard for roads. When they did, the legislators would remind the realtors that the state constitution forbade inheritance taxes, in itself a factor in attracting the wealthy to the state and keeping them there as permanent residents. In order to build highways, money would have to be raised, and they observed that the best source might be new taxes on estates. By threatening a state constitutional convention to change the inheritance laws, they stilled the highway lobby. At the time, of course, Fisher and others like him were convinced Florida would remain a playground for the wealthy, while the middle class would remain at home.

extremely pretty and smartly-dressed girls under brightly-coloured parasols; it was quite an attractive site."

Then, south of Palm Beach, Weigall saw one of the large subdivisions that dotted the coastline in 1925, and the people in cars along the Dixie Highway, making the great trek southward.

> The train was off again, and now we were wending our way through a different sort of scenery; an unending series of perfectly flat subdivisions, with perfectly straight streets lined with electric lamps heading down towards a perfectly blue sea a mile or so away on our left, and here and there quite considerable little collections of houses in the prevailing white and red, with occasionally a big hotel, semi-completed. The Dixie Highway had changed sides now, and on our right the cars were still pouring by, with the passengers in their back seats pulling about among their luggage and preparing for the end of their journey. The numbers of the triumphal archways and the ornamental concrete bridges had become legion now, and everywhere vistas of the inevitable "White Way Lights" stretched away over the grass-covered flats.

Such trips were novel experience for middle-class Americans, who prior to the advent of the moderately priced automobile had viewed travel as a chore undergone to seek employment, certainly not for pleasure. As children, such people had gone to railroad stations to watch the trains come and go. Now they had their own vehicles, and most who took the Florida trip in the early 1920s did so as their first major expedition from home. There were no motels in those days—the word had not even been coined—and only a few "tourist cabins," which in any case most of the new travelers avoided. Nor did they want to eat at diners along the road, fearing strange foods, contamination, meeting strange new people, and paying what might be outlandish prices. So they packed boxes of canned and packaged foods to eat along the roadside, and slept in the cars or in blankets in open fields. They had a name for themselves—tin can tourists.

Kenneth Roberts, who later would become a celebrated American novelist, was a magazine writer in the early 1920s, specializing in "Florida stories," often for *The Saturday Evening Post,* the most popular magazine of the day. Roberts investigated the tin can tourists in 1920–1921, traveled the roads with them, and told his readers of their activities. They would travel about in Florida, he said, spending most of their vacation on the road. "The tin-canner spends, for his winter of travel, about the same amount of money that a seasoned Palm Beach mixer frequently spends in a couple of days."

> The ordinary tin-canner . . . is content with an ordinary, small touring car, which, when in motion, has a part of his camping outfit attached to every exposed part of his machine. The tent and a couple of suit-cases are attached to one running board; mattresses and blankets are attached to the other; cases of canned goods, kitchen utensils, and other odds and ends are fixed to the rear or concealed beneath a false floor in the tonneau. . . . When the ordinary tin-canners break out their camping outfit, the tent extends out at right angles from the side door of the car, so that the occupants of the tent can use the car as a combination lavoratory, sitting-room, chiffonier, clothes closet, pantry and safe-deposit vault.

These were the kinds of people that came to Miami and the Beach after the war. They were hardly the class Fisher expected, but he welcomed them nonetheless.

The tin-canners represented a new phenomenon in another way, one which would not be clearly discerned until the mid-1920s. Prior to the war most of them would have been classified as "working class," with little in the way of tangible assets. If they had jobs in factories, their wages barely covered living costs. They lived in a cash economy, since no one, with the possible exception of the corner grocer, would extend them credit. Since most of their purchases were for food and material for clothing, they would not have thought to ask for credit. Some owned their own homes, purchased with a mortgage from the bank; the mortgage was short term by today's standards, and feared by the family as though an ogre were living in the basement. Paying off the mortgage was a major goal of their lives, and its final elimination as great a reason for celebration as a marriage or birth. People like these had little money, and what they had would not be used for such frivolous things as vacations, automobiles, and the like.

The war changed all this. The economy boomed from 1914 to 1918, especially during the neutrality phase prior to 1917. Full employment at high wages was the rule in a labor-short economy. Anyone with a modicum of skills and ambition could find a job and at far higher wages than were available prior to the war. Consumer spending rose, but savings increased at a far more rapid pace. Many purchased savings bonds, the patriotic thing to do in wartime, and opened savings accounts for the first time in their lives. The result was a sizable increase in what might be called the "moneyed proletariat." Poverty was still a problem in America, though largely unrecognized at the time. Half of the American people lived in farm areas, subjected to periodic depressions, and the slums in the large cities were no better than before. What was recognized as early as 1919 was the notable increase in the number of people who could put a down payment on a house and automobile, take a vacation, splurge on factory-made clothes, or attend college. This was not a temporary phenomenon; it would last throughout the 1920s, and conditions would get better in most years.

It was an age, too, where "having a good time" was not considered immoral. The prosperity of the 1920s encouraged a consumer ethic, which began replacing the work ethic of the previous generation. The sons and daughters of people who admired Andrew Carnegie and read Horatio Alger would make heroes of Rudolph Valentino and Gloria Swanson, and try to ape their ways of living. The moneyed proletariat could not take a cruise to Europe, play polo, or vacation at Palm Beach—they lacked the status and background for such activities, even if they had the money. But they could and did take up golf and tennis, and get into their Fords for vacations, perhaps to Miami. They had enough money to do so, or at least enough for a down payment on a set of clubs—and perhaps enough money to buy a plot of land at Miami Beach on time payment plans.

Flagler would not have thought a man like Fisher suitable for Palm Beach. In 1918, Fisher did not calculate on the tin-canners. Had Flagler lived long enough, he might have adjusted in time to the idea that Fisher's *nouveaux riches* had earned a place in the sun. Fisher lived through the 1920s boom and became one of its enduring symbols. He did accommodate himself to the situation in which the moneyed proletariat wanted a vacation in Miami Beach and perhaps would buy a small plot of land. It did not take him long to realize that the postwar economy was throwing up many fairly wealthy people, such as stockbrokers, advertising men, salesmen, junior executives in large corporations, and stock speculators who not only wanted exotic vacations but perhaps vacation homes as well. These people would provide a far larger market for Fisher and other developers than would the polo players and yachtsmen Fisher catered to in 1919.

Why did it happen in Florida? Why didn't these people go on European tours, vacation in southern California or other tourist areas, or buy land in the Northeast and Midwest? In other words, why did the Miami Beach of *that* period develop in that state? After all, wildcatters went to Spindletop because the oil was there, and miners to Washoe because it contained silver ore. Why did the moneyed proletariat and the *nouveaux riches* of postwar America find themselves drawn to southern Florida?

To understand the reasons, one must consider the unusual interlude of the early postwar years, a period of disorientation for many, one in which there appeared reason to be optimistic about the future, and pessimistic, too, but more strongly so in both directions than is usually the case. There were reasons for hope, but equally strong sentiments of cynicism.

Those who saw the bright side of things could note that the United States had emerged from the war the most powerful nation on earth, in effect the only winner. The economy appeared sound, even though there was a sharp and short dip in 1920. The following year, talk of limitless prosperity was heard, and it would continue for the rest of the decade or at least until the fall of 1929. The future was in America, and the thought was witnessed by the election returns of 1920 in which Harding and "normalcy" won a record majority, by reports of "Bolshevism" on the old continent, and by a carry-over of the fervent patriotism of the wartime era.

George Babbitt, the hero of Sinclair Lewis' 1922 novel, was as good a symbol as any of this sentiment. Babbitt boasted that his hometown distrusted foreigners, loved the "good old U.S.A.," and yearned for challenge to overcome. In his own way, Babbitt was a pioneer, but one without a frontier to conquer. Toward the end of the novel, Lewis indicates he is poetic in an age of material progress, a person who might have been quite different in appearance and action a half century earlier. But Babbitt wore his button ("Boosters—Pep" is what it read) and went on to try to conquer Zenith, his hometown and the "greatest little city in the world." Zenith will not be little if George Babbitt has anything to do with it. Nor will the U.S.A. take any guff from foreigners. George Babbitt, middle-aged patriot, a real-estate salesman in a boom period, was a natural for Miami.

In the novel he remains in the Midwest; in the Florida land boom, thousands like him motored into town, seeking an American vacation, an American winter place, and Americans with whom to meet and joke. At a time when the nation finally had produced a large class of people who might have taken "the European tour," such individuals decided to remain at home.

Yet all was not well. The changes had come so quickly, and many Americans could not handle them. For decades America had played at having a world role; now it was real, and in the months of debate on the League of Nations, the role was rejected. Was the Russian Revolution the wave of the future? Or was the American way destined to conquer the world? The Babbits of America said they had no doubts of victory, but underneath it all, they did. And if they did fight and win, was the prize worth the effort? What would the nation be like in the future? At one time there seemed little doubt that the goal was Jefferson's nation of freemen, the "happy republic" so publicized in the 1840s and even after the Civil War. Now many were no so sure they could realize these ambitions. The 1920 census shov ed that, for the first time, more Americans lived in urban areas than in rural and on farms. After two decades of reformism, the big corporations were bigger than ever, and increasingly coming to dominate national life. Wall Street, not Pennsylvania Avenue or Main Street, was the locus of power, or at least so it seemed. Many Americans, seeking to recapture a past that may not have ever existed and to hold onto values that were rarely applied, and who had the money and means of going to places where they could be realized, thought of Florida. In its own strange way and for the first time in an urban, modern setting, the nation searched for a utopia, for a new America when the old seemed ending and the main features of the new were unclear. Such individuals, too, came to Florida.

There were good business reasons to make the move. The motion-picture industry was growing rapidly, and seemed to be centering in Hollywood, California. Eastern investors, reluctant to take regular long train rides to the West Coast, thought Florida offered everything California did and was closer—only a day away by fast train. These men and others like them helped plan Picture City on the Atlantic coast, north of Miami, which was supposed to become the motion-picture capital of America. If the climate was excellent, the financial climate was just as good. Florida had no inheritance laws, no state income tax, no sales tax, and was conservative politically. California, on the other hand, had a long reform tradition, and the state's most potent political figure, Senator Hiram Johnson, was considered little better than a socialist by conservative businessmen. This, too, drew business to Florida.

Prohibition was a factor in the Florida boom. The "noble experiment" began in 1919, at a time when the land boom was gathering steam anyway, and Prohibition added glamour and excitement, intrigue and action, to Miami and southern Florida in general. Other towns and cities throughout the nation flaunted the Prohibition statutes, but none so flagrantly as Miami. Weigall noted that Florida was the wettest state in the nation. In fact, Prohibition wasn't even an issue in the state—"people had simply forgotten about it altogether."

* * *

> I should say that during the boom there must have been more alcohol per head consumed in Florida than in any other country in the world. The organization of the liquor traffic was so complete and so elaborate that it was difficult to see how it could ever be eradicated even if anyone wanted it to be; and personally, I never met anyone who did. . . . In Miami there were at least two proper oldfashioned saloons, with polished counters, brass hand-rails and stocks of bottles ranged on wooden shelves behind the bar. One of them was within 200 yards of the central police station, and there was a constable on . . . duty directly opposite its entrance.

There is good reason to believe that, on the whole, Americans drank less during Prohibition than they did prior to 1919. Liquor prices rose when drink became illegal, and the poor couldn't afford the cost. On the other hand, there were some Americans who drank little when they could get booze, and resented any law that told them they couldn't do something. So they imbibed more heavily than before, reflecting perhaps that forbidden fruits are the sweetest. A finger of Scotch was a drink in 1918; in 1920, it was a status symbol.

Carl Fisher was one of those who began to drink heavily after the law was passed. "Not even the United States Government could tell Carl Fisher what he should or should not eat or drink," said his wife Jane. He bought up all the liquor he could find before the law went into effect, and afterward went on "cruises to Nassau" to purchase additional supplies.

South Florida became one of the two greatest bootlegging areas in the United States during the Prohibition era—the other was the Great Lakes. Fishing or cruise boats, like Fisher's, would go to Nassau and pick up a load of Scotch at $24 a case. The liquor could be wholesaled in Miami at $40, and retailed at from $100 to $120 to tourists, who would then take "the real stuff" home and perhaps let a friend have a fifth for $20.

Other British islands in the Caribbean began to compete with Nassau for the business. They did so not on a price basis, but rather on reliability and on payoffs to the biggest bootleggers in town. By 1922 Bimini took the lead, and the American fishing boats would line up in the harbor waiting for stevedores to load them up for the return trip. Capture by federal agents was rare. As Kenneth Roberts wrote at the time:

> There seems to be an idea in the North that rum-running from Bimini and Cuba to the Florida coast can be easily stopped by Prohibition agents. This is a mistaken idea; for the rum-runner has several hundred miles of uninhabited coastline and keys on which to land his cargo. It was among these keys that the most notorious pirates of the early days concealed their vessels and their treasures, and eluded pursuit for years. It would be as easy to catch a rum-runner among the Florida keys as to locate a red ant in the Hippodrome.
>
> Any Prohibition enforcement agent that didn't have lead in his shoes and a daub of mud in both eyes, however, could easily get the goods on twenty or thirty Miami bootleggers in a day.
>
> One good result of comparatively cheap whiskey in Miami is the apparently total disappearance of beer-making and other home-brewing activities. There seems to be no market for hops, malt, prunes, raisins or wash-boilers—which would seem to make Miami an unusually healthy city in which to live.

Cuba itself was the final lure. In this period Cuba was a virtual protectorate of the United States, a place where American citizenship was a badge for special privilege, where the American dollar reigned supreme. Also, Cuba was considered somewhat sinful, exciting, and exotic. So tourists there had the advantages of adventure but none of the dangers. Finally, Cuba was spoken of as a fine area for investment. This was a time when Cuban stocks were featured on the Curb Market in New York, and brokers shuttled back and forth seeking new listings.

Tourists and businessmen would go to Cuba by steamship, but a faster and less rocky route was to take the train to Miami and from there board a Caribbean steamer for the short hop to Havana. Miami in the early 1920s was a bustling seaport as well as a place for pleasure. Many of those who came for business stayed for pleasure, and this, too, added to the Florida boom.

Any one of these factors would have helped realize Fisher's dream of a Miami bonanza. Now all of them came at the same time—just after the signing of the Armistice in 1918. The exodus from the North and Midwest began the following winter. It would gather steam during the next four years and reach a crescendo in 1924–1925. By then, all the country would be talking of Florida, and, in particular, of Miami Beach.

The boom would affect Wall Street in New York and London's Lombard Street, and even the French Riviera, Monaco, and other European resorts. Serious American commentators, trying to understand just what the phenomenon implied, no longer dismissed it as just another craze. Unable to fathom the future at a time of great social and economic change, some believed Florida held the key to the American destiny. It was as though some master hand had lifted the nation by the Midwest and shaken its inhabitants to the South, said one, while another believed that, by 1970, Florida would be the most populated state in the nation, with some hundred million Americans living there. A third, Frank Bohn, wrote seriously of a new kind of culture developing in what he called "The American Mediterranean." In time Americans would look to the South for growth, he claimed, and to Latin America, not Europe, for neighbors. All would learn Spanish as a second language, just as educated Cubans and Mexicans had to learn English as theirs. In time the rest of the South would follow Florida's lead, and then the other sections would fall in line.

> Eventually our Nordic type must be as changed here as were the Longobards and the Normans in Italy. New England will probably remain as our Scotland. But our Italy and Spain will evolve and mellow with the passing centuries. Indeed, in all our Southland our race is destined to go on in this refining process.

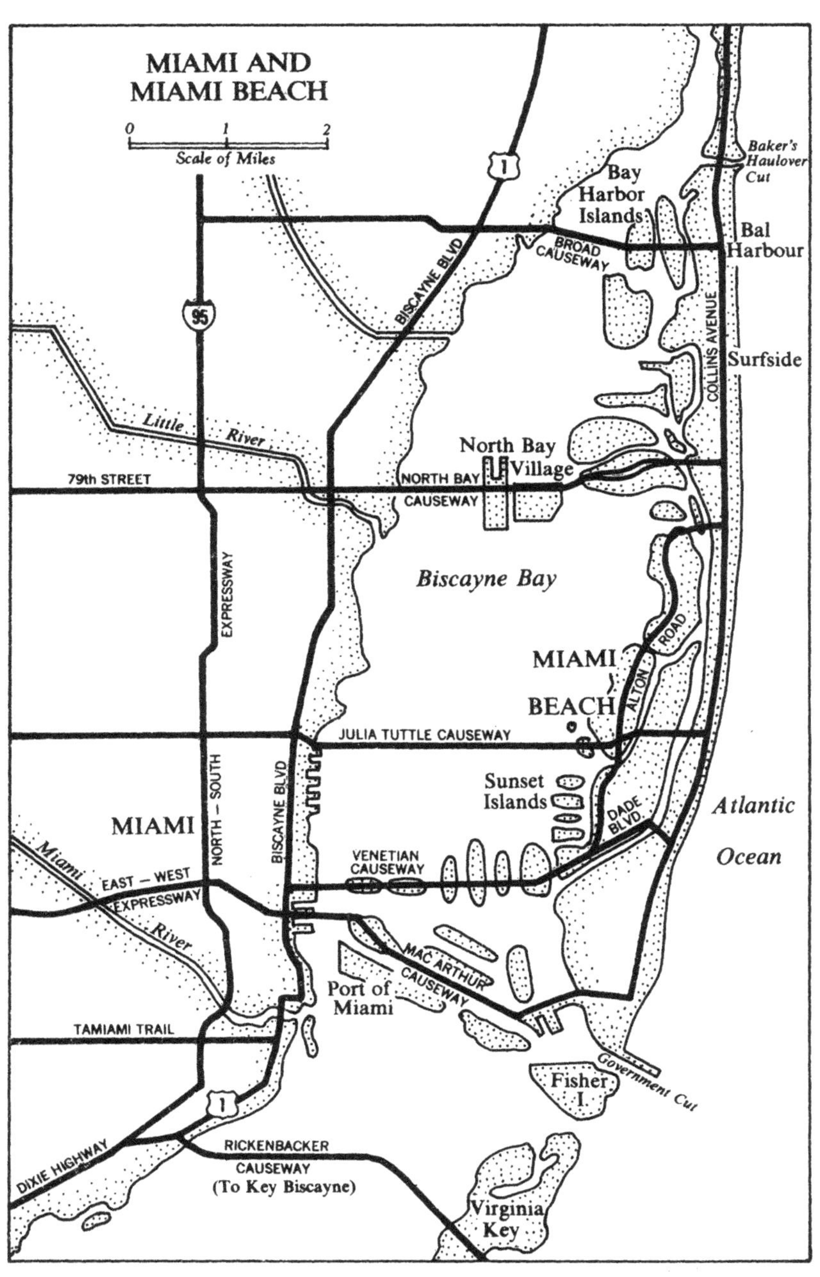

MIAMI AND
MIAMI BEACH
0
1
2
Scale of Miles
1
95
Baker's
Haulover
Cut
Bay
Harbor
Islands
Bal
Harbour
BROAD
CAUSEWAY
BISCAYNE BLVD
COLLINS AVENUE
Surfside
Little
River
North Bay
Village
79th STREET
NORTH BAY
CAUSEWAY
EXPRESSWAY
Biscayne Bay
ROAD
MIAMI
BEACH
ALTON
JULIA TUTTLE CAUSEWAY
Sunset
Islands
NORTH – SOUTH
BISCAYNE BLVD
MIAMI
DADE
BLVD.
Atlantic
Ocean
VENETIAN
CAUSEWAY
Miami
EAST – WEST
EXPRESSWAY
River
MAC ARTHUR
CAUSEWAY
Port of
Miami
TAMIAMI TRAIL
Government Cut
Fisher
I.
1
DIXIE HIGHWAY
RICKENBACKER
CAUSEWAY
(To Key Biscayne)
Virginia
Key

It is to be one of the major cultural evolutions of Western Civilization.

Such musings came after the boom had peaked and resulted from extrapolating events into the distant future. Visions that appear at the beginning or end of great enterprises rarely are reliable, especially when one is not sure the enterprise is great, or if one is at the beginning or end.

Dating the beginning of such a boom is impossible, for there was no single dramatic event to mark the start. Rather, it was a continuation of what had gone before, and an acceleration of forces already in existence. Despite the recession of 1920 and the recovery phase of the following year, the tourists and travelers came, but it was not until full recovery, in 1922, that the great floods of people would begin to arrive, with the boom phase coming in 1924–1925. The visitors came to look in 1922–1923, and they returned to buy in 1924–1925.

Operating Statistics of the Florida East Coast Railroad, 1919-1926

Year Ending December 31	Total Operating Revenues Per Mile of Road (Unit: $1,000)	Tons of Freight Traffic (Unit: 1 million tons)	Number of Passengers Carried One Mile (Unit: 1 million passengers)
1919	11.231	411.894	101.222
1920	15.196	478.621	117.418
1921	15.059	340.777	96.400
1922	14.893	342.141	92.833
1923	17.767	450.600	113.256
1924	22.351	589.835	142.929
1925	31.828	792.738	241.121
1926	29.377	842.680	241.463

Source: Vanderblue, *"The Florida Land Boom,"* p. 116.

The state was inundated with outsiders, but most of the activity was centered in a hundred-mile-long strip of land on the coast running from Palm Beach to Coral Gables. The big draws there were the reputation of Palm Beach, to which was added the work of Addison Mizner, the ballyhoo of Miami and Miami Beach, for which Fisher bore the greatest responsibility, and the creation of new suburbs, Coral Gables—the work of George Merrick—being the most famous.

The Palm Beach episode was the least typical of the Florida phenomena of the 1920s, but the most publicized. It really began with Parris Singer, one of the several illegitimate children of the founder of Singer Sewing Machines. Parris was a pre-World War I playboy, most of whose activities were in Europe, where he spent several years consorting with dancer Isadora Duncan. The two vacationed at Palm Beach, which Singer liked as a place in which to recuperate from his wild flings. In the post-Flagler period, Palm Beach had become somewhat old fashioned, with the aging friends of the Standard Oil tycoon maintaining their residences, but their children going elsewhere for vacations and pleasures.

It was at Palm Beach that Singer met Addison Mizner, a man who had participated in the Alaska Gold Rush, lived in various countries around the world, and knew the "right people." Mizner was an architect, though he had no formal training and seemed to do most of his work on the strength of intuition and a keen sense of what the Palm Beach rich wanted.

One day in January 1917, Mizner and Singer were talking of their various ills on the porch of Flagler's Royal Poinciana at Palm Beach. Singer told Mizner he had gone there to die, "but I'm damned if I feel like it." Mizner asked Singer what he wanted to do about it, to which Singer responded with a wry smile. "I tell you what I'd do," said Mizner. "I'd build something that wasn't made of wood, and I wouldn't paint it yellow," looking about at the now-decaying hotel.

Singer then commissioned Mizner to design and build a hotel for convalescent servicemen, which became the Everglades Club. It was a great success, and led to other commissions, most of them for private homes. All were pretty much the same—as Mizner put it, "More Spanish than anything you'll find in Spain." The Mizner "cottages" were laden with stucco and dark woods, hanging gardens, and furnished with heavy "antiques," some of which were imported from Spain, the rest manufactured in a factory Mizner established for the purpose. And they had Spanish names. El Mirasol, constructed at a cost of over a million dollars, was commissioned by the Stotesburys. It had thirty-seven rooms, a garage that could hold forty automobiles, and high ceilings, with the paint properly aged so as to seem like a room out of a period motion picture. El Mirador, Amado, Casa Bendita, El Solano, and other similarly named millionaires' "cottages" followed, as Mizner became the most famous architect in Florida, setting a style that survives to this day. Before he was through, Mizner and other architects who imitated him had remade Palm Beach. Money was no object, neither to the old rich nor the new who made Palm Beach the most famous and exclusive watering place in the nation. Life was a round of tennis, golf, parties, and dressing. Always there was the dressing. The latest fashions were unveiled at Palm Beach, and the world's best-dressed women congregated there to show off their gowns and jewels.

Palm Beach was not the Florida boom, only a small part of the edge of it. "Nobody should come to Palm Beach who doesn't have money," said one of the Beach's millionaires. By money, he meant fortunes in the seven figures, and individuals who could afford million-dollar homes and vacations that cost $100,000. There were enough of them to make Palm Beach a dazzling place in the 1920s. But most were older than the general run of people attracted to Florida in that period. As one of these individuals put it, "The trouble with Palm Beach is that by the time you can afford it, you're too old to enjoy it."

Addison, his brother Wilson, and a promotional genius named Harry Reichenbach were responsible for the development of a new resort, which Addison placed halfway between Miami and Palm Beach. Boca Raton—Spanish for Rat's Mouth, although the translation was rarely offered—was to be even more exclusive than Palm Beach, and loaded with Mizner architectural creations. The Mizner Development Corporation, whose directors included many prominent political, financial, and industrial leaders, was to "screen" candidates for home ownership as well as pass on Mizner's projects, most of which were to be on or near Boca Raton's main highway, El Camino Real, which ran less than half a mile but was twenty lanes wide. The homes would be situated on canals, which Addison spent fortunes on in a vain attempt to make them blue rather than muddy brown. Eventually the company imported gondoliers who would ply their trade up and down the waterways, singing Italian ballads as they glided past mossy, Spanish-style mansions inhabited by American businessmen and their wives. It was very elegant (a much-used word in that place and time).

Mizner began planning for Boca Raton in 1923, and lots were ready for sale in May 1925. On the first day $2.1 million in sales were recorded. Within two weeks Reichenbach sold $14 million worth, and Addison had begun work on his palazzi. By then sales offices had been opened in all the large eastern and midwestern cities, and Mizner had broken ground for the Ritz-Carlton Hotel, which he claimed would cost more than $6 million and be the finest in Florida. From all indications, Boca Raton seemed destined for long life and great success.

The Mizners stressed exclusivity at Boca Raton. Only the best people, and those Protestants and proper denominations, could apply for purchases. George Merrick wanted his community, Coral Gables, to be open to all who could afford it, again assuming they were white Protestants. But the prices would be high. Still, there were plenty for him to appeal to.

Coral Gables was to be a completely planned city, or to be more precise, a suburb of Miami. The roofs of the houses would be made of coral-colored tiles, and the walls tinted pale pink. Coral Gables would have country clubs, canals, shopping malls, excellent transportation, and anything else its residents might desire so long as money could buy it. One entered the suburb through Douglas Entrance, a rocky area with an impressive archway, which led into the main streets. Once within the confines, there were fountains, flamingos, plazas, and other signs which in that period bespoke affluence. Visitors and prospective buyers motored past coral pools, bulldozers knocking down scrubby pines and cutting canals, one of which would go into Biscayne Bay, and builders at work on large pink "bungalows." They were all given copies of an advertising brochure, which described

Merrick's vision of a city such as this. As a boy Merrick grew up on a Florida farm, and he heard voices in the night that told him what to do. "The boy Merrick listened, and as he grew older, his dream took shape. He built a *city*. His city is set among pines and palms, and flaming poincianas, and he called it Coral Gables. It is indeed a city of coral gables, and of soft tinted coral walls. Upon the fields he used to till, the stones have blossomed; those ragged stubborn rocks he used to curse, he has called to bloom into an eternal flower."

In this way, Merrick united the dreams of Horatio Alger with the life-style of George Babbitt.

Coral Gables was to be the "Venice of America." Each of the new towns sprouting in Florida in 1923–1926 had its own name, something Spanish, Italian, or musical to the ear, and a subtitle to go with it. Indrio was to be "Florida's Newest and Most Beautiful"; Hollywood, the "Golden Gate of the South"; Orlando, "The City Beautiful"; St. Petersburg, "The Sunshine City"; and Fort Lauderdale, "The Tropical Wonderland." Naples, Venice, Los Gatos, Rio Vista, Pasadena, Cedar Keys, and Riviera were other "communities of the future today."

Leading them all was Miami and Miami Beach, "The Magic City." In 1923 alone Fisher sold $3 million in lots, and this figure doesn't include construction efforts. Sales rose to $8 million the following year and $12 million in 1925. Mansions, shopping centers, hotels, and country clubs crowded the narrow sandbar, until some feared it might collapse. There seemed only two kinds of people in town—real-estate salesmen and would-be buyers. Tin-canners would enter an office "Just to look and talk." They would be told of how easy it could be to buy a lot. All that was needed was a binder, usually less than 20 percent of the purchase price, and the deed was theirs. Such customers would be told of how busboys became millionaires within a few weeks by selling part of their holdings to those who came later, or former farmers who had "more money than they knew what to do with" by selling a few acres. "Why stop at one lot," was the cry. "Buy several, sell off a few, and the rest would be free."

The "binder boys" did well at such deals. They would take down payments, sometimes as little as 5 percent of the price, with the next payment to be 25 percent, at which time the deal would be closed. Then they would sell off their interest and use the capital for additional ventures. The buyers did well too. Since the land offices were so overcrowded, the second payment might not be required for weeks or even months. In the meantime, they would resell the land in the same fashion, becoming binder boys on their own. Then the process would be repeated, perhaps several times, so that the final deed might have a half-dozen or more binders on it, with several individuals making money on each transaction. It was though a massive chain letter was being set into motion. Today's binder boy was the customer of yesterday, and the person to whom he sold a lot would be a binder boy tomorrow.

Ballyhoo was the order of the day. Orchestras and dance bands were imported to amuse the customers, baseball teams were enticed to take spring training in Florida, and celebrities from all parts of the world were drawn there, as a place of action, excitement, and fortune. William Jennings Bryan, now retired to the lecture circuit and a Florida resident for some years past, was paid $250 a lecture to talk to visitors of the glories of the state. For a while Bryan considered running for the Senate from Florida, but abandoned the idea after a bit of thought. But he did deal in real estate, and as a result of Florida investments was able to leave an estate of almost a million dollars, a trifle embarrassing for the Great Commoner.

Those wishing to hear Bryan or see Gilda Gray or others of the many attractions Miami and Miami Beach had to offer had to find their ways around construction sites. Before the boom ended, the Beach alone would boast 56 hotels with more than 4000 rooms, as well as 178 apartment houses, 308 shops and offices, 8 casinos, 3 schools, 4 polo fields, 3 motion-picture theaters, and 2 churches (Community and Methodist). In addition, 858 private homes were built on the Beach, which became the home of the *nouveaux riches* as well as some of the tin-canners.

The boom was nationwide. Salesmen for Florida real estate appeared in all states, seeking buyers who willingly took high mortgages on unseen land, some planning to build, but many expecting to sell at a profit. Advertisements in Florida and northern papers carried the message, along with coupons to clip and send in, with checks, for land deeds. One such advertisement, typical of hundreds of the 1924–1925 period, read:

> This is a straight-from-the-shoulder message to MY FRIENDS. –GET IT AND GET IT QUICK! I had to make a rush trip to New York, and, believe me, I am glad to be back in time to get my friends in on the BEST THING YET. . . . NOW GET THIS QUICK! . . . When I discovered Lake Stearns I knew I had found the best land in Florida. . . . With me is Mr. Walter T. Spaulding, President of the Spaulding Construction Company of New York and Miami . . . a nationally known constructor. . . . He has put his OWN money into this proposition and will handle the construction of all utilities at Lake Stearns.
>
> MR. WALTER DUNHAM . . . a man of great vision, will direct the selling campaign of this property to the public.
>
> These two associates and I are going to PUT THIS OVER, and YOU are COMING IN ON IT. . . . YOU are coming in with me on the first $150,000 we are going to put in because you KNOW ME and believe in my judgement. I want $5000 out of you for this proposition. . . . NOW DON'T WRITE ME. I WON'T HAVE TIME TO SCRATCH A PEN. I have given you the facts and am offering you a FINAL OPPORTUNITY to get in RIGHT NOW. SEND ME YOUR CHECK, and I will put it in the BANK. . . . This is a personal message from me to YOU. You want to make some REAL MONEY now. Get in and come on while the PROPOSITION IS HOT.

The money did flow in. While no clear estimate of the amount of investment capital can be reconstructed, it was assumed at the time that in 1925 alone some $1 billion from outside sources went into Florida projects of various kinds.

The money came from several sources. Some arrived from Wall Street, and from investors seeking even bigger killings in Florida than in stocks and bonds. As a result, the market dipped for a while in 1925, before recovering and going on to new highs. More money arrived from small towns and cities across the country, as formerly conservative people withdrew their savings and sent it on to buy lots and homes in Florida. A great deal came from New England and Ohio, and banks and real-estate firms in those areas suffered deeply, with several banks going out of business as a result. By 1925 stories of thievery in Florida appeared, followed by others regarding the coming crash of values in the state. Florida real-estate dealers investigated these reports and found that most came from Ohio, with Massachusetts in second place. In addition, foreign interests became concerned with the Florida boom and tried to end it. The French Riviera and Italy reported bad winter seasons, the result of tourists choosing Florida over their accustomed resorts. Talk of a new Fisher-backed gambling palace in Miami Beach caused tremors to pass through Monaco, as even Monte Carlo leaders thought their casino might bow before the Miami wave.

How long could it last? By 1925 many were asking such questions, even as the lines formed at Miami real-estate offices and swamps were selling for absurd prices. "Allow ten years for the Miami Boom," said T. S. Knowland of New York, one of the leading realtors of the city.

> There are certain lots in Miami which were sold two years ago at $3,000. Their present selling price is $25,000. No wonder, then, that the market is brisk with buyers and sellers. The point is, how much higher will these prices go? Nobody knows, for at every turn one is met by the fact that Florida is different from anything of its kind that has gone before. Past booms are a good guide in a general way, but they cannot serve as an exact measure for the present movement.
>
> For one thing, the whole wealth of the United States is interested in Florida. Almost everybody of consequence appears to have a large holding there, and vast sums are being

> brought from other States for industrial and developmental purposes. The significance of the fact is this: That such names tend to generate deep confidence.

The big names indeed did go to Florida, and respected financial commentators said they would not allow the boom to end. Roger Babson, who since 1921 had said Wall Street was due for a crash, was a longtime Florida enthusiast, and he, too, thought the boom was solid enough, though overdone. In time values would decline, said Babson, who was listened to by more small, conservative investors than any other man in the mid-1920s. But that would be a long way off. The Florida boom would last as long as the stock-market bull market continued, said Babson in 1925. Even then, after Wall Street recovered, Florida would go on to even greater heights. Such words were soothing, coming as they did from a man who in the past had been skeptical of booms.

In the summer of 1925 Miami Beach residents put up signs on their front lawns reading, "This Property Not for Sale." The would-be buyers came early that year, and were going from door to door, at odd hours, trying to purchase houses. N. B. T. Roney paid $3 million for a stretch of beach, and within a week resold it for $12 million. That fall the railroads announced they could no longer carry shipments to Miami due to overcrowding. Steamship lines joined in an embargo against furniture; there simply wasn't enough room for all who wanted to go that year. Biscayne Bay was clogged with ships of all description; the Dixie Highway became one long line of cars, stretching hundreds of miles north of the border. In January 1926, it was learned that over $2 billion in Miami Beach real estate passed hands the previous year. What did this mean? How much were sales, resales, and further resales? Did a 5-percent down payment on a $10,000 lot count for $10,000, or for $500? Federal tax inspectors were in Miami, investigating the matter, and vowing to end abuses. Even then, the boom seemed to be rolling on.

But it wasn't. Suddenly, Florida was becoming less fashionable than it had been in the past. Bookings on Europe-bound steamers were high; sales at Boca Raton slipped, and several important Palm Beach leaders announced they were bound for the Riviera. Now that Florida had become fashionable for the middle class, Palm Beach was no longer as desirable for the old American aristocrats, and Boca Raton was yesterday's news. Besides, Mizner's once-impressive Spanish-style buildings were too stylish and modish to last as status symbols. His public tired of them, and Mizner had nothing more to offer. In addition to this Mizner was engaged in a squabble with General T. Coleman du Pont, who claimed Boca Raton had used his name without permission. Wealthy America had made Florida popular, and the middle and lower classes had aped the style setters. Now society's leaders were bored with Florida. What would their followers do?

Carl Fisher didn't seem to care. Miami Beach no longer excited him, now that the challenge of pioneering was ended. Fisher would not remain there in 1925, when all that was needed was a secretary to take orders.

Seeking new challenges, Fisher traveled to Long Island in New York. There, at the eastern end, was Montauk, a rather scrubby area, with not much in the way of natural beauty to recommend it. More a part of New England than New York, and the home of fishermen and farmers, Montauk seemed unlikely as a site for the Fisher enterprises. But it was close to New York City, had a decent natural harbor that could be deepened and widened, and a climate in the summer that was bracing at a time when the city sweltered. Here, thought Fisher, was the site for a new Newport, if not a Palm Beach. Turning to his friends, many of whom made fortunes as a result of investing in Miami Beach, Fisher raised $2.5 million and in the summer of 1925, purchased almost 10,000 acres at Montauk. The Montauk Beach Development Corporation, which owned the land and would construct hotels, homes, and roads at Montauk, was designed to be a far larger version of Miami Beach Improvement. Thoughts of Montauk, not Florida, interested Fisher and other Miami leaders in the summer of 1925.

Miami was hectic in the spring and summer of 1926, but not as much as it had been a year earlier. Federal agents were in town, and the binder boys were lying low for the time being. People who had purchased sites for $20,000 expecting to sell them for $30,000 in a few months found some would-be buyers, but they were offering from $15,000 to $18,000 for the land. Needing cash, they took the offer. Florida real-estate prices were falling, though not so much as to indicate a crash. But there were stories of ruin. Roberts noted: "One man, who had bought some lots for $125,000 in the late summer, refused an offer of $325,000 for them in November [of 1925]. He was holding for the January market, when he expected to get $425,000. They were conservatively appraised at $150,000, but appraisals weren't bothered with in those hectic days of the boom. In February he couldn't sell his lots at any price. In April he took $50,000 cash."

Newspapers and magazines began publishing articles on the end of the Florida boom. None of these predicted the state would return to where it had been prior to World War I. Rather, they observed that too much had happened too rapidly. People had been attracted to Florida for the right reasons, but they had begun speculating in land rather than using it to live on. Now the speculative phase was ending, and the real growth could proceed. In other words, the binder boys were leaving–some for Montauk–and their places were being taken by builders.

M. S. Rukeyser, who for four years had criticized the excesses, spoke glowingly of Florida's future in March of 1926, at a time when he could have assumed a triumphant attitude of a proven prophet of doom. As he saw it, the state's future growth lay in three directions: industry, tourism and winter homes, and agriculture. Of the three, agriculture was the most promising. As for the tin-canners and others who thought of Florida as a new Eldorado, they would remain, but attract few others like them.

> At a price, Florida will remain attractive to increasing numbers of residents in colder climates who wish to escape the winters. At boom quotations, however, Florida competed with the

> Italian and French Rivieras, Southern California, the Gulf resorts, and the West Indies.
>
> What of the boom cities, the creations of realtors during the time of inflation—places like Boca Raton, Coral Gables, and Hollywood, municipalities that were made to order? The strongest of these are surviving, but at present are floundering under the stress of financial burdens. They contain ghosts in the form of uncompleted structures that are monuments to the earlier economic folly.

The situation was far from grim in early September 1926, as tin-canners and tourists arrived seeking bargain rates on land and houses. Coming late to the boom, they came late to the decline as well. If land was worth $30,000 in 1924 and $60,000 in 1925, it was surely worth $90,000 in 1926. And such land was being sold at only $40,000. The middle class bought, and continued to buy, as September sales boomed.

Then, on the morning of September 18, the skies darkened. A hurricane, originating in Nassau, was on its way. Old-timers gathered food and clothing and put up shutters, while the newer Floridians hardly knew what to do, but followed their example. The storm hit after midnight, in fury, combining with floods. For the first time the new Floridians learned what a hurricane could do to their land. Flooding occurred over the coastal areas; homes were destroyed; trees were uprooted and thrown against half-completed palazzi. It was the first major hurricane in Florida since 1910, and certainly not the worst in history. But in 1910 there had been little in the way of property to be destroyed, or people to be killed. The situation was quite different in 1926, when 392 died, 6,281 were injured and treated at hospitals, and tens of millions of dollars in property damage occurred.

Still, it wasn't as bad as might seem. Few of the hotels were badly damaged, and within hours of the winds' abatement, reconstruction was begun. But coming as it did at a time when Florida tourism was already in decline, the hurricane served to end whatever remained of the boom. State political leaders assured the press that all was well; Carl Fisher and others ran advertisements telling tourists that Florida was healthier than ever, in every way. These statements only served to frighten away some who might have come. The Florida resorts did not recover in the winter of 1926–1927, conditions remained bad the following summer, and remained poor in 1927–1928. Then came a second hurricane in 1928, causing a further decline. The stock-market crash of 1929 was the conclusion to the Fisher phase of the state's history.

Of course, Florida would recover. All the factors that made Florida appealing prior to World War I still operated after World War II. Those who held on to property acquired in 1925 could have sold at multiples of the price a quarter of a century later. Today that $60,000 lot in Miami Beach is worth almost $1 million.

Henry Flagler, who ruled Florida during the railroad age, lived to see the beginning of the state's automobile age, although he never met Carl Fisher. Florida's next boom, in the aviation age, was dimly perceived by Fisher, though he did nothing to rush it. In any case, he would have been in no condition, financially or otherwise, to do so after 1926. Although not completely wiped out, Fisher was no longer wealthy. Miami had served him well, but he lost all in Montauk. In 1935 the Carl G. Fisher Company was taken over by creditors. Fisher began to drink more heavily than before. He went into comas, delivered drunken orations, spoke of "the good old days" as though they still existed, and, in 1939, he died.

CHAPTER 9

Conglomeritis

When J. P. Morgan created United States Steel in 1901, observers and students of the business scene were awed by the new giant's scope and power. U.S. Steel not only dominated its industry—it engulfed it. The firm owned railroads, coal mines, limestone quarries, fleets of ships, and whatever else fitted into the needs of the steel empire.

But it was, basically, a *steel* corporation, headed by men well versed in the nature of the industry. The same could be said of almost all the men who had headed its component parts. Carnegie, though engaged in other activities at the beginning of his career, was wholly identified with steel at its end, and he was typical in this respect.

Not so John Gates. Although Gates had been associated with wire and steel prior to the merger, he had also worked in other areas, and later on would be engaged in railroading, petroleum, land development, and any other enterprise that interested him and in which he could turn a quick profit. Morgan never liked Gates personally, but he had worked with others of his kind when necessary. He could not forgive what he considered Gates's cavalier attitude toward business: Morgan felt comfortable with professionals, men who were experts in one or another field of endeavor. Gates was not that kind of man. Instead, he seemed to be in the business of opportunity, snatching whatever came his way, so long as it seemed a good buy at the time. It was for this reason, as much as anything else, that Gates was excluded from the U.S. Steel giant.

Morgan, whose life had been spent in trying to bring order out of chaos, would have as little as possible to do with this chaotic person. He dreamed of an age in which giant corporations, headed by responsible gentlemen knowledgeable in their own fields, would cooperate with other like-minded individuals at other firms engaged in similar activities to create a harmonious whole. Above all would be the investment bankers, also experts and powerful men, who would orchestrate the advance of civilization. There were a fixed number of industries and a right way to harmonize each. Investment bankers would sort things out and perfect the pattern which would have emerged in any case, and do so with a minimum of disruption. Business to Morgan was like a giant game of solitaire, and while at ease Morgan would play game after game of cards, treating the suits in much the same way he did firms in industries.

This seemed the drift of the times, and it also represented progress to Wall Streeters like Morgan in 1901. They had come too far to allow men like Gates to drag them back to a barbaric and disorderly state of business.

Gates seemed thoroughly "modern" in his tastes, love of the novel, and "loose morality." Yet in his attitude toward business he was closer to that of eighteenth-century entrepreneurs than those of the early twentieth century. The men who operated out of small shops in New York, Boston, and Philadelphia just before and immediately after the Revolution were not specialists, and for good reason: there were no industries large enough to specialize in, which at the same time could be controlled by their limited capital, and through the poor means of transportation and communication that existed.

Business was chancy, and failures common. Should a merchant put all his capital in one venture—a mine, an insurance plan, a bank, a shipyard, or whatever—and that venture failed, he would be wiped out. Rather than risk all on a roll of the dice, he would take shares in major ventures, spreading the risks with others like him. So the "sedentary merchant" of 1795 New York would sit in his shop on Wall Street, awaiting news of a cargo of slaves in which he had a 10-percent share, of progress on a ship being constructed at his shipyard, in which he had an 8-percent share, or a land speculation in the West, in which he owned a quarter of the stock, and so on.

The men who speculated on the Vandalia Company's shares were in this category. Unless and until they had greater resources, a safer political environment, and better means of transportation and communication, they could not take over great enterprises, and would instead share in smaller ones.

The march of civilization (and business) seemed in that direction in the nineteenth century, and it appeared to have culminated in U.S. Steel, or at least that was the general view on Wall Street. What did a Gates, who might have been at home with George Croghan and Samuel Wharton but not with a Morgan or Charles Schwab, have to do with this new industrial giant? For all his talk of progress and the need for innovation, Gates, in 1901, seemed a throwback to a distant past, the last of his breed, destined to fall before the power of the new industrialists and investment bankers. Just before his death in 1913, Morgan remarked that this was his view of things and boasted that one of his greatest accomplishments had been to exclude such men from responsible business activity.

He was wrong. A half century later men like Gates would be the darlings of Wall Street, admired by business writers and considered heroes in business schools, while the older kind of entrepreneur feared their approach. Gates may have been a throwback to the eighteenth century, but he was also the precursor of a new breed: the conglomerater.

During the 1960s the business and financial pages were filled with stories of conglomerates, the men who organized and ran them, and their seeming methods of operation. To some, such individuals were corporate raiders and irresponsible jugglers, a view Morgan might have appreciated had he been alive. Others considered the conglomeraters a creative force in business, men who brushed aside the old and made possible a new form of enterprise best able to deal with the complex business world of the future.

Interestingly enough, few journalists and scholars spent much time and effort in defining what they meant by a conglomerate. They were content to define it as a group of nonrelated businesses operating under a single corporate roof. Horizontal expansion took place when a business engaged in new functions in an area related to already existing business, such as an automobile company entering the manufacture of trucks and golf carts, or a soap company setting up a subsidiary to produce detergents. Vertical expansion occurred when a steel company enlarged its activities to include coal mining or construction. Both U.S. Steel and Standard Oil had elements of vertical and horizontal growth, as did most major American firms. This had become quite common, and was recognized as such in the universities and governmental agencies. At the same time, the companies tended to remain within their own spheres, such as steel and oil. So it was possible for regulators and industrialists alike to talk of "industries" and "communities of interest."

What, then, was a conglomerate? According to most writers and observers, the category included all companies and activities that were neither horizontal nor vertical, hardly a precise or useful definition. Yet David Kamerschen, a respected student of the subject, quoted with approval just such a definition set forth by H. Igor Ansoff, one of the nation's leading experts on the question, as late as 1970:

> A vertical consolidation builds the firm's capabilities either "forward" toward its markets or "backwards" toward the sources of supply. A horizontal consolidation rounds out the firm's product line by increasing the line of goods sold to its customers. A conglomerate is the complement of the above two to the complete set; it describes "all other" mergers and in popular parlance describes them as "unrelated."

Conglomerates could be in a variety of nonrelated fields at the same time—producing textiles, watchbands, power tools, helicopters, fasteners, agricultural products, and whatever else might benefit the firm. Their methods of expansion differed from those of most old-line companies. Horizontal and vertical growth after 1920 and prior to World War II took place either through the establishment of new subsidiaries or a merger with an already existing company, with the former method being the rule. Conglomerates, on the other hand, rarely branched out on their own. Rather, they would seek an already existing company and, through negotiations with management or a direct appeal to stockholders, take it over and add it to the mixed bag of firms already under their corporate umbrellas. U.S. Steel's leaders could say they were in the steel business, while Standard Oil executives clearly were in petroleum. But the leaders of Litton Industries, a major conglomerate, boasted somewhat sententiously that they were in the business of opportunity. Gates would have approved. Or to put it another way, U.S. Steel and Standard Oil appeared rational and directed, and were compared to works of art by their creators. Litton seized opportunities when they presented themselves. And Litton's founder, Charles "Tex" Thornton, once compared his company to a domino game.

Those who wrote of and studied conglomerates dealt more with conditions than with contexts. Rarely did students of the subject consider why conglomeritis struck when, how, and where it did and, even when they made the attempt, such individuals did not generally explore any deeper. They tended to accept part of the conglomeraters' claims that they appeared to advance "the state and level of management," which was by no means the whole story, or even an important part of it. And they tended to ignore the two factors that made this new management form possible, perhaps even predictable, and enabled conglomerate corporations to become the focus of a high-powered money mania in the 1960s: the nature of American political and economic reformism in the twentieth century, and the uncertainties of the business climate after World War II.

Ever since the late 1880s big business has been a target for reformers, whether populist, progressive, New Deal, Fair Deal, New

Frontier, Great Society, and even, in some cases, Modern Republican. Although the Sherman Antitrust Act had been passed in 1890, it had little effect, due to the unwillingness of most Presidents to use their powers, the courts to support executive actions, and the legislature to strengthen the act itself. In 1912, however, Woodrow Wilson benefited from a split in the Republican party to win the Presidency. Wilson campaigned on a platform that included pledges of new antitrust legislation and vigorous prosecution of big business, and in 1914 three measures were introduced in the House to redeem that pledge. One of these, drawn up by freshman Congressman Sam Rayburn of Texas with the help of famous anti-big business lawyer Louis Brandeis, called for the strengthening of the Interstate Commerce Commission, which would be granted powers to regulate the issuance of new securities. A second measure, identified with Representative James H. Covington of Maryland, would merely add to already existing investigatory agencies, while a third, sponsored by Alabama Representative Henry D. Clayton, would outlaw specific practices and make interlocking directorates illegal.

Wilson seemed to favor the Clayton proposal, and in preparation for its passage the Morgan interests began withdrawing from directorships in railroads and industrial corporations. During debate on the measure, however, two additional bills were introduced. One, sponsored by more radical Democrats, would bring the securities exchanges under federal supervision, and declare that no corporation or holding company would be allowed to control more than 30 percent of the production of its industry. The second, introduced by Representative Raymond B. Stevens of New Hampshire, provided for the creation of a federal trade commission, which would supervise all of business and have the power to *prevent* unfair business practices even prior to their implementation.

The final battle in Congress was between those who favored the Stevens and more radical approach on the one hand and the backers of the Clayton proposal on the other. Congressmen who opposed all control measures, and those who wanted a weak bill, such as Covington's, now accepted the Clayton draft, which with modifications passed both houses of Congress and was signed by Wilson.

The Clayton Antitrust Act, then, was a moderate victory. Some of the other measures considered in 1914 indicated the drift of progressive, liberal, and radical thought, which would persist for the next half century. In time bills embodying the other ideas would be passed, some in the 1930s, the rest in 1950. Yet none would be adequate to deal with the issue of conglomerates.

Insofar as big business was concerned, Section 7 of the Clayton Act was its most significant part. It read:

> . . . no corporation engaged in commerce shall acquire, directly or indirectly, the whole or any part of the stock or other share capital of another corporation engaged also in commerce, where the effect of such acquisition may be to substantially lessen competition between the corporation whose stock is so acquired and the corporation making the acquisition, or to restrain such commerce in any section or community, or tend to create a monopoly of any line of commerce. . . .

The Clayton Act had little effect on big business. World War I began soon after its passage, and Wilson was loath to apply it when he needed large-scale enterprise to prepare for the conflict. In large part because of the war, American big business was more powerful in the early 1920s than it had been during the Age of Morgan. Then, when a new merger wave began in the mid-1920s, pro-business Presidents and courts all but ignored the act. Banks and utilities in particular, but industrial firms as well, grew rapidly in the late 1920s; the antitrusters were a small minority in Congress and the nation.

The situation changed after the beginning of the Great Depression, and more particularly with the election of Franklin Roosevelt in 1932. Much of what Sam Rayburn had wanted in 1914 was passed into law during the early years of the New Deal, in the form of measures regulating the securities industry. The Public Utilities Holding Company Act of 1935, sponsored by Rayburn, forbade the pyramiding of utilities holding companies and seemed a preview of future legislation geared to provide the same kind of controls for industrial corporations. Legislation embodying the radical proposals of 1914 was readied, and might have passed Congress were it not for Roosevelt's political difficulties in 1937 and the recession of that year. Updated versions of the Stevens draft act of 1914 were in the works, too, and although these were shunted aside in 1938, Assistant Attorney General Thurman Arnold embarked on the most sweeping antitrust crusade yet seen in the nation. In that year Roosevelt established the Temporary National Economic Committee, charging it with making a complete study of the American economy and business, and bringing in recommendations for reform. Eventually the TNEC recommended a tough antitrust law, but by the time the report was ready, World War II had begun, and antitrust became a dead issue. Like Wilson before him, Roosevelt needed big business to provide the nation with the instruments of war. In a replay of what had occurred during World War I, the giant corporations expanded and grew yet more powerful. From 1939 to 1945 they were virtually free from prosecution under the antitrust laws, even encouraged to take monopoly positions in some instances "in the national interest."

The end of the war changed this situation, and the new climate was signaled by Circuit Court of Appeals Judge Learned Hand, who in 1945 handed down a decision in a long-running suit the government had brought against Aluminum Corporation of America. The Justice Department had held that Alcoa had become a monopoly through the use of unfair practices, in particular by conspiring with European and Canadian producers. The government lost its case in the District Court, but the decision was reversed by Hand. Admitting that the government hadn't proved Alcoa guilty of any illegal activity, or of intent to monopolize, Hand stated that "we disregard any question of 'intent.' "

> . . . the whole issue is irrelevant anyway, for it is no excuse for "monopolizing" a market that the monopoly has not been used to extract from the consumer more than a "fair" profit. The Act has wider purposes.

In other words, it made no difference *how* a monopoly had been achieved, or whether the monopoly was innocent of law violations. According to Hand, its very existence, for any reason whatsoever, was justification for action under the antitrust laws.

The decision and its implications were thought to have opened a new era in antitrust prosecutions. For the time being, however, one did not take place. Businessmen had learned several important lessons in dealing with the government in such matters, and these were applied in the next few years. They realized that all antitrust measures were compromises, worked out between two or more factions, and put together in a crazy-quilt fashion. None of the antitrust measures on the books was carefully written and explicit. There were wide differences of opinion on the bench as to their meanings, as indicated in the Hand decision. So the giant corporations retained large and well-paid legal staffs, one of whose key functions was to deal with government agencies, to find flaws in regulations, and advise management how best to get around old and new legislation. One of their major tasks was to keep the corporations out of the courts in antitrust matters. In the mid-1940s, they did their jobs well.

Business leaders also realized that war and preparation for war tended to lessen or even end antibusiness sentiments in Washington, along with demands for antitrust measures. Finally, many businessmen and investment bankers had come to realize that most of the antitrust and related legislation was framed and backed by agrarian representatives and senators, men who often knew little of the actual methods by which big business functioned, and whose images of business techniques often were decades behind realities. The approaches tended to respond to yesterday's wrongdoing, not today's or tomorrow's. The Clayton Act of 1914 was directed against the Big Steel merger of 1901, and as has been seen Standard Oil was broken up a decade after it had ceased to monopolize the American petroleum industry. Similarly, many New Deal measures were directed at ending abuses of business practiced in the 1920s, which had come to an end with the Depression.

Businessmen of the late 1940s would oppose future attempts at regulation and the passage of new antitrust legislation. But even had they failed, they seemed confident of finding loopholes in any law the congressional reformers might pass. If Congress insisted on regulating the corporations of the 1940s, business leaders would find new forms of organization not covered by the laws. It was from such attitudes, on the part both of businessmen and congressional reformers, that the conglomerate movement began.

If the duel with government helped promote the conglomerate movement, the nature of the postwar economy made it possible. World War II had transformed a sluggish, chronically underutilized physical plant into a modern industrial miracle. The gross national product in 1938, the last full peacetime year, had been $85.2 billion, with 10.4 million workers, or 19 percent of the work force, unemployed. The nation's gross national product in the last year of the war, 1945, was $213.6 billion, while fewer than a million workers, or less than 2 percent of the labor force, were categorized as being unemployed. This change was due to federal spending, which rose from $6.8 billion in 1938 to $98.4 billion in 1945, as Department of War expenditures alone went from $644 million to $50.5 billion.

The end of the war and the beginning of conversion to a peacetime economy created economic instabilities, as had been expected. In 1948 federal expenditures stood at $33 billion, with the Department of the Army taking $7.7 billion of that sum. The gross national product was $259.4 billion, a goodly increase over the 1945 figure, but far slower a rate of growth than that of the previous seven years, while the unemployment level was at 3.4 percent, and would rise to 5.5 percent in the recession of the following year.

The picture for corporate profits in this period was quite different. The government reported that industrial profits after taxes were $3.3 billion in 1938, the lowest since 1934, and a result of the 1937 depression. Then profits rose sharply, reaching $12.2 billion in 1943 before declining due to federal controls and additional taxes. Some of these controls and taxes were removed or reduced with the coming of peace, and profits soared once more, to $22.5 billion in 1948, as consumers rushed to buy formerly rationed goods.

Not all companies did well in the immediate postwar period, however. Aircraft companies, for example, slumped badly when the procurement program ended. Non-aircraft firms which had produced planes during the war had relatively few problems. Ford Motors, which manufactured bombers during the war, could convert to automobiles and have no trouble selling them. But what of a firm like Avco Manufacturing, the nation's third largest defense company? During the war Avco manufactured 33,000 airplanes, nine aircraft carriers, the battleship *South Dakota*, and the bodies for almost all the Jeeps produced in the United States. Avco would obviously have to cut its size drastically or seek new businesses.

Avco president, Victor Emanuel, was convinced the nation would be in for a long period of peace and demobilization. For that reason, he decided to get out of the military hardware business as rapidly as possible. The fastest way this could be done was through the acquisition of firms in the civilian and civilian-related market.

In 1945 Emanuel purchased New Idea Corp., a small factor in the farm machinery field, and Crosley, which manufactured appliances, radios, owned some radio stations, and was a very small producer of automobiles. Avco paid cash for the acquisitions, $27.2 million for New Idea and Crosley. The funds came from retained wartime earnings and the sale of stock Avco owned in American Airlines. Other purchases followed—American Central Manufacturing in 1946, Nashville Corp. in 1947, Bendix Home Appliances in 1950, and a television station in 1951, among others. By 1953 Avco was a minor but growing force in appliances, broadcasting, farm equipment, and laundry equipment, while at the same time concentrating its major efforts in its primary business, that of aircraft engine manufacturing.

These mergers were made to stabilize and save a large enterprise whose sole customer no longer needed its only product. By diversifying, Avco was preparing for the changing economic and political climate of the postwar world. In the process Avco became a conglomerate, even before the term was in common currency. Yet Emanuel and his successors had not entered into their diversifications in order to become one. The executives had not formulated a philosophy of management different from what had existed before. Most of their acquisitions had been made for cash; there had been no attempt made at financial manipulation, tax avoidance, or even concern with the antitrust laws. As far as they were concerned, Avco was still an engine company, but one that was hedging its bets.*

Corporations in situations similar to Avco's, cash rich as a result of war profits, eagerly sought nondefense business during the immediate postwar period. Later on, other defense firms, Electric Boat being the most important, would try another approach, merging with small- and medium-sized firms in the same industry to create a major corporation, one that would concentrate on obtaining government contracts, in the belief that in such a business climate, only the giants could survive.

Electric Boat was founded in 1899; in 1952 the company's president, J. J. Hopkins, changed its name to General Dynamics and began an acquisition program that would make G.D. a billion-dollar giant in less than a decade. The new name was significant, if for no other reason that it signified nothing in particular. The name "Avco" had been derived from Aviation Corporation; there was no problem in identifying the main business of General Motors, International Business Machines, U.S. Steel, and other like-titled firms. What was General Dynamics' main area of interest and activity? Anything

*This is not to say that Avco was the first conglomerate, or its managers the first to face such problems. Rather, it was one of several defense firms obliged to diversify at the time, and their managers had learned diversification methods during previous periods of stress and opportunity, especially the 1920s. In discussing structural change in large corporations prior to 1940, a leading student of the subject wrote:

> Strategic growth resulted from an awareness of the opportunities and needs—created by changing population, income, and technology—to employ existing or expanding resources more profitably. A new strategy required a new or at least refashioned structure if the enlarged enterprise was to be operated efficiently. The failure to develop a new internal structure, like the failure to respond to new external opportunities and needs, was a consequence of overconcentration on operational activities by the executives responsible for the destiny of their enterprises, or from their inability, because of past training and education and present position, to develop an entrepreneurial outlook.
> —Alfred D. Chandler, Jr., *Strategy and Structure* (Cambridge, 1962), pp. 15-16.

Hopkins wanted, was the obvious answer. Yet for the time being at least, General Dynamics concentrated its efforts in the defense area. In this respect, it was not a true postwar conglomerate.*

In the late 1940s, then, two movements were growing, separate from one another and yet interrelated. Business was expanding, seeking new outlets for energies, attempting to survive the problems of conversion and isolate new markets and products to exploit and, in the process, perhaps develop a new form of management organization. At the same time antitrusters in Congress were taking up the movement where they left off in 1939, and noting as they did that concentration in American industry was greater than it had been prior to the New Deal. The Hand decision in the Alcoa case had been followed by others, taking a similar stand, so it appeared any new regulatory legislation would find favor in the courts. It was at this point that the careers and thoughts of three men converged to form the rationale and beginnings of modern day conglomeritis. Each acted for different reasons, but the work of one served to reinforce that of the others.

Peter Drucker, a professor at New York University, was the first of them to catch the public eye. Already recognized as one of the nation's most important thinkers in the field of management, and certainly one of the best known both to business and the intellectual community, Drucker had conducted several studies of major American firms, and he put some of his conclusions down in a work entitled *The New Society: The Anatomy of Industrial Order,* which was published in 1949. In this book Drucker wrote that "It is management's first responsibility to decide what economic factors and trends are likely to affect the company's future welfare," which by itself was not startling. But he followed this up by saying that "*it is management's responsibility to decide what business the enterprise is really in.*"

*By 1966 G.D. was a conglomerate, in appearance if not in philosophy. Yet a quarterly report of that year read, "Over the past decade some 85 percent of our sales have gone directly or indirectly to government, with the bulk of that for the military. The balance is a miscellany of commercial business. . . ." Roger Lewis in *General Dynamics: Report to the Share Owners, for the nine months ended September 30, 1966.*

> This may seem pointless. Surely it needs no rigamarole and analysis to find out what a company's business is. Is it not even, in most cases, stated in the name of the company? Actually, the decision what business an enterprise is really in—that is, the decision what its product is, what its market is, and what its outlook is—is anything but obvious. It requires careful and difficult analysis of a very high order. It also implies a very difficult decision what business the company should aim to be in. Only a few managements have so far been able to answer these questions.

For example, is General Motors in the automobile or transportation business? If it is the former, then why was the firm so deeply involved in the production of tractors, locomotives, diesel engines, airplane engines, and other non-passenger car operations? Clearly, G.M. was a transportation company, and not solely an automotive concern.

Drucker suggested that the old classifications of industries made little sense. Railroads were in the business of land development, food companies, in machinery, and business machine firms, in financing. These diversifications went beyond vertical and horizontal expansion, and Drucker was not certain he knew where it all would end. He realized in 1949 that the old order of things was changing, and indeed had changed greatly while the managers themselves had so far failed to realize it. He could not foresee, however, that within a few years new managers, and some of the old, would take his words quite literally, and go into the business of opportunity as conglomeraters.

The junior senator from Tennessee, Estes Kefauver, was the second of the three men. He had entered the Senate in 1949, at the age of forty-six, after serving for ten years in the House of Representatives. Kefauver had been born on a farm, and had a raw-boned, somewhat ungainly appearance, but he was one of the more sophisticated members of the legislature, graduating from Yale Law School after attending the University of Tennessee and becoming a leader of the Chattanooga bar. He had entered politics as a member of the Crump-McKellar machine, one of the most powerful in the section, but within three years had broken with Crump to run as an independent Democrat.

Kefauver was a maverick, but he shared with the state's senior senator, Kenneth McKellar, a deep distrust of big business. The struggles over the Tennessee Valley Authority in the 1930s had raised a generation of New Deal Democrats in the state, and Kefauver was one of their leaders. While in the House he had tried to amend the Clayton Act to "give it more teeth," and in the fight had the support of other reformers, as well as leaders at the Federal Trade Commission. In 1948 the commission surveyed the business landscape and concluded that the new merger movement was threatening competition. The agency supported a proposed amendment to the Clayton Act, one that would further limit combinations and corporate size. There must be "some effective means of preventing giant corporations from steadily increasing their power at the expense of small business," read the annual report for 1948. "Therein lies the real significance of the proposed amendment to the Clayton Act, for without it the rise in economic concentration cannot be checked nor can the opportunity for a resurgence of effective competition be preserved."

In 1950 the reformers framed a new measure, known as the Celler-Kefauver Act, which passed Congress and was signed into law. The act amended Section 7 of the Clayton Act, which had been interpreted prior to 1945 as forbidding monopolies, with the condition investigated *after* the fact. The Celler-Kefauver Act would put restraints on growth *prior* to corporate expansion or merger, in this way putting legislative sanction behind the gist of the Hand decision in the Alcoa case. The key paragraph read:

> That no corporation engaged in commerce shall acquire, directly or indirectly, the whole or any part of the stock or other share capital and no corporation subject to the jurisdiction of the Federal Trade Commission shall acquire the whole or any part of the assets of another corporation engaged also in commerce,

> where in any line of commerce in any section of the country, the effect of such acquisition *may be* [emphasis added] substantially to lessen competition, or to tend to create a monopoly.

In commenting on the measure, the House Judiciary Committee stated that it was not intended to prohibit all mergers, but only those that resulted in lessened competition. Its report went on to offer several examples, all of which were of a vertical or horizontal nature. Almost as an afterthought, the committee concluded that "The same principles would, of course, apply to backward vertical and conglomerate acquisitions and mergers."

The reformers in Congress didn't quite know what to make of conglomerates, or even why they existed. Neither did the Federal Trade Commission, whose first statement on conglomerates, made two years earlier, was rather vague.

> Conglomerate acquisitions, sometimes referred to as circular acquisitions, are those in which there is little or no discernible relation between the business of the purchasing and the acquired firm. Of all the types of mergers, the reasons for this particular form of acquisition are the most difficult to ascertain. Intent to remove a troublesome competitor or to become the leading producer of a particular product, so often present in horizontal acquisitions, generally does not exist in conglomerate acquisitions. Desire to acquire sources of supplies or end-product fabricating facilities, which characterizes vertical acquisitions, is not a factor in conglomerate mergers. Instead, the motives underlying conglomerate acquisitions appear to include such diverse incentives as desires to spread risks, to invest large sums of idle liquid capital, to add products which can be handled with existing sales and distribution personnel, to increase the number of products which can be grouped together in the company's advertisements, etc.

None of these last "motives" was declared illegal under the new Celler-Kefauver Act. Nor did the government understand the intent of the conglomeraters, nor could it foresee how conglomeritis would change as it spread.* In retrospect, however, we can see that by ignoring conglomerates, Kefauver had left a large hole in his new law, one through which the entrepreneurs of the 1950s and 1960s would drive. Once again, Congress had passed a law to prevent past abuses, not those of the present or future.

Kefauver had attempted to strengthen the antitrust laws, and in so doing forced managers to seek new ways of growth for their firms. By questioning the current concepts of the corporation, Drucker presented the bones of a theory that would be discussed, debated, and fleshed out in schools of business and in management seminars for years to come.

The third of the key figures present at the creation of the conglomerate movement was Royal Little. He seemed unconcerned with congressional actions and court decisions and, if he read Drucker, gave little evidence of it. Instead, Little was engaged in the more practical task of salvaging his corporation, Textron, whose sales in 1949 were half those of two years earlier. Textron had also just posted the largest deficit in its history.

Little was fifty-three years old in 1949, and a veteran of the textile industry's wars.† Little had entered the business in Massachusetts, and after some false starts, helped form Franklin Rayon in 1928 by bringing together several near-defunct firms. The company barely survived the Depression, operating as a marginal unit in a sick industry. Like many other similar firms, Little's company, renamed Atlantic Rayon in 1939, was saved by war orders, in this case for parachutes.

*The only conglomerate cited as evidence in 1948 was American Home Products, which since its inception in 1926 had acquired sixty firms, thirty-two of these from 1940 to 1948. A.H.P. produced both ethical and proprietary drugs, floor wax, coffee, Italian foods, lubricating oil, cheese products, insecticides, and beauty preparations, but did not have a dominant position in any one of these. As a result, the corporation had little to fear from antitrusters.

†Royal Little was the nephew of Arthur D. Little, one of the country's leading industrial chemists and the founder of the management consulting firm that bears his name. Arthur Little raised Royal after the boy reached the age of fourteen, and hoped they would go into business together after Royal graduated from Harvard and M.I.T. But Royal was a poor student, and dropped out of Harvard to join the Army.

Little realized Atlantic's prosperity would end with peace, so as early as 1943 he began to formulate a strategy for survival. He was helped in this by the tax laws, which enabled a prosperous company to shift most of its profits to unsuccessful subsidiaries, in this way avoiding the heavy excess-profits levy. At the time many small textile firms were failing. Little's idea was to take them over at cheap prices, shift Atlantic's profits to their books, and in this way have the government help finance the merger through a lower tax bill. Then Little would invigorate the other firms, merge their operations into Atlantic's, and so enlarge his company at little or no cost. In the end, he wanted a textile giant, one that could challenge the industry's leaders, and, more to the point, survive.

To signal his intent, Little dropped the Atlantic name and changed it to Textron, Inc., selecting the new one because it was "something that says textile products made of synthetics." But it would be more than that. Textron would convert synthetic yarns to cloth, finish it, produce clothing and other items, and sell them to the public. In other words, at war's end, Little dreamed of making Textron a major vertically integrated textile company.

On the way toward this goal, however, Little picked up other firms, utilizing his knowledge of the tax laws learned during the war. Cleveland Pneumatic Tool Co., a leading producer of aircraft landing gear struts, was in a peculiar situation, but one not uncommon in the postwar world. It had done very well with war contracts, but these had ended. The company showed few orders on the books, but it had a good balance sheet and a large amount of retained earnings. In 1948 Cleveland's lawyers told management that either the company must pay out a large dividend or forfeit much of its undistributed profit to the Internal Revenue Department. Neither made much sense, so Cleveland looked for a merger partner. Little was there, made an offer that was accepted, and Textron obtained a nontextile subsidiary, almost by accident, due more to the tax laws than Little's grand design.*

*Under the terms of its charter, Textron could not enter the nontextile areas. Little got around this by having Textron's pension fund buy Cleveland Pneumatic. Subsequent to a change in the charter, the fund sold the shares to Textron.

In 1950 Textron obtained Pathé-Industries, Inc., a newsreel and real-estate company. This was followed by F. Burkart Manufacturing, a producer of cotton batts and pads. Dalmo Victor, a manufacturer of radar equipment, followed in 1953, and MB Manufacturing the following year, along with Homelite, a prewar pump manufacturer which had just gone into the chain saw business. A plywood company was obtained in 1955, along with more machine tool firms. Textron was becoming a hodgepodge of small, unrelated firms, although Little insisted his goal remained that of becoming a textile giant.

In 1954 Little maneuvered for a key merger, one that would transform Textron into just such a firm. He would acquire American Woolen Corp., a major factor in the industry but one suffering from poor management, then buy out Bachmann Uxbridge Worsted Corp., a smaller firm but one with excellent management, and merge the two into Textron, with the Bachmann Uxbridge staff taking charge at American Woolen. Things went badly from the start, as American Woolen fought the merger and take-over with every weapon in its possession. Little won out in the end, taking in Robbins Mills as well, to form Textron American, his long-desired giant textile company. The newly re-formed firm had assets of $162 million, and Textron's sales rose from $99.7 million in 1954 to $191.6 million in 1955 as a result. Little predicted sales of $300 million in a few years, at which time Textron would dominate the industry.

But the new firm was not well-integrated, and at the same time textiles went into one of their regular nose dives. At the end of 1955 Little had a large, sick, textile operation and a grab bag of small, unrelated firms. As a result of the American Woolen merger, he also had a huge tax-loss credit as well as a good cash position.

It was then that Little decided to turn from textiles to other fields. In effect, he was doing what he seemed to succeed in. Ever since the war he had thought he was in the textile business. Actually, Textron was doing best in the business of managing diverse companies, seeking out new merger candidates, and taking them in under a broad company umbrella. His only failure in this regard had been American Woolen. Little vowed never again to try to take over a company against its will. Writing of Textron's policies in 1956, he said:

> What interests me . . . is why they sell to Textron. And I think I know why our batting average has been so high on acquisitions. It has been our policy to buy only well-managed businesses and to give the old management complete autonomy except for financial control. Many of these former owners feel that under our plan they can have their cake and eat it too; in many cases they can convert ordinary income into capital gains and still have the fun of running their own businesses.
>
> We believe in management incentives, and one of the greatest incentives for anyone is happiness in his work. That we aim to provide. For unless real incentives are maintained, the operating results probably will be disappointing to the buyer. Any fool can buy businesses—all *that* takes is money. The important question is whether the business you buy will continue to be successful after you purchase it.

Little's attitude and this kind of statement were illustrations that might have come from one of Drucker's articles. They were also statements of Textron's rationale, as one of the first conglomerates. A few years later Textron would sell off its textile business and concentrate entirely on the management of its diverse enterprises, as well as the acquisition of new ones.

The Textron experience would not be a guide for other conglomerates, however. Each conglomerate manager seemed to have his own philosophy, his own way of diversifying, that depended on the man, the nature of the corporation he began or took over, the opportunities present at the time, and the power and influence of his advisers, especially his investment banker.

For example, in his statement Little refers to the mistaken belief that money alone can bring businesses into the fold, stressing instead the importance of techniques he developed. Textron did buy out companies, at least in the beginning, by paying cash. The money came from reserves, short-term borrowings, the flotation of bonds, cted Statistics for Textron, Inc., 1939-1969

Sales	Earnings	Shares	Earnings Per	Price Range, Common	
(millions of dollars)		Outstanding	Share	Low	High
7.5	.1	not available	$0.54	not available	
7.5	(.02)	not available	(0.14)	not available	
8.1	.2	not available	0.67	not available	
11.9	.3	not available	1.08	3	4-7/8
23.8	.5	not available	2.22	4-1/2	8-1/2
26.3	.6	not available	2.65	7-1/4	12-5/8
46.9	4.4	583,000	(0.22)*	13-1/4	25-1/2†
113.0	17.0	978,000	6.16*	9-1/2	26-3/4
124.8	6.3	1,133,000	5.35	13-5/8	15-1/4
98.8	6.9	1,133,000	5.77	10-3/8	20-3/8
67.9	(0.9)	1,133,000	(1.89)	8	11-1/4
87.5	3.1	1,133,000	2.38	10	19-3/8
98.3	4.7	1,196,000	3.66	16-1/8	23-1/2
98.7	(3.5)	1,196,000	(3.33)	10-1/2	18-3/4
71.0	(0.2)	1,206,000	(0.57)	6-1/4	12-3/8
99.7	1.3	1,332,000	0.52	6-3/8	12-1/4
191.6	9.5	2,896,000	3.26	12	25-5/8
245.8	6.5	3,530,000	1.73	20-1/4	29-3/4
254.6	8.7	3,501,000	2.25	10	21-1/2
244.2	10.8	4,349,000	2.30	9-7/8	21-7/8
308.2	16.6	4,784.000	3.38	19-3/4	29-5/8
383.2	14.2	4,672,000	2.94	18-3/4	24-3/4
473.1	10.5	4,904,000	2.06	21-1/2	29-1/2
549.5	14.8	4,842,000	2.96	22-1/2	31-1/4
587.0	18.0	5,161,000	3.42	29-1/2	40-3/4
720.2	22.1	5,350,000	4.08	39-3/4	54
851.0	29.1	11,038,000	2.62	25-7/8	47-3/8†
1,132.2	43.9	12,399,000	3.54	38-1/2	53-3/4
1,446.0	61.5	26,320,000	2.06	38-3/8	55†
1,704.1	74.0	26,905,000	2.26	40	57-7/8
1,682.2	76.1	27,287,000	2.31	23-1/4	45

fter special items connected with demobilization after World War II.

fter two-for-one stock split.

ce: *Moody's Handbook of Common Stocks*, 1958, 1967 editions.

and other conventional debt securities, such as convertible debentures. As a result, Textron's bonded debt rose from $16.8 million in 1953 to $78.9 million in 1956, after the first phase of Little's mergermania had ended. Textron could not use its own common stock to pay for acquisitions because its price was too low. In 1955, for example, Textron could be purchased for as little as four times earnings. Yet common stock, expecially if it paid no dividend, would have been far preferable to cash, not only to the company that acquired a sell-out candidate, but also to the seller himself. The seller would not face large capital gains taxes, since under the Internal Revenue code such a transaction could be considered a pooling of interests, while the acquiring firm would be able to retain cash needed for expansion. Try as he might, Little was unable to raise Textron's price/earnings ratio. Had he done so, doubtless stock would have been used, as it was later on.

Part of Textron's problem lay in the area of "image." Long after it had left the textile field, investors continued to think of it as a fabric manufacturer. Historically such firms had low price/earnings ratios. Even those who knew of the firm's transformation were not overly impressed, for Textron was in few glamour areas, such as business machines, electronics, space, and drugs, and these were the fields investors were intrigued with in the 1950s. Rarely did Textron common reach twenty times earnings, with fifteen or so more often the case. Meanwhile, glamour issues sold for over one hundred times earnings at bull market peaks in the 1950s.

Textron's second problem was its genesis date: it had been born "too soon." The transformation, which began slowly in the late 1940s and gathered steam in the early 1950s, came at a time when stock prices were rising, but not as fast as good economic news and higher earnings might have justified. The "Eisenhower Bull Market," which began in 1953 and continued into the late 1960s as the "Kennedy Bull Market" and "Johnson Bull Market," provided an entirely different investment climate, one in which stockholders scrambled to buy issues at what in the immediate postwar period would have been considered ridiculously high prices. Yet they continued to rise, making acquisitions with such "paper" all the easier, and providing fuel for the conglomerate movement.

Yearly Highs and Lows of Dow-Jones Industrials, 1948-1969

Year	High	Low
1948	193.16	165.39
1949	200.52	161.60
1950	235.47	196.81
1951	276.37	238.99
1952	292.00	256.35
1953	293.79	255.49
1954	404.39	279.87
1955	488.40	388.20
1956	521.05	462.35
1957	520.77	419.79
1958	583.65	436.89
1959	679.36	574.46
1960	685.47	566.05
1961	734.91	610.25
1962	726.01	535.76
1963	767.21	646.79
1964	891.71	766.08
1965	969.26	840.59
1966	995.15	744.32
1967	943.08	786.41
1968	985.21	825.13
1969	968.85	769.93

Source: *Barron's*, July 17, 1972.

Many conglomerates formed and flourished in this period, but the most famous of those appearing in the mid-1950s was Litton Industries, and its managers provided a variation and "scientific version" of the Little format.

Litton was organized by Charles "Tex" Thornton, who became the firm's chairman, and to a slightly lesser extent by Roy Ash, later on its president. Thornton graduated from Harvard Business School—the spawning ground for many of the new conglomeraters of the 1950s—before World War II. From there he went into the Army Air Corps, where he earned a reputation for efficiency, innovation,

One Conglomerater's Views of "Old" vs. "New" Management Methods

1. Authoritarian planning: "Central Management makes plans, budgets, forecasts."	Cooperative planning: "Planning and budgeting is decentralized as much as possible."
2. "From the Top" management: Staff sets goals, controls, checks.	"From the Roots" management: Line develops the goals, self-controls, checks.
3. Exaggerated requisitions and forecasts: Request twice as much as you need—predict half as much as you can produce.	Non-bargaining allocations: Costs are mutually arrived at and requests reflect actual needs and are economically supportable.
4. Line-staff conflict: All line-staff contact a competitive win-lose clash.	We win—you win. Line is responsible; its judgement prevails, while staff serves and supports. Both aim for common goals, sound growth, and qualitative-quantitative improvements.
5. Line fights the system: System imposed by staff to suit its wishes; line tries to beat it.	Line needs the systems: Staff offers innovative, professional support. Line and staff agree on best.
6. Minimum supplementary education.	Maximum education: Greatest help possible in meeting new standards, ever higher goals.
7. "Bargain Counter Theory": How little can we pay?	What is the MOST a man can make and be more valuable to the company?
8. How far can we go and get away with it? Line personnel in informal conspiracy to outwit accounting.	Self-controlled expenses: Line profit responsibility and participation creates self-control and absolute intra-structural honesty.
9. Secret financial data: "What you don't know won't hurt you."	Fullest disclosure of any information that affects individual's area of concern, or over which he exercises control, as well as to our outside partners-shareholders.

10. Damn the shareholders—they are all outsiders.	We own our company and work for ourselves as well as our public-owners, who share our confidence in our company.

Source: Nicholas M. Salgo (Chairman of the Board, Bangor-Punta Corporation), "Conglomerates: Another Wave of Business Development or the Beginning of a New Era?" *St. John's Law Review,* Spring, 1970, p. 787.

and charm. After the war he and a group of like-minded and educated officers went into Ford's top management, and the so-called "whiz kids"—which included Robert McNamara and future Ford president Arjay Miller—helped revive the then moribund company. After Ford, Thornton worked at Hughes Aircraft, where he developed some of his management ideas as well as his concept of conglomerates.

Throughout his career Thornton had been known as an "idea man," a promoter who was best able to exploit the talents of others. Thornton would organize teams of executives, give them his ideas, and set them to work on their own. His experiences in the Air Corps and Ford taught him that most large organizations were inefficient, and a major reason for this was overstructured management. He may well have studied Little's performance in this period, and the Textron experience may have helped perfect some of his own ideas. More than Little, Thornton believed in throwing out old rules and creating new ones as needs arose.

Thornton was also more sophisticated in his knowledge of the stock market than most early conglomeraters. He understood the need to preserve capital, and acquire new firms through the issuance of high-priced, nondividend-paying common stock. Early in his career he formed an association with the banking house of Lehman Brothers and obtained its cooperation in his ventures.

Thornton left Hughes in 1953 and purchased a small electronics company, Electro-Dynamics. Then, through an exchange of stock, he acquired an even smaller firm, Litton Industries, and changed the name of the mother company to that of the newly engulfed unit. Thornton hunted for small electronics firms in the next few years, taking them over with newly issued stock. In this way Ahrent Instruments, USECO, West Coast Electronics, and Automatic Sereograph were added. Then, in 1958, he added a major company, Monroe Calculating Machine, which was down on its luck. From that point on, the Litton mergers became larger and more diverse. With the Monroe merger, Litton grew from a small firm with $3 million in sales in 1953 to one with $83.2 million. Mostly with the help of mergers, Litton crossed the billion-dollar mark in 1966, and the $1.7-billion level a year later.

Selected Statistics for Litton Industries, 1954-1966

Year	Sales (millions of dollars)	Earnings (millions of dollars)	Shares Outstanding*	Earnings Per Share	Price Range, Common Low	Price Range, Common High	Price Earnings Ratio
1954	3.0	.2	525,000	$0.28	not available		not available
1955	8.9	.4	967,000	0.44	10	16-3/4	19.0
1956	14.9	1.0	1,047,000	0.97	14-3/4	32-1/4	24.2
1957	28.1	1.8	1,194,000	1.51	29-1/2	56-5/8	28.5
1958	83.2	3.7	2,059,000	1.76	29	75	29.9
1959	125.5	6.0	4,372,000	1.16	30-1/2	63-1/2†	34.3
1960	187.8	7.5	4,944,000	1.48	48-1/2	83-1/2	44.4
1961	250.1	10.2	5,065,000	1.96	57	143	55.1
1962	393.8	16.3	10,131,000	1.48	34	67-3/4†	34.1
1963	553.1	23.3	11,197,000	2.08	52	80-1/2	32.0
1964	686.1	29.8	11,317,000	2.58	58-1/4	79-4/8	25.1
1965	915.6	39.6	11,490,000	3.28	74-5/8	150-1/2	33.3
1966	1,340.0	71.3	25,323,000	2.13	56-5/8	86-1/2†	32.0

*Excluding 2½-percent stock dividends, 1959–1966.
†After two-for-one stock split.

Source: *Moody's Handbook of Common Stocks,* 1958, 1967 editions.

In this period Litton acquired an interesting array of companies. In 1958, in addition to Monroe, Thornton took over Maryland Electronics, Airtron, Westrex, and several minor electronics companies. But the greatest growth was yet to come, at least in terms of acquisitions.

Thornton, Ash, and others at Litton and Lehman Brothers realized that little of this could have been done without high-priced stock to use as bait in acquisitions. So the publicity department at Litton was

Acquisitions of Litton Industries, 1959–1966

Year	Company
1959	Times Facsimile Co.
	Svenska Dataregister
1960	Western Geophysical Co.
	Servomechanisms (Canada)
	Integrated Data Processing, Inc.
	Fritz Hellige & Co. (West Germany)
1961	A. Kimball Co.
	Applied Communication Systems
	London Office Machines (United Kingdom)
	C. Plath, K.G. (West Germany)
	Simon Adhesive Products Co.
	Cole Steel Equipment Co.
	Eureka Specialty Printing Co.
	Aero Service Corp.
	Ingalls Shipbuilding Corp.
1962	Poly-Scientific Corp.
	McKiernan-Terry Corp.
	Emertron, Inc.
1963	Winchester Electronics, Inc.
	Pyne Moulding Corp.
	Century Boulevard Corp.
	Adler Electronics, Inc.
	Bruder & Co., Inc.
	Clifton Precision Products Co.
1964	Fitchburg Paper Co.
	Advance Data Systems
	Streater Industries, Inc.
	Profexray, Inc.
	Mellonics Systems Development, Inc.
1965	Magnuson X- Ray Co.
	Royal McBee Corp.
	Hewitt-Robins, Inc.
	The Leopold Co.
1966	Electra Motors, Inc.
	Analogue Controls
	Alvey Furguson Co.
	Everett Waddey Co.
	Maverick-Clark Co.
	McCray Refrigeration Co.
	Fenix Mfg. Ltd. (United Kingdom)
	Willy Feiler Zaehl-Und Rechenwerke GmbH (West Germany)

Acquisitions of Litton Industries, 1959–1966 (1966—continued)

	Sturgis Newport Business Forms, Inc.
	Imperial Typewriter Ltd. (United Kingdom)
1967	Wilson Marine Transit Co.
	Louis Allis Co.
	Jefferson Electric Co.
	American Book Co.
	Stouffer Foods Corp.
	Saphier, Lerner, Schindler, Inc.
	Burton Crescent Corp.
	Kester Solder Co.
	Marine Consultants and Designers, Inc.
	Chainveyer Co.
	Rust Engineering Co.
	Business Equipment Holdings Ltd. (Australia)
	Eureka X-Ray Tube Corp.
	Hampton Corp.
	Allen Hollender Co., Inc.
	Dentists' Supply Co.

Source: *Moody's Industrial Manual,* 1972.

one of the company's key offices. The higher the stock's price, the more attractive it would be for takeover candidates, and the fewer shares would be needed for the merger. Other firms might note that Litton's production and profit results were only adequate, and that, without the mergers, earnings per share moved upward rather slowly. But all would agree that Litton's publicity office was one of the best in the field. One executive, unhappy with his own company's situation, compared it with Litton's:

> I don't know how in the world we can increase our p/e ratio . . . we have a very conservative board; they don't want to do anything that anyone can interpret as a promotion. . . . I think many of these companies like Litton have done a terrific job in promoting the heck out of their company. . . . Every time they get an order you pick up the paper and Litton did so and so, Litton hired a new vice president for this company, and Litton did so and so, Litton, Litton, Litton. . . . I'm sure that has a great

deal to do with getting that p/e ratio up there higher which puts them in a wonderful position to make these acquisitions and keep the ball rolling.

Thornton and Ash also worked hard to impress securities analysts, either going to Wall Street themselves, inviting them to their California offices, or sending topflight aides to conventions. This resulted in Litton's being touted in financial columns and stock-market advisories, which during the bull market of the 1950s and 1960s were read with great care and often acted upon. *Barron's,* the conservative financial magazine that often frowned on conglomerate manipulations, ran a column by John Wall in 1968 called "Want to Get Rich Quick? An Expert Gives Some Friendly Advice on Conglomerates," in which the new conglomeraters were "taken apart." Bitingly, Wall suggested:

> Get hold of the speeches and annual reports of the really savvy swingers, who know the lingo and make it sing. . . . You have to project the right image to the analysts so they realize you're the new breed of entrepreneur. Talk about the synergy of the free-form company and its interface with change and technology. Tell them you have a windowless room full of researchers . . . scrutinizing the future so your corporation will be opportunity-technology oriented. . . . Analysts and investors want conceptually oriented (as opposed to opportunistic) conglomerates, preferably in high-technology areas. That's what they pay the high price-earnings ratios for, and life is a lot less sweaty with a high multiple.

Thornton and Ash denied allegations of opportunism, insisting the Litton acquisitions were purposeful, and patterned. For example, the conglomerate acquired Ingalls Shipbuilding not so much to get into the marine field, but rather as a customer for its electronics products. Vice-President Harry Gray said that at one time Litton considered acquiring a brewing company in order to gain the brains and patents of its subsidiary, which was engaged in advanced work in ceramics. Ash observed, too, that Litton never took over a firm that was a leader in its industry. The reason, he said, was that leading companies have less room for growth than those that trailed behind. He added, however, that another reason was antitrust considerations. Like Textron, Litton wanted to avoid prosecution or even investigation by the Federal Trade Commission, and went so far as to discuss potential mergers with the commission prior to their being consummated.

Litton gave its leading executives a great deal of freedom and encouraged them to "use imagination" in dealing with problems. Publicity releases stressed "the new breed of executives," and this, too, helped boost stock prices. It also encouraged Litton executives to seek their own conglomerates, or go off on their own. By the mid-1960s new conglomerates were formed every week, or old-line firms announced they were becoming conglomerates. Many of the new leaders were Litton graduates, and Litton itself was characterized as a "school for conglomerates," just as dozens of corporation presidents "graduated" from General Electric and General Motors in previous years.

Fred Sullivan, who took Walter Kidde & Co. and made it into a conglomerate in the safety, lighting, office equipment, textile, and aerospace industries, was one such Litton graduate—or "Lido," as they were called. Another was William E. McKenna of Hunt Foods & Industries, which produced food stuffs, containers, paint, and plywood, and had stock interests in steel and publishing firms. George T. Scharffenberger went from Litton to City Investing, and helped turn a small land company into a real estate-defense contractor-franchise-container-banking-insurance giant, with more than half a billion dollars in sales by 1969. Russel McFall took the chairmanship of Western Union, offered by a board of directors who hoped he could perform the Litton miracle at the then moribund communications company. Frank Moothart went to Republic Corporation, Seymour Rosenberg to Mattel, and Frederick Mayo to American Export. Crosby M. Kelley set up his own operation, Crosby M. Kelley Associates. Henry Singleton helped found Teledyne, a company in the Litton mold, which began with next to nothing in 1961 and had sales of over a quarter of a billion dollars in 1966. All the while, Ash would promote new men to the posts vacated by the old—an "old-timer" at Litton was a man who had been there more than three years, while remaining at a key post for more than two was regarded as having reached a dead end. "We not only accept the idea that some executives will leave," said Ash, "but we recognize it as a way of revitalizing the organization."

So it was in the go-go world of the mid-1960s. By then there was little doubt in the minds of Wall Streeters as to what company was or was not a conglomerate. Most would say these firms were engaged in many businesses at the same time, not necessarily related to one another (if they were, the firms were dubbed by some as "congenerics"). The conglomerates were managed by a "new breed" of entrepreneur and were concerned with acquisitions. Critics of conglomerates charged them with using "funny arithmetic" in reporting earnings, and indeed it was shown that their accountants could manipulate figures to report almost any kind of earnings performance that might be desired.

Above all, the conglomerates were considered new and exciting, "the wave of the future," a cliché that received new circulation at the time. Litton, Textron, City Investing, Teledyne, and the others were unlike the stodgy old firms of preconglomerate days, such as Borg-Warner, General Electric, Rexall, and Chrysler.

But the definition was troublesome. If a conglomerate was a firm in many unrelated fields, then some of the older companies were also conglomerates. Still operating according to pre-World War II guidelines and preconglomerate philosophy, the federal government divided all business activity into what were known as standard industrial classifications (SICs). There were seventy-eight major classes, and these supposedly provided the FTC with antitrust ammunition. If a firm obtained too great a position in one of the SICs, it would become a candidate for an antitrust suit.

As one might expect, the conglomerates fell into several categories, not surprising since one reason for their existence was avoidance of

Celler-Kefauver and other laws. But they were not alone in this. Indeed, some of the nation's oldest, largest, and most mature firms not only matched the conglomerates in SICs, but outdid them.

SICs of Selected American Industrial Corporations, 1967

Company	SICs
Allied Chemical	9
American Machine & Foundry	10
Armour	11
Bendix	10
Borg Warner	12
Chrysler	9
Firestone Tire & Rubber	10
General Electric	14
Rexall	10
Conglomerates	
General Tire	17
Gulf & Western	8
International Telephone & Telegraph	13
Kaiser Industries	8
Kidde (Walter)	11
Litton Industries	18
Textron	13

Source: *Fortune,* June 15, 1967, p. 177.

The other features most easily recognized as being special to conglomerates, including the charisma of their leaders, the use of securities to negotiate mergers, and the rather bizarre accounting procedures, either were not actionable or were within the bounds of the law. The government was faced with a crisis in antitrust policy. Throughout the early 1960s many cases under federal legislation were decided against firms wanting to merge, but no clear principle was ever enunciated by any judge that could be employed as a guide for future decisions. It appeared to many constitutional lawyers that judges were breaking up mergers they didn't like for political reasons, and allowing those they did. An air of uncertainty surrounded the issue; no solution seemed in sight.

It was then that the third wave of conglomeritis became most noticeable. In the first, Royal Little had diversified to salvage an old-line textile company, and in the process created a conglomerate. Then Tex Thornton and Roy Ash, and their followers, using ballyhoo, bookkeeping devices, and inflated stock had taken over smaller firms and made them parts of ever-growing corporate giants. Now new men and techniques came to the fore. Charles Bluhdorn, James Ling, and Harold Geneen, magnifying the practices of Thornton and Ash and each adding major twists of his own, threatened to transform the face of American industry within a decade, and capture major as well as minor corporations in their conglomerate nets.

In 1956, at the age of twenty-nine, Bluhdorn joined the board of directors at Michigan Plating and Stamping Co. He had been a coffee trader and had little direct business experience when he took the post, but this did not seem a drawback for a small firm, which at the time had sales of little over a million dollars and assets of less than $3.5 million, and was, after all, just a minor factor in the automotive aftermarket.

During the next eight years Bluhdorn concentrated on expanding this automobile-related operation, acquiring smaller firms in the business, in a fashion not unlike others who sought horizontal growth. Most of the time Bluhdorn used common stock for his purchases, even though its price and its price/earnings ratio were low. Often the acquisitions cost more than they appeared worth, but Bluhdorn hoped to turn the companies around, integrate them with existing operations, and so increase sales volume, and hopefully profits and profit margins as well.

In 1958, when Bluhdorn changed his firm's name to Gulf & Western Industries, sales were at the $8.4-million mark. G & W passed the $100-million level in 1964, and the following year *Steel* magazine ran an article entitled: "Gulf & Western's Goal: Become the GM of Partmakers." At the time some 90 percent of the company's business was in auto parts. Bluhdorn was recognized as an excellent businessman and manager. He was not considered a conglomerater.

Late in 1965 Bluhdorn announced a merger of Gulf & Western and New Jersey Zinc, a firm that had had sales of $135.5 million and net earnings of $7.5 million the year before. Zinc prices had fluctuated wildly over several years, and the acquired firm's management felt the need for a wider corporate umbrella. Bluhdorn's statement on the merger was not unusual:

> G & W management feels that G & W has now reached the size and financial position where, for the long term, it should broaden the base of its operations to include major participation in basic industries, such as those in which Zinc Co. is engaged. . . . G & W's Board of Directors believed that the merger of the two corporations will provide the desired diversification to a great extent and under more favorable conditions than would be possible through the acquisition of a number of smaller enterprises.

To all intents and purposes, the merger had taken place for reasons of diversification, and not to transform G & W into a conglomerate on the Litton or Textron model. Following established precedents, Bluhdorn had paid cash and stock for Zinc, and then consolidated the two companies' earnings statements. Later on, however, the merger would be recognized as the initiation of a new policy at the company.

In mid-1966 Bluhdorn began buying shares of Paramount Pictures, acquiring 18.5 percent of its capitalization. The motion-picture company, then faced with several suitors, merged into G & W in October, with Bluhdorn's stock a key factor in the decision. Bluhdorn did the same with South Puerto Rico Sugar, which had sales in 1966 of $61 million, and it became part of Gulf & Western in July 1967.

The sugar merger was greeted on Wall Street as a sign that G & W had indeed become a conglomerate. But it would be different from its predecessors. Rather than concentrate on the purchases of many small firms and a few medium-sized ones—the Litton pattern that most conglomerates then were following—Bluhdorn would seek major firms in depressed fields. He would accumulate stock in these companies prior to the merger, and use his holdings as a lever in "convincing" management to join G & W. There was little of the "synergy" of the Litton mergers in Bluhdorn's. At the time, Thornton and Ash were talking of perhaps buying American Motors—to provide Litton companies with vehicles for internal use. Bluhdorn resembled more the corporate raiders of the old school, or at least that was how he was portrayed in the business press at the time. It seemed difficult to determine where he would strike next. Bluhdorn was known to be accumulating stock in several companies, but their identities were kept a closely guarded secret.

The blow came in January 1968, when within a period of three weeks Bluhdorn announced three major acquisitions. Machinery manufacturers E. W. Bliss (1967 sales: $160 million), Universal American (1967 sales: $200 million), and Consolidated Cigar Corporation (1967 sales: $175 million) were added to Gulf & Western. The parent corporation's sales, which had been $649 million in 1967, would rise to $1.3 billion the following year, in large part the result of these and a few smaller mergers. Gulf & Western was now among the hundred largest industrial corporations in the United States.

What, then, would Bluhdorn's next move be? Talk on Wall Street had it that G & W owned some $2 billion in the common stock of other companies, in preparation for take-over moves. This may have been somewhat of an exaggeration, but it was certain that Bluhdorn had not yet finished conglomerating.

A new pattern developed in the early months of 1968. G & W would purchase a sizable block of stock in a company and offer tenders for the rest. Or Bluhdorn simply would allow rumors of his interest to float down through Wall Street. The raided firm's management would protest vigorously and make their own appeals to stockholders. Other conglomeraters might join in the scramble, and two or three groups would be bidding for the same stock, which would rise rapidly as a result. Bluhdorn let it be known that he was interested in acquiring Armour & Co., the meat-chemical-industrial equipment company with sales of over $2.2 billion a year. He purchased 23 percent of the stock of Brown Co., a $215-million-a-

Selected Statistics for Gulf & Western Industries, 1956-1969

Year	Sales	Earnings	Shares Outstanding*	Earnings Per Share	Price Range, Common Low	High
	(millions of dollars)					
1956	1.2	(0.02)	265,000	(0.64)	4-1/2	6-5/8
1957	6.5	.2	265,000	0.74	3-3/4	5
1958	8.4	nil	265,000	nil	3-1/4	10
1959	15.4	.3	406,000	0.78	8-1/2	13-1/4
1960	24.0	.4	721,000	0.60	9-1/4	12-3/8
1961	33.8	1.0	1,046,000	0.96	9-7/8	36
1962	65.6	1.8	1,288,000	1.37	20	44-3/8
1963	92.5	2.6	1,542,000	1.71	25-1/8	35-1/4
1964	117.2	3.5	1,845,000	1.87	24	32
1965	182.1	5.5	2,111,000	2.61	31-1/8	102
1966	317.5	20.1	7,328,000	1.98	17-1/2	41-3/8†
1967	649.5	46.2	11,964,000	2.85	28-7/8	60-5/8
1968	1,320.5	69.8	12,047,000	3.13	37-3/4	64-1/4
1969	1,563.6	72.1	15,438,000	3.15	17-1/2	50-1/4

*Adjusted for stock dividends, 10% 1956, 5% 1959–63, 3% 1964–66, 1969.
†Adjusted for 3-1 stock split.
Source: *Moody's Handbook of Common Stocks*, 1960, 1969 editions; *Moody's Industrial Manual*, 1957–1969.

year paper and forest products company (the Wall Street joke was that Bluhdorn would need paper to wrap his meat in). Then he made offers for Security Insurance Company of Hartford and Security Connecticut Life Insurance. Other bids followed, but none of these large firms ever were merged into G & W. Instead, Bluhdorn would hold on to the stock as he did with Brown, or he would lose the contest for control and sell out at a large profit. G & W did well in such forays. Although profits from operations slipped badly in 1969, Bluhdorn more than made up the difference in securities transactions, so that the company actually posted a slightly higher earnings figure than it had had in 1968.

G & W performed erratically as a conglomerate, although Bluhdorn did succeed in turning some of his acquisitions around. Still, his record seemed impressive. Through wheeling and dealing, he had made conglomerate construction an industry in itself. And, at the same time, he sparked interest at the Justice Department, where antitrusters began sharpening their axes.

In 1958, the year Bluhdorn renamed Michigan Plating and formed

Gulf & Western, Harold Geneen became president of International Telephone & Telegraph Corp. Geneen was forty-nine years old at the time, and already considered one of the brightest executives in the nation. He had taken a job as a Wall Street page boy at the age of sixteen, while studying accounting at night. Geneen then worked for a New York accounting firm, left to take a job as accountant at American Can, and from there became controller at Bell & Howell. In 1950 he was at Jones & Laughlin Steel as assistant to the vice-president, and then on to Raytheon as executive vice-president. Geneen was credited with putting that company back on its feet, but he constantly clashed with Raytheon President Charles Francis Adams, who made it clear Geneen would never succeed him. So when an opening developed at ITT, Geneen accepted.

Gulf & Western Operating and Financial Results, 1965-1969

Year	Net Earnings on Operations	Per Share	Net Earnings On Securities Sales	Per Share
1965	$ 5,514,000	.79	nil	nil
1966	19,306,000	1.90	$ 811,000	.08
1967	45,411,000	2.80	788,000	.05
1968	67,208,000	3.00	2,634,000	.13
1969	50,982,000	2.15	21,068,000	1.00

Source: Charles Gilbert, ed. *The Making of a Conglomerate* (Hempstead, N.Y., 1972), p. 259.

The ITT of 1956 was an unusual company, molded by a remarkable man, Sosthenes Behn. Born of a Danish father and French mother, who gave him a name that meant "of sound strength" in Greek, Behn was working as a sugar merchant in Cuba in 1914 when he began buying up small telephone companies on the island. In 1920 he brought them together to form International Telephone & Telegraph, and proceeded to acquire similar communications companies in other countries, so that within two decades he commanded a network that stretched halfway around the world, from Britain to China. Some of the ITT companies were seized during World War

II, but Behn managed to sell several just prior to the German attack on Poland, and so had sufficient funds to embark on new ventures. He used them to buy defense and related companies in the United States, with which ITT prospered during the war. Now, for the first time, the company had an American base. Behn enlarged upon it when the war ended and he, like Emanuel and other industrialists, found he needed additional civilian business to maintain operations. Behn purchased radio and phonograph companies, electric appliance manufacturers, a switchboard firm, and others, all related in one way or another to the use of electricity. He also continued to sell foreign utilities companies, plowing the receipts into new manufacturing acquisitions, both in the United States and overseas.

Behn's insistence on having sole direction of the firm chafed others at ITT; when several of his mergers went sour and the common stock declined, they were able to convince Behn to move up to the chairmanship. In 1948, William Henry Harrison, a vice president at American Telephone & Telegraph, was named to the ITT presidency and set out to remold it into a telephone equipment firm that could challenge Western Electric, the AT&T subsidiary, among the independent telephone companies. Behn opposed this change, and for the next six years he and Harrison clashed almost daily. Harrison was able to sell off most of the Behn manufacturing acquisitions in this period, but his own plans never fully matured. In 1954 he gained the upper hand at ITT, but within two years he died, and Behn died a year later.

Edmund Leavey succeeded Harrison, but he was an elderly man at the time; he realized his major task would be to find a man to take command and to straighten out the jumble of companies and finances left over from the Behn-Harrison years. This was to be Geneen's major task, or at least that was the idea in the minds of the men who offered him the post in 1958. Geneen accepted, but instead of rationalizing ITT, he quickly set about making it more complex than it had been before, and more so than any other company in the world. Geneen took over a conglomerate-by-accident with $653.5 million in sales in 1957, and within twelve years had made it into the ninth largest company in industrial America, with sales of $5.5 billion.

Like most of the other conglomerates, ITT came to be fashioned in the image of its founder. Litton's free-form management, interrelated units, and image of modernity were a result of the Thornton-Ash philosophy of enterprise, one that had roots at Harvard Business School. Little's grab bag of diverse companies, each with a vice-president with a great range of powers, reflected his belief that once you found a good man you gave him his head. Bluhdorn's razzle-dazzle sweeps made him appear a real-life version of a motion-picture tycoon, and it was not by accident that he acquired Paramount, or that it became his favorite subsidiary. These men each represented a "type" of conglomerater, and would have imitators, some even more successful than the original.

Geneen would have few imitators; those who tried, failed. His management techniques and operations would not become a beacon for other conglomeraters, for they lacked his unique combination of audacity, imagination, energy, and training. Alone of the conglomeraters of the period, Geneen was described as a genius, a term he accepted as his due. Although ITT became the largest of the conglomerates by far, and by many measures the most successful, it remained a Geneen creature, one he controlled from the top. ITT divisional presidents and vice-presidents had less autonomy than their counterparts at smaller firms or large, old-line industrial corporations. On one occasion Geneen spoke of his resentment of the fact that the day was only twenty-four hours long. Given another ten hours, he allowed, he could manage the entire ITT operation.

This same attitude existed in his acquisitions program. In many cases Geneen would select firms to be approached, plan the takeover, arrange financing, and carry through negotiations. By 1969 ITT had some two hundred operating subsidiaries scattered throughout the world, and some had subsidiaries of their own. ITT was essentially a management concern, presiding over an array of operating firms, as well as several "captive conglomerates."

Geneen spent most of his first year in office restructuring the company and bringing in new men as his aides. Then he embarked on an acquisitions program, concentrating at first on small- and medium-sized firms in fields related to already existing operations. Then, in 1963, he began making larger mergers, in unrelated fields as well. A merger with American Broadcasting Corporation fell through, and in 1965 ITT had its first important antitrust encounter and was obliged to divest itself of part of the business of a subsidiary, Avis, the automobile renter. In some months ITT would swallow a dozen small firms at a time, usually without the fanfare and publicity attendant upon a Litton or a Gulf & Western merger.

Selected Statistics for International Telephone & Telegraph, 1947-1969

Year	Sales (millions	Earnings of dollars)	Shares Outstanding	Earnings Per Share	Price Range, Common Low	High
1947	173.3	.2	6,399,000	0.03	9-1/2	17-3/4
1948	215.4	6.8	6,399,000	1.07	8-3/4	16-1/2
1949	233.4	4.7	6,539,000	0.72	7-1/2	11-1/8
1950	253.1	15.6	6,539,000	2.38	9-1/4	16
1951	298.0	18.0	6,919,000	2.60	13-1/8	19-1/8
1952	397.6	22.1	7,177,000	3.09	15	20-3/4
1953	408.0	22.4	7,177,000	3.12	13-1/2	20-1/4
1954	423.8	20.1	7,177,000	2.80	13-7/8	26-3/4
1955	502.8	23.1	7,177,000	3.21	23-3/4	31-1/8
1956	599.6	28.1	7,177,000	3.92	29-1/4	37-3/8
1957	653.5	22.4	7,177,000	3.12	25-3/4	37-3/4
1958	687.5	26.6	7,363,000	3.70	29-1/4	65-1/4
1959	765.6	29.0	15,530,000	1.80	28	45-1/2*
1960	811.4	30.6	15,681,000	1.96	32	48-7/8
1961	930.5	36.1	16,375,000	2.19	44-3/4	60-7/8
1962	1,090.2	40.7	16,629,000	2.41	33	58-1/2
1963	1,414.1	52.4	18,462,000	2.69	41-3/4	55-5/8
1964	1,601.5	66.8	19,933,000	3.16	53-5/8	61-1/2
1965	1,782.9	76.1	20,265,000	3.58	48-3/4	70
1966	2,121.3	89.9	21,084,000	4.04	58	79-1/2
1967	3,577.8	153.8	28,785,000	4.38	72-1/2	124
1968	4,066.5	180.2	59,059,000	2.58	44-7/8	62-1/2*
1969	5,474.7	234.0	65,371,000	2.90	46-1/4	60-1/2

*Two-for-one stock split.

Source: *Moody's Handbook of Common Stocks,* 1958, 1965, 1971.

The ITT mergermania reached what at the time seemed a climax in 1969. In that year Geneen acquired:

ITT Acquisitions, 1969.

Month	Business	Primary Product or Service
January	Thorp Finance	Financing, insurance
February	Hopkins Airport Hotel	Hotel
	Temple School	Correspondence school
March	Liberty Investors Benefit Insurance	Insurance
	Marquis—Who's Who	Reference books
	United Homes	Construction
April	Joseph B. Giglio Enterprises	Rental automobiles
	Canteen Corporation	Food services
May	United Building Services	Building maintenance
	City Window Cleaning	Building maintenance
	Office Training School	Secretarial training
August	Minnesota School of Business	Business school
	American Electric Manufacturing	Outdoor lighting
September	G. K. Hall	Printer and publisher
	Wadsworth Land	Real estate
	Maria Isabel Hotel	Hotel
October	Grinnell	Auto supplies,plumbing
	Southern Wood Preserving	Creosoted products
	Nova, Appareils	Household appliances
	Zuid Hollandse Grofuco	Foods
	American House & Window	Building maintenance
	Allied Industries	Building maintenance
	American Building Services	Building maintenance
	Alton Canteen	Vending service
November	Pearson Candy	Candy manufacturer
December	Jacques French Restaurant	Restaurant

Source: *Moody's Industrials.*

A pattern could be discerned in many of these acquisitions, which were part of Geneen's master plan for ITT. When asked later on for a rationale of his diversification program, Geneen wrote that the corporation's purposes were:

1. To diversify into industries and markets which have good prospects for above-average, long-term growth and profitability;

2. To achieve a sound balance between foreign and domestic earnings;
3. To achieve a sound balance between high-risk, capital-intensive manufacturing operations and less risky service operations;
4. To achieve a sound balance between high-risk engineering-labor-intensive electronics manufacturing and less risky commercial and industrial manufacturing;
5. To achieve a sound ratio between commercial-industrial products and services and consumer products and services;
6. To achieve a sound ratio between government-defense-space operations and commercial-industrial-consumer products and services in both foreign and domestic markets; and
7. To achieve a sound balance between cyclical products and services.

Most conglomeraters had similar ambitions, but few had been able to carry them out as successfully.

ITT did have problems, however, and one was Geneen himself. All would be well so long as he headed the company. But what would happen should he die suddenly? Or after his retirement? Geneen had put together a good management team, but none of those in the upper echelon seemed capable of assuming command. Geneen would not train anyone to take his place, guarding his powers and relinquishing as few as possible. He insisted on filling the posts both of chairman and president, an unusual situation even for conglomerates. As a result, many executives left ITT for other companies; they would praise Geneen, but note that ITT in the 1960s was not unlike Raytheon in the 1950s, when Geneen himself was blocked from advancement by men unwilling to share or relinquish power. Those who remained either were good staff men or managers. The former lacked field experience, and the latter a view of the conglomerate as a whole. Only Geneen had both, and in 1969 he was unwilling to name a crown prince.*

*In December, 1972, Geneen selected Francis J. "Tim" Dunleavy to become president of ITT. It was said this was done to allay fears of chaos should he die. But it is still not clear

The company's large debt worried some Wall Streeters. When Geneen arrived in 1958 ITT had a bonded debt of $199.5 million and working capital of $234 million. The debt in 1969 was $1.6 billion, against working capital of only $773 million. Much of the debt had been entered into as a result of the mergers, and ITT had a long series of convertible bonds outstanding that worried investment analysts. Nor were they pleased with the fact that Geneen often refused to take advice from his investment bankers. As a former accountant, he may have felt he knew at least as much about financing as they.

ITT's third problem came from government. The company's size attracted the antitrusters, although Geneen had been careful in obeying the letter of the law. The Grinnell merger was barely announced when the Justice Department warned ITT that it would face divestiture action if and when the acquisition took place. When Geneen announced a major tender offer for Hartford Fire Insurance, the department attacked the plan and sought an injunction against it. In mid-1969 it appeared the government would attempt to force Geneen into a series of divestitures. Undaunted, he went ahead with the acquisitions, and prepared to battle the government in court.

ITT's earnings increased regularly and at a rapid pace. Yet the company's common stock did not sell at a price/earning multiple that would put it in the "growth" category. ITT rarely sold for above twenty times earnings, on par with Textron but far below Litton in that company's palmiest days. This irked Geneen, but did not interfere with his activities, as he continued to seek out likely merger candidates.

For all his abilities, Geneen was unknown to the man in the street, and indeed to many investors as well. Bluhdorn and Thornton had better publicity, but neither had become a major symbol of the conglomerate movement. That star role was held for a time by James Ling, head of Ling-Temco-Vought, a Horatio Alger hero who captured the imagination of the investing portion of the nation and the only man who might have challenged Geneen for the title of top

that Dunleavy has any real power. Geneen continued to rule with an iron hand, and some Wall Streeters compared ITT under Geneen to the U.S.S.R. under Stalin—a major power without a clear method of succession.

conglomerater. Indeed, Ling was more inventive than Geneen, if less steady as a businessman. For a while, LTV seemed to have all the advantages of ITT and none of its drawbacks. Toward the end of the decade, however, Ling would prove less resourceful than Geneen. He was the most exciting person in the early conglomerate movement, but he made it appear more like a roller coaster than a serious business.

Although Ling is thought of as a Texan, he was born in Oklahoma, and did not settle in Dallas, his home base, until he was almost twenty. Before that he had an indifferent schooling, was a self-confessed "bum," and knocked around the country. Later on he would be called a "typical Texas millionaire," but this was not so. If anything, the Lings were at the edge of poverty, and young Ling had to scrape for what he could get. And, along the way, he had to educate himself, for no one else would do it for him.

Ling drifted into the trade of electrician in Dallas and worked for a while at the office of a small electrical contractor. While there he learned the business, which included estimating contract costs and arranging for work to be done. In 1944, at the age of twenty-one, he became a journeyman electrician. That same year he joined the Navy, which sent him to electrical school. On his discharge in 1946, Ling returned to Dallas and founded Ling Electric Company in January 1947 with a capital of $3,000.

The Texas economy had been in the doldrums after war contracts had been canceled in 1945. But things were picking up in 1947, with new defense contracts and the beginning of a building boom in Dallas. Ling Electric was able to win a few small contracts and one major one, so that its first year's gross was $70,000. The company did $200,000 worth of business the following year, and $400,000 in 1949. The Lings, who had lived in rooms above the shop at first, were now able to move to their own home.

Ling Electric grossed $1.5 million in 1955, and Ling was wealthy, with a large income that was heavily taxed. Because of this, and to raise capital for expansion, he decided to register Ling Electric as a public company. The offering went well, and armed with new funds,

Ling began to seek acquisitions. The first of these was L.M. Electronics, a small West Coast manufacturer of testing equipment. Ling now changed his company's name for the first time, calling it Ling Industries, Inc., and renaming his subsidiary Ling Electronics. Then he sold more stock and purchased United Electronics and Calidyne Company. Without waiting to consolidate these companies, Ling floated a $2.2-million issue of convertible bonds and purchased Altec Companies, University Loudspeakers, and Continental Electronics. Once again he changed his company's name, to Ling-Altec Electronics.

In this series of swift moves, Ling had taken his $1.5-million company of 1955 and transformed it into a $48-million conglomerate with net earnings of $1.9 million by the end of 1959. He had also learned the methods of conglomerates, and was prepared to apply them on a major scale. Then he embarked on the second phase of his business career, one that would last for less than five years, and raise Ling's gross to a third of a billion dollars in 1964.

Ling acquired nine companies in the period from July 1960 to June 1964, hardly a record or even impressive in the light of what other conglomeraters were doing in the same years. And of the nine, only two were significant. The first was Temco Electronics and Missiles in 1960, after which Ling-Altec became Ling-Temco, and the second being Chance Vought, a large but ailing aircraft company, which resulted in yet another name change, to Ling-Temco-Vought. Ling disposed of some of Chance Vought's operations for cash, and once again sought new financing.

It was then that Ling entered a third phase of his career, the major one, which would demonstrate his imagination and daring as a conglomerater, and would be his most important original contribution to the movement.

In December 1964, Ling announced "Project Redeployment." Ling-Temco-Vought would be restructured into three separate, and for the time being wholly-owned, companies: LTV Aerospace, LTV Electrosystems, and LTV Ling-Altec. The aerospace company would be the largest, while the other two would be minor units. Now

Ling-Temco-Vought was a holding company, with little more than a central office and a portfolio of stocks in three operating corporations.

Ling's next step was to announce the sale of some of Ling-Temco-Vought's stock holdings, or to be more precise, the exchange of the holdings for stock in the parent company. For each share of Ling-Temco-Vought tendered to the parent company, the stockholder would receive a half share apiece in each of the three subsidiary companies and nine dollars in cash.

The offer would have three major results. First of all, it would establish public markets for the subsidiaries' securities, which Ling fully expected would be higher *in toto* than the equivalent price of Ling-Temco-Vought at the time of the offering. Next, it would result in a lowering of the number of Ling-Temco-Vought shares outstanding, and in this way cause the earnings per share to rise. Ling thought investors would take note of this, and the fact that Ling-Temco-Vought's net asset value per share was also higher, the result of investors' favorable evaluations of successor company securities.

Finally, Ling believed Project Redeployment's success would enable him to borrow more money than before. Not only would he be able to use Ling-Temco-Vought for this purpose, but the subsidiary companies as well.

It was an intriguing idea, and it did work. Ling repeated the procedure in 1965, when after taking over Okonite Corp. from Kennecott Copper he sold off 14 percent of the common stock. After all the manipulations were completed, the mother company had fewer shares outstanding, a larger debt, and a major equity position in yet another subsidiary. Ling appeared intent on lowering the amount of shares outstanding in Ling-Temco-Vought whenever possible, increasing the debt, and gobbling up new firms. Wall Street hadn't seen such imaginative use of leverage since the 1920s, and before he was through, Ling would make his predecessors of that period appear amateurish. The public appreciated his daring, and the fact that as a result of the switches, his company's earnings rose dramatically. So did the stock. "LTV" common soared on the New York Stock

Exchange, and was a darling of the rampaging bull market of 1965 and 1966.

Clearly a celebrity, Ling acted the part. He was an open, attractive individual, willing to explain his system to even the most obtuse reporter who came to interview him. More acquisitions were in the works, he said. He would use long- and short-term borrowing, divestitures and amalgamations, and continual restructuring. In the process, he expected LTV to become the largest industrial in the nation.

Ling's methods were criticized, but he dismissed objections by saying his opponents didn't understand the business climate of the 1960s. Still, there were weaknesses in LTV's debt structure. Ling brushed these aside. But he could not answer those who asked what he would do if and when the bull market ended, or when money rates began to rise.

This was the trouble with the LTV situation. So much of the corporation's net worth consisted of holdings in subsidiaries, at the time highly valued in the bull market of 1966. What would happen if the market fell? More than any other conglomerate, LTV resembled the infamous holding companies of the 1920s, most of which collapsed shortly after the market crash of 1929.

While Wall Street analyzed the situation and LTV common fell from 75 1/2 to 40 3/7 in part because of the uncertainties, Ling moved ahead in Dallas. Carefully he pursued his next candidate, Wilson & Co., which had sales of over a billion dollars, most in meat-packing, but with important representation in drugs, soap, and sporting supplies. At the time, LTV's sales were under $500 million. Undaunted, Ling began buying Wilson shares on the open market, and then he made a tender offer for the rest. In January 1967, he had over half the shares, and moved to merge the company into LTV.

Most of the money Ling used for the tenders came from short-term borrowings, funds he would have to repay quickly. So he offered the remaining Wilson stockholders a new convertible LTV bond in return for their stock and he received most of the remaining shares that way. But he would have to move quickly to obtain funds to repay his loans and prepare for payments on the bonds.

Ling did so by breaking down Wilson as a meat-packer might carve a carcass. He created three new companies, Wilson & Co. (meat-packing), Wilson Pharmaceutical & Chemical (drugs and soap), and Wilson Sporting Goods. It was not long before the three were dubbed "meatball, goofball, and golfball."

LTV retained most of the stock in all three and sold the rest to new investors, in return obtaining $44.5 million, almost all of which was used to repay the short-term notes. Then, as LTV common remained low, Ling floated a rumor to the effect that he planned to purchase his own company's stock with more borrowed money. In this way, he would further increase LTV's debt, while lowering the amount of shares outstanding. This would result in higher earnings per share. When the speculating public saw this, he believed, they would bid LTV to new highs, and then he could use the stock to obtain yet additional companies. As had been the case previously, Ling activities were not secret or a violation of any statute. True, they were complicated, but by then he was considered a genius by many investors, who proceeded to act exactly as he believed they would. LTV began to rise once more.

It was the height of mergermania on Wall Street, and Ling was its hero. In 1967 manufacturing and mining mergers registered a 50-percent gain over the previous year—going from 996 mergers to 1496—with the rate of activity accelerating each quarter.

The man of the moment, Ling lost no time in consolidating his gains, but rather sought new ones. Troy Post, chairman of the board at Greatamerica Corporation, was one of his closest friends and greatest admirers. Greatamerica was a Texas-based insurance and banking conglomerate, which also owned majority interests in Braniff Airways and National Car Rental, as well as several small firms, among which were computer-related operations. Post was eager to retire, and James Ling was interested in acquiring Greatamerica. So they came together to make a deal, one of the biggest of the period.

Early in 1968 Ling made a tender offer to Greatamerica

shareholders that had Post's appoval. For every hundred shares of Greatamerica. he would exchange $3,000 in LTV debentures paying 5-percent interest and a warrant to buy ten shares of LTV common at $115. News of the offer caused LTV stock to jump to over 125, and the offer looked better all the time. It was accepted by most stockholders, at a cost to LTV of $500 million in bonds.

Once again, there was more to the merger than appeared on the surface. Greatamerica had some $150 million in cash, and this made the price seem more reasonable. And Ling sold off several of its banks and insurance companies to realize another $126 million. Still, the merger left LTV with an uncomfortably large debt, and Ling acted to reduce it in a typically grandiose way.

In October, Ling announced an exchange offer that confused the public and amazed Wall Street. He established what he called a "package" of securities. This consisted of 1.1 LTV warrants exercisable at 103.35, 0.6 share of National Car Rental, one share of National Car Rental class A stock, one share of Braniff Airways special A stock, and 0.33 share of Computer Technology.

LTV would exchange these units in the following manner:

1.1 units for one share LTV common stock.

9.75 units for $1,000 of LTV 6.5-percent notes.

10 units for $1,000 of LTV 6.75-percent debentures.

6.7 units for $1,000 of LTV 5-percent debentures.

9.5 units for $1,000 of LTV 5.75-percent debentures.

It was a free-for-all on Wall Street, as owners of LTV paper called their brokers to find out what it all meant, while the brokers made their own calls to friends and analysts, who couldn't reply for hours. Even then, the meaning of the offers was clouded and complicated by another one of Ling's moves.

While completing the Greatamerica take-over, Ling made a tender offer for the common stock of Jones & Laughlin, one of the country's major steel firms. Ling's offer was $85 a share. The previous day Jones & Laughlin was selling for around $35 less. The price jumped immediately, on heavy demand, and shares poured into the LTV underwriter's offices. By June, Ling had more than 63 percent of the stock, acquired at a cost of almost $500 million.

Within a few months, then, Ling had paid almost as much for two companies as Morgan had for the components that went to make up United States Steel. The operations were grander than Bluhdorn's, and in comparison the Thornton and Little acquisitons seemed penny ante. Only Geneen, who had recently offered a bundle of securities worth in the neighborhood of $1.5 billion for Hartford Fire Insurance, could rival Ling. But such actions were expected from Geneen and not from a high-school dropout from Dallas who, even then, was on the prowl for additional companies.

And additional capital. The mergers required massive borrowings of short-term capital at high rates in the United States and Europe. Ling seemed a man on a financial tightrope. Would he fall? He seemed confident, but Wall Street wasn't so sure. LTV's total debt in early 1969 reached $1.8 billion; in 1965 it had been less than $100 million. Servicing the debt would be difficult. A bad year, bearable by most large firms, could throw LTV into grave straits, including passing interest payments on bonds and perhaps even bankruptcy. It didn't seem likely, but Wall Street had learned to expect unexpected things from Ling by then.

The Ling-Temco-Vought Debt, 1964-1969
(thousands of dollars)

Year	Short-Term Debt	Long-Term Debt	Total
1964	$ 21,700	$ 37,012	$ 58,712
1965	57,000	50,274	97,274
1966	47,640	94,755	143,413
1967	160,938	202,586	363,524
1968	413,970	1,236,693	1,650,663
1969	358,394	1,500,972	1,859,366

Source: *Ling-Temco-Vought Annual Report*, 1969.

Ling was an unsettling influence, not only on Wall Street and in world banking centers, but in Washington as well. The antitrust movement was stirring once more, the result of court decisions and the activities of Bluhdorn, Geneen, and Ling. In retrospect, it would appear that conglomeritis reached its fever pitch in the summer and autumn of 1968, with Bluhdorn's acquisition of Armour and stock purchases in other companies, the speedup of the ITT merger operations, and the Ling takeover at Jones & Laughlin and his complicated scheme for exchanges of Greatamerica securities. At the same time, the courts, congressional critics, and the FTC, as well as the Justice Department, were preparing to slow the movement down, if not halt it completely. To complicate matters, 1968 was an election year, and although conglomeritis was not a major issue, it was being discussed.

Selected Statistics for Ling-Temco-Vought, 1957-1969

Year	Sales (millions of dollars)	Earnings (millions of dollars)	Shares Outstanding	Earnings Per Share	Price Range, Common Low	Price Range, Common High	Price Earnings Ratio
1957	130.1	3.2	2,632,000	$1.59	3-5/8	7-5/8	3.2
1958	132.9	3.0	2,349,000	1.30	5	19-7/8	9.1
1959	148.7	3.0	2,429,000	1.16	16-1/4	44-1/2	26.3
1960	148.4	3.1	2,553,000	1.25	20	42	24.8
1961	192.8	(13.1)	2,775,000	(4.82)	23-1/8	42-1/2	–
1962	325.4	8.7	2,784,000	3.03	15	25-7/8	6.7
1963	329.0	7.1	2,825,000	2.44	13-1/2	19-1/8	6.7
1964	322.9	4.9	1,850,000	2.32	14-1/2	20-1/4	7.5
1965	336.2	6.0	1,765,000	2.82	17-1/4	58	13.3
1966	468.3	13.7	1,936,000	6.47	38-1/8	80-3/8	9.2
1967	1,833.3	32.2	4,669,000	6.85	76-3/4	203*	19.8
1968	2,769.7	29.4	4,894,000	5.01	80	135-3/4	40.2
1969	3,750.3	(38.3)	3,764,000	(10.15)	24-1/8	97-3/4	–

*Three-for-two stock split.

Source: *Moody's Handbook of Common Stocks*, 1964, 1971; *LTV Annual Report*, 1967.

Throughout the early and mid-1960s FTC and Justice Department cases against large corporations involved in mergers were argued in the courts. Prosecution under existing legislation, which had

Ling-Temco-Vought Subsidiary Companies, 1969

LTV Research Center	100%	owned
LTV Jet Fleet	100%	
LTV International	100%	
Wilson & Co.	89%	
Okonite	86%	
Wilson Sporting Goods	75%	
Wilson Pharmaceutical	75%	
LTV Ling-Altec	73%	
LTV Electrosystems	69%	
LTV Aerospace	63%	
Braniff Airways	55.4%	
Jones & Laughlin	81%	

Source: *Moody's Industrial Manual*, 1970.

been written with horizontal and vertical mergers in mind, was vigorous. In the government arguments and court decisions, doctrines involving conglomerates were enunciated and accepted. Donald F. Turner, head of the Antitrust Division of the Justice Department and later professor of law at Harvard, argued that an increase in market power *alone* would suffice to bring his lawyers into a merger situation.

This produced interesting results. In 1966, for example, the Supreme Court disallowed a merger of Von's Grocery and Shopping Bag Foods, even though their combined sales in their market was only 7.5 percent of the total. A more significant case was argued the following year, when an FTC action against Procter & Gamble to disallow that firm's acquisition of Clorox Corp. reached the Supreme Court. In its argument the FTC claimed that P & G's resources were such as to "dwarf the entire liquid bleach industry," and could "hardly be bested."

> . . . the remaining firms may now be motivated to seek affiliation by merger with giant companies. The practical tendency of the instant merger, then, is to transform the liquid bleach industry into an arena of big business competition only, with the few small firms falling by the wayside, unable to compete with their giant rivals.

The FTC conceded that Procter & Gamble had brought efficiencies to the industry, along with lower prices. The consumer had benefited in some ways. Still, "the kind of 'efficiency' and 'economy' produced by this merger is precisely the kind that—in the short as well as the long run—hurts, not helps, a competitive economy."

Procter & Gamble's attorneys argued that competition in the bleach sector had not been harmed by the merger. They challenged the very idea that there was such a category as "liquid bleach industry," noting that the product competed with others that did the same tasks. Finally, the company claimed it had not broken any statute, since bigness by itself was not deemed a violation under the Clayton or Celler-Kefauver acts.

The Court found for the government. The merger was dissolved.

The business community and press reacted strongly, charging the FTC with having embarked on a witch-hunt. Turner, now in private life, agreed. As early as 1965 he had written:

> I do not believe Congress has given the courts and the FTC a mandate to campaign against "superconcentration" in the absence of any evidence of harm to competition. In light of the bitterly disputed issues involved, I believe that the courts should demand of Congress that it translate any further directive into something more formidable than sonorous phrases in the pages of the Congressional Record.

Congress indeed was considering new legislation, although it had a low priority at a time when the country was debating the Vietnam War and civil rights. From 1965 on, Senate and House committees and subcommittees investigated the merger movement, especially that part of it involving conglomerates. If nothing else, the committees and the FTC documented allegations that the movement had indeed grown rapidly since the end of World War II, and that many companies which in the past had developed their own subsidiaries were relying instead on take-overs. The growth of this kind of activity had been steady if irregular in the 1950s, with the greatest growth taking place in the next decade, especially the mid- and late-1960s.

Assets of Large Acquisitions Compared with New Investment, Manufacturing and Mining, 1948-1968*

Year	New Investment	Assets of Large Acquisitions	Acquired Assets as Percent of New Investment
	(billions of dollars)		
1948	10.01	.130	1.3
1949	7.94	.067	0.8
1950	8.20	.173	2.1
1951	11.78	.201	1.7
1952	12.61	.327	2.6
1953	12.90	.679	5.3
1954	12.02	1.425	11.9
1955	12.40	2.129	17.2
1956	16.19	2.037	12.6
1957	17.20	1.472	8.6
1958	12.37	1.107	8.9
1959	13.06	1.960	15.0
1960	15.47	1.710	11.1
1961	14.66	2.129	14.5
1962	15.76	2.194	13.9
1963	16.73	2.917	17.4
1964	19.77	2.798	14.2
1965	23.75	3.900	16.4
1966	28.46	4.100	14.4
1967	28.11	8.222	29.2
1968	28.27	12.616	44.6
1969			

* "Large" is defined as acquisitions with assets of $10 million or more.

Souce: Bureau of Economics, FTC, *Current Trends in Merger Activity, 1968*, p. 17.

The FTC also demonstrated statistically that the conglomerate type of merger, which had been utilized by large firms in the prewar period, was becoming practical for smaller ones, too. Whether as a result of economic benefits to be derived from such mergers, or the "glamour" that came with being considered a conglomerate in the 1960s, the movement was gathering steam, and in time might come to dominate business organization in the United States.

Rise of the Conglomerates, as Reflected in *Fortune's* Roster of the Five Hundred Largest America Industrial Corporations*

Conglomerate	Rank						
	1969	1968	1967	1966	1965	1964	1963
International Telephone & Telegraph	9	11	21	28	30	31	31
Ling-Temco-Vought	14	25	38	168	204	186	168
Tenneco	34	39	39	58	56	—	—
Litton Industries	39	40	44	57	72	85	102
Textron	57	47	49	61	81	80	95
Gulf & Western	64	69	135	247	341	—	—
Signal Companies	74	68	57	95	105	105	149
Teledyne	84	124	191	293	—	—	—
U.S. Industries	105	163	284	425	444	460	465
Ogden	109	94	104	130	134	128	140
Avco	129	78	84	134	157	139	111
Studebaker-Worthington	141	118	382	325	—	—	—
Walter Kidde	143	176	204	283	—	—	—

*This list is not meant to be all-inclusive, and takes into consideration the fact that to this day, a clear definition of what is or is not a conglomerate has not been made, either by the Justice Department or by scholars. Rather, the rankings indicate relative growth among some firms that have been labeled as conglomerates over the years.

Source: *Fortune*, 1964-1970.

The FTC and the various congressional committees concluded that the conglomerate philosophy was accepted by many "old line" companies. Increasingly, the larger mergers were of the conglomerate rather than the vertical or horizontal type. In 1964 there had been 91 mergers involving manufacturing and mining firms with assets in excess of $10 million. Of these, 62 were of the conglomerate variety while 29 were classified as horizontal or vertical. In 1969 there were 192 such mergers, with 161 being conglomerate. The total assets of these merged companies were $12.6 billion, with the conglomerate variety accounting for $11.2 billion of the amount.

Still, the country had no law dealing with such mergers, and public policy on the matter was fuzzy. Indeed, government agencies still were debating definitions of conglomerates, even while the FTC and Justice Department were attacking them.

Percentage Distribution of Mergers by Type and Period, 1926-1968

Type of Merger	1926-1930	1940-1947	1951-1955	1956-1960	1961-1965	1966-1968
Horizontal	75.9	62.0	39.2	30.1	22.5	8.6
Vertical	4.8	17.0	12.2	14.9	17.5	9.8
Conglomerate	19.3	21.0	48.6	55.0	60.0	81.6

Source: Staff Report of the Federal Trade Commission, *Economic Report on Corporate Mergers,* Hearings on Economic Concentration, Subcommittee on Antitrust and Monopoly, U.S. Senate, 91st Cong., 1st Sess. (Washington, D.C., 1969); p. 63.

Notwithstanding this, important government officials mounted an attack on conglomerates in 1969, shortly after the Nixon Administration took office. There was talk that the attack was political. Old-line business leaders tended to be Republican, while several important conglomeraters, the most visible being Ling, supported Hubert Humphrey in the 1968 election. Old-line antitrusters, led by House Judiciary Committee Chairman Celler, joined new Nixon appointees to blast conglomeritis. Securities and Exchange Commission Chairman Hamer Budge called for immediate action, while the new assistant attorney general in charge of the Antitrust Division, Richard McLaren, promised action.

The first target would be James Ling, and the issue would be the Jones & Laughlin take-over.

On April 14, 1969, McLaren filed an antitrust action to force LTV to divest itself of a substantial part of Jones & Laughlin. At the time of the merger, LTV had no business directly involved with the steel industry. Yet the suit charged the merger would destroy competition, create unfair opportunities for reciprocal dealings between LTV subsidiary companies and Jones & Laughlin, and, most significantly, McLaren claimed the very increase in LTV's size would constitute a violation of the antitrust laws. McLaren's case was weak, but he pressed it nonetheless.

At the time of the suit Ling was preparing to take over the rest of Jones & Laughlin's stock and then break the company down into subsidiaries, as he had done with Wilson & Co. It was vital that he do so as fast as possible, so as to obtain funds needed to pay off short-term borrowing necessitated by the tender offer. Unable to take the time to fight a lengthy action, Ling accepted a compromise settlement in March, one that affected not only Jones & Laughlin, but also other parts of the LTV empire.

LTV would not be allowed representation on the Jones & Laughlin board, and agreed to cease attempts to break down the company's several operations. There would be no dealings between LTV concerns and the steel company for ten years. Ling would either divest himself of Jones & Laughlin or Braniff and Okonite within three years. And most important insofar as Ling's conglomerating activities were concerned, LTV agreed not to acquire any company with assets in excess of $100 million during the next ten years, unless it first divested itself of Jones & Laughlin.

LTV had been described as a "bicycle company," not because it was in the business of making or distributing bikes, but rather because it was akin to a moving bicycle. So long as it was going, all was well. But when it stopped, the bike would fall to one side. LTV was stopped, and there was fear it would soon collapse, unable to pay off its debts.

To make for an even more depressing picture, the stock market was in grave difficulties. The Dow-Jones Industrials fell from a high of 968.85 to a low of 631.16 between May of 1969 and May of 1970. It was the sharpest drop since 1937, and the closest Wall Street had come to panic and failure since 1929. Money rates soared, and the cheap paper with which the conglomeraters had taken over companies was now undesirable.

To this was added new antitrust investigations of conglomerates, with ITT a prime target. The Justice Department filed a suit attempting to force the firm to divest itself of Canteen Corp. This was followed by an action directed against Northwest Industries, a large and rising conglomerate, then in the process of attempting to force Goodrich into a merger. McLaren promised more of the same.

Many leaders of take-over candidates, such as those at Goodrich, were delighted by the actions, while conglomeraters called the attacks politically inspired and blamed the Justice Department for the stock market collapse. McLaren denied both charges, the second more effectively than the first. But he did call upon Congressman Celler to hold new hearings in order to frame a revised antitrust act, conceding indirectly that his actions were weakly based. Celler agreed to do so, and scheduled them for 1970.

In the meantime the mania aspects of conglomeritis had clearly passed. McLaren noted this in October 1969, when he wrote, in an article entitled, "Anti-Trust, Republican Style":

> The very large mergers that were causing us concern have definitely slowed down. But a lot of smaller mergers of the conglomerate type are continuing to be negotiated and closed. I think this is a very healthy thing.

McLaren added that "the basic idea of a diversified corporation, which is really what you're talking about when you say conglomerate, is an excellent one." Were the conglomerates of the 1960s merely "diversified corporations"? If so, what would one classify U.S. Steel of 1901, General Motors of 1925, or General Electric of 1945? These firms, too, were diversified, but their methods, approaches, philosophy, and leadership were quite different from those of LTV, ITT, and Gulf & Western. McLaren said that "It's the big, anticompetitive and potentially anticompetitive kind of merger that we're worried about." But the Justice Department was never able to show how the conglomerate mergers restricted competition in what the department itself classified as "industries."

The Antitrust Subcommittee of the House Judiciary Committee could do no better. Celler held hearings as promised, and the subcommittee report was released early in 1971. In it was a strong blast at LTV, noting that it had become, through its acquisitions program, a debt-ridden, unstable corporation. ITT was charged with having overstated its earnings through devious accounting procedures, and the charge was extended to other conglomerates as well. The corporations dutifully replied that their accounting was within the law and "accepted practice," and all but dared the government to bring actions against them for fraud. None was forthcoming, as accountants disagreed among themselves as how to handle conglomerate accounting.

As for Ling, he no longer remained in control at LTV. The corporation suffered a bad loss in 1969, primarily as a result of a deficit at Jones & Laughlin which, like most steel firms, did poorly that year. Ironically, the merger that brought the Justice Department down on LTV also caused it to come to the edge of destruction financially.

By 1971 Ling was busy at his new conglomerate, Omega-Alpha, where supposedly he would create another LTV. Omega-Alpha did not "move" like the giant company, for the atmosphere of the early 1970s was wrong for conglomerates. Attacks and problems came from all sides. Ralph Nader, the consumer crusader, called for a breakup of ITT and other large conglomerates. Government investigations of ITT continued, and these were followed by charges that the company had attempted to influence the Republican party through a donation. Litton posted a deficit, and its stock skidded badly. Other conglomerates pulled in their horns. Some, which had proudly boasted of their go-go attributes in the late 1960s when conglomerates were all the rage, now denied that they were in that field. "Our company is a *congeneric,*" said one businessman, while another firm attempted to win the tag "synergistic."

The major conglomerates remained in business and some thrived. But the combination of Ling's antics, Justice Department action, falling stock prices, higher interest rates, and a new anti-big-business mood in the nation, served to lower the temperature considerably. There would be no new antitrust laws, but by 1973 none was really necessary. The cause for earlier consternation was no longer present. The latest of the great U.S. money manias was over.

But, assuming the past as a guide to the future, there would be others.

Conclusion: The Mood for Mania

The conglomerate craze subsided in the spring of 1969, exactly two centuries after Samuel Wharton and William Trent arrived in London to seek backers for the Vandalia scheme. These two hundred years saw more and greater social, economic, and political change than that of any equivalent period of time. Wharton's life was equidistant from those of Queen Elizabeth and Richard Nixon, from the sea beggars of the Spanish Main and the astronauts. His views of life and the world were far closer to the former than to ours. Wharton and Trent might have found places in the London business scene of 1569. They would have been completely alien to the Wall Street and Dallas in which James Ling operated, or the world of Harold Geneen.

Yet these men, as well as the others who participated in and led the money manias discussed in this work, did share certain common characteristics, the most obvious of which was the desire for money and power. Too, with the exception of the slave traders, they thought of themselves as men of vision, convinced that their activities would benefit not only themselves, but also society as well. Of course, the vision changed as the nation was transformed from a small agrarian colony to a complex superpower in the two centuries being considered. In the late eighteenth and nineteenth centuries, the vision was in land, what romantics called "the westward sweep of empire." Washington, Clinton, Sutro, and Mackay, as well as the cattle barons, spoke feelingly of the land, and their desire to develop its potential.

As the nation industrialized, manias appeared in that area. Carnegie always considered himself a man of vision, and would have preferred that title to one of industrialist. Higgins, Lucas, and the men of Spindletop who followed them, wanted wealth and power, but also realized they were filling a major need for an industrializing nation. Similarly, Flagler and Fisher hoped to develop Florida in order to create a new kind of playground, for a people increasingly interested in such things. Finally, the conglomeraters thought of themselves as pathfinders and creators of a new business form, one more suited to the needs of the nation in the late twentieth century than the corporate form refined a century earlier.

The conglomerate executives talked much of the business of opportunity. Perhaps in that phrase can be found the reason why America has witnessed so many manias involving money and power. The twin forces of freedom and opportunity allowed, even impelled, the ambitious and intelligent to enter into grandiose schemes, to win the applause and often the fear and hatred of their fellows. In much the same way the restrictive atmosphere of nineteenth-century Prussia encouraged similar individuals to enter the army and civil service, while frustrated ambition in Russia led to a generation of great artists and authors in the late nineteenth century, and the absence of the capitalist spirit and limited social vision in the Middle Ages produced geniuses in the area of religious speculation. In America, the person who might have become an office manager in Prussia, a novelist in Russia, or a religious philosopher in medieval France or Italy went into the business of opportunity. In other words,

America seemed to have an atmosphere that from the start encouraged money manias.

This was noted during the colonial period and after the Revolution. Americans took it for granted, though those who visited Europe remarked how the people there seemed placid, cultured, conventional, and polite when compared with their neighbors and themselves. Foreigners coming to the new nation saw the difference, too. In 1843 Felix Grund, a perceptive European visitor wrote:

> There is, probably, no people on earth with whom business constitutes pleasure, and industry amusement, in an equal degree with the inhabitants of America. Active occupation is not only the principle source of their happiness, and the foundation of their national greatness, but they are absolutely wretched without it. . . . Business is the very soul of America; the American pursues it, not as a means of procuring for himself and his family the necessary comforts of life, but as the fountain of all human felicity; and shows as much enthusiastic ardor in his application to it as any crusader ever evinced for the conquest of the Holy Land, or the followers of Mohammed for the spreading of the Koran.

Along with the craving for wealth and power, the individuals at the center of the money manias wanted status and respectability. In Europe, where vestiges of a feudal past remain even to this day, status was far more clearly defined than in the United States. It derived from one's position in the social order, and this often came through birth. Such was not the case in America, with no aristocracy or established church. As Alexis de Tocqueville put it:

> When the prestige attached to what is old has vanished, men are no longer distinguished, or hardly distinguished, by birth, standing, or profession; there is thus hardly anything left but money which makes very clear distinctions between men or can raise some of them above the common level. Distinction based

on wealth is increased by the disappearance or diminution of all other distinctions.

Finally, many men of mania were driven by senses of inadequacy. In a society such as that which developed in the United States, poverty itself became a cause for shame and lack of distinction a reason for distress. It was no coincidence that so many of the leaders of money manias began their lives poor, and sought wealth. This certainly was the case with George Croghan and Isaac Franklin, the men of Comstock and the cowboys of the beef bonanza, the steel millionaires and the wildcatters who flocked into Beaumont, and Carl Fisher of Florida and Indiana.

It is worth noting that most of those involved in manias in America came from the North, Midwest, and Far West; there were few southerners among the leaderships of manias, and those who were, more often than not were from the fringes, not the center, of "southern civilization." So we have James Ling, the poor Catholic from Oklahoma and George Merrick, the penniless boy from backwater Florida, seeking respectability in areas of the "new South," recognizing perhaps that they had little chance to do so in the old, which more than any other part of the nation resembled feudal Europe. James Ling's story might have been written by Horatio Alger, and Merrick's appears right out of a Norman Vincent Peale sermon. Sophisticated Americans think little of Alger and Peale, but to most, they articulated the American Dream, one that linked Carnegie to Geneen, Croghan to Carl Fisher.

As a people, Americans have mixed emotions regarding the men who led the manias or rode their crests. It is as though we recognize in them our own virtues and defects, though often exaggerated to be sure, and applaud the former while despising the latter. Was George Croghan a pioneer or an exploiter? Were Carnegie and Morgan robber barons or captains of industry? Did Fisher open a vacationland for the common man or create a garish and tasteless amusement park that destroyed the environment? Some would have us believe that Geneen, Bluhdorn, Thornton, and others of their kind reinvigorated old enterprises, while critics have made them out to be industrial pirates. One cannot simply say that when the men of mania succeeded, they were called heroes, and when they failed, scoundrels, for some of the heroes were rejected while there have been heroic losers in abundance in the nation's history.

Money manias often result from the American Dream, one so popular in the nineteenth century but which has faded among some segments of American society today. Most middle-class Americans appear to cling to the work ethic, the dream of striking it rich when the proper opportunity presents itself. To lose the race is not the worst disaster that can happen to a person. Rather, not to try, to fail to compete, is somehow "un-American." The men of mania all attempted to seize the main chance when it came their way. It was an effort most Americans could understand.

Then there are those who criticize the ethic itself, calling it antisocial and destructive, and money manias themselves a sign of avarice and greed. They are relatively few, but influential. Whether their call for a sense of community against the cry for individualism will succeed is in doubt. Both points of view can be argued effectively.

Nevertheless, we have not seen the end of money manias in America. As the country evolves, and the economy and society change, new opportunities will be opened to the kinds of people described in this book. Given the American past, as we have seen, individuals will arise to seek advantage, power, status, and wealth, by leading and participating in them. Whether they are beneficial or harmful is an issue that cannot be resolved, or perhaps is even irrelevant, since one hardly can legislate against what appears to be a national attribute. We do know that money manias have been with us since the continent's discovery, and have provided a *leitmotiv* for the nation's development, and that of its people.

Selected Bibliography

Descriptive studies of crowd or mass psychology interest few sociologists and psychologists today. At least this is the conclusion one is forced to draw from the literature. There is no shortage of analytical and quantitative works, both books and articles, but researchers in this area seem more interested in enumeration and classification than in discovering complex interactions between individuals in times of high excitement. The best work in the field remains Charles Mackay's *Extraordinary Popular Delusions and the Madness of Crowds*, more than a century old, and reprinted regularly. Mackay wrote interesting accounts of English, Dutch, and French bubbles, but although he knew of the Vandalia scheme and the canal mania in the United States, and indeed had visited America, he wrote nothing of the subject in this book and only referred to them briefly in other works. The closest we have to a study of American money manias is A. M. Sakolski's *The Great American Land Bubble*, first published in

1932. Sakolski has little to say of Vandalia, his work on the canal boom has been superseded by later studies, and the same is true for his chapters on other land booms in the nineteenth century. Sakolski's chapter on the Florida speculations is fresh, however, and, although written shortly after the event, is the best part of the book.

Because of the lack of overarching studies of money manias, each chapter has had to be considered as separate from the others, although there were overlapping sections for several. In the following bibliography is contained the most significant works for each mania. Articles and newspapers have been omitted for all but the last two chapters, which for the most part were based on such specialized and current material. The Florida boom was covered by every major general magazine in the nation, and I have selected the most important articles for those interested in future work in the field, or additional reading. The same is true for the conglomerates, only more so. Scarcely an issue of *Business Week, Fortune,* or other financial publications of the 1960s would fail to contain references to one conglomerate or another, or to different aspects of the movement. The best bibliography on the subject is in Charles Gilbert, ed., *The Making of a Conglomerate,* and the list there is thirty-two pages long, consisting mostly of articles. Rather than duplicate that admirable bibliography, which provided me with an invaluable guide to the subject, I commend it to those who wish additional material on the subject.

The Wall Street Journal, of course, has been used for the chapter on conglomerates, while *The New York Times, New York Herald, New York Tribune* (and, of course, the *Herald Tribune* later on), *New York Journal*, and *New York World* were referred to for post-1860 manias. The *Rocky Mountain News* was explored for the Washoe and beef bonanzas, as was the *San Francisco Chronicle* for the former mania.

Chapter 1: The Vision of Vandalia

Abernethy, Thomas Perkins. *Western Lands and the American Revolution.* New York, 1959.

Alden, William B. *New Governments West of the Alleghenies Before 1780.* Madison, 1897.

Alvord, Clarence W. *The Illinois Country, 1673–1818.* Chicago, 1922.

———. *The Mississippi Valley in British Politics.* 2 vols. Cleveland, 1917.

Ambler, C. H. *George Washington and the West.* Chapel Hill, 1936.

Ashton, John. *Old Times: A Picture of Social Life at the End of the Eighteenth Century.* London, 1885.

Bagehot, Walter. *Lombard Street.* London, 1873.

Bailey, Kenneth P. *The Ohio Company of Virginia and the Westward Movement, 1748–1792.* Glendale, Calif., 1939.

Bond, Beverley W. *The Foundations of Ohio.* Vol. I. Columbus, 1941.

Burton, Elizabeth. *The Pageant of Georgian England.* New York, 1967.

Cameron, Rondo, Crisp, Olga, Patrick, Hugh, and Tilly, Richard, eds. *Banking in the Early Stages of Industrialization.* New York, 1967.

Chazanof, William. *Joseph Ellicott and the Holland Land Company.* Syracuse, 1970.

Clark, Thomas. *Frontier America.* New York, 1969.

Cleland, Hugh. *George Washington in the Ohio Valley.* Pittsburgh, 1955.

Dyer, Albion M. *First Ownership of Ohio Lands.* Baltimore, 1969.

Erleigh, Viscount. *The South Sea Bubble.* New York, 1933.

Fernow, Berthold. *The Ohio Valley in Colonial Days.* Albany, 1890.

Fitzmaurice, Edmund. *Life of William, Earl of Shelburne.* Vols. 2 and 3. London, 1875–1876.

Gipson, Lawrence. *The British Empire Before the American Revolution.* Vol. XI. *The Triumphant Empire: The Rumbling of the Coming Storm.* New York, 1965.

Hale, John P. *Trans-Allegheny Pioneers.* Cincinnati, 1886.

Homer, Sidney. *A History of Interest Rates.* New Brunswick, 1963.

Imlay, George. *A Topographical Description of the Western Territory of North America, etc.* London, 1793.

James, Alfred P. *The Ohio Company: Its Inner History.* Pittsburgh, 1959.

Lester, William S. *The Transylvania Colony.* Spencer, Ind., 1935.

Lewis, George E. *The Indiana Company, 1763–1798: A Study in Eighteenth Century Frontier Land Speculation and Business Venture.* Glendale, Calif., 1941.

Livermore, Shaw. *Early American Land Companies: Their Influence on Corporate Development.* New York, 1939.

Lord, John. *Capital and Steam-Power, 1750–1800.* London, 1966.

Mantoux, Paul. *The Industrial Revolution in the Eighteenth Century.* New York, 1928.

Mershon, Stephen L. *English Crown Grants.* New York, 1918.

Mohr, Walter H. *Federal Indian Relations, 1774–1783.* Philadelphia, 1933.

Morgan, E. Victor, and Thomas, W. A. *The London Stock Exchange: Its History and Functions.* London, 1962.

Namier, Lewis. *England in the Age of the American Revolution.* London, 1963.

———. *The Structure of Politics at the Accession of George III.* 2 vols. London, 1929.

Pares, Richard. *King George III and the Politicians.* Oxford, 1953.

Paxton, Frederic L. *History of the American Frontier, 1763–1893.* New York, 1924.

Pound, Arthur, and Day, Richard E. *Johnson of the Mohawks.* New York, 1930.

Powell, Ellis T. *The Evolution of the Money Market, 1385–1915.* London, 1915.

Richards, R. D. *The Early History of Banking in England.* London, 1929.

Savelle, Max. *George Morgan: Colony Builder.* New York, 1932.

Smith, Warren H. *Horace Walpole: Writer, Politician, and Connoisseur.* London, 1967.

Sosin, Jack M. *The Revolutionary Frontier: 1763–1783.* New York, 1967.

———. *Whitehall and the Wilderness: The Middle West in British Colonial Policy, 1760–1775.* Lincoln, Nebr., 1961.

Steuart, A. F., ed. *The Last Journals of Horace Walpole During the Reign of George III from 1771–1783.* 2 vols. London, 1910.

Volwiler, Albert T. *George Croghan and the Westward Movement, 1741–1782.* Cleveland, 1926.

Wainwright, Nicholas B. *George Croghan: Wilderness Diplomat.* Chapel Hill, N.C., 1959.

Watson, John F. *Annals of Philadelphia and Pennsylvania, in the Olden Time.* I-II, Philadelphia, 1850.

Chapter 2: A Great National Project

Albion, Robert. *The Rise of New York Port, 1815–1860.* New York, 1939.

Ambler, Charles H. *George Washington and the West.* Chapel Hill, N.C., 1936.

———. *A History of Transportation in the Ohio Valley.* Glendale, Calif., 1932.

Andreades, A. *History of the Bank of England, 1640–1903.* London, 1924.

Beard, Charles A. *An Economic Interpretation of the Constitution of the United States.* New York, 1913.

Bogart, Ernest. *Internal Improvements and State Debt in Ohio.* New York, 1924.

Calhoun, Daniel H. *The American Civil Engineer: Origins and Conflict.* Cambridge, 1960.

Catterall, Ralph C. *The Second Bank of the United States.* Chicago, 1903.

Cawley, James, and Cawley, Margaret. *Along the Delaware and Raritan Canal.* Cranbury, 1970.

Davis, Joseph S. *Essays in the Earlier History of American Corporations.* 2 vols. Cambridge, 1917.

Dunbar, Seymour. *History of Travel in America.* New York, 1937.

Ellis, David. *Landlords and Farmers in the Hudson-Mohawk Region, 1790–1850.* New York, 1967.

Evans, Paul D. *The Holland Land Company.* Buffalo, 1924.

Flexner, James T. *George Washington and the New Nation, 1783–1793.* Boston, 1969.

Gilbart, James W. *The History of Banking in America.* London, 1837.

Goodrich, Carter, ed. *Canals and American Economic Development.* New York, 1961.

———. *Government Promotion of American Canals and Railroads, 1800–1890.* New York, 1960.

Gray, Ralph D. *The National Waterway: A History of the Chesapeake and Delaware Canal, 1769–1965.* Chicago, 1967.

Grayson, Theodore J. *Leaders and Periods of American Finance.* New York, 1932.

Hadfield, Charles. *British Canals: An Illustrated History.* London, 1950.

———. *The Canal Age.* New York, 1969.

Hammond, Bray. *Banks and Politics in America: From the Revolution to the Civil War.* Princeton, 1957.

Hidy, Ralph W. *The House of Baring in American Trade and Finance: 1763–1861.* Cambridge, Mass., 1949.

Howden Smith, Arthur D. *John Jacob Astor: Landlord of New York.* Philadelphia, 1929.

Huntington, C. C., and McClelland, C. P. *Ohio Canals, Their Construction Cost, Use, and Partial Abandonment.* Columbus, Ohio, 1905.

Jenks, Leland H. *The Migration of British Capital to 1875.* New York, 1938.

Klein, T. B. *The Canals of Pennsylvania and the System of Internal Improvements.* Harrisburg, Pa., 1901.

McGrane, Reginald C. *Foreign Bondholders and American State Debts.* New York, 1935.

Meade, Robert. *Patrick Henry: Practical Revolutionary.* New York, 1969.

Miller, Nathan. *The Enterprise of a Free People.* Ithaca, N.Y., 1962.

Moulton, Harold G. *Waterways Versus Railways.* Boston, 1926.

Myers, Margaret. *The New York Money Market.* New York, 1931.

North, C. Douglass. *The Economic Growth of the United States, 1790–1860.* New York, 1961.

Poor, Henry V. *Sketch of the Rise and Progress of Internal Improvements and of the Internal Commerce of the United States of America.* New York, 1881.

Porter, Kenneth W. *John Jacob Astor: Business Man.* Cambridge, Mass., 1931.

Rachlis, Eugene, and Marqusee, John. *The Land Lords.* New York, 1963.

Redlich, Fritz. *The Molding of American Banking: Men and Ideas.* 2 pts. New York, 1968.

Sakolski, A. M. *The Great American Land Bubble.* New York, 1932.

Sanderlin, Walter S. *The Great National Project: A History of the Chesapeake and Ohio Canal.* Baltimore, 1946.

Scheiber, Harry N. *Ohio Canal Era: A Case Study of Government and the Economy, 1820–1861.* Athens, Ohio, 1969.

Severence, Frank H., ed. *The Holland Land Company and the Erie Canal.* Buffalo, 1910.

Smith, Walter B. *Economic Aspects of the Second Bank of the United States.* Cambridge, Mass., 1953.

Tanner, Henry. *A Description of the Canals and Rail Roads of the United States.* New York, 1840.

Taylor, George R. *The Transportation Revolution, 1815–1860.* New York, 1951.

Treat, Payson J. *The National Land System, 1785–1820.* New York, 1910.

Chapter 3: Speculation in Slaves

Andrews, Ethan A. *Slavery and the Domestic Slave-Trade in the United States.* Boston, 1836.

Bancroft, Frederic. *Slave-Trading in the Old South.* Baltimore, 1931.

Bennett, Hugh H. *Soils and Agriculture of the Southern States.* New York, 1921.

Christy, David. *Cotton Is King, and Pro-Slavery Arguments.* Augusta, Ga., 1860.

Cohn, David L. *The Life and Times of King Cotton.* New York, 1956.

Coleman, J. Winston. *Slave Times in Kentucky.* Chapel Hill, N.C., 1940.

Collins, Winfield H. *The Domestic Slave Trade of the Southern States.* Port Washington, N.Y., 1904.

Conrad, Alfred, and Meyer, John. *The Economics of Slavery.* Chicago, 1964.

Cotterill, Robert. *The Old South.* Glendale, Calif., 1939.

De Bow, J. D. B. *Industrial Resources of the Southern and Western States.* 3 vols. New Orleans, 1852–1853.

Eaton, Clement. *The Growth of Southern Civilization, 1790–1860.* New York, 1961.

———. *A History of the Old South.* New York, 1966.

Elkins, Stanley. *Slavery.* Chicago, 1959.

Genovese, Eugene. *The Political Economy of Slavery.* New York, 1965.

Gray, Lewis C. *History of Agriculture in the Southern United States to 1860.* 2 vols. New York, 1941.

Hammond, Matthew B. *The Cotton Industry.* New York, 1897.

Jenkins, William S. *Pro-Slavery Thought in the Old South.* Chapel Hill, N.C., 1935.

Jordan, Weymouth. *Hugh Davis and His Alabama Plantation.* Montgomery, Ala., 1948.

Mooney, Chase. *Slavery in Tennessee.* Bloomington, Ind., 1957.

Moore, John H. *Agriculture in Ante-Bellum Mississippi.* New York, 1958.

Olmsted, Frederick L. *The Cotton Kingdom: A Traveller's Observations on Cotton and Slavery in the American Slave States.* New York, 1953 ed.

———. *A Journey in the Back Country.* New York, 1970 ed.

Parsons, C. G. *Inside View of Slavery.* Boston, 1855.

Phillips, Ulrich B. *American Negro Slavery: A Survey of the Supply, Employment and Control of Negro Labor as Determined by the Plantation Regime.* New York, 1918.

Stampp, Kenneth. *The Peculiar Institution.* New York, 1956.
Starobin, Robert S. *Industrial Slavery in the Old South.* New York, 1970.
Stephenson, Wendell H. *Isaac Franklin: Slave Trader and Planter of the Old South.* Baton Rouge, 1938.
Stowe, Harriet Beecher. *The Key to Uncle Tom's Cabin.* New York, 1968 ed.
Sydnor, Charles S. *Slavery in Mississippi.* Baton Rouge, 1966.
Taylor, Joe G. *Negro Slavery in Louisiana.* Baton Rouge, 1963.
Taylor, Orville W. *Negro Slavery in Arkansas.* Durham, N.C., 1958.
Taylor, Roser H. *Slaveholding in North Carolina: An Economic View.* Chapel Hill, N.C., 1926.
Woodman, Harold D. *King Cotton and His Retainers.* Lexington, Ky., 1968.
———, ed. *Slavery and the Southern Economy.* New York, 1966.

Chapter 4: The Comstock Lode
Altrocchi, Julia. *The Spectacular San Franciscans.* New York, 1949.
Angel, Myron. *History of Nevada, with Illustrations and Biographical Sketches of Its Prominent Men and Pioneers.* 1958 ed. Berkeley, Calif., 1958.
Becker, George. *Geology of the Comstock Lode and the Washoe District.* Washington, 1882.
Browne, J. Ross. *A Peep at Washoe and Washoe Revisited.* 1959 ed. Balboa Island, 1959.
Dana, Julian. *The Man Who Built San Francisco.* New York, 1936.
Fatout, Paul. *Mark Twain in Virginia City.* Bloomington, Ind., 1964.
Geismar, Maxwell. *Mark Twain: An American Prophet.* Boston, 1970.
Hawgood, John. *America's Western Frontiers.* New York, 1967.
Holmes, Eugenia. *Adolph Sutro: A Brief Story of a Brilliant Life.* San Francisco, 1895.
Hulse, James. *The Nevada Adventure.* Reno, 1969.
Johnson, Clifton. *Highways and Byways of the Rocky Mountains.* New York, 1910.
King, Joseph. *History of the San Francisco Stock and Exchange Board.* San Francisco, 1910.
Lavender, David. *The Rockies.* New York, 1968.
Lewis, Oscar. *Silver Kings: The Life and Times of Mackay, Fair, Flood and O'Brien.* New York, 1947.

Lillard, Richard. *Desert Challenge: An Interpretation of Nevada.* New York, 1949.

Lord, Eliot. *Comstock Mining and Miners.* Washington, 1883.

Lyman, Richard. *Ralston's Ring: California Plunders the Comstock Lode.* New York, 1955.

———. *The Saga of the Comstock Lode.* New York, 1934.

Older, Fremont, and Older, Cora. *The Life of George Hearst, California Pioneer.* San Francisco, 1933.

Ostrander, Gilman. *Nevada: The Great Rotten Borough, 1859–1964.* New York, 1966.

Paul, Rodman. *Mining Frontiers of the Far West, 1848–1964.* New York, 1963.

Phelps, Alonzo, ed. *Contemporary Biographies of California's Representative Men.* 2 vols. San Francisco, 1881–1882.

Rickard, Thomas. *A History of American Mining.* New York, 1932.

Shinn, Charles. *The Story of the Mine, as Illustrated by the Great Comstock Lode of Nevada.* New York, 1896.

Smith, Grant. *The History of the Comstock Lode, 1850–1920.* Reno, 1943.

Spence, Clark. *Mining Engineers and the American West.* New Haven, Conn., 1970.

Stone, Irving. *Men to Match My Mountains, The Opening of the Far West, 1840–1900.* New York, 1956.

Twain, Mark. *Roughing It.* 1913 ed. New York, 1913.

Wright, William (Dan De Quille). *The Big Bonanza: An Authentic Account of the Discovery, History, and Working of the World-Renowned Comstock Lode of Nevada.* Intro. by Oscar Lewis. 1947 ed. New York, 1947.

Chapter 5: Beef Bonanza

Arrington, Leonard. *The Changing Economic Structure of the Mountain West, 1850–1950.* Logan, Utah, 1963.

Athearn, Robert. *High Country Empire.* New York, 1960.

Bartlett, Richard. *Great Surveys of the American West.* Norman, Okla., 1962.

Bray, Charles. *Financing the Western Cattle Industry.* Fort Collins, Colo., 1928.

Brisbin, James. *The Beef Bonanza; or, How to Get Rich on the Plains.* 1959 ed. Norman, Okla., 1959.

Burton, Harley. *A History of the J.A. Ranch.* Austin, 1927.

Clay, John. *My Life on the Range.* 1962 ed. Norman, Okla., 1962.

Coburn, Walt. *Pioneer Cattleman in Montana: The Story of the Circle C Ranch.* Norman, Okla., 1968.

Craig, John. *Ranching with Lords and Commons.* Toronto, 1903.

Dale, Edward E. *Cow Country.* Norman, Okla., 1942.

———. *The Range Cattle Industry: Ranching in the Great Plains from 1865 to 1925.* Norman, Okla., 1930.

Dobie, J. Frank. *The Longhorns.* New York, 1941.

Dodge, Richard. *The Plains of the Great West and Their Inhabitants.* 1959 ed. New York, 1959.

Dykstra, Robert. *The Cattle Towns.* New York, 1968.

Fletcher, Baylis. *Up the Trail in '79.* Norman, Okla., 1968.

Fletcher, Robert. *Free Grass to Fences, the Montana Cattle Range Story.* New York, 1960.

———. *Organization of the Range Cattle Business in Eastern Montana.* Bozeman, Mont., 1932.

Fowler, Bertram. *Men, Meat, and Miracles.* New York, 1952.

Gard, Wayne. *The Chisholm Trail.* Norman, Okla., 1954.

Gressley, Gene. *Bankers and Cattlemen.* New York, 1966.

Hagedorn, Hermann. *Roosevelt in the Bad Lands.* New York, 1921.

Hale, Will. *Twenty-four Years a Cowboy and Ranchman in Southern Texas and New Mexico.* Norman, Okla., 1959.

Haley, V. Evetts. *The XIT Ranch of Texas and the Early Days of the Llano Estacado.* 1953 ed. Norman, Okla., 1953.

Holden, W. C. *The Spur Ranch.* Boston, 1934.

Hopkins, John, Jr. *Economic History of the Production of Beef Cattle in Iowa.* Iowa City, 1928.

Jackson, W. Turrentine. *The Enterprising Scot: Investors in the American West After 1873.* Edinburgh, 1968.

———, Frink, Maurice, and Spring, Agnes. *When Grass Was King.* Boulder, Colo., 1956.

James, Will. *Lone Cowboy.* New York, 1930.

Larmer, Forrest. *Financing the Livestock Industry.* New York, 1926.

Lea, Tom. *The King Ranch.* 2 vols. Boston, 1957.

McCoy, Joseph. *Cattle Trade of the West and Southwest.* Kansas City, 1874.

Mackenzie, Agnes. *Scotland in Modern Times, 1720–1939.* London, 1941.

Marwick, W. H. *Economic Developments in Victorian Scotland.* London, 1939.

Mothershead, Harmon. *The Swan Land and Cattle Company, Ltd.* Norman, Okla., 1971.

Nevins, Allan. *Grover Cleveland: A Study in Courage.* New York, 1964.

Nordyke, Lewis. *Cattle Empire, the Fabulous Story of the 3,000,000 Acre XIT.* New York, 1949.

———. *Great Roundup: The Story of Texas and Southwestern Cowmen.* New York, 1955.

Osgood, Ernest. *The Day of the Cattleman.* Minneapolis, 1929.

Payne, Peter, ed. *Studies in Scottish Business History.* London, 1967.

Peake, Ora. *The Colorado Range Cattle Industry.* Glendale, Calif., 1937.

Pearce, W. M. *The Matador Land and Cattle Company.* Norman, Okla., 1964.

Pelzer, Louis. *The Cattlemen's Frontier.* Glendale, Calif., 1936.

Putnam, Carleton. *Theodore Roosevelt.* Vol. I, *The Formative Years, 1858–1886.* New York, 1958.

Quiett, Glenn C. *They Built the West.* New York, 1934.

Richthofen, Walter, Baron von. *Cattle-Raising on the Plains of North America.* 1964 ed. Norman, Okla., 1964.

Sandoz, Mari. *The Cattlemen.* New York, 1958.

Sharp, Paul. *Whoop-Up Country.* Minneapolis, 1955.

Smythe, William. *The Conquest of Arid America.* New York, 1899.

Spence, Clark. *British Investments and the American Mining Frontier, 1860–1901.* Ithaca, N.Y., 1958.

Stewart, Edgar, ed. *Penny-an-Acre Empire in the West.* Norman, Okla., 1968.

Streeter, Floyd. *Prairie Trails and Cow Towns.* New York, 1963.

Tait, J. S. *The Cattle Fields of the Far West.* London, 1884.

Towne, Charles, and Wentworth, Edward. *Cattle and Men.* Norman, Okla., 1955.

Wagoner, J. J. *History of the Cattle Industry in Southern Arizona, 1540–1940.* Tucson, 1952.

Webb, Walter. *The Great Plains.* Boston, 1931.

Yost, Nellie, ed. *Boss Cowman: The Recollections of Ed Lemmon, 1857–1946.* Lincoln, Neb., 1969.

Chapter 6: The Steel Millionaires

Allen, Frederick Lewis. *The Lords of Creation.* New York, 1935.

Baker, Charles. *Monopolies and the People.* New York, 1899.

Basset, William. *Operating Aspects of Industrial Mergers.* New York, 1930.

Beebe, Lucius. *The Big Spenders.* New York, 1966.

Bridge, J. H. *The Inside Story of the Carnegie Steel Company.* New York, 1903.

Bridges, Hal. *Iron Millionaire: Life of Charlemagne Tower.* Philadelphia, 1952.

Burns, Arthur. *Production Trends in the United States Since 1870.* New York, 1934.

Carnegie, Andrew. *Autobiography of Andrew Carnegie.* Boston, 1920.

———. *Empire of Business.* Buffalo, 1907.

Carosso, Vincent. *Investment Banking in America.* Cambridge, Mass., 1970.

Casson, Herbert. *The Romance of Steel.* New York, 1907.

Cotter, Arundel. *The Authentic History of the United States Steel Corporation.* New York, 1916.

———. *United States Steel: A Corporation with a Soul.* New York, 1921.

Dewing, Arthur. *Corporate Promotions and Reorganizations.* Cambridge, Mass., 1924.

Edwards, George. *The Evolution of Finance Capitalism.* New York, 1938.

Ely, Richard. *Monopolies and Trusts.* New York, 1912.

Evans, Henry. *Iron Pioneer: Henry W. Oliver, 1840–1904.* New York, 1942.

Faulkner, Harold U. *The Decline of Laissez Faire, 1897–1917.* New York, 1951.

Fetter, Frank. *The Masquerade of Monopoly.* New York, 1931.

Hacker, Louis. *The Triumph of American Capitalism.* New York, 1940.

Harvey, George. *Henry Clay Frick: The Man.* New York, 1936.

Hatcher, Harlan. *A Century of Iron and Men.* New York, 1950.

Hendrick, Burton. *The Age of Big Business.* New Haven, 1919.

———. *The Life of Andrew Carnegie.* 2 vols. New York, 1932.

Hidy, Ralph, and Hidy, Muriel. *Pioneering in Big Business, 1882–1911.* New York, 1955.

Hoffmann, Charles. *The Depression of the Nineties.* Westport, Conn., 1970.

Holbrook, Stewart. *The Age of the Moguls.* New York, 1953.
———. *Iron Brew: A Century of American Ore and Steel.* New York, 1939.
Hoyt, Edwin. *The House of Morgan.* New York, 1966.
Hughes, Jonathan. *The Vital Few: American Economic Progress and Its Protagonists.* Boston, 1966.
Jenks, Jeremiah, and Clark, Walter. *The Trust Problem.* New York, 1929.
Jones, Eliot. *The Trust Problem in the United States.* New York, 1921.
Josephson, Matthew. *The Robber Barons: The Great American Capitalists, 1861–1901.* New York, 1934.
Kirkland, Edward. *Industry Comes of Age, 1860–1897.* New York, 1962.
Kolko, Gabriel. *The Triumph of Conservatism.* New York, 1963.
Lundberg, Ferdinand. *America's 60 Families.* New York, 1937.
McCarthy, George. *Acquisitions and Mergers.* New York, 1963.
Maurer, Herrymon. *Great Enterprise: Growth and Behavior of the Big Corporation.* New York, 1955.
Moody, John. *The Masters of Capital.* New Haven, Conn., 1921.
Morell, Parker. *Diamond Jim: The Life and Times of James Buchanan Brady.* New York, 1934.
Myers, Gustavus. *History of the Great American Fortunes.* New York, 1907.
National Industrial Conference Board. *Mergers and the Law.* New York, 1929.
———. *Mergers in Industry.* New York, 1929.
Nelson, Ralph. *Merger Movements in American Industry, 1895–1956.* Princeton, N.J., 1959.
Nevins, Allan. *Abram S. Hewitt, With Some Account of Peter Cooper.* New York, 1935.
Noyes, Alexander. *Forty Years of American Finance.* New York, 1909.
Nutter, G. Warren, and Einhorn, Henry. *Enterprise Monopoly in the United States, 1899–1958.* New York, 1969.
Poor's Railroad Manual Co. *Poor's Manual of Industrials, 1910.* New York, 1910.
Reid, Samuel. *Mergers, Managers, and the Economy.* New York, 1968.
Ripley, William Z. *Trusts, Pools and Corporations.* Boston, 1905.
Satterlee, Herbert. *J. Pierpont Morgan: An Intimate Portrait.* New York, 1939.
Seligman, Ben. *Business and Businessmen in American History.* New York, 1971.

Stevens, William. *Industrial Combinations and Trusts.* New York, 1922.
Tarbell, Ida. *The Life of Elbert H. Gary.* New York, 1933.
Temin, Peter. *Iron and Steel in Nineteenth-Century America.* Cambridge, Mass., 1964.
United States. Commissioner of Corporations. *Report on the Steel Industry.* Pt. I, *Organization, Investment, Profits, and Position of United States Steel Corporation, July 1, 1911;* pt. II, *Cost of Production, Preliminary Report, January 22, 1912;* pt. III, *Cost of Production, Full Report, May 6, 1913.* Washington, D.C., 1911–1913.
———. Congress. House of Representatives. House Report No. 1127. *Hearings Before the Committee on Investigation of United States Steel Corporation.* 62nd Cong., 2nd sess. Washington, D.C., 1911.
Walker, J. Bernard. *The Story of Steel.* New York, 1926.
Wall, Joseph F. *Andrew Carnegie.* New York, 1970.
Warshow, Robert. *Bet-A-Million Gates.* New York, 1932.
Wendt, Lloyd, and Kogan, Herman. *Bet A Million! The Story of John W. Gates.* New York, 1948.
Wilgus, H. L. *A Study of the United States Steel Corporation in Its Industrial and Legal Aspects.* New York, 1901.
Winkler, John. *Morgan the Magnificent.* New York, 1932.

Chapter 7: Spindletop

American Association of Petroleum Geologists. *Structure of Typical American Oil Fields.* II, 1929. Tulsa, 1950.
American Guide Series. Harry Hansen, ed. *Texas: A Guide to the Lone Star State.* New York, 1969.
Ball, Max. *This Fascinating Oil Business.* New York, 1940.
Beaton, Kendall. *Enterprise in Oil: A History of Shell in the United States.* New York, 1957.
Boatright, Mody. *Folklore of the Oil Industry.* Dallas, 1963.
———, and Owens, William. *Tales from the Derrick Floor.* New York, 1970.
Clark, J. Stanley. *The Oil Century.* Norman, Okla., 1958.
Clark, James, and Halbouty, Michel. *Spindletop.* New York, 1952.
Connelly, W. L. *The Oil Business As I Saw It.* Norman, Okla., 1954.
Cotner, Robert. *James Stephen Hogg: A Biography.* Austin, 1959.
De Chazeau, Melvin, and Kahn, Alfred. *Integration and Competition in the Petroleum Industry.* New Haven, Conn., 1959.

Finty, Tom, Jr. *Anti-Trust Legislation in Texas.* Dallas, 1916.
Halbouty, Michel. *Salt Domes: Gulf Region, United States & Mexico.* Houston, 1967.
Harvard Graduate School of Business Administration. *Oil's First Century.* Cambridge, Mass., 1960.
Henriques, Robert. *Bearsted: A Biography of Marcus Samuel.* New York, 1960.
Hidy, Ralph, and Hidy, Muriel. *History of the Standard Oil Company (New Jersey): Pioneering in Big Business, 1882–1911.* New York, 1955.
Holbrook, Stewart. *The Age of the Moguls.* Garden City, N.Y., 1954.
James, Marquis. *The Texas Story: The First Fifty Years.* New York, 1953.
Johnson, Arthur. *The Development of American Petroleum Pipelines: A Study in Private Enterprise and Public Policy, 1862—1906.* Ithaca, N.Y., 1956.
King, John. *Joseph Stephen Cullinan.* Nashville, 1970.
Knowles, Ruth. *The Greatest Gamblers.* New York, 1959.
Kolko, Gabriel. *The Triumph of Conservatism.* New York, 1963.
Landes, Kenneth. *Petroleum Geology.* New York, 1959.
Larson, Henrietta, and Porter, Kenneth W. *History of Humble Oil and Refining Company: A Study in Industrial Growth.* New York, 1959.
Leven, David. *Done in Oil.* New York, 1941.
McLean, John, and Haigh, Robert. *The Growth of Integrated Oil Companies.* Cambridge, Mass., 1954.
Marcosson, Isaac. *The Black Golconda.* New York, 1924.
Nash, Gerald. *United States Oil Policy, 1890–1964.* Pittsburgh, 1968.
Nevins, Allan. *John D. Rockefeller.* 2 vols. New York, 1940.
O'Connor, Harvey. *The Empire of Oil.* New York, 1955.
———. *Mellon's Millions.* New York, 1933.
O'Connor, Richard. *The Oil Barons.* Boston, 1971.
Rister, Carl. *Oil! Titan of the Southwest.* Norman, Okla., 1949.
Spence, Hartzell. *Portrait in Oil: How the Ohio Oil Company Grew to Become Marathon.* New York, 1962.
Taylor, Frank, and Welty, Earl. *Black Bonanza: How an Oil Hunt Grew Into the Union Oil Company of California.* New York, 1950.
Thompson, Craig. *Since Spindletop: A Human Story of Gulf's First Half-Century.* Pittsburgh, 1951.
Tugendhat, Christopher. *Oil: The Biggest Business.* New York, 1968.

United States. Bureau of Corporations. *Report of the Commissioner of Corporations on the Petroleum Industry.* Pt. I, *Position of the Standard Oil Company in the Petroleum Industry;* pt. II, *Prices and Profits.* Washington, D.C., 1907.

Warner, Charles. *Texas Oil and Gas Since 1543.* Houston, 1939.

Warshow, Robert. *Bet-A-Million Gates.* New York, 1932.

Wendt, Lloyd, and Kogan, Herman. *Bet A Million! The Story of John W. Gates.* New York, 1948.

Williamson, Harold F., and Daum, Arnold R. *The American Petroleum Industry: The Age of Illumination, 1859–1899.* Evanston, Ill., 1959.

———, Andreano, Ralph, Daum, Arnold, and Klose, Gilbert. *The American Petroleum Industry: The Age of Energy, 1899–1959.* Evanston, Ill., 1963.

Chapter 8: The Great Florida Boom

Allen, Frederick Lewis. *Only Yesterday.* New York, 1931.

American National Red Cross. *The Florida Hurricane: September 18, 1926.* Washington, 1929.

Amory, Cleveland. *The Last Resorts.* New York, 1948.

Babson, Roger. *Actions and Reactions.* New York, 1935.

Barbour, Ralph. *Let's Go to Florida.* New York, 1926.

Coletta, Paolo. *William Jennings Bryan.* Vol. III, *Political Puritan, 1915–1925.* Lincoln, Nebr., 1969.

Fox, Charles D. *The Truth About Florida.* New York, 1925.

Grey, Robert. *The Power and the Glory: Some Tinsel Also.* Tallahassee, Fla., 1965.

Grismer, Karl. *The Story of St. Petersburg.* St. Petersburg, Fla., 1948.

Hopkins, James. *Fifty Years of Citrus: The Florida Citrus Exchange, 1909–1959.* Gainesville, 1960.

Jahoda, Gloria. *The Other Florida.* New York, 1967.

James, Marquis. *Alfred I. Du Pont: The Family Rebel.* Indianapolis, 1941.

Johnston, Alva. *The Legendary Mizners.* New York, 1953.

Lummus, John. *The Miracle of Miami Beach.* Miami, 1940.

Martin, Sidney. *Florida's Flagler.* Athens, Ga., 1949.

Mayo, Nathan. *Florida: An Advancing State.* St. Petersburg, Fla., 1928.

Muir, Helen. *Miami, U.S.A.* New York, 1953.

Nash, Charles. *The Magic of Miami Beach.* Philadelphia, 1938.

Rachlis, Eugene, and Marqusee, John. *The Land Lords.* New York, 1963.

"Rambler." *Guide To Florida* (1875 edition). Gainesville, Fla., 1964.
Redford, Polly. *Billion Dollar Sandbar: A Biography of Miami Beach.* New York, 1970.
Roberts, Kenneth. *Florida.* New York, 1926.
———. *Sun Hunting.* Indianapolis, 1922.
Sakolski, A. M. *The Great American Land Bubble.* New York, 1932.
Sessa, Frank. *Real Estate Expansion and Boom in Miami Beach and Its Environs During the 1920's.* Unpublished Ph.D. dissertation, University of Pittsburgh, 1950.
Small, John. *Eden to Sahara: Florida's Tragedy.* Lancaster, Pa., 1929.
Sullivan, Mark. *Our Times, The United States, 1900–1925.* Vol. VI, *The Twenties.* New York, 1935.
Tebeau, Charlton. *A History of Florida.* Coral Gables, Fla., 1971.
Weigall, Theyre. *Boom in Paradise.* New York, 1932.

Articles

Babson, Roger. "Florida's Future." *Review of Reviews,* November 1925.
Cason, N. H. "The New Florida." *Munsey's Magazine,* February 1909.
Chamberlain, Lucy. "Behind the Boom in Florida." *Survey,* February 1, 1926.
"D.R." "The Blue Sky's the Limit." *Independent,* January 23, 1926.
Jordan, John. "What's Left in Florida." *World's Work,* September 1926.
McCullagh, Francis. "Miami." *Nineteenth Century,* February 1926.
Payne, Will. "Capturing the Simple Life; or, the Boom in Florida." *The Saturday Evening Post,* June 20, 1925.
Rukeyser, M. S. "Is Florida Coming Back?" *World's Work,* March 28, 1926.
Shelby, Gertrude. "The Crisis of Florida Fever." *Outlook,* May 5, 1926.
Stockbridge, Frank. "The Florida Rush of 1925." *Current History Magazine, New York Times,* November 1925.
Tindall, George. "The Bubble in the Sun." *American Heritage,* August 1965.
Townsend, Reginald. "The Gold Rush to Florida." *World's Work,* June 1925.
Vanderblue, Homer. "The Florida Land Boom." *Journal of Land and Public Utility Economics,* May 1927.
"Human Flotsam of the Florida Hurricane." *Literary Digest,* October 9, 1926.

"Thrills and Humors of Florida's 'Gold Rush.' " *Literary Digest*, June 20, 1926.

Chapter 9: Conglomeritis

Alberts, William, and Segall, Joel. *The Corporate Merger.* Chicago, 1966.

Ansoff, H. Igor, Brandenburg, Richard, Portner, Fred, and Radosevich, Raymond. *Acquisition Behavior of U.S. Manufacturing Firms, 1945–1965. Nashville, 1971.*

Asch, Peter. *Economic Theory and the Antitrust Dilemma.* New York, 1970.

Barber, Richard. *The American Corporation.* New York, 1970.

Barmash, Isadore. *Welcome to Our Conglomerate—You're Fired!* New York, 1971.

Butters, J. Keith, Lintner, John, and Cary, William. *Effects of Taxation on Corporate Mergers.* Boston, 1951.

Chandler, Alfred D., Jr. *Strategy and Structure.* Cambridge, Mass., 1962.

Crum, William. *Corporate Size and Earning Power.* Cambridge, Mass., 1939.

Donaldson, Gordon. *Corporate Debt Capacity.* Cambridge, Mass., 1961.

Drayton, Clarence, Jr. *Mergers and Acquisitions: Planning and Action.* New York, 1963.

Evans, George, Jr. *Business Incorporations in the United States, 1800–1943.* New York, 1948.

Fortune. The Conglomerate Commotion. New York, 1970.

Garoian, Leon, ed. *Economics of Conglomerate Growth.* Corvallis, Oreg., 1969.

Gilbert, Charles, ed. *The Making of a Conglomerate.* Hempstead, N.Y., 1972.

Gort, Michael. *Diversification and Integration in American Industry.* Princeton, N.J., 1962.

Gorman, Joseph. *Kefauver: A Political Biography.* New York, 1971.

Hacker, Andrew, ed. *The Corporation Take-Over.* New York, 1964.

Hennessy, J. H., Jr. *Acquiring and Merging Businesses.* New York, 1966.

Kelley, Aemon. *The Profitability of Growth Through Merger.* New York, 1967.

Kefauver, Estes. *In a Few Hands.* New York, 1965.

Kripke, Homer, ed. *Conglomerates and Congenerics.* New York, 1969.

Lynch, Harry. *Financial Performance of Conglomerates.* Boston, 1971.

Nelson, Ralph. *Merger Movements in American Industry, 1895–1956.* Princeton, N.J., 1959.

Nutter, G. Warren, and Einhorn, Henry. *Enterprise Monopoly in the United States: 1899–1958.* New York, 1969.

Sauerhaft, Stan. *The Merger Game.* New York, 1971.

St. John's Law Review. Conglomerate Mergers and Acquisitions: Opinion and Analysis. New York, Spring 1970.

Trebling, Harry. *The Corporation in the American Economy.* New York, 1970.

United States. Federal Trade Commission. *Report of the Federal Trade Commission on the Merger Movement.* Washington, D.C., 1948.

———. Federal Trade Commission. *Report of the Federal Trade Commission on Corporate Mergers and Acquisitions.* Washington, D.C., 1955.

———. House of Representatives. House Report No. 2337. *Report of the Securities and Exchange Commission on the Public Policy Implications of Investment Company Growth.* 89th Cong., 2nd Sess., 1966.

———. House of Representatives. Committee on Ways and Means. *Summary of Testimony on Corporate Mergers at Public Hearings, February 18–April 24, 1969, on the Subject of Tax Reform.* 91st Cong., 1st Sess., 1969.

———. Senate. Committee on the Judiciary. *Hearings Before the Subcommittee on Anti-Trust and Monopoly.* 89th Cong., 1st Sess., 1965.

Vance, Stanley. *Managers in the Conglomerate Era.* New York, 1971.

Weston, J. Fred, and Peltzman, Sam, eds. *Public Policy Toward Mergers.* Pacific Palisades, Calif., 1969.

Journals

Barron's

Business Week

Commercial & Financial Chronicle

Dun's Review

Economist

Financial Chronicle

Financial Executive

Forbes

Fortune

Harvard Business Review

Harvard Law Review
Iron Age
Journal of Accounting
Newsweek
Quarterly Review of Economics and Business
Time
U.S. News & World Report

Index

Abandoned mines, stock shares in, 121–122
Aberdeen, earl of, 159
Abilene, Kan., 137, 139–140
Abolitionism, 71, 73, 96, 99, 100
Abraham, Chief, 20
Adams, John, 40
Adams, John Quincy, 42, 63, 177
Adams, Samuel, 22
Adler Electronics, Inc., 323
Advance Data Systems, 323
Aero Service Corporation, 323
Ahrent Instruments Company, 321–322
Airlie, earl of, 155
Airton Company, 322
Alabama, 251
 slavery, 70, 81
Alaska Gold Rush, 285–288
Albany, N.Y., 45, 47, 50–51, 147, 178
Albany-Erie Canal, 47–48
Albany Iron Works, 178
Alexander III, Czar, 129
Alexandria, Va., 87, 88
Alger, Horatio, 276, 288, 359
Allen Hollender Company, 324
Allied Chemical Company, 328
Allied Industries, 337
Alpha-Omega Company, 355
Alta Californian (newspaper), 110, 117
Altec Companies, 341
Alton Beach, Fla., 268
Alton Canteen Company, 337
Aluminum Company of America (ALCOA), 208, 304
Alvey Furguson Company, 323
American Airlines, 307
American Beef Packers, 77
American Book Company, 324
American Bridge Company, 193
American Broadcasting Corporation, 336
American Building Services, 337
American Car & Foundry Company, 193
American Cattle Company, 156
American Central Manufacturing, 307
American Colonies, *see* Colonial period
American Electric Manufacturing, 337
American Export Company, 326
American Gasoline Company, 241
American-Hawaiian Steamship Company, 243
American Home Products Corporation, 313
American House & Window Company, 337
American Iron & Steel Manufacturing Company, 193
American Machine & Foundry Company, 328
American Revolution, 15, 30, 32, 43, 45, 358
American Sheet Steel Company, 191, 192, 193
American Steel & Wire Company of New Jersey, 188, 190, 191, 192, 193, 196, 198
American Steel and Wire of Illinois, 188, 193
American Steel Hoop Company, 191, 192, 193
American Telephone & Telegraph (AT&T), 334

American Tin Plate Company, 191, 192, 193
American Woolen Corporation, 315
Ames, Joseph, 148
Amherst, Lord Jeffrey, 8–9
Analogue Controls Company, 323
Andreano, Ralph L., 248
Andrews, Samuel, 212
Angelina County (Texas), 220
Anglo-American Cattle Company, 155
Anglo-American Oil Company, 239
Annapolis Conference of 1786, 39
Ansoff, H. Igor, 300
Anthrax (cattle disease), 149
Applied Communications Systems, 323
Arapaho Indians, 138
Archbold, John D., 220, 221, 238
Argentite, 100
Arkansas Company, 160, 161, 170
Armfield, John, 86–87, 89
Armour & Company, 328, 331
Arnold, Thurman, 304
Arthur, Chester A., 162
Ash, Roy, 319, 325, 326, 327, 331
Astor, John Jacob, 51, 59
Atlantic Monthly, 216
Atlantic Rayon Company, 313
Atwood, Melville, 106
Auction Lunch Counter (San Francisco), 126–127
Austin, Texas, 159
Austrian Naval Academy, 227
Austro-Hungarian Empire, 218, 227
Authentic History of the United States Steel Corporation (Cotter), 200
Automatic Sereograph Company, 322
Automobiles, 266
  number registered (1907), 233
  production of, 271
Avco Manufacturing Company, 307–308, 351

Babcock, Amos, 159
Babson, Roger, 292
Bachmann Uxbridge Worsted Corporation, 315
Bacon, Robert, 197
Baker's Haulover Cut (Florida), 270–271
Baku oil fields (Russis), 217–218
Ballard, Rice C., 86, 89
Ballard & Company (R.C.), 87
Ballard, Franklin & Company, 86, 89
Baltimore & Ohio Canal, 66
Baltimore & Ohio Railroad, 55, 64, 66
B. & O. Railroad bonds, 66
Bancroft, Frederic, 96–97
Bank of California, 123, 124, 125, 130
  reorganized, 130
Bank of Nevada, 130
Bank of the United States, 60, 65
  end of, 62
  opposition to, 61
Barbed wire fences, 138–139
Baring Brothers, 51, 59, 65, 66
Barron's (publication), 325
Bayard, William, 50
Baynton, Wharton & Morgan, 12, 13, 16, 20
Beaumont, Texas, 224–233, 234, 241, 243, 245
Beaumont Stock Exchange, 232
Beckett, Hugh, 159
Beebe, Lucius, 201, 202
Beef Bonanza, The: How to Get Rich on the Plains (Brisbin), 142
Behn, Sosthenes, 333–334
Belcher Company, 121
Belmont, August, 110
Bendix Company, 328
Bendix Home Appliances, 307
Berrien, John, 97
Bessemer Steamship Company, 194–195
Bessemer Steel Association, 185
Bessemer steel process, 177, 178, 179, 180, 181, 212
Bethlehem, Pa., 178
Bethlehem Iron Company, 178
Bethlehem Steel Company, 185, 206
Bevan, David, 50
Beveridge, Albert, 266
Big business, reformers of, 301–302
Big Bonanza, The (Wright), 129
Biggs, Asa, 97
Big Spenders, The (Beebe), 202
Binder boys, 288–289, 294
Bingham, Gladys, 226
Biscayne Bay, 258, 259, 263, 264, 265, 267, 269, 287, 292
Bishop, John, 103
Blaine, James, 162
Bliss Company (F.W.), 331
Bluhdorn, Charles, 329–33, 335, 339, 346, 347, 359
Board of Trade (London), 11, 13–14, 15, 23, 26–27, 149, 175
Boca Raton, Fla., 286–287, 293
Bolshevism, 278
Book value, concept of, 199
Boone, Daniel, 9
Bootlegging industry, 280–281
Borg-Warner Corporation, 327, 328
Boston, 40, 55, 144, 148, 298
Boston Stock Exchange, 192
Boston Tea Party, 29
Bouquet, Henry, 15
Bozeman, Mont., 105

Brady, James B. "Diamond Jim," 202
Brandeis, Louis, 302
Brandon Bank (Georgia), 77–78
Braniff Airways, 344, 345, 348, 353
Breakers, The (hotel), 257
Brickell, W. B., 258
Brisbin, General James S., 142, 144, 146
British Economic Growth, 1688–1867, Trends and Structure (Dean and Cole), 3
British Empire, 150
British Investment and the American Mining Frontier, 1860–1901 (Spence), 157
British Linen Company Bank, 158
Brown, Ethan Allen, 58
Brown Company, 331–332
Bruder & Company, 323
Brush, J. L., 143
Bryan, William Jennings, 190, 207, 289
  "Cross of Gold" speech, 175
Bubble Act of 1720, 4
Buchanan, James, 66, 112
Budge, Hamer, 352
Buffalo, N.Y., 45, 48, 52
Buffalo range (in the West), 138, 145
Bullion Company, 121
Bureau of Corporations, 198
Burkart Manufacturing Company (F.), 315
Burning Moscow Company, 120–121
Burton Crescent Corporation, 324
Business Equipment Holdings Ltd., 324
Byrd, Richard Willing, 82

C. & O. Canal, 64, 66
Calderhead, William, 97
Calhoun, John C., 97
California, 136, 279
  gold rush, 99–100, 101, 102, 106, 116, 137
  oil fields, 220, 246
California Mining Company, 128, 129, 133
Cambria Iron Works, 178
Cambria Steel Company, 182, 185, 206
Campbell, Walter L., 95–96
Campbells (B.M. & W.L.), 95–96
Canada, 218
Canal Fund, 51
Canal transportation, 33–68, 70, 177, 207
  benefits of, 67
  debts, 64–66
  farmers and, 40, 45, 53
  Gallatin's *Report on Roads and Canals*, 41–42, 43
  government financing of, 41–42, 43
  maintenance and repairs, 63
  mileage (1850), 67
  Potomac venture, 36–40, 42, 54, 68
  securities markets and, 55, 68
  slave labor, 77
  technology, 38, 48, 63
  turnpike system, 40, 42, 48, 61, 63
  Watson's proposal for, 46–47, 48, 49
  in western New York, 43–53
  westward movement and, 55, 60
  See also names of canals
Canteen Corporation, 337
Cape of Good Hope, 100
Capitalist ethic, xiv, 276
Capitol Freehold Land and Investment Company Limited, 159–160
Carey, Mathew, 53
Carnegie, Andrew, 179–190, 192–198, 202, 204–205, 207, 208, 211, 212, 214, 216, 236, 276, 297, 359
Carnegie, Thomas, 182
Carnegie Brothers & Company, 181–182, 186
  profits of, 182, 183
Carnegie Company, 197–198
Carnegie Company of New Jersey, 196
Carnegie, McCandless & Company, 181
Carnegie, Phipps & Company, 183
Carnegie Steel Company, 186–187, 194, 196, 202, 205, 209
Carson City, 105, 111
Carson Valley, 101
Carter, Robert, 11
Caspian & Black Sea Company, 218
Casson, Herbert, 182, 200
Cattle industry, 134–172, 207
  beef prices, 136–137, 139, 140, 165–166, 171, 174
  blizzard of 1886, 166–169
  boom of 1880's, 154–156
  buffalo ranges, 138
  company shares (1886–87), 170
  company statistics, 160, 170
  Eastern investments in, 145, 157–158
  epidemic of 1867, 139
  exports, 150
  farmers and, 138–139, 155, 164
  foreign investors in, 149–163, 171
  Indian wars, 137–138, 145, 163
  joint-stock companies, 148–149, 153
  partnership ventures, 147–148
  price decline, 165–166
  railroads and, 137, 141–143, 154, 165
  ranch foreclosures, 170
  Rosenbaum's aid to, 171
  sheepmen and, 163
  steer population, 135, 136
  types of speculation in, 158
Cattle Raising on the Plains of North America (Richthofen), 164
Cattle Ranche Company, 160

Catts, Sidney, 272, 273
Cavalier, J. B. E., 118
Cayuga Indians, 20
Cazenove, Theophile, 44, 45
Celler-Kefauver Act, 311–312, 349
Census of 1920, 278–279
Central Pacific Railroad, 114, 137
Century Boulevard Corporation, 323
Chainveyer Company, 324
Chance Vought Company, 341
Chandler, Alfred D., Jr., 308
Change Alley, 4
Charleston, S.C., 251, 252
Charleston & Savannah Railroad, 78
Charleston Mercury, 94
Charlotte, Queen, 27
Chenaugheata, Chief, 20
Cherokee Indians, 137
Chesapeake & Ohio Canal, 54
  cost of, 63
Chesapeake and Ohio Canal Company, 42
Cheves, Langdon, 51
Cheyenne, Wyo., 148, 156–157
Cheyenne Club, 156–157
Cheyenne Indians, 138
Chicago, 61–62, 135, 136, 144, 145, 149, 157, 159, 176, 190–191, 203
Chicago Fire of 1871, 154
Chicago, Lake Shore & Eastern, 190
Chicago Stock Exchange, 191
China, 159, 333
Chollar Company, 113–114, 121
Chollar-Potosi (mining stock), 133
Chrysler Corporation, 327, 328
Church of Jesus Christ of Latter Day Saints, 101, 116
Cincinnati, Ohio, 58
Citrus fruit industry, 255, 256, 257
City Investing Company, 326, 327
City Window Cleaning Company, 337
Civil rights movement, 349
Civil War, 71, 72, 83, 96, 98, 100, 107, 108, 118, 136, 137, 139, 145, 149, 176, 179, 211, 212, 249, 268, 278
Clark & Rockefeller (commission house),
Clay, John, 150–151, 155, 169, 170–171
Clayton, Henry D., 302
Clayton Antitrust Act, 302–303, 305, 311, 349
Cleveland, Grover, 162, 163–164, 165
Cleveland, Ohio, 58, 155, 212, 229
Cleveland Pneumatic Tool Company, 314
Clifton Precision Products Company, 323
Clinton, DeWitt, 49, 51, 52, 58, 59, 67, 357
Clinton, George, 45
Clorox Corporation, 348
Coast-to-Coast Rock Highway, 266
Cobb, Howard, 118
Coeur d'Alene, Idaho, 216
Cole, W. A., 3
Cole Steel Equipment Company, 323
Collins, John S., 262–263, 267
Colonial period, 5–32
  agriculture, 8
  exports, 7
  frontier land speculators, 9–32
  fur trade, 7, 8, 10, 12, 16
  Indians, 5, 6, 7, 8–9, 10–12, 13, 16, 18–20, 27
  industry, 8
  land values, 6–7
  population growth, 5, 6
  taxes, 14–15
  westward movement, 5–6, 17
Colorado, 132, 137, 164
  cattle industry, 139
Colorado Mortgage and Investment Company of London, 155
Colorado Ranche Company Limited, 155
Colorado Stock Growers Association, 142
Columbus, Christopher, xiii
Committee for Plantation Affairs (England), 27
Company of Military Adventurers, 11
Computer industry, 199, 345
Computer Technology Corporation, 345
Comstock, Henry T. P., 102–103, 104, 105, 106, 131
Comstock Lode, 99–133, 174, 175, 201, 232, 249, 277, 359
  air temperature of, 108–109
  decline of, 132–133
  depression of 1869–72, 126
  discovery of, 102–104
  feet (shares), 116–119, 129
  first owners of, 105
  flood problems, 109, 126
  fortunes made from, 107–108, 111, 115, 122–124, 129, 131
  miner strikes, 110, 111
  Ophir site, 104, 108, 109, 120, 125, 127
  pipeline, 109
  price of shares, 129, 131, 133
  production capacity (1875), 129
  prospectors and miners, 106–108
  shaft timbers, 108
  stake claims, 111–114
  stock manipulations, 119–120
  Sutro Tunnel scheme, 109–111
  veins, 105, 108, 111, 112, 119, 128
  ventilation and drainage, 109–110
  wealth of, 105–106
Comstock Mining and Miners (Lord), 106
Concord, Battle of, 30

Confederate States of America, 136, 137, 138
Conglomerates, 297–355
  beginning of, 307–309
  business attitude toward, 299–300
  categories, 327–328
  critics of, 326
  distribution of mergers by type and period (1926–1968), 352
  government regulation and, 301–306, 311–312
  horizontal growth, 300, 301, 351
  Justice Department and, 304, 332, 347, 348, 351, 352–354
  management methods of, 320, 322
  meaning of, 300, 351
  mergers, 307, 312, 315, 318, 328, 330, 349
  rise of (1963–1969), 351
  types of, 301
  vertical growth, 300, 301, 351
  See also names of conglomerates
Connecticut Land Company, 59
Conquistadores, xiii–xiv
Conrad, Alfred, 72
Consol bonds (England), 5
Consolidated Cigar Corporation, 331
Consolidated Steel and Wire Company, 188
Consolidated Virginia Company, 108, 120, 128–129, 130, 133
  price of shares (1874), 128–129
Continental Cattle Company, 169
Continental Congress, 37
Continental Electronics Company, 341
Converse, James, 148
Conway, General Henry Seymour, 17, 18
Cooper, Peter, 110
Cooper, Thomas, 78
Coral Gables, Fla., 284–288
Corbett, James J. "Gentleman Jim," 130
Corey, William, 202
Corsicana, Texas, 221, 224, 229, 230, 232, 243
Corsican Pet Company, 224
Corsicana Water Development Company, 222
Cotter, Arundel, 200, 206
Cotton gin, invention of, 70
Couper, John, 73–74, 75
Covington, James H., 302
Craigie, Andrew, 44
Croghan, George, 9–16, 19–20, 22, 25–26, 27, 30–31, 55, 299, 359
Crosby M. Kelley Associates, 326
Crosley Company, 307
Crossfield Stephen, 45
Crown and Anchor Tavern, 24
Crown Point Company, 121, 126
  abandoned stock shares, 121–122
Crucible Steel Company of America, 193, 209
Crump-McKellar (political machine), 311
Cuba, 17, 136, 260
  tourism, 281–282
Cullinan, Joseph, 223, 228, 233, 234, 236, 242, 243, 244–245
Cullinan & Company (J.S.), 223–224, 243
Curb Market (New York), 201, 232, 281
Custer, General George A., 138, 145
Cyclops Iron Company, 179

Dalmo Victor Manufacturing Company, 315
Dartmouth, earl of, 26
Darwin, Charles, 146–147, 150
Davis, Jefferson, 97
Davis, Joseph S., 44
Day of the Cattleman, The (Osgood), 160
Daytona, Fla., 254, 255, 256
Deacon, John, 50
Dean, Phyllis, 3
DeBillier, Frederic, 148
Declaration of Independence, xiv
Declarations of Rights and Grievances, 15
Deidesheimer, Philip, 108
Delaware, 81
Delaware Indians, 19, 27
Democracy in America (Tocqueville), xv, xvii
Dentists' Supply Company, 324
Denver, 137, 176
Denver Journal of Commerce, 143
De Quille, Dan, 129
De Soto, Hernando, 225
Dew, Thomas, 71, 92
Diamond Match Company, 191, 245
Dickinson, John, 15
Dilke, Charles, 135
Dinwiddie, Robert, 11
District of Columbia, 81, 87
Dixie Highway, 268, 269, 272, 274, 292
Dixie Highway Pathfinders' Tour, 268
Dodd, Samuel, 221
Drake, Colonel, 231
Drucker, Peter, 309, 310, 313, 316
Duer, William, 44
Dumble, Robert, 227
Dundee Mortgage and Trust Investment Company, 157
Dunleavy, Francis J., 338–339
DuPont, General T. Coleman, 293

East India Company, 21, 23, 31
Eastman Kodak Company, 199
Economic Report on Corporate Mergers, 352
Economics of Slavery, The (Conrad and Meyer), 72

Economist (publication), 161
Eddy, Thomas, 50
Edgar Thompson Steel Works, 181
Edmunds, George, 161–162
Eisenhower, Dwight D., 318
El Camino Real, 286–287
Elcho Oil Company of Pennsylvania, 243
Election of 1896, 175–176
Election of 1912, 302
Electra Motors, Inc., 323
Electric Boat Company, 308–309
Electro-Dynamics Company, 321
Elgin, Joliet & Eastern, 190
Ellicott, Joseph, 50
Emanuel, Victor, 307–308
Emerton, Inc., 323
Empire Steel & Iron Company, 193
England, 203, 238, 239, 333
  canal technology, 38, 46
  cattle investors, 149–150
  economic growth, 203
  steel industry, 178, 181
Enterprising Scot, The: Investors in the American West After 1873 (Jackson), 153
Erie Canal, 49–53, 54, 55, 58, 62, 174
  construction of, 50–51
  cost of, 52
  funds for, 49–50
  toll revenues, 51
Essays in the Earlier History of American Corporations (Davis), 44
Eureka Specialty Printing Company, 323
Eureka X-Ray Tube Corporation, 324
Evans, Paul D., 68
Evansville, Ind., 59
Everett Waddey Company, 323
Everglades Club, 285
Excelsior Works, 212

Fair, James, 127–131, 132
Fairbanks, Charles, 266
Fairfax, George, 11
Farwell, Charles, 159
Farwell, John, 159
Federal Highways Act, 272
Federalists, 40
Federal Steel Company, 190, 192, 193
Federal Trade Commission (FTC), 311, 312, 326, 327, 347–350, 351
Fenix Manufacturing Limited, 324
Fennimore, James, 102–103, 104, 131
Field, Elnathan, 263
Finger Lakes, 43
Firestone Tire & Rubber Company, 328
Fisher, Carl, 265–271, 275, 280, 284–285, 288, 291, 293, 296, 357, 359
Fisher, Mrs. Carl, 265, 266, 280
Fisher Automobile Company, 265–266
Fisher Body Company, 266
Fisher Company (Carl G.), 296
Fitchburg Paper Company, 323
Five Civilized Tribes, 137
Flagler, Henry, 248–249, 250–262, 263, 265, 271, 272, 277, 285, 296, 357
Flagler, Mrs. Henry, 250–251, 252
Flagler, Mrs. Henry (Ida Alace Shourds), 252–253, 259
Flagler, Mrs. Henry (Mary Lily Kenan), 259–260
Fleming, Francis, 255
Flood, James, 126–131
Florida, 250–296, 357, 359
  hurricane of 1926, 295–296
  slavery, 81, 84
Florida East Coast Railroad, 257, 260
  operating statistics, 261, 270, 284
Florida Keys, 258
Florida land boom, 250–296
  binder boys, 288–289, 294
  Cuba and, 281–282
  end of, 292–296
  Flagler era, 250–262, 263, 265, 271, 272, 277, 285, 296
  highway transportation, 266–269, 271–272, 273, 286–287
  out-of-state investments (1925), 290–291
  Prohibition era, 279–281
  prosperity of 1920s, 276, 277–278, 284, 292
  railroad transportation, 254–255, 256, 257, 259, 272
  reasons for, 277–292
  salesmen, 289–290
  tin can tourists, 274–276, 288, 289, 295
  See also names of cities
Florida Special (train), 254, 255
Florida Steamship Line, 251
Flower, Roswell, 221
Folger, Henry, 223–224, 228, 229
Ford, Henry, 209
Ford Motor Company, 247, 307
Fort Cumberland, 36
Fort Lauderdale, Fla., 288
Fortnightly Review, 171
Fort Stanwix, Treaty of, 18–20, 22, 23, 25, 26, 30
Fortune (magazine), 248, 351
France, 5, 7, 62, 357
Francis Smith & Company, 157
Franklin, Benjamin, 9, 16–18, 21, 24–25 26, 29, 31–32
Franklin, Isaac, 86–87, 98, 359

Franklin, William, 16–17, 18, 19, 20, 24–25, 26, 27
Franklin & Armfield, 86–89, 90
Franklin Rayon Company, 313
Frasch, Herman, 219–220
Fredericktown, Md., 87
Freedom Iron Company, 180
Freedom Iron & Steel Company, 180
Free Soil Party, 99
French and Indian War, 9, 12, 24, 36
Frick, Henry Clay, 182–184, 186, 187, 189, 194–196, 205–206, 208, 216
Frick Coke Company, 182–183, 186, 195
Fritz Hellige & Company, 323
Fruit and Vegetable Growers Association, 259
Fur trade, 7, 8, 10, 12, 16

Galey, James, 236
Galey, John, 222, 229, 233–236, 238
Gallatin, Albert, 40–42, 48, 60
Galloway family, 27
Galveston, Texas, 136, 137, 228–229, 231
Gardner, James, 147–148
Gary, Elbert H., 187–188, 190
Gates, John "Bet-A-Million," 187–188, 192, 196–198, 244, 245, 297–299
Gaustarax, Chief, 20
Geneen, Harold, 326, 333–339, 347, 356, 359
General Dynamics Corporation, 308–309
General Electric Company, 326, 327, 328, 354
General Motors, 247, 308, 310, 326, 354
General Tire Company, 328
Genovese, Eugene, 72
George III, King, 15
George Kephart & Company, 87, 88
Georgia, 41, 42, 43, 251
    slavery, 70, 71, 77, 81, 90, 91
Germania Mining Company, 214
Germany, 62
Gist, Christopher, 11
Gladys City Oil, Gas and Manufacturing Company, 226, 227, 228, 229
Gold Canyon, 101–102, 103, 105–106, 107
Gold Hill, 103, 107
Gold Ring of 1869, 118
Gold standard, 175
Goodyear Tire & Rubber, 266
Gorham, Nathaniel, 43, 44
Gould, George, 197
Gould, Jay, 141, 142
Gould & Curry Mining Company, 106, 107, 121, 125, 128
Government bonds, 5, 41
Gower, Lord, 23
Grand Ohio Company, 24–25, 26–29, 30, 31
Grant, U. S., 109, 176
Gray, Gilda, 289
Gray, Harry, 325–326
Greatamerica Corporation, 344–345, 347
Great American Land Bubble, The (Sakolski), 43
Great Depression, 303, 306, 313
Great Florida Boom, 250–296
Great Kanawha Valley, 33–34, 35
Great Lakes, 42, 46, 51, 197
Great Ohio Company, 29
Great Plains, The (Webb), 140
Great Salt Lake, 101
Green Cove Springs, 250
Grenville, George, 23
Grinnell Company, 337
Grosch, Allen and Hosea, 102, 131
Grund, Felix, 358
Guffey, James McClurg, 222, 229, 233, 234, 235–241, 243
Guffey Petroleum Company (J.M.), 235–236, 237
Gulf & Western, 328, 329–333, 336, 351, 354
    operating and financial results, 333
    statistics for, 332
Gulf Oil Corporation, 238
Gulf Refining Company of Texas, 236, 238

Haines, Charles, 58, 59
Hale, Daniel, 154
Hale & Norcross, 121, 127–128, 133
Hale & Norcross and Savage pumps, 109
Hall Company (G.K.), 337
Hamill, Al, 229, 230–231, 233
Hamill, Curt, 229, 230–231, 233
Hamill, Jim, 230–231, 233
Hammond, Matthew, 94–95
Hampton Corporation, 324
Hanbury, John, 11
Hand, Learned, 304, 305, 309, 311
Hand-Book of Wyoming. . . (Strahorn), 142
Hansford Land and Cattle Company, 156, 160, 170
Harder, Cary, 272–273
Hardin County (Texas), 220
Hardy, J. H., 113
Harkness, Mary, 249
Harrisburg Chronicle, 53–54
Harrison, B. A., 104
Harrison, Benjamin, 215
Harrison, William Henry, 334
Hartford Fire Insurance Company, 339, 346
Hatch, Rufus, 158
Hay, John, 239
Hayes, C. Willard, 228–229

Haynes, C., 85
Hayward, Alvinza, 122, 126
Head, A. E., 106
Hearst, George, 106, 108
Hearst, William Randolph, 106
Helena, Mont., 171
Henry, Patrick, 15, 36
Henry Cazenove & Company (J.), 44
Hertford, Lord, 23
Hewett, Abram, 187
Hewitt-Robins, Inc., 323
Higgins, Patillo, 226–229, 233, 257
Highway construction, 271–272
Hillman Iron Works, 78
Hillsborough, Lord, 13, 15, 18, 19, 20, 21, 22, 23–24, 25, 26
History of the Standard Oil Company, The (Tarbell), 247
Hogg, James, 221, 241–243
Hogg-Swayne syndicate, 242–243
Holland Land Company, 44–45, 47, 49–50
  stock issues, 67–68
Holland Land Company, The (Evans), 68
Hollicot, John, 169
Hollywood, Cal., 279
Hollywood, Fla., 288
Homelite Company, 315
Homestead strike of 1892, 186, 195, 216
Homestead Works, 182, 183
Hope & Company, 65
Hopeton (plantation), 73–74, 76, 77
Hopkins, J. J., 308–309
Hopkins, James, 245
Hopkins Airport Hotel, 337
Houston, Texas, 231–232
Hudson River, 42, 43, 46, 47, 58
Hudson Valley, 48
Hughes Aircraft, 321
Huges & Downing, 89, 90
Humphrey, Hubert, 352
Hunt Foods & Industries, 326

Idaho, 132
Illinois, 14, 16, 122, 159
  oil fields, 246
  population growth, 55
Illinois Steel Company, 190
Illinois-Wabash Company, 11
Imperial Typewriter Limited, 324
Independence, Mo., 137
Indiana, 157, 266
  canal construction, 59–60, 66
  oil fields, 220, 238
  population growth, 55
Indiana Company, 15–16, 19, 20
Indianapolis, 157
Indianapolis Motor Speedway, 266
Indian Creek, Fla., 267
Indians, 101, 119
  British regulation of affairs, 14
  buffalo range economy, 138
  cattlemen and, 137–138, 145, 163
  colonial period, 5, 6, 7, 8–9, 10, 12, 13, 16, 18
  Fort Stanwix meeting, 18–20
  Ohio Valley uprising, 27
  treaties, 10–11, 18–20
  U.S. policy toward, 138
  wars in the West, 137–138, 145, 163
Indrio, Fla., 288
Information Concerning a Negotiation of Lands of America, 44
Ingalls Shipbuilding Corporation, 323, 325
Integrated Data Processing, Inc., 323
Internal Revenue Department, 314
International Business Machines Corporation (IBM), 199, 308
International Telephone & Telegraph (ITT), 328, 333–339, 340, 354–355
  acquisitions program, 336–338
  debts, 339
  formed, 333
  mergers, 347
  statistics for (1947–1969), 336
  World War II, 333–334
Interstate Commerce Commission, 302
Intolerable Acts, 29
Investment and speculation, 1–32
  difference between, 1–2
  eighteenth century, 2–32
Investment trusts, 153
Iron Clad agreements, 184–185, 196, 201
Iroquois Confederacy, 8–9
Iroquois Indians, 12, 14, 18
Isthmus of Panama, 100
Italy, 357

Jackson, Andrew, 60–61, 62, 63, 97, 99
Jackson, Henry, 168
Jackson, Richard, 23
Jackson, W. Turrentine, 153
Jacksonville, Fla., 251, 253, 255, 262
Jacksonville, St. Augustine, and Halifax Railroad, 254
Jacques French Restaurant, 337
James F. Purvis & Company, 88
James River, 6, 33–34, 35
James River Canal Company, 36–37, 39
Japan, 218
Java, 218
Jefferson, Thomas, 5, 36, 37, 40–42, 97
  slaves of, 82
Jefferson Electric Company, 324

Jeffersonianism, 48
Johnson, Andrew, 110
Johnson, Hiram, 279
Johnson, Lyndon B., 318
Johnson, William, 12–20, 22, 24–25, 31
Johnson Company, 190
Johnstown, Pa., 178
Joliet, Ill., 178
Joliet Steel Works, 178
Jones, Eliot, 193, 206
Jones, John P., 122, 126, 132
Jones, Samuel M., 242
Jones & Laughlin, 178, 182, 185, 206, 345–346, 347, 348, 352, 353, 355
Joseph B. Giglio Enterprises, 337

Kaiser Industries, 328
Kamerschen, David, 300
Kansas, 137, 157
  cattle industry, 139–140, 141, 149
  oil fields, 220, 246
Kansas City and Southern Railroad, 244
Kansas Pacific Railroad, 137
Kavanaugh, Dr. B. T., 225–226
Keene, James, 119, 201
Kefauver, Estes, 310–311, 313
Keith, R. C., 142
Kelley, Crosby M., 326
Kelly steel process, 177
Kenan, Mary Lily, 259–260
Kennecott Copper Company, 342
Kennedy, John F., 318
Kennedy, William, 227
Kentuck (mine), 127, 133
Kephart, George, 89
Kerosene, 213, 217, 218, 219, 220, 221, 233, 237, 247
Kester Solder Company, 324
Keystone Bridge Company, 179, 180
Key West, 260, 264
Kimball Company (A.), 323
King, Wilson, 217
King Ranch, 141
Kirkwood, Samuel, 162
Kloman & Phipps, 179
Klondike gold rush, 231
Knowland, T. S., 291–292
Kuhn, Loeb Company, 188

L. M. Electronics, 341
Lake Champlain, 47
Lake Erie, 43, 45, 196
Lake Ontario, 43, 47
Lake Pontchartrain, 77
Lake Superior Consolidated Iron Mines Company, 194–195
Lake Tahoe, 114
Land speculation, 1–68
  American Colonies, 1–32
  canal era, 33–68
  Great Florida Boom, 250–296
  Jacksonian era, 61–62
  in Middle Ages, 5
Lapham brothers of New York, 243
Laramie Boomerang (newspaper), 144
Latham, Dr. Harry, 141–142, 144
Lawson, Thomas, 158
Lawton, Franklin, 116, 118
League of Nations, 278
Leavey, Edmund, 334
Lee, Arthur, 23, 25
Lee, Colonel Thomas, 11
Lee, Richard, 11
Lee, Robert E., 176
Lee family, 27
Lehman Brothers, 321
Leopold Company, The, 323
Lewis, Roger, 309
Lewis, Sinclair, 278
Lexington, Ky., 83–84, 89
Lexington, Battle of, 30
Liberty Investors Benefit Insurance Company, 337
Lima, Ohio, 219
Lincoln, Abraham, 83–84, 99, 112
Lincoln Highway, 268
Ling, James, 326, 339–347, 352, 355, 356, 359
Ling Electric Company, 340–341
Ling-Temco-Vought (LTV), 339–347, 351, 354, 355
  acquisitions program, 341–343
  antitrust actions against, 352–353
  debts in, 346
  statistics for (1957–69), 347
  subsidiary companies, 348
LTV Aerospace Company, 341, 348
LTV Electrosystems Company, 341, 348
LTV International Company, 348
LTV Jet Fleet Company, 348
LTV Ling-Altec Company, 341, 348
LTV Research Center, 348
Little, Arthur D., 313
Little Big Horn, Battle of, 138
Little Kanawha River, 19
Little, Royal, 313–318
Litton Industries, 301, 319–326, 327, 328, 330, 331, 335, 336, 339, 351, 355
  acquisitions of, 323–324
  statistics, 322
Lloyd, Henry Demarest, 216, 217
Locke, P. B., 114
Logan, Samuel, 85, 86
London Morning Chronicle, 65

London Office Machines Company, 323
London Times, 52
Long, Charles de, 113, 115
Lorain Steel Company, 190
Lord, Eliot, 106
Louis Allis company, 324
Louisiana, 227, 230
slavery, 73, 76, 81, 84, 91
Louisiana Purchase, 6
Lovejoy, Francis, 204
Low, Charles, 122, 126
Lucas, Captain Anthony F., 227–230, 233, 234, 357
Lucas, Mrs. Anthony F., 229–230
Lucky Dime Company, 234
Lucy Furnaces, 182
Lumber & Flume Company, 129
Lumber industry, 226
Lummus Brothers, 267
Lusitania (liner), 269
LX Ranch, 169
Lyell, Charles, 73

McCalmont & Bros., 111
McCandless, Gardiner, 182
McClellan, George, 147–148
McClure's Magazine, 247
McCormick, Robert, 256
McCoy, Joseph, 137, 139–140
McCray Refrigeration Company, 323
McFall, Russel, 326
Machinery Manufacturers, 331
Mackay, John, 127–131, 359
McKellar, Kenneth, 311
McKenna, William F., 326
Mackenzie, Colin J., 158–159
McKiernan-Terry Corporation, 323
McKinley, William, 190
McLaren, Richard, 352, 354
McLaughlin, Patrick, 103, 104, 105, 130
MacLeane, Lauchlin, 21
McNamara, Robert, 321
Macomb, Alexander, 44, 45, 46
Madison, James, 37, 42, 97
Magnuson X-Ray Company, 323
Maine-Georgia Turnpike, 42
Mainline canals, 53–54, 55, 66
Mangum, Willie, 97
Manhattan Island, purchase of, 10
Maria Isabel Hotel, 337
Marine Consultants and Designers, Inc., 324
Marquis—Who's Who, Inc., 337
Martin, John, 273
Maryland, 7, 40
canal system, 36–40, 41, 54–55, 64, 66
slavery, 76, 81, 84, 88, 95
Maryland Electronics Company, 322
Mason, George, 70
Massachusetts, 21, 41
Matador Company, 160, 161, 170
Matador Land and Cattle Company, 155–156
Maverick-Clark Company, 323
Mayo, Frederick, 326
Mechanics and Farmers Bank of New York, 50
Meek, John, 85, 86
Mellon, Andrew, 208–210, 235, 240
Mellon, Richard, 235
Mellon, Thomas, 208
Mellon, William, 235, 237
Mellon, William Lorimer, 209
Mellon brothers, 235–237, 242
Mellon & Sons (T.), 208
Mellonics Systems Development, Inc., 323
Memphis, Tenn., 157
"Men of the Western World" (Wordsworth), 65
Menzies, William, 153–154
Mercer, George, 20, 23, 24, 25, 26
Merrick, George, 285, 287–288, 359
Merritt brothers, 194
Mesabi range, 194, 201
Mexican (mining stock), 133
Mexican War, 71, 90, 99, 112
Meyer, John, 72
Miami, Fla., 256, 258–259, 264, 269, 270, 275, 278, 279, 282, 284, 288, 289, 293–294
Miami and Erie Canal, 58
Miami Beach, 263–264, 265, 267–268, 269, 270, 271, 275, 277, 282, 284, 287, 289, 291, 292, 296
Miami Beach Improvement Company, 264, 267, 293
Miami River, 258, 259
Michigan Plating and Stamping Company, 326, 332
Middle Ages, 5
Miller, Arjay, 321
Mills, Darius Ogden, 124, 130
Minnesota Iron Company, 190
Minnesota School of Business, 337
Minuit, Peter, 10
Mississippi & Alabama Railroad, 78
Mississippi Company, 11, 23
Mississippi River, 33–34, 54
Mississippi Supreme Court, 83
Mississippi Valley, 6
Missouri Land and Livestock Company, 156
Mizner, Addison, 285–288, 293
Mizner, Wilson, 286–287
Mizner Development Corporation, 286–287
Mobil Oil, 247–248
Mohawk Indians, 20

Monckton Hall (estate), 16, 30
Monroe, James, 42
Monroe Calculating Machine Company, 322
Montana, 105, 162, 168
  cattle industry, 139, 171
Montauk Beach Development Corporation, 293
Monte Carlo, 205, 291
Moody, John, 190–191
Moore, William and James, 191, 192, 196
Moore Company, 192
Moothart, Frank, 326
Mores, Marquis de, 165
Morgan, George, 29
Morgan, J. P., 188–199, 200–201, 205, 207, 208, 211, 212, 214, 215, 247, 297, 298, 299, 300, 302, 359
Morgan & Company (J.P.), 211
Mormons, 101, 116
Morris, Robert, 43–44, 46
Morrison, Thomas, 204
Motion-picture industry, 279
Mount Davidson, 105–106, 109, 120
Mutual funds, 153

Nacogdoches County (Texas), 220
Nader, Ralph, 355
Napoleon I, xv, 2, 67
Nashville Corporation, 307
Natchez, Miss., 86, 89
National Biscuit Company, 191
National Car Rental, 344, 345
National Enameling & Stamping Company, 193
National Intelligencer, 87–88
National Land System, 1785–1820, The (Treat), 43
National Steel Company, 191–192, 193
National Transit Company, 214, 215, 220
National Tube Company, 193, 196, 198
National Turnpike, 41
Nebraska, 137, 166
Neches River, 224
Nevada, 112, 130
  Comstock Lode, 99–133
  statehood, 132
Nevada Bank, 130
Nevada City, 106, 113
Nevada Territory, 112
New Deal, 301, 303, 305, 309, 311
New Frontier, 301–302
New Idea Corporation, 307
New Jersey, 19, 21, 42
New Jersey Zinc Company, 330
New Orleans, 34, 36, 54, 84, 136
  slave trade, 71, 86, 87, 88, 95, 96
Newport, R. I., 253, 254, 261, 293
New Society, The: The Anatomy of Industrial Order (Drucker), 309
New York, 7, 40, 42, 144, 145, 149, 176, 203, 229, 298
  canal system, 43–53, 54, 55, 58, 62
  cattle industry, 135, 136, 137
  realty values (1837), 62
New York Evening Post, 204
New York Herald, 177
New York State Bank, 50
New York Stock and Exchange Board, 50, 116, 118, 132, 145
New York Sun, xv
New York Times, The, 162
New York University, 309
Nixon, Richard, 352, 356
Nobel, Alfred, 218, 219
Nobel, Ludwig, 218, 219
Nobel, Robert, 218, 219
Nobel Brothers Naphtha Company, 218
Nobel's Explosive Company, 159
North, Judge James A., 113–114
North, Lord, 18
North America Mining, 123
North Dakota, 132, 145–146, 165, 166
  cattle industry, 139
Northern Canal, 48
Northern Inland Lock Navigation Company, 47, 49
Northern Pacific Railroad, 145, 165
Norwalk, Ind., 266
Nova, Appareils (company), 337
Nova Scotia, 14
Nye, Bill, 144
Nye, James, 132

O'Brien, William, 126–131
Ocean Beach, Fla., 268
Ocklawaha River, 251
Office Training School, 337
Ogden Company, 351
Ohio, 58–59, 219–220
  antitrust actions, 215
  canal system, 58–59
  oil fields, 219–220, 228, 238
  population growth, 55
Ohio and Erie Canal, 58
Ohio Canal, 58, 59
Ohio Company, 22–23, 34, 36
Ohio Company of Virginia, 11, 18, 19, 20, 25
Ohio Indians, 19
Ohio Oil Company, 220
Ohio River, 19, 20, 33–34, 51, 58
Oil industry, 180, 194, 207, 211–249, 277
  beginning of, 212
  crude oil production (1900–1919), 246
  exports, 217, 218

Hogg-Swayne syndicate, 241–243
kerosene market, 213, 217, 218, 219, 220, 221, 233
markets (1870), 213
prices, 213
production (per barrel), 220, 222, 245–246
railroads and, 213, 214, 234
Shell-Guffey deal, 238–241
Spindletop discovery, 226–231
wildcatters, 234
See also names of companies
Oil Springs, Texas, 221
Oklahoma oil fields, 246
Okonite Corporation, 342, 348, 353
Oliver, Henry, 194
Olmsted, Frederick Law, 78, 94
Omaha, Neb., 137
Omaha Herald, 141
Oneida Indians, 20
Onondaga Indians, 20
Onondaga Lake, 46
Ophir Mining Company, 121, 125, 133
Ophir-Burning Moscow case, 120–121
O'Riley, Peter, 103, 104, 105, 130
Orinoco River, xiii
Ormond, Fla., 255, 257, 258
Orr, John, 101
Ottowa Indians, 9
Overman Company, 121, 123

Pacific Mill and Mining Company, 129
Pacific Stock Exchange, 118
Pacific Wood Company, 129
Packard Motor Car Company, 266
Palm Beach, 255–257, 258, 259, 261, 269, 271, 284–285, 286, 293
Pancoast, Thomas, 264–265, 270
Pancoast, Mrs. Thomas, 264
Panic of 1837, 62, 63, 73, 86, 91
Panic of 1857, 212
Panic of 1873, 139, 140–141, 145, 149, 150, 181
Panic of 1893, 194, 226
Panic of 1901, 204
Panic of 1903, 204
Panic of 1907, 171, 205
Paramount Pictures, 330, 335
Pastoral Company, 160
Pathé-Industries, Inc., 315
Pauper Alley (San Francisco), 131–132
Payne, Calvin, 223–224, 228, 229
Peacock, Alexander, 202, 203–204, 236
Peale, Norman Vincent, 359
Pearson Candy Company, 337
Peculiar Institution, The (Stampp), 72
Pennsylvania, 7, 15, 19, 23, 53, 54, 158
canal era, 53–54, 64–65, 66
oil discovery (1859), 212
oil fields, 212–213, 217, 219, 220, 222, 223, 228, 231
Pennsylvania Council, 10
Pennsylvania Railroad, 179, 211
Pennsylvania Society for the Promotion of Internal Improvement in the Commonwealth, 53
Pennsylvania Steel Company, 185
Penrod, Emmanuel, 103, 105
Peoria, Ill., 83–84
Perkins, Simon, 59
Perley, D. W., 113
Phelps, Oliver, 43, 44
Philadelphia, 40, 52–54, 55, 144, 298
Phillips, Ulrich, 96
Phillips, William, 229
Phipps, Henry, 186, 195, 196
Pinckney, C. C., 70
Piper and Shiffler Company, 179
Pittsburgh, 53, 178, 196, 197, 201, 203, 207, 211, 229, 232, 235, 236, 238, 241
Pittsburgh Petroleum Stock Exchange, 209
Pittsburgh Reduction Company, 208
Pittsburgh Steel, 209
Plantation system, *see* Slavery
Plath, (C.) K.G., 323
Plumb, Preston, 162
Polaroid Company, 199
Political Economy of Slavery (Genovese), 72
Polk, James K., 98
Poly-Scientific Corporation, 323
Ponce de Leon Hotel, 254
Pontiac, Chief, 9
Pools (steel industry), 185–186, 187
Populist Party, 111, 216, 301
Port Arthur, Texas, 236, 238, 244
Port Arthur Land and Townsite Company, 244
Post, Troy, 344–345
Potomac Company, 36–40, 42, 54
shares, 37–38
toll revenues, 39
tonnage hauled (1800–1811), 39
Potomac River, 36
Potosi Company, 113–114, 121
Powder River Company, 160, 161
Power, Tyrone, 77, 78
Pownall, John, 21
Pownall, Thomas, 21
Prairie Cattle Company, 155, 160, 161, 170
Pressed Steel Car Company, 193
Prest-O-Lite Corporation of America, 266
Prime, Ward & King, 59

Prime, Ward & Sands, 51
Proclamation of 1763, 11
Procter & Gamble, 349
Producers Oil Company, 244–245
Profexray, Inc., 323
Progress: Its Law and Causes (Spencer), 147
Progressive Party, 301
Prohibition, 279–281
Prouse, William, 101
Prussia, 357
Public Utilities Holding Company Act, 303–304
Pullman, George, 180
Pullman Sleeping Car Company, 180, 181
Pure Oil Company, 215
Puritan ethic, 248
Pyne Moulding Corporation, 323

Quakers, 11

Railroads, 40, 53, 66, 124, 180, 188, 190, 197, 207, 309
  cattlemen and, 137, 141–143, 154, 165
  construction of, 63–64
  Great Florida Boom, 154–255, 256, 257, 259, 272
  mileage, 67, 176
  oil industry and, 213, 214, 234
  steel industry and, 176, 177
  Thoreau on, 64
  use of slave labor, 78
Ralston, William Chapman, 110, 122, 123, 124–126, 128, 130, 132
Randolph, Thomas Jefferson, 92
Rathbone & Lord (banking firm), 59
Rayburn, Sam, 302, 303
Raytheon Corporation, 338
Reardon, Thomas B., 113
Recession of 1920, 284
Red Cloud, Chief, 138
Red River, 136
Redwood, Boverton, 218
Reichenbach, Harry, 286, 287
Report on Roads and Canals (Gallatin), 41–42, 48
Republic Corporation, 326
Republic Iron & Steel Company, 193
Rexall Company, 327, 328
Rhett, R. Barnwell, 97
Richthofen, Baron Walter von, 164, 165
Ritz-Carlton Hotel, 287
Robards, Lewis C., 89–90
Robbins Mill Company, 315
Roberts, Kenneth, 275, 281
Rochford, Lord, 23
Rockefeller, John D., 193–194, 195, 197, 205, 207, 209, 210, 211–213, 217–221, 224, 228, 234, 237, 241
Rockefeller, Nelson, 210
Rockefeller & Andrews, 212, 249
Rock Life Assurance Company, 50
Rocky Mountains, 100, 101, 134
Romance of Steel, The (Casson), 182, 200
Roney, N. B. T., 292
Roosevelt, Theodore, 145–146, 165
Rosenbaum, Joseph, 157, 170, 171
Rosenberg, Seymour, 326
Rothschild, Baron Alphonse de, 218
Rothschild family, 219, 241
Royal Commission on Agriculture, 155
Royal Dutch Petroleum, 218, 241
Royal Exchange Assurance Company of London, 50
Royal McBee Corporation, 323
Royal Palm Hotel, 259
Royal Poinciana Hotel, 256–257, 285
Ruffin, Edmund, 92
Rukeyser, M. S., 294–295
Rumsey, David, 38
Russia, 357
  oil fields, 217–218
Russian Revolution, 278
Rust Engineering Company, 324

Sacramento, Cal., 101, 104, 124
St. Augustine, Fla., 250, 251, 253–254, 255, 257, 258, 269, 271
St. Elmo's fire, 225
St. Johns River, 250, 251
St. Louis, Mo., 144
St. Louis Post-Dispatch, 232
St. Petersburg, Fla., 288
Sakolski, A. M., 43
Salgo, Nicholas, 321
Salt Lake City, 112
Samuel, Marcus, 238–240
Samuel & Company (M.), 218
San Antonio, 157
San Francisco, 131–132, 176, 231
  brokerage community (1850s), 116–118, 120, 121, 128
  growth of, 115–116, 124
  silver rush (Comstock Lode) and, 100, 107, 110, 111, 115–118, 120, 121, 126–128, 129, 131–132
San Francisco Exposition, 266
San Francisco Mining and Scientific Press, The, 117
San Francisco Stock Exchange, 118–119
Saphier, Lerner, Schindler, Inc., 324
Saquarisera, Chief, 20

Sargent, John, 25
Saturday Evening Post, The, 275
Saunders & Company (J.M.), 87
Savage & Company, 226–227
Savage Mining Company, 121, 133
Savannah, Ga., 40, 79, 251, 252
Scharffenberger, George T., 326
Schiff, Jacob, 188
Schlaet, Arnold, 243–244, 245
Schuyler, General Philip, 47
Schwab, Charles, 184, 196, 197–198, 205–206, 236, 299
Scotland, 179, 186, 189
  banking techniques, 152–153
  joint-stock companies, 153
Scott, John, 182
Scott, Thomas, 179, 180, 211
Scottish-American Investment Company, 154
Scottish-American Mortgage Company, 154, 155, 157
Scranton Iron & Steel, 185
Seaboard Air Line Railroad, 269
Second Bank of the United States, 51
Securities and Exchange Commission (SEC), 4, 352
Security Connecticut Life Insurance, 332
Security Insurance Company of Hartford, 332
Segregated Belcher (mining stock), 133
Seiberling, Frank, 266
Seneca Indians, 19, 20
Sennghois, Chief, 20
Servomechanisms Company, 323
Seton-Karr, Henry, 159
Seven Years' War, 5
Sewickley Heights mansions, 203
Sharon, William, 122–124, 128, 130, 132
Shawnee Indians, 19, 27
Shelburne, earl of, 17, 18
Shelby Steel Tube Company, 193
Sheldon, Henry, 154
Shell-Guffey Oil deal, 238–241
Shell Oil Company, 238–241
Shell Transport & Trading, 218, 238–240
Sheridan, General Philip, 145, 163
Sherman Antitrust Act, 190, 215, 302
Shibaieff Company, 218
Shopping Bag Foods, 348
Shreveport, La., 136
Sibley, Joseph, 228
Sierra Nevada Mountains, 100, 102, 109, 121
Signal Companies, 351
Silver ore, 100, 101–102, 175
Simon Adhesive Products Company, 323
Simons, Trent, Franks & Company, 16, 19
Simpson, Gilbert, 35
Simpson's Mill, 35
Singer, Parris, 285
Singer Sewing Machines, 285
Singleton, Henry, 326
Sioux Indians, 138
Six Mile Canyon, 103, 104, 105
Slavery, 69–98, 100, 107
  breeding for sale, 91–96
  colonial period, 71
  concubinage, 90
  cotton production and, 70, 71, 73, 76, 80, 81, 90–91, 95, 98
  death rate, 76, 79
  investment and returns, 76–77, 79, 86
  plantation economy, 72–77
  population, 81, 97
  prices, 70–71, 72, 80, 90–91, 94, 97
  rental prices, 77
  runnways, 76, 79, 85, 86, 90, 93, 94
  Washington's attitude toward, 64–70
  westward movement, 81–82
  Slavery and the Southern Economy (ed. Woodman), 72
Slave trade, 4, 8, 69, 82–98, 174, 299, 356
  advertisements, 87–88, 94, 96
  Alexandria-Tennessee-New Orleans triangle, 86–89
  auctions, 84, 85, 90, 95
  as big business, 96–98
  Constitution on, 80
  end of, 98
  firms dealing in, 85–90
  Lincoln on, 83–84
  New Orleans, 71, 86, 87, 88, 95, 96
Slave-Trading in the Old South (Bancroft), 96–97
Slidell, John, 97
Sloss-Sheffield Steel & Iron, 193
Smith, Francis, 157–158
Smith, James Duncan, 154
Smith, James Guthrie, 154, 161
Smith, Reverend Sydney, 65
Social Darwinism, 146–147, 150, 186, 214
Socrates, 147
Sons of Liberty, 15
Soulé, Pierre, 97
South Carolina, 7, 21, 51
  cattle industry, 135
South Carolina Railroad, 78
South Dakota, 132, 145–146, 165, 166
  cattle industry, 139
South Dakota (battleship), 307
Southern Oil Company, 222, 223
Southern Pacific Railroad, 114
Southern Wood Preserving Company, 337
South Puerto Rico Sugar Company, 330
South Sea Bubble, 3–4, 21

Spanish law, 111–112
Sparks, William, 163
Specie circular of 1836, 62
Spence, Clark C., 157
Spencer, Herbert, 147, 150, 186
Spindletop Springs, Texas, 226–231, 234, 235, 236, 237, 238, 240, 242, 243, 245, 247, 248, 277, 357
Springfield, Ill., 137
Stadnitzki, Peter, 44
Stamp Act, 17, 23
Stamp Act Congress, 15
Stampp, Kenneth, 72
Standard industrial classifications (SICs), 327–328
Standard Oil, 186, 193, 194, 216–221, 223, 224, 229, 231, 234, 237–238, 247–249, 253, 255, 265, 300, 301, 305
- antitrust suits against, 247
- earnings, 216
- foreign competition with, 218–219
- production statistics, 248

Standard Oil of California, 248
Standard Oil of Indiana, 248
Standard Oil of New Jersey, 215, 224, 239, 247, 249
Standard Oil of New York, 214–215
Standard Oil of Ohio, 212–214, 215, 249
Standard Oil of Pennsylvania, 215, 224
Standard Oil Trust, 214–215, 216
State banking, growth of, 61
State of Texas v. *John D. Rockefeller et al.*, 221
Steel (magazine), 329
Steel industry, 173–210, 212, 214, 359
- Bessemer process, 177, 178, 179, 180, 181, 212
- foreign competition, 178
- Iron clad agreements, 184–185, 196, 201
- Kelly process, 177
- mergers, 190, 202, 207, 305
- non-Carnegie amalgamations (1898–1900), 193
- number of ingots produced (1867), 177
- opposition to organized labor, 186, 187
- pools, 185–187
- rail costs, 181
- railroads and, 176, 177

Steele, W., 51
Stephens, Alexander, 97
Stevens, Raymond B., 302, 304
Stewart, David, 182
Stewart, William M., 113–115, 123, 125 131, 132
"Stock Broker's Prayer" (Twain), 115
Stock certificates, 5
Stock-jobbers, 4
Stouffer Foods Corporation, 324
Strahorn, Robert, 142, 144
Strategy and Structure (Chandler), 308
Streater Industries, Inc., 323
Strikes, 110, 126, 186, 195, 215–216
Stuart, Granville, 168
Studebaker-Worthington Company, 351
Sturgis Newport Business Forms, Inc., 324
"Suffering traders," the, 12–13, 14
Sullivan, Fred, 326
Susquehannah Company, 11
Sutro, Adolph, 109–111, 125, 357
Sutro Tunnel Company, 109–111, 132
Sutter's Mill, 99, 104, 113
Svenska Dataregister Company, 323
Swan, Alexander Hamilton, 158–159
Swan Company, 160, 161, 170
Swan Land and Cattle Company, Limited, 158–159
Swan Ranch, 159, 160, 171
Swayne, James, 241–243
Synthetic Philosophy (Spencer), 147

Taft, William Howard, 266
Tagaaia, Chief, 20
Talbott, Harold, Jr., 270
Tammany Hall, 49
Tampa, Fla., 251
Tarbell, Ida, 247
Taxes, 14–15, 49, 306
Taylor, Abner, 159
Taylor, Babcock & Company of Chicago, 159
Teacle, Elisha W., 116, 118
Teledyne Company, 326–327, 351
Temco Electronics and Missiles, 341
Temple School Company, 337
Temporary National Economic Committee (TNEC), 304
Tenneco Company, 351
Tennessee Iron and Coal Company, 206
Tennessee Valley Authority (TVA), 311
Teschemacher, Hubert, 148
Teschemacher & deBillier Cattle Company, 148
Texaco, 245
Texas, 70
- annexation of, 71–72
- cattle industry, 136, 137, 139, 141, 144, 171
- oil industry, 209, 220–241, 247

Texas Company, 160, 170, 245
"Texas fever," 139
Texas Fuel Company, 243, 244, 245
Texas Land and Cattle Company, 155
Texas longhorns, 137, 139, 144
Texas Mineral Company, 226–227
Texas Oil and Development Company, 242

Texas Petroleum Company, 222, 223
Texas shorthorns, 144
Texas Supreme Court, 221, 223
Textron, Inc., 313–326, 327, 328, 330, 339, 351
 statistics (1939–1969), 317
Thomas M. Jones Company, 88
Thoreau, Henry, 64
Thornton, Charles "Tex," 301, 319–326, 331, 339, 346, 359
Thorp Finance Company, 337
Tick disease, 164
Times Facsimile Company, 323
Tin can tourists, 274–276, 288, 289, 295
Tin Plate Trust, 191
Tocqueville, Alexis de, xv, xvii, 358–359
Toledo, Ohio, 58, 59
Toombs, Robert, 97
"To the Pennsylvanians" (Wordsworth), 65
To the Rockies and Beyond . . . (Strahorn), 142
Totten, Joseph, 45
Townshend Acts, 16
Traders Company, 15–16, 18
Treat, Payson, J., 43
Trent, William, 19, 20–21, 22, 23, 26, 29–32, 356
Tribune (slave ship), 88
Trimble, Allen, 58
Trotter, Alexander, 62–63
Trust Problem in the United States, The (Jones), 193, 206
Turner, Donald F., 348
Turner, George, 114
Turner, Reverend Jesse H., 94
Turnpike system, 40, 42, 48, 61
 cost of, 63
Tuscarora Indians, 20
Tuttle, Mrs. Julia, 258–259
Twain, Mark, 110, 115
Tweeddale, marquis of, 160
Tyson, Job, 54

Uncle Sam Mines, 123
Underlying assets, concept of, 199
Underwood, Frank L., 157
Union Carbide Corporation, 266
Union Consolidated (mining stock), 133
Union Iron Mills, 179, 180, 181, 182
Union Mill and Mining, 125
Union Pacific Railroad, 137, 141, 145, 180
Union Transfer & Trust Company, 208–209
United Building Services, 337
United Electronics and Calidyne Company, 341
United Homes Company, 337
United States Cast-Iron Pipe & Foundry Company, 193
United States Constitution, xiv, 39, 80
United States Geological Survey, 228
United States Industries, 351
United States Leather Company, 243, 244
United States Steel (Cotter), 206
United States Steel Corporation, 198–200, 205–207, 209, 210, 235, 247, 297, 298, 299, 300, 301, 308, 346
 profits and securities (1901–10), 206
United States Supreme Court, 30, 247
Universal American Company, 331
University Loudspeakers Company, 341
University of California, 124
University of Tennessee, 310
University of Texas, 229
Utah, 101, 112

Van Buren, Martin, 99
Vandalia Company, 299
Vandalia scheme, 1–32, 149, 174, 356
Vanderblue, Homer B., 261, 284
Vandervort, John, 182
Vanneck, Sir Joshua, 21
Victoria, Queen, 238
Vietnam War, 349
Virginia, 6, 7, 11, 19, 30, 62
 canal era, 36–40, 41
 cattle industry, 135
 slavery, 70, 71, 78, 79–80, 81, 84, 85, 88, 91–92, 95
Virginia and Truckee Railroad, 125, 129
Virginia City, 104, 110, 112–115, 118–121, 124, 127, 132, 232
 growth of, 106–108
 lawyers and judges, 113–115, 120–121
 legal actions in (1862–67), 121
 population of, 107
 See also Comstock Lode
Virginia City Stock Exchange, 118
Virginia Iron, Coal & Coke Company, 193
Von's Grocery, 348

Wabash and Erie Canal, 59–60, 66
Wadsworth Land Company, 337
Walker, Robert, 97
Walker, Thomas, 19, 20
Wall, John, 325
Walpole, Horatio, 21
Walpole, Sir Robert, 21
Walpole, Thomas, 2–3, 7, 9, 21–25, 27, 30, 31
Walpole Associates, 24–25, 26–27, 29
Walter Kidde & Company, 326, 328, 351
War of 1812, 39, 42, 48, 67, 73, 81, 86
Washington, Bushrod, 82
Washington, George, 5, 8, 9, 11, 60, 71, 72, 97, 357

acres of land owned by, 33
attitude toward slavery, 69–70
canal venture, 33–40, 68
legal suit against squatters, 35
Potomac Company venture, 36–40, 42, 54, 68
Washington, Lawrence, 11
Washington family, 27
Washoe district, 100
See also Comstock Lode
Washoe mules, 109
Waters-Pierce Company, 221, 223
Watson, Elkanah, 46–47, 48, 49
Wattel Company, 326
Wealth Against Commonwealth (Lloyd), 216
Webb, Walter Prescott, 140
Weigall, T. H., 273, 279
West Coast Electronics Company, 322
Western American Cattle Company, 156
Western Canal, 48
Western Company, 48, 49, 50
Western Electric Company, 334
Western Geophysical Company, 323
Western Inland Lock Navigation Company, 47
Western Land Company, 160, 164
Western Ranche Company, 160, 170
Western Union, 326
West Palm Beach, 256–257, 273–274
Westrex Company, 322
West Virginia, 226
oil fields, 220
Wharton, Samuel, 12–13, 19, 20–30, 58, 299, 356
White, Canvass, 48
Wildcatters, 277, 359
Williams, Charles H. S., 113
Williamson, Harold F., 248
Willy Feiler Zaehl-Und Rechenwerke GmbH, 324
Willys-Overland Company, 266
Wilson, James, 159
Wilson, Woodrow, 302, 303
Wilson & Company, 343, 344, 348
Wilson Marine Transit Company, 324
Wilson Pharmaceutical & Chemical Company, 344, 348
Wilson Sporting Goods, 344, 348
Winchester Electronics, Inc., 323
Wood Brothers, 157
Woodman, Harold, 72
Wordsworth, William, 65
World War I, 269, 271, 294, 296, 303, 304
World War II, 296, 301, 304
expenditures, 306
Wright, Benjamin, 48
Wright, William, 129
Wyoming, 137, 144, 147
cattle industry, 139, 149, 150–151
Wyoming Cattle Ranche Company, 156, 161

Xerox Company, 199
XIT Ranch, 159, 160

Yellow Jacket Mining Company, 121
Youghiogheny River, 35, 54
Young Ladies Oil Company, 234
Yukon gold strike, 132

Ziegfeld Follies, 273
Zuid Hollandse Grofucco Company, 337